THE BOOK
OF
JACK LONDON

BY

CHARMIAN LONDON

ILLUSTRATED WITH
PHOTOGRAPHS

VOLUME II

CONTENTS

LIST OF ILLUSTRATIONS

THE BOOK
OF
JACK LONDON

THE
BOOK OF JACK LONDON

CHAPTER XXV

RETURN FROM KOREA; DIVORCE

Autumn, 1904

ON June 30, 1904, still in the ocean aboard the incoming *S.S. Korea*, from Yokohama, Jack London was served with papers for "separation and maintenance." Moreover, he learned from the inhospitable messenger that an attachment had been levied by the plaintiff upon his personal property, even to his books, "My very tools of trade," as he designated his library. The attachment spread to whatever funds might be due from his publishers, and covered his balance with *The Examiner* for the war articles—all of it revenue which in his provident integrity he had sought almost solely for the benefit of his dependents.

He was generous until taken advantage of, and then—divinely generous still, even to generosity becoming, in the nature of things, a mere duty. When questioned as to a seemingly short-sighted attitude that might work disadvantage to himself, his philosophy dictated the following:

"If ——— should sell off everything I possess, I would say, 'cheap at the price.' The dollars do not amount to anything to me where human relations are concerned. I think I am the same way with my neck. I would trust it willingly to a friend, a dear friend, and if that friend should chop off my head, my head, rolling on the ground, would say, I am sure, 'Cheap at the price.' So I shall let certain powers remain in So-and-So's hands. If such power is misused, why, what of it? The extent of its misuse would be as nothing to the fact that So-and-So had misused it, and I prefer to give the chance."

To Cloudesley he sent a scribbled note: "Am back, rushed to death, and trying to straighten things out. At present all money tied up (earned and unearned) and don't know where I'm at."

And this was not the worst. A dear and wonderful friend had been ruthlessly named as co-respondent in the separation complaint and of course there ensued all the malodorous notoriety which accompanies such attacks. A hue and cry went up from a hypocritical capitalist press, quite as if Jack London were the first youth who ever repented of a marital mistake.

The girl's chief reply to the astonishing accusations, as recorded in the Bay dailies, was that the same were "merely vulgar." Jack, grieved to the heart that his beloved friends should be soiled in his unfortunate affairs, declined to comment upon the latter otherwise than: "I refuse to say a word about my separation. . . . A man's private affairs are his private affairs." And as might be surmised, the "Herbert Wace" of the "Letters" was widely quoted. To the girl herself, Jack wrote, in part:

"I do most earnestly hope that your name will not be linked any more with my troubles. It will soon die away, I believe. And so it goes, I wander through life delivering hurts to all that know me. . . . And so one pays . . . only, it is the woman who always pays.

"Unspoilt in your idealism? And think of me as unsaved in my materialism. . . . However, I am changed. Though a materialist when I first knew you, I had the saving grace of enthusiasm. That enthusiasm is the thing that is spoiled, and I have become too sorry a thing for you to remember."

The original complaint, a lengthy arraignment abounding in curious charges, was eventually withdrawn and another, this time for complete divorce instead of mere separation and maintenance, and on the ground of simple "desertion," went before the court on August 2, 1904. This was allowed by default, Jack London not appearing. Property interests were adjusted out of court.

Shortening down already insufficient sleep, beating his head with his fist to keep awake, Jack plunged deeper than ever into work. For he must immediately start building the new home for his little girls; and this home, in addition to his other driven obligations, he personally superintended. As if all this were not enough, the death of Mammy Jennie's husband made it incumbent upon him to take over her affairs.

The events of this summer of 1904 threw Jack into a melancholia that he tried to conceal under a carefree manner when with the "The Crowd" picnicking in the hills, or rollicking in the Piedmont swimming baths—his main recreations. A letter to me aired his depression over the minuteness of human generosity and fair play:

"It's sometimes a dreary thing to sit and watch the game played in the small and petty way. One who not only takes a hand in the game, but calmly sits outside as well and watches, usually sees the small and petty way, and is content to face immediate losses, knowing that the ultimate gain is his. It is so small, so pitifully small, that at worst it can produce only a passing glow of anger, and after that, pity only remains, and tolerance without confidence.—Oh, why can't the men and women of this world learn that playing the game in the small way is the losing way? They are always doomed to failure when they play against the one who plays in the large way."

So bleak was his spirit for a while, that more than once he considered, though with a terrible cheerlessness, returning to the old order, what of love and sorrow for the babies. In a letter: "Believe me, . . . it has taken all the resolution I could summon to prevent my going back, for the children's sake. I have been sadly shaken during the last forty-eight hours—so shaken that it almost seemed easier for me to sacrifice myself for the little ones. They are such joys, such perfect little human creatures." But in after years he reviewed his state at that time: "If I had gone back, it would have meant suicide or insanity."

As it was, he was with the children frequently, either in their home or his own.

My people wrote to me, in the east, that he had come to spend a week at Wake Robin Lodge, and his regard for the beautiful mountainside had only extended.

Manyoungi, the brightest Korean in Jack's train with the Japanese First Army, had been brought by him to California, for he needed just such a servitor to relieve him of all domestic friction in the little flat. This boy, resourceful and comely, took prideful charge from kitchen to study, and made entertaining an irresponsible pleasure to "Master," as he continued to designate his employer, to the playful horror of jeering friends, radical and otherwise. Finding it useless, Jack gave up trying to dissuade Manyoungi from his long-time custom with European travelers to Korea, and submitted willingly to the ministrations of the perfect servant who assumed entire care of his wardrobe, even to dressing him in the morning. Jack's attitude upon personal service was to the effect that it saved him priceless minutes for work and reading. "Why tie my own shoes when I can have it done by some one whose business it is, while I am improving my mind or entertaining the fellows who drop in!"

And many were the fellows who dropped in, persons from near and far flocking to look upon the face and hang upon the speech of the young writer. Jack, jealously conserving his every moment, saved hours by meeting them at mealtime:

"Manyoungi, there'll be two to dinner this evening—" or a dozen, or six; and the table blossomed forthwith by virtue of a complete set of exquisite Haviland china, with silver and crystal and napery as faultless; to all of which beauty Jack, hospitality in his eye, had treated his longing soul upon taking up bachelor life.

"If I had to be a servant," he would muse, "I'd be just such an one as Manyoungi. He possesses what I understand as 'the spirit of service' to the finest degree."

"The spirit of service"—he appeared to love the quality, despite the popular idea of his socialism. Out of his own mouth: "If I were a servant, I'd make myself the finest servant in the world."

"The Faith of Men," another series of Klondike yarns, and ninth volume on the stretching shelf, had been published by Macmillans in the spring, and autumn saw "The Sea Wolf" beside it. The latter was given especially high acclaim by the reviewers. However, they persisted in pigeonholing it as essentially "a man's book—a book women would not care for;" and it was with loud glee that Jack later on received word that *The Ladies' Home Journal* had purchased several thousand copies to be used as premiums to subscribers. Meanwhile, he tried his hand at writing a play, based upon his short story "Scorn of Women"— frankly an experiment. This play at various times intrigued the fancy of one and another of "America's foremost actresses," but was never performed. Referring to the comment of one star, Jack wrote me:

"——, in suggestion of making a struggle between Freda and Mrs. E. for Capt. E., violates the eternal art canon of UNITY. It is ANOTHER story.

"I violated all the conventional art-canons, but not one eternal art canon.

"I wrote a play without a hero, without a villain, without a love-motif, and with two leading ladies."

And to Anna Strunsky:

"Am on third and last act of play, adapted from 'Scorn of Women,' to be called 'The Way of Women.' Not a big effort.

Wouldn't dare a big effort. An experiment merely—lots of horse-play, etc., and every character, even Sitka Charley, is belittled."

Then, in another paragraph, concerning his health:

"I have been working hard, and what of my physical afflictions have been a pretty good recluse. . . . Yes, I am thin—seven pounds off weight, and soft, which is equivalent to twelve pounds off weight altogether. My grippe was followed by a nervous itch, which heat aggravated, and I was prevented from exercising for weeks."

The "nervous itch" referred to gave Jack much disquietude both mental and physical, and to the skin- and nerve-specialists not a little thought and experimentation. Under the most minute scrutiny, the skin revealed nothing that would lead to a diagnosis. Remained only to go into the question of nerves. The patient's dynamic habits of overwork in every department of his intellectual life, and his relentless limitation of repose, afforded good reason; on the other hand, he had pursued this system for many years, with no such warning as the present.

By a process of elimination common to his drastic fashion, he hit upon an apparently innocent custom indulged for some months past—that of munching salted pecans and almonds while reading in bed. Possibly he had saturated himself with an excess of salt. (Physicians often reduce sodium chloride in the tissues and fluids for remedial purposes, a method known as dechloridation.) He dropped this saline element from his dietary. The itch disappeared. Resuming the nut-refreshment, the affliction took a new lease of his hypersensitive surfaces, which flamed intolerably at the slightest exertion. So acute was the disorder, that even the thought of it precipitated an attack.

After convincing himself that salt was the offending factor, Jack went gaily to the specialists with his findings, and they agreed with his conclusion. His diagnosis was verified to his entire satisfaction when in tropic climes relapses followed long exposure to salt air and water; and even under a bright California sky in long periods of mid-winter yachting.

But there was no diminishing of his work; rather, he increased the staggering pace. Having reeled off an article entitled "The Yellow Peril" (now in collection "Revolution"), in which his sage views on the Asiatic situation were presented, he tackled a short novel. This was "The Game," which might be termed a prizefight idyl—its overarching motif being man's eternal struggle between woman and career. He wrote me:

"Am slowly weaving 'The Game.' You would n't think it difficult if you read it. Most likely a failure, but it is a splendid exercise for me. I am learning more of my craft. Some day I may master my tools."

He loved the writing of it, for, like Keats, he loved a fair contest between man and man. It was not for the prize nor for brutality's sake, but for the cleanness of a scientific game—Anglo-Saxon sport, square and true, as say against some other national sports like bull-fighting, where as a rule one contestant is doomed through trickery of superior intelligence.

He enjoyed the creating of Genevieve, line for line. "Why, you'd never guess where I got my model for her," he said to me afterward. "She was a candy-girl in a poor little sweet-shop in London. I never saw such a skin—sprayed with color like your Duchesse roses out the window there. I used to hunt up a thirst for gallons of soft drinks just for excuse to go and sit at the dingy little counter and look shyly at her face, as a silly boy might. I did not even want to touch her—and she hadn't a thing in her yellow head to talk about. It was just an abandonment to the prettiness and fragility of her English bloom."

"The Game" was serialized in *The Metropolitan Magazine*, illustrated by Henry Hutt in water-colors. And Jack had been right: it was for the most part a failure, so far as concerned the American public. For readers listened to the uncomprehending words of space-writers who totally missed the big motif, and neither knew nor cared to know aught of "the game" itself. Timely to the subject, I quote entire a letter Jack London wrote on August 18, 1905, to the editor of the New York *Times:*

"As one interested in the play of life, and in the mental processes of his fellow-creatures, I have been somewhat amused by a certain feature of the criticisms of my prize-fighting story, 'The Game.' This feature is the impeachment of my realism, the challenging of the facts of life as put down by me in that story. It is rather hard on a poor devil of a writer, when he has written what he has seen with his own eyes, or experienced in his own body, to have it charged that said sights and experiences are unreal and impossible.

"But this is no new experience, after all. I remember a review of 'The Sea Wolf' by an Atlantic Coast critic who seemed very familiar with the sea. Said critic laughed hugely at me because I sent one of my characters aloft to shift over a gaff-topsail. The critic said that no one ever went aloft to shift over a gaff-topsail, and that he knew what he was talking about because he had seen many gaff-topsails shifted over from the deck. Yet I, on a seven-months' cruise in a topmast schooner, had gone aloft, I suppose, a hundred times, and with my own hands shifted tacks and sheets of gaff-topsails.

"Now to come back to 'The Game.' As reviewed in the New York *Saturday Times,* fault was found with my realism. I doubt if this reviewer has had as much experience in such matters as I have. I doubt if he knows what it is to be knocked out, or to knock out another man. I have had these experiences, and it was out of these experiences, plus a fairly intimate knowledge of prize-fighting in general, that I wrote 'The Game.'

"I quote from the critic in the *Saturday Times:*

" 'Still more one gently doubts in this particular case, that a blow delivered by Ponta on the point of Fleming's chin could throw the latter upon the padded canvas floor of the ring with enough force to smash in the whole back of his skull, as Mr. London describes.'

"All I can say in reply is, that a young fighter in the very club described in my book, had his head smashed in this manner. Incidentally, this young fighter worked in a sail-loft and took remarkably good care of his mother, brother and sisters.

"And—oh, one word more. I have just received a letter from Jimmy Britt, light-weight champion of the world, in which he tells me that he particularly enjoyed 'The Game,' 'on account of its trueness to life.'

"Very truly yours,
"Jack London."

Jack always remained a champion of this book of his, not only in view of its subject but also of his workmanship. When Great Britain received it with intense appreciation, placing "this cameo of the ring" alongside other favorites like "Cashel Byron's Profession," the author was exultant with vindication. And yet, only the other day in fact, I picked up an American newspaper clipping in which "The Game" was tossed aside as "that Jack London novel without an excuse!"

With reference to some tentative and evidently shortsighted criticism I had made of the manuscript, he responded:

"And, by the way, remember that anybody, by hard work, can achieve *precision of language,* but that very few can achieve *strength of style.* What knocks E——? Precision. To be precise he has pruned away all strength. What the world wants is strength of utterance, not precision of utterance. Remember that about all the precise ways of saying things have already been said; the person who would be precise is merely an echo of all the precise people who have gone before, and such a person's work is bound to be colorless and insipid. Think it over. Let us talk all these things over."

I remember, when he referred to a rusty pipe as "a streak of rust," wishing that I had thought of it first!

Ere the ink was dry on the packet that inclosed his manuscript of "The Game" to the editor, he was busy upon memoranda for his next novel in mind, "White Fang." On December 6, I received a handful of notes by mail, with the following comments:

"Find here, and please return, the *motif* for my very next book. A companion to 'The Call of the Wild.' Beginning at the very opposite end—evolution instead of devolution; civilization instead of decivilization. It is distinctly NOT to be a sequel. Merely same length, dog-story, and companion story. I shall not call it 'Call of the Tame,' but shall have title quite dissimilar to 'Call of Wild.' There are lots of difficulties in the way, but I believe I can make a crackerjack of it—have quit the play for a day to think about it.

"May go East in January after all for two or three months—lecturing."

By now, I was back from the east and living at Wake Robin Lodge with my Aunt, putting in hours a day at the piano. Meanwhile my services were offered to Jack in the matter of relieving him of typewriting, a suggestion that met with glad response; and I was thus brought into closer touch with his work and aims. My remuneration—and that a treasure—was the possession of his handwritten pages. Except for a few short stories and articles, the play "Scorn of Women" was my first typing for him, and by mail we exchanged some lively discussions of its technique before final completion. One of his letters contains this lamentation:

"I did 1000 words (dialogue and direction) on the first act of the play to-day. Oh, how it puzzles me and worries me, that play. Sometimes all seems clear (and good) and next it seems all rot and a rotten failure. But I do n't care. Though I never get a cent for it, I'm learning a whole lot about play-writing."

Here are the last two 1904 communications to Cloudesley Johns:

> "1216 Telegraph Avenue,
> "Dec. 8, 1904.
>
> "I had to tell *Black Cat* that the idea of my story was not original [this was 'A Nose for the King,' published in *The Black Cat* for March, 1906, and collected in 'When God Laughs'] having been told me by a Korean. So I don't know whether my chance is spoiled or not.
>
> "Sure, I'll come to stay with you—if I can bring Manyoungi. Only too glad. Expect to be down in first part of January.
>
> "I went to look at the *Spray* to-day. First time since that night we came in from Petaluma. Won't be able to get out on her this year."

I have heard Jack London remark that Miss Mary Shaw, whom he met after a San Francisco performance of "Mrs. Warren's Profession," was the most intellectual actress he had ever talked with. And to Cloudesley:

> "Yes—met Miss Shaw—went to dinner. Liked her better than any actress ever met."

Every moment energy incarnate, he rushed and crowded as if to preclude thinking of aught except the work or recreation of the moment. Speed, speed—and he began saving for a big red motor-car to mend the general pace. He fell ill—another severe attack of grippe that compelled him to ease up; but the instant his brain cleared of dizziness, his incredible activities were resumed. And he always made it a religious duty personally to answer every letter received. Often I read the following, at the end of hastily scrawled notes to me: "This is the last of 30 [or 40, or 50] letters I have just reeled off."

And this:

"I never had time to bore myself—Do you know I never have a moment with myself—am always doing something when I am alone—I shall work till midnight to-night, then bed, and read myself to sleep."

To which I, tinged with sorrow and foreboding:

"You make me sad. You have n't time to live; so what's the use of living?"

One of Jack's relaxations, if the word can apply to the tense interest he took in game and sport, and his unquench-able joy in the pard-like beauty of an athlete, was following the monthly boxing bouts at the West Oakland Athletic Club, the scene of the prizefight in "The Game." A char-acteristic incident has been offered me by a newspaperman, Mr. Fred Goodcell, who made his acquaintance one day when Jack had, for the first time in years, dropped in to see his old friend Johnny Heinold in the First and Last Chance. I give Mr. Goodcell's version of one evening that Jack described to me at the time:

"It was some weeks later that I met Jack again. I call him Jack, not because close acquaintanceship would permit, but because I believe all the world thinks of him in that intimate way. He was n't a man to be Mistered.

"This second meeting was at the box office of the West Oakland Athletic Club. The bouts were staged in an upstairs hall, far too small for the crowds that came, a fire trap that would make a Hun bomb thrower envious, but sweating, shouting, smoking fight-fans gathered there and cheered the 'ham and egg' boys as they slugged through four rounds, unless a knockout brought earlier surcease.

"Jack was at the box office trying to buy a front seat. There was none to be had. Just then I arrived and with an extra press ticket in my pocket invited Jack to be my guest. He accepted and we occupied ringside seats.

"On the card this night there was one fighter called 'The Rat.' I never knew him by any other name. I knew 'The Rat' to be an Italian huckster. . . . To me he was a fifth-rate fighter, lacking brains to be anything better. But Jack became enthusiastic:

" 'What a beauty,' he remarked.

" 'That's 'The Rat,' I answered.

" 'A beauty,' he resumed, enthusiastically. 'A perfect speci-

men. Can't you see it? Beautifully molded, young, full of life;
the cautious tread of an animal and perfect symmetry in every
limb.''

"As a matter of fact, 'The Rat' possessed a face that became
a fighter accustomed to taking the short end of the purse. He was
homely—his face was, but Jack London looked and saw beauty in
the perfection of his naked body. To me he was 'The Rat' and he
was homely; to Jack he was 'a beauty.' He had seen beauty where
I had missed it. Perhaps that is one of the secrets of his success—
his ability to see more than the rest of us, to pick out the beauty
from the drab.

"The fight over, I asked Jack to write me a brief account of the
show. He agreed, but his 150 or 200 words were about 'The Rat.'
His story, signed 'By Jack London,' was published in the Oakland
Herald. The one story led to others. London yearned for the
ringside seats, not because of any ambition to be 'up in front,' but
because from the ringside he could have an unobstructed view of
the ring, could watch every blow, see everything that took place.
And so we made a deal, I to supply a ringside seat for each show
and London to write a signed story regarding the show, or some
feature of it. This continued three or four months and the Jack
London stories became big features, features that are undoubtedly
to-day prized by many old-time fighters, too old now to enter the
padded arena, but proud that Jack London wrote about them.''

In addition to all else, he dashed off requested "stories"
for *The Examiner*, one of which was "The Great Socialist
Vote Explained"—a similar article going to *Wilshire's
Magazine*. Many an evening was filled with a reading or
a lecture at this club and that. One night he talked at the
Home Club of Oakland, on Japan; on another, he spoke at
the Nile Club, in acknowledgment of an honorary membership; he read to the New Era Club, the men's league of the
Methodist Church, from "The People of the Abyss"; "The
Call of the Wild" of course was often asked for; and
whenever Mr. Bamford sent out invitations to a Ruskin
Club dinner, Jack was expected to be on the program. At
one dinner he gave them "The Class Struggle," and again

"The Scab." Both these papers were later collected in "War of the Classes," proof-sheets of which in the spring he sent me for correction. In among Jack's correspondence with me is laid away a little handwritten sheet from which he made a statement to the Ruskin Club of his Socialistic position:

"I am a socialist, first, because I was born a proletarian and early discovered that for the proletariat socialism was the only way out; second, ceasing to be a proletarian and becoming a parasite (an artist parasite, if you please), I discovered that socialism was the only way out for art and the artist."

The Ruskin Club several times mentioned was composed of what might be termed the intellectual aristocracy of the socialists about the Bay. Its father and moving spirit was Professor Frederick Irons Bamford, "the lion-hearted one," Jack lovingly called him, for despite an agonizingly supersensitive nature he was made of the stuff of martyrs. And to Comrade Lyon Jack one evening observed: "Bamford is the only man in the Ruskin Club who makes me feel small." The Club would meet here and there, at irregular intervals, say at Piedmont Park Clubhouse, or the Hotel Metropole of "Martin Eden" fame. Notable were these affairs, often in honor of big men in the movement, as well as in honor of men whom the Club strove to convert to its banner.

He would even go out of the Bay region to lecture, perhaps to San José where, as guest of Professor Henry Meade Bland, he addressed the State Normal; or to Vallejo where ashore from the *Spray* he had made friends; once or twice to Stockton, making headquarters with Johannes Reimers. One of Mr. Reimers' sons found himself abruptly unpopular with his teachers because of his father's firebrand socialist guest; a circumstance in which Jack's quick natural regret was tempered by the reflection: "That young fellow is the stuff that opposition will make a man of!"

Perhaps I have not mentioned that Jack never attended any lectures except his own. "I do not waste my time listening to lectures," he put it. "I'd rather read. I get more for myself, without the personality of the speaker coming between. And I cover more ground." The following, from another's pen, seems to expess what Jack meant: "To attend a motion picture play is to be primitive; to listen to an orator is to be a cave man; to read is to be civilized!"

In a vast ledger, clipping-book of 1904, pasted by his children's mother and Eliza Shepard, I find several humorous newspaper squibs upon Jack's being made a member of the Bohemian Club despite his soft-collared silk shirt and other ineradicable preferences. Indeed, this was not the first capitulation of clubdom to his apparel. And the press was often the reverse of reliable, as in the case of a certain affair in Jack's honor given by the exclusive feminine Ebell Club of Oakland, when, it is to this day firmly believed by newspaper readers, he lectured in a red flannel shirt. I have Jack's word that outside of those brilliant Klondike undergarments, and possibly while stoking a steamship passage, never in his whole existence did he affect scarlet flannel. When he did don woolens at all, as say at sea, it was of navy-blue. Even his trusty sweater, though as described in my Prologue he early wore it in making social calls on his bicycle, never appeared upon the platform. A white, soft shirt, with flowing tie, worn with a black, sack-coated suit, was his evening dress.

Handling the item of Jack London's entrance into the Bohemian Club, one San Francisco sheet, *The Wasp*, avoided the humorous note to such a virulent extent as to defeat its ends. Being by all counts the most venomous slam in all the scrapbooks, it is too comical not to quote entire—especially in view of the fact that at about the date of its publication a portion of "The Call of the Wild" had been incorporated into a text-book on English used in the

University of California, forerunner of others of his books to be adjudged "classics" by that institution:

"Jack London's Shirt Vindicated.

"The Bohemian Club has relented toward Jack London's negligée shirt and taken the novelist into membership—honorary membership at that. Why honorary, I cannot say. Certainly, it is not on the strength of Mr. London's 'The Call of the Wild,' which deserves to take rank as an average Sunday supplement story in a yellow newspaper. Neither can it be his 'Sea Wolf' that has raised him into a niche in the Bohemian Temple of Honor beside Charles Warren Stoddard, Henry Irving, and Joaquin Miller. *The Wasp* would be only too glad to help in placing laurels on the brow of Mr. London if he deserved them, but he must furnish better evidence of his literary quality before this journal will assist in decorating him. *The Wasp* decorates as masters no apprentices whose work is more conspicuous for its blemishes than its finish. I have said that Mr. Jack London's 'Call of the Wild' belongs to the Sunday supplement order. His 'Sea Wolf' is better adapted as a serial for the *Coast Seamen's Journal* and the habitues of the 'Fair Wind' and the 'Blue Anchor' saloons on the city front than for the shelves of libraries or the tables of reading rooms frequented by people of even superficial culture. It lacks every essential of a thoroughly good novel except nice binding, careful printing, and excellent illustrations. The best that can be said of it is that it is a poor and clumsy imitation of the new Russian school of tramp literature, which has given to the world a series of novels dealing with the scum of humanity, with brutal frankness. When one has waded through 'The Sea Wolf' by a laborious effort the conviction is irresistible that the author shows more fitness for the post of second mate of a whaler than a leader of the great army of imaginative scribblers.''

While on the theme, I might say in passing that Jack London was not at any period a zealous clubman. He belonged to no large club bodies otherwise than the Bohemian; and the famous rooms in San Francisco saw him little and at prolonged intervals, when he chanced to be in the neighborhood for some other purpose. After the Great Earthquake and Fire, the new clubrooms and the Sultan Turkish Baths were rebuilt in close proximity. We often, Jack and I, finished off a theater night at the Baths, but first he would drop in at the Club for poker or pedro or bridge, and I can still hear his drowsy-happy voice over the Baths telephone from the men's floor, telling me of his luck—for the voice was sure to be happy from his pleasure in the game, be luck good or ill. And whenever feasible, our world-wanderings led homeward in midsummer, that he might spend at least one week of High Jinks at Bohemian Grove, situated but a few miles from the Ranch. For he dreaded foregoing the marvelous annual Grove Play, words and music, acting and staging, all done by members of the Club only.

January, 1905, was an especially full month. The first week saw Jack in Los Angeles, visiting Cloudesley Johns in the quaint rambling home at 500 North Soto Street, where he reveled in the companionship of his friend's family. The grandmother, Mrs. Rebecca Spring, was Jack's particular joy. She was one of California's most remarkable women, friend of Margaret Fuller, Emerson, Holmes, Longfellow; and she subsequently died in dissatisfaction with Life, because Life cheated her by a few short weeks of attaining her centenary.

He also visited the Mathers in Pasadena, for the daughter of the house, Miss Katherine, had been a fellow passenger on the *Siberia* to Japan. And of course he attended the yearly winter Rose Carnival of her city. This vacation, like his life in Oakland, was without repose of spirit or body—rush, rush from daybreak to even-fall, and for the best hours of the night. While in Los Angeles, he spoke for the Socialists, who rented the Simpson Auditorium for the occasion. Miss Constance L. Skinner, poet and historian, another member of the Johns' fascinating household, who evoked Jack's admiration and regard, ably reported the lecture, which was on the subject of "Revolution," for the *Los Angeles Examiner*. Strangely enough, the radicals of the "City of Angels," when publishing their favorite picture of Jack, replaced the sweater by a formal suit and collar, drawn quite to order, beneath which Jack scratched a disgusted comment.

His introduction at that meeting was not to his liking, according to his comrade J. B. Osborne, of Oakland: "The Chairman introduced him as a ripe scholar, a profound philosopher, a literary genius and the foremost man of letters in America. . . . When London arose, dressed in good clothes but wearing a soft shirt, he said:

"Comrade Chairman and Fellow Workers: I was not flattered by all the encomiums heaped upon me by the chairman, for the reason that before people had given me any of these titles which the chairman so lavishly credits me, I was working in a cannery, a pickle factory, had my application in with Murray and Ready for common labor, was a sailor before the mast, and worked months at a time looking for work in the ranks of the unemployed; and it is the proletarian side of my life that I revere the most and to which I will cling as long as I live."

Once more in his home town, Jack set others than the County of Alameda by the ears by consenting to an oft-repeated request from the President of the University of California, Dr. Benjamin Ide Wheeler (in 1919, Emeritus), to address the students in Harmon Gymnasium. And "choose your own subject—anything at all," Jack was left to consult his fancy. Now was his big chance to let loose a thunderbolt in the sacred groves, and he armed for the fray.

The day was the 20th of January. Humming across the campus from North Berkeley in the morning sunlight, fresh from an hour with my piano teacher, Mrs. Fred Gutterson, herself pupil of Bauer and Leschetizsky and Carreño, I turned westerly toward the "Gym" where I had danced so many an evening away. And who should come stepping along with a smile in his eyes but our young friend, who explained that he had come out early in order to think quietly upon what he was going to say and how he was going to say it.

At the entrance we parted, I to become one of the several thousand, students and citizens, who packed the huge elongated octagon, Jack London to take his seat with the faculty convened upon the platform. President Wheeler presented the speaker, and the speaker went into action without preamble, head high, eyes grave and dark, voice challenging as he rapped out the short crisp sentences:

"I received a letter the other day. It was from a man in Arizona. It began, 'Dear Comrade.' It ended, 'Yours for the Revolution.' I replied to the letter, and my letter began, 'Dear Comrade.' It ended 'Yours for the Revolution.'"

The house thereupon settled to listen spellbound to the strangest statement of facts and opinions ever enunciated within the college walls. Dr. Wheeler, conventional embodiment of what by all tradition the head of a great university should be, sat aghast at what he had done. But it must be said that he was game; for when Jack, on the stroke of noon, realizing he was over his time, paused on tiptoe and asked, "Shall I stop?" the President came back hurriedly and with perfect courtesy: "No, go on—go on."

The last words of unequivocal indictment of society's mismanagement of society rang out clear from the upraised young face that had been imperially stern throughout, "The revolution is here, now. Stop it who can!" The audience, from whatever mixture of emotions, resounded in mighty applause. This was followed by a rouse from the Glee Club, composed for the renowned ex-student of the college. Meanwhile the faculty crowded about him, some in protest, some in curiosity, all with keen interest from one motive or another.

One humorous incident crept in: Jack in the course of his indictment had attacked the antiquated methods common to institutions of learning. When he stepped from the rostrum, according to one who stood near, "Professor Charles Mills Gayley greeted him and congratulated him upon his literary success. The author during their conversation reiterated his opinion of the deficiencies in teaching methods. He said:

" 'Dr. Gayley, permit me to make the criticism that English is not being taught in the right way. You are giving the students for their textbooks such antiquated authors as Macaulay, Emerson and others of the same school. What you need in your course is a few of the more modern types of literature——'

"Here Dr. Gayley interrupted with a dry smile:

" 'Perhaps you are not aware, Mr. London, that we are using your own "Call of the Wild" as a textbook in the University?' "

Jack surrendered, laughing with the others.

The evening papers and their morning associates treated the lecture with unexpected leniency. But when the press in general (Jack meantime repeating the speech at every opportunity) had had time to catch its breath, there was nothing too vicious nor unfair that could be printed of his utterances. There were exceptions, to be sure, the *Oakland Tribune* being one of those which remained loyal to "our own Jack." But the majority deliberately distorted his words, and robbed of its context the *quoted* phrase "To Hell with the Constitution"—notorious exclamation made by Sherman Bell, when that capitalistic leader of troops for the employers in Colorado, during the recent scandalous labor war that had raged there, was reproved for riding roughshod over the Constitution. Jack was held up as a dangerous anarchist—the same platitudinous old charge of the capitalist press against the socialist. And carefully editors refrained from embodying in their columns the statement that the social revolution was, as announced by the speaker, "to be fought, not with bombs, but with votes."

Nor did President Wheeler escape his share of criticism for having allowed so incendiary a character to sully the choice air of Berkeley. Again he was game, if a little condescending as befitted the dignity of his years and position, and the closing sentence in this excerpt from his letter to *The Argonaut* held him inviolate as concerned misapprehension of his own views:

"I think you ought to know that we never stipulate or inquire concerning the subject a speaker is to discuss at such a meeting. We intend to ask only such to speak as have by achievement earned the personal right to be heard. We seek the man and not the subject. I conceive it to be of highest value for students to meet and hear men who have honorably wrought and done in various fields. I introduce *them* to the students, and rarely, if ever, mention any subject. Jack London is a former student of the university, and has surely won an honorable distinction in the field of letters. And, after all, is it best for us to start an *Index* of tabooed subjects? One way to deal with a hard boiling tea-kettle is to take off the lid."

One paper, however, noted that Jack London, socialist, affected illustrious company, naming amongst others, H. G. Wells and George Bernard Shaw.

Some of the students of the old Oakland High wanted Jack to lecture, but promptly went up against the bars shut by Superintendent of Schools McClymonds and Principal Pond. Also, was he not a divorced man, inimical to the sanctity of hearth and home? How pitifully trivial and pettish all this hullabaloo of little editors' squeaks amidst the slashing, smashing events following the World War!

On the 29th of January Jack read "The Tramp"—another "War of the Classes" article, at Socialist Headquarters in Oakland. And a few weeks afterward I wrote him:

"Probably you already know it, but I'll repeat it anyway—that following your lecture at the University a few of the students organized a socialist club. This was announced at the Ruskin Club dinner last Friday evening. I know it will please you—I remember what you said to me the day of your lecture: that you would be satisfied if perhaps only a half dozen of the students were impressed.''

This club was the nucleus of the subsequent Intercollegiate Socialist Society, of which Jack London was elected the first President.

Near the end of January, he went one evening to see Blanche Bates at the Macdonough Theatre in Oakland, in ''The Darling of the Gods.'' Turning over in his mind the suitability of Miss Bates to the character of Freda Moloof in his own play ''Scorn of Women,'' he attended three consecutive performances from front-row vantage, the eager-eyed boy studying the young star carefully to this end. And naturally, by the time he had schemed an introduction, called upon her at the Hotel Metropole, and given a dinner in her honor, the papers had blazoned their plighted troth— the vigorous denials of both parties rendering new headlines in the next issues, and causing no end of mirth to the pair as well as the public.

It was not until the first week in February, 1905, that Jack and Cloudesley got the *Spray* up-river. Just before sailing from Oakland City Wharf, Jack accepted the socialist nomination for Mayor of Oakland. On the same ticket were Austin Lewis for City Attorney, with J. B. Osborne councilman for third ward. And who should be nominee for Mayor on the Independent Ticket, but John London's old friend John L. Davie? On the morning of election, one local sheet had it: ''All the nominees for Mayor, with the exception of Jack London, socialist candidate, were conspicuous about the polls.'' And Jack polled 981 votes at that. Knowing how personally distasteful the holding of public office would be to him, I once asked:

"What would you do if you should accidentally be elected to some of these political positions you let yourself in for?"

"There's not the least chance, my dear," he replied; then realizing he had not answered my question, he laughed, "I wouldn't let my name be used if I thought there was the slightest possibility of winning. If I did by chance get elected, I guess I'd run away to sea or somewhere with you!"

Meantime, I had taken to my room with an abscess in the left ear, made doubly torturing by neuralgia. For it is a nipping winter one may experience on Sonoma Mountain. The trouble was assumably due to long hours swimming and diving in the Oakland baths on cold days, and more especially a certain oft-repeated, twenty-two-foot jump in which Jack had coached me. Such an anomaly as unhealth on the part of "the Cheery One," as he liked to call me, was sufficient to make Jack desert the sloop somewhere along Petaluma Creek, leaving his friend and Manyoungi aboard, and footing it to the nearest railway for Glen Ellen. Reaching Wake Robin Lodge after nightfall, he stood for long contemplative minutes at the low casement of the red-wooded living room, gazing in at the unwonted spectacle of said Cheery One supine upon a couch, her head swathed in warm bandages.

Two days he remained, reading aloud to me by the hour; and I can vouch that no one ever knew tenderer nurse. So improved was I that on the second evening I rose hungry for the first time in weeks, and joined my nurse in a stealthy raid upon Auntie's sweet-smelling pantry. Returning to the big fireplace with our spoils of honey and biscuits and sun-dried figs, we feasted and giggled like truant schoolfellows. Truly, in our long years together, so few are the memories of irresponsible tranquil hiatuses in Jack's driven habit, that they stand forth in relief apparently out of all proportion to their importance. Not so, however; they showed him capable of the purest enjoyment of that sheer nonsense which relaxes a brain ordinarily over-conscious.

I recall an uproarious afternoon a few months later, when we two spent hours in a hammock under the laurels, doing nothing more profitable than manufacturing the most absurdly banal of limericks. Again, years afterward, I see in memory the twain of us, replete with picnic luncheon and good nature, prone upon the green outer declivity of a fern-lined crater in Hawaii euphoniously styled Puuhuu-luhulu. We peered over-edge into the giddy emerald cup and planned, in very extravagance of lazy foolishness, all the details of a country home in the pit, even to an adjustable glass roof against tropic showers!

Pain and house-confinement were happily mitigated by Jack's sympathy, both during his visit and thereafter, when such notes as these drifted to me from the *Spray's* pleasant course up the Sacramento river:

"Rio Vista, Feb. 10, 1905.

"I think continually of you, lying there through the long days and longer nights, and I look forward almost as keenly as you, I am sure, for the blessed time when you will be up and around and your old self again.

"Got here last night. The river is booming. Flood tide is not felt at all. Current runs down all the time. Expect to go to Walnut Grove and then down through Georgiana Slough to the San Joaquin and up to Stockton."

"Rio Vista, Feb. 11, 1905.

"Your short note just received. I am haunted right along by seeing you lying there, the bandage around your head and the cloth over your eyes. I do so look for improvement, and yet the north wind is blowing to-day which is bad for you. Do let me know every bit of improvement as soon as it comes.

"I have nothing to write in the way of news. Am working hard. Did 1000 words to-day. We have been here two days now, and I have not yet been ashore, though the town is interested in my existence. Have already 3 invitations to dinner, etc., and a launch is expected off in a few minutes with admirers (!). Also, Brown came aboard with a bunch of violets in his collar, sent, so Cloudesley avers, by the prettiest girl in California.

"Guess I'll take up one dinner invite to-night."

This mention of Brown calls to mind that Jack had become unexpectedly possessed of "twa dogs," one, a valuable lost Chow who presented himself at the front door, and tarried entirely at home for some weeks, when his rightful owner was discovered. The other was an Alaskan wolf-dog, a true "husky," brown-and-white of furry coat and fine of brush, with slant, watchful eyes and pointed ears, and a limp in the off hind-leg that was eloquent of sled and trail. His master, an old Klondiker, had lately died; and though strangers to Jack London, the relatives asked him if he would accept "Brown." Jack was willing, but the animal had other views, and sought every loophole to escape from the little yard at the rear of the flat (which sometimes was the ring for spirited bouts with the gloves), or from the front door when he was entertained within, to return to his loved one's house. Jack, after trying every cajolement to win him over, and going himself or sending his nephew or Manyoungi countless times to retrieve the estray, swore roundly that when Brown again ran away he could stay. But the dog had been making his own adjustment, and the next fruitless pilgrimage to the old home was his last. From the second story window Jack saw him cantering cheerfully back, and bounded downstairs to welcome him right comradely. Thenceforth Brown attached himself with the mute adoration of a soul disillusioned of all else in the world. Mute? Why, that dear lonely dog-fellow of our first married year was never heard to bark except upon two occasions when he thought Jack imperilled by a fractious horse. One day in the summer I asked:

"Now, what do you suppose Brown Wolf would do, if his old master should suddenly pop up beside *you?*"

"A story right there—don't breathe another word for a minute," Jack flashed at me, scribbling like mad on a note-pad, his deep mouth-corners turned up pleasedly with the scent of a new motif. The tale "Brown Wolf," in collection "Love of Life," was the sequel of the incident. That pleased expression recalls that always when lost in his morning's work, no matter how reluctantly begun, there was a half-smile lurking about his lips the while he bent concentrated over the broad tablet upon which the inky-wet characters sprawled and sprawled.

CHAPTER XXVI

1905

THE *Spray's* ramblings were to lead aside into Napa River to the pretty city of the same name that lies in the next inland valley to Sonoma. Here Jack was to visit the Winships, friends made on the voyage to Japan; and he sent me word that he would ride across the hills to spend several days with us at Wake Robin Lodge. He arrived on February 12, a showery Sunday, astride a harassing livery hack, both horse and horseman much the worse for the twenty miles. Jack wore a nerve-racked look, and my Aunt and I were solicitous, although we avoided advertising the same. The boy was in veritable distress, never quiet for a moment. His great-pupiled eyes were haunted with a hopeless weariness, and glassy as from fever. He talked very hard, as if against time, or in fear of silence. In the evening, as we clustered about the fireplace, my Aunt asked:

"Jack, my dear, why don't you get out of the city for a while, bring your work, and Manyoungi to look after your wants, take a little cottage here and rest and work far away from excitement and people?"

The eyes he raised to her face were as of some creature hunted. He shifted uneasily, almost as if embarrassed, and the corners of his mouth drooped like a child's on the verge of tears. Yet when he replied it was with a tinge of impatience, though a pitiful tiredness lay under the tone:

29

"Oh, Mother Mine—thank you. . . You're kind. . . But. . . but I think that the very quiet would drive me crazy."

It was a wail to be left alone in his impotence, and no further reference was made to the matter until the night before he departed.

The only recurrence of the temperamental joyance that was a large part of his nature was when he related the *Spray's* experience. For no sadness of soul could ever rob Jack London of his native delight in a boat. In relation to this very trip, I am tempted to quote from "Small-Boat Sailing" (in "The Human Drift"):

"After all, the mishaps are almost the best part of small-boat sailing. Looking back, they prove to be punctuations of joy. There are enough surprises and mishaps in a three-days' cruise in a small boat to supply a great ship on the ocean for a full year. I remember taking out a little thirty-footer I had bought. In six days we had two stiff blows, and, in addition, one proper south-wester and one ripsnorting southeaster. The slight intervals between these blows were dead calms. Also, in the six days, we were aground three times. Then, too, we tied up to a bank on the Sacramento river, and, grounding by an accident on the steep slope of a falling tide, nearly turned a side somersault down the bank. In a stark calm and a heavy tide in the Carquinez Straits, where anchors skate on the channel-scoured bottom, we were sucked against a big dock and smashed and bumped down a quarter of a mile of its length before we could get clear. Two hours afterward, on San Pablo Bay, the wind was piping up and we were reefing down. It is no fun to pick up a skiff adrift in a heavy sea and gale. That was our next task, for our skiff, swamping, parted both towing painters we had bent on. Before we recovered it we had nearly killed ourselves with exhaustion, and certainly had strained the sloop in every part from keelson to truck. And to cap it all, coming into our home port, beating up the narrowest part of the San Antonio Estuary, we had a shave of inches from collision with a big ship in tow of a tug."

Once, during his five-days' stay, I prevailed upon him to walk up the tree-embowered mountain road that skirts Graham Creek; but, to my hidden sorrow, he appeared to have grown blind to the beauty he had so loved. His tongue ran on and on incessantly—we were discussing the English poets. It was an exquisite sunset that bathed us in its waves of colored light, and upon a green eminence I halted Jack and his speech and stretched my arm toward the valley to the east, welling to its rosy wall-summits with a purple tide of shadow from the mountain on which we stood. To an earnest query if the loveliness of the world meant nothing to him any more, he stilled for a moment, then let fall very sadly:

"I don't seem to care for anything—I'm sick, my dear. It's Nietzsche's 'Long Sickness' that is mine, I fear. This doesn't seem to be what I want. I don't know *what* I want. Oh, I'm sorry—I am, I am; it hurts me to hurt you so. But there's nothing for me to do but go back to the city. I don't know what the end of it will be."

During my late convalescence at Wake Robin, slowly working at the typing and word-counting of his play, "Scorn of Women," and brooding not a little over his mental condition, I had received from Jack several of Nietzsche's books, of which he had written me:

"Have been getting hold of some of Nietzsche. I'll turn you loose first on his 'Genealogy of Morals'—and after that, something you'll like—'Thus Spake Zarathustra.'"

But I liked them all—"ate them up," as he said; and after digging through "Genealogy of Morals," "The Case of Wagner," "The Antichrist," and others, I polished off with "Zarathustra," which just happened to fill a need and accomplished more than any tonic to clear my own surcharged mental atmosphere and set my feet on the road to recovery. Here is a favorite bit I quoted to Jack: "At the foot of my height I dwell. How high my summits are?

How high, no one hath yet told me. But well I know my valleys."

At Jack's side upon the grassy promontory with the west-wind in our hair, I called attention to the wholesome philosophy of Zarathustra. In return I was reminded by Jack of Nietzsche's ultimate fate. Oh, no—he was not "playing to the gallery," nor inviting sympathy to his spiritual dole. That was not his custom; he was but frankly, soul to soul, letting me know what was true of him at the time, and vouchsafing a glimpse at the worst symptom—his own uncaring attitude concerning it.

On the eve of parting I played my last stake—recurred to my Aunt's suggestion, picturing the sweetness of the spring and summer he might pass there among the redwoods by the brook that once had soothed, and the work we could accomplish. But the warning unrest leaped into his eyes and voice and he implored:

"No, no; it doesn't seem that I can. I could not stand the quiet, I tell you. I could not. It would make me mad."

"Very well, then," I gave up, with my best cheer; "the thing for you is to do what you feel you must, of course.— And we won't say any more about it."

He started, flushed, turned and looked at me. Reaching for my hand, in a hushed, changed tone that meant volumes, he breathed:

"Why—why—you're a woman in a million!"

That night he slept an unbroken eight hours, unprecedented repose for Jack at any time, and for many weeks he had been working on but three or four hours nightly—sufficient alone to account for his sorry plight.

In the morning I offered to pilot him a different way from the one he had come. It was up through Nunn's Canyon, a lovely defile out of Sonoma Valley to the east. Jack appeared pleased; in fact presented a much brighter aspect for his long night of rest, and I hoped vainly that he would have reconsidered the matter of coming to Wake Robin for the season.

Away we rode together, he and I, one of us with a heavy heart, no inkling of which was allowed to pass eyes and lips. For I felt this was the last of Jack, that he was slipping irrecoverably from us who loved and would have helped him; and, what was more grave, slipping away from himself. Flesh and blood and brain could not support much longer this race he was waging against the sum of his mental and physical vitality.

But a charm was working in him, although I think he did not know it. The morning was one of California's most blessed, a great broken blue-and-white sky showering prismatic jewels and sungold alternately. Even the jaded livery hack responded to the brightness as he vied with my golden Belle over the blossoming floor of that bird-singing vale and up the successive rises of narrow Nunn's Canyon, where, on its rustic bridges, we crossed and recrossed the serpentine torrent a dozen times.

As we forged skyward on the ancient road that lies now against one bank, now another, the fanning ferns sprinkling our faces with rain and dew, wild-flowers nodding in the cool flaws of wind, I could see my dear man quicken and sparkle as if in spite of himself and the powers of darkness. The response to my own mood in the earth's enchantment, which had been so lamentably absent from him in the few days gone by, kept mounting and bubbling and presently was overflowing in the full measure I knew so gloriously of him. Truly, as the summit drew near, I do believe he still did not know that the crisis had been reached and passed in his Long Sickness for which the mad German philosopher had given him a name, and that he had staved off despair and death itself for many a splendid, fruitful year to come.

And now, could I credit my ears?—he was talking quite naturally with his old engaging enthusiasm, as if pursuing an uninterrupted conversation upon his intention to spend the year at Wake Robin; he would rearrange the interior of the tiny shingled cabin under the laurels and oaks, and ship up this and that piece of fruniture, and such and such books, dwelling upon certain of these he wanted to read to me. What fun Manyoungi would have getting settled and keeping house; and could he, Jack, dictate his damned correspondence to me? "And say, can you, do you suppose, find me a good horse? All the riding I've ever done was what my mare Belle taught me in Manchuria, and I know I'd love riding if I had another horse as good. I've got $350.00 for the *Black Cat* story—could you get me a horse for that? . . . How I wish I'd had that mare sent me from Korea!" and he launched into reminiscence of her virtues.

Not by word nor look did I treat his reviving humor as if it had not been the same throughout his visit. *Now* was the thing—he had come over and out by some sweet miracle, I cared not what, from his valley of the shadow. Far be it from me to disturb the ferment of the magic. Out of a pleasant, sunny silence as we climbed the grade, Jack suddenly reined in and laid his hand upon my shoulder. It was one of the supreme moments of my life. I met a look deeper than thankfulness, and in my heart for ay will abide his voice from the mouth that was like a child's surprised in emotion:

"You did it all, my Mate Woman. You've pulled me out. You've *rested* me so. And rest *was* what I needed— you were right. Something wonderful has happened to me. I am all right now. Dear My Woman, you need not be afraid for me any more."

My face must have answered, for I know I said no word. Solemnly at the green height of the pass, we clasped hands and kissed good-by, solemnly, joyfully, all in one. And there was that in his eyes which brought tears to mine. But it was the happy rain of a new day, for me, for him, and my heart for one ached with the joy of it. Loath to part,

Jack broke out: "Why not come on the rest of the way?
No, never mind that you're not fixed up—the Winships are
good sports and will welcome you with open arms."

Long we waved and waved until a descending bend into
the hinterland buried him from sight, and I turned and re-
traced the royal road we had come together, hardly able to
contain myself. Years thence, the Winships and Cloudeslev
told me that another man than the Jack who had left them
five days, rode in that afternoon on the same dispirited
steed. But Cloudesley knew; once they were aboard the
Spray he was told of the miracle.

Winding up his voyage mid-March in Oakland, Jack
discovered through Dr. Nicholson that he was suffering
from a tumor consequent upon an old injury he had thought
of little moment, and which should be removed as soon as
he could be put in proper condition. The red-cheeked
physician had him to bed at the flat, on a diet, and "no
cigarettes, young man, for a week." The "young man"
compromised, of course—or was it the practitioner who
compromised?

I bought a rose-pink lawn frock for his pleasure, and
went daily to help a very gay patient with his piled up correspondence, dictated from high pillows. After the
operation, when I called at the hospital, Jack told me he
was greatly relieved by the report that his tumor had been
pronounced non-malignant, and the assurance there would
be no relapse—an opinion that time corroborated. "I wonder," the bedridden philosopher speculated with a half-
abashed grin, "how much of my intellectual 'Long Sickness' could have been traceable to this damned thing draining my system?" Then suddenly grave, he rejoined: "No,
my dear—I won't belittle the real diagnosis. I know, and
you know, that when the sudden healing of that malady
took place, it was before I even knew I had a physical ail-
ment. . . . My dear, my dear."

Back at the little flat, he resumed his dictations, and

our readings progressed. During these days Jack made the better acquaintance of Tennyson, and, for the first time, "Idylls of the King," never ceasing to mourn that he had not "grown up with them" and their pure glamour of poesy. "And I never knew the gnomes and fairies as you did, either, to my loss," he regretted.

With boyish raptures he looked forward to summer at Wake Robin, and once interrupted himself in the middle of a sentence to say: "Oh, for the days when you can play, play for me!" One warm late afternoon, listening for the end of a pause in his dictation, something caused me to raise my eyes to Jack's face. His thread of thought lost, he had forgotten all else in the world but the wonder of loving:

"I'm quite mad for you, my dear, my dear," he repeated in the rare golden voice that returned in shaken moments. "Indeed, quite mad—with all the old madness of before the Long Sickness. And so we poor humans, weak and falli-ble, and prone to error, condemn ourselves liars, for I would not have believed I could be so mad twice!"

Then and then only, was I quite assured that he was saved to himself. But perhaps, when all is said, the best influence I had for him was the repose he said I brought—a repose that otherwise life seemed to have denied. Often I was reminded by him of the first story in which he employed any portion of his many-sided love for me. It was "Negore the Coward," last of the "Love of Life" collection, and will be found at the ending in one of Jack London's masterly depictions of death:

"And as even the memories dimmed and died in the darkness that fell upon him, he knew in her arms the ful-filment of all the ease and rest she had promised him. And as black night wrapped around him, his head upon her breast, he felt a great peace steal about him, and he was aware of the hush of many twilights and the mystery of silence."

I have before me the letter of the editor to whom the

author first submitted this manuscript. And he comments with surprise and delight upon the intangible "new touch" in Jack's work.

In the fly-leaf of "Love of Life" stands his inscription, of date November 23, 1909:

"Dear Mate-Woman:—

"There is within these pages a story you wot of well, wherein, long ago, I told of my love for you, and, more and better, of all that you and your love meant, and mean, to me."

My friend recovered rapidly—so rapidly that the surgeon was horrified to hear from the irrepressible's smilingly-rebellious, smoke-wreathed lips that he intended to ride his new horse as soon as ever he got to Glen Ellen, which would be on the 18th of April. The first time he left the house, was to walk around the corner to look over the beautiful animal which I brought for him to see. For I had bought the horse—Washoe Ban, blue-blooded Thoroughbred, his veins of fire throbbing through a skin of purest chestnut-gold. He was owned by Dr. H. N. Miner of Berkeley, and I had ridden him a number of times in the past. Two hundred and fifty dollars of Jack's *Black Cat* prize went for Ban, and I rode him from Berkeley to Oakland, thence by ferry to San Francisco, river steamer to Petaluma, where I slept, and next day sat the incomparable, exhaustless creature the twenty-two undulating green miles to Glen Ellen.

Jack further reminded Dr. Nicholson that before he spurned the haunts of men he had given his word to deliver "Revolution" in Shattuck Hall, Berkeley, on the 14th, and at the Alhambra Theatre in San Francisco on the 21st; also a talk at a Ruskin Club dinner to the Social Progress Club of the University of California. It was at one Ruskin dinner that year he "made the members take notice" most unexpectedly. Mr. Bamford had charged each guest to be ready with a definition of "Happiness." To me Jack said:

"What's yours going to be?" And I: "I haven't thought it out yet. What's yours?" "A coöperative commonwealth!" he grinned. "I'd like to speak up with 'Just loving,' " I laughed. "Great!" shouted Jack, "couldn't be better. Tell you what: I'll trade with you." "Done," said I. And at the banquet, upon the heels of Anna Strunsky's "Happiness is *adjustment*," my borrowed witticism raised the expected applause. "And yours?" Mr. Bamford called upon Jack London:

"*Just loving*," that wicked person breathed softly, his long-lashed eyelids demurely drooped.

A blank silence was broken by a smothered "Just WHAT?" from Mrs. A. A. Dennison, and Jack, raising his eyes, looked calmly about the company with a charming "What-are-you-going-to-do-about-it" expression as he repeated, "Just loving."

In passing, I want to relate, as nearly as possible in his own words, an occurrence that crystallized Jack London in certain personal habits more than any other self-argument. He put it something this way:

"You remember Dr. Nicholson? He was a magnificent specimen of a man, you will agree? Tall, straight, with the beauty of the athlete—girl's complexion and all that; not a vicious habit—drink, nor tobacco—not an injurious leaning. And he warned me that this and that vice of mine would ruin my health in a short time. Well, listen: Only a few short months after he talked so seriously to me, he died in screaming agony—rheumatism of the heart or some such horribly excruciating thing. Probably he had exposed himself in his practice; I don't know. But what I do know, is, that there are all sorts of bad habits in this world, and he must have landed on one of them peculiar to his way of life, or it landed on him. Cigarettes, or overwork—I tell you it's all one; one's as bad as the other; and I'll bet you 'even' money that cigarettes don't kill me!"

A man's argument, verily, and one that supersedes man's finest logic.

Washoe Ban and my Belle were housed amicably in a little shack-barn on a small property across the road from Wake Robin Lodge. This was the Caroline Kohler Ranch, familiarly known as the Fish Ranch because it had once been the scene of an ambitious failure in fish-hatchery. Jack had painstakingly considered the type of my Australian saddle, but decided upon a McClellan tree that we found in San Francisco, which had been fitted with a horn. Ultimately, however, he adopted my model. And he was almost as good as his challenge to Dr. Nicholson, for it was but a few days after his arrival on the 18th that he actually mounted and took his first lesson in Ban's easy, rocking-horse stride. I had yet to learn the man's giant recuperative power, and was fully as apprehensive as the man of medicine, but made no protest.

Not long afterward, at a request from Oakland, he bought a mare and surrey for his children and their mother. The animal later developed an incorrigible balk, and the family tiring of this kind of recreation, Jack brought the whole outfit up-country, where the mare came eventually to do light work and to negotiate the mountain trails under saddle. I am minded of the day she inconveniently lay down and rolled with her rider, none other than Johannes Reimers, in a pestiferous hornet-nest in the grass, as a means of escape from the stinging.

Jack's abrupt relinquishment of the city occasioned considerable press comment, with which I was connected, but even *The Examiner* failed to command any statement from either of us relating to matrimonial intentions. Jack informed the paper's representatives that when he had anything to say in the matter, he would give them the ''scoop,'' and with this they had to be content.

As for his new choice of residence he said to reporters: "I have forsaken the cities forever; winter and summer I shall live at Glen Ellen."

Would to heaven-upon-earth that every mating pair of men and women could know the privilege of the illuminating sort of experience which was Jack's and mine this six months before marriage. In the course of strenuous work and play of whatsoever nature, by our wedding date in November there was little of which we did not have a fair inkling as concerned each other's temperament and idiosyncrasies.

For the most part the study was smooth sailing, though at times beset by snags. Once, I shall never forget, it came to light that I had been accused by friends of Jack's, whom I had believed my own, of disloyalty and unveracity. With his invincible courage in seeking and gaging truth, he put even his Love impartially on the stand. To be other than sanely judicial even in so intimate a situation was contrary to his nature and method. True to what he called his "damned arithmetic," he undertook to thresh out the difficulty. Oh, he staked his love and his proudest judgment upon my guiltlessness; and, having satisfied himself, he set his every faculty to demonstrating to my detractors, if he perished in the attempt, that they were wrong on every count. All this not so much for personal gratification as for the pleasure of confounding them with my innocence and his faith. To be sure, he had taken the chance in a million that I prove false to his firm idea of my integrity. I met his infinitely sincere eyes on that, and laid at his disposal all that I had, and was. Amongst other expedients at my hand, a little pocket diary routed the most important charge that had been preferred. Well, indeed; but better still, when Jack, excitedly fishing up his own notebook for the same year, found it tallied with mine. Other evidence dove-tailed to his entire enlightenment of heart and brain, and I stood unassailable to our mutual joy, and the vindication of his "damned arithmetic."

"If you only knew—you can't *possibly* know—" he burst out one day near the end of the discussion by mail, "what it means to me to have some one fighting with me shoulder to shoulder, fighting my own fight, in my own way!"

When it was all over and certain apologies demanded by him had been written me by the unhappy complainants:

"Let me tell you something," he said. "This matter was broached to me sometime ago, before I went on the *Spray* trip. I want to show you a bit of my philosophy, in general as regards mankind, in particular as concerns you alone and in relation to me:

"When friends, ostensibly for my own good, came to me with a tale about you, I told them, first, that it was a pity they should soil their hands in gutter politics; and then I earnestly tried to help them know me a little better, as a matter of pride if you will, by telling them that even were these absurd things true—and I would stake my best judgment and my soul that they were not—they would make no possible difference to me. I said to them: 'I love Charmian, not for anything she may or may not have done, but for what I find her, for what she is to me. I know human beings pretty well—I make my living through my understanding of them—and I know Charmian better than to credit these calumnies. But the point is: Charmian might have murdered her father and mother, and subsisted solely upon little roast orphans—it is what I know of her, now, what she now is, that counts with me.'"

"And really," he once confessed in our married years, "I could almost have wished you'd had a past like my own, or worse, if you'd been just the same as when I knew I loved you. It would have made you seem almost greater to me—I mean, if you could have come up through degrading experiences that did not degrade but left you as I have always seen you!"

Since there was no way of actually manifesting how he would have regarded me in this suppositious premise, the question remained a moot one.

He always pleaded not guilty to the passion of jealousy, despising and deriding it as a low, bestial trait. With an exceptional capacity for tolerance toward almost every human weakness save disloyalty, he could not harbor any sympathy with that calamity of the ages, sheer animal jealousy. "Should you turn from me to another man, if I could not make you happy, I'd give that man to you on a silver platter my dear," he would declare, "and say 'Bless you, my children.'—But I don't believe *I* could send *you* on a silver platter to a man—quite!"

What better place than this, further to interpret Jack London's relation toward the element feminine? I, who have known the clasp of his soul, known him at his highest, can yet withdraw from that passionate fellowship and regard his masculinity as a whole. Asking my reader to bear in mind earlier manifestations of his philosophy and emotions toward the little woman of his adolescence, I shall enlarge upon his attitude.

He was not prone to allow women to interfere with the business of life and adventure. He liked to think of himself as in Augustus's class—that women could not make nor mar. In short, he was not a man who lost his head easily. "God's own mad lover dying on a kiss" was an appealing line to his sense of poesy; but Jack preferred to live, rather than die, on that kiss! Love, in brief, should be a warm and normal passion that made for fuller living. At one period, after soaking himself in the vast accumulation of erotic literature, pro and con, he told me, with a shake of his fine shoulders, that he felt himself lucky to have been born so rightly-balanced, that no abnormalities of his early rough days, nor contact with decadences of super-civilization, had touched him to his hurt. The alienists interested him intellectually, but he was nicely avert to perversion of any stripe.

I had supposed that there would be little of the proprietary in the regard of so broad-minded an individualist. One of my most vital surprises was to find that Jack was as delightfully medieval as many another lover in this world when it came, say, to matters financial. Having been myself independent, and believing that he would take this into consideration, I looked for him to make no matter of a separate bank account, or at least the "allowance" loved of wives, that I might not suffer a sense of bondage. But no—like the bulk of men his was the pleasure of spending his own money upon the "one small woman." Any other arrangement was frowned upon—at the suggestion a frost seemed to spread over his face. And, seeing that it was he, I found the bondage sweet.

Jack charmed women of all classes; and while he held a reserved opinion as to the intellectuality of the average female brain, he could not abide a stupid woman. His adventurous mentality had made him pursue women in curiosity, and learn them too well for his own good. He was of two distinct minds about them, and swung from one to the other: their innate goodness and staunchness commanded his worship, while their pitiable frailty and smallness wrung his spirit. "Pussy! Pussy!" I can hear him purr in the ear of any backbiting among his friends. Women, weighed by his biological judgment, represented the Eternal Enemy, and he liked the line:

"Her narrow feet are rooted in the ground,"

from Arthur Symons's "The Dance of the Daughters of Herodias." Yet this very concept, not always voiced without contempt, must have given rise to his pronouncement in "John Barleycorn": "Women are the true conservators of the race."

He has been heard to speak of woman as "the immodest

sex." And "Men are far more modest than women!" he would step into the heated air of argument, bringing down storms upon his unrepentant head. But he considered that he had several blazoned names to bear him out, among them Jean Paul, who said: "Love increases man's delicacy, and lessens woman's" and Bernard Shaw: "If women were as fastidious as men, morally and physically, there would be an end of the race!"

I must admit that I have seen him play down, not always up, to women and their vanity; but to his credit and theirs, he never left them long deceived. And he would not try to deceive those who spoke his own language, though he made it extremely difficult for them to understand his.

He had struggled against misogyny, winning out because he had had experience enough with exceptional women of conscience and brain to keep him healthy in viewpoint. Besides, in the last extremity, he was a one-woman man, glorying in the discovery of this. In my copy of "Before Adam," in 1907 he wrote: "I have read Schopenhauer and Weininger, and all the German misogynists, and still I love you. Such is my chemism—our chemism, rather." He showed an actual reverence for the woman who "informed" her beauty, or, better, her lack of beauty, who waged incessant warfare upon her imperfections, who wrought excellently with the material at her hand.

Jack owned to annoyance that the public denied he could write convincingly about women. "And yet," he would say, "I know them too well to write too well about them! I'd never get past the editor and the censor!"

Despite that he would often merely appear to take women at their own valuation and act as if he gave them credit for logic, he was possessed of a fine sense of chivalry. As instance: Once, bound to a foreign country, war-corresponding, a girl friend, who had received a similar commission, informed him that they would be sailing on the same boat. Jack was in despair because he knew, from knowledge of her want of practicality, that she would be on his already full hands. "What *would* you have done?" I asked him once. He reflected, working those brows that were like a sea-bird's wings: "I'd have had to marry her before I got through with it, I suppose!" "But," I expostulated, "but you loved another woman!" "Surely," he rejoined; "but what is a man to do? Her reputation would have been shattered—so I say, what can a man do in such circumstances, but marry the girl!"

Women have loved Jack London, aye, and died for love of him. And I can imagine, had he been situated so that it would have been possible, that his chivalry and sweetheartedness could have led him into marrying such, for their own happiness.

Once, I asked him how he had behaved himself toward the girls of yesterday, as he passed beyond them into the world that he was making his—the Lizzie Connollys, the Haydees. "I saw them occasionally," he said. "One must be kind, you know."

Little of love had he bought in his life, except in the course of laying his curiosity. A passion, with him, must be mutual, else worthless.

And so I became conversant with that "swarm of vibrating atoms" which men knew as Jack London, the youthful literary craftsman who had, as one critic put it, "Lived with storms and spaces and sunlight like a kinsman."— That was it; the dominant note of him was spaciousness, for the inflowing and out-giving of all available knowledge and feeling—the blood of adventure, physical and mental, scorching through life's channels.

"Visualization is everything for the teacher," he said, "and I love to teach, to transmit to others the ideas and impressions in my own consciousness."

It always seemed to me, observing, that while others were merely scratching the surface of events, Jack was getting underneath them, deeper and deeper into their significances.

Religion, as the average man knows religion, had no part in him. Spiritualism had been the belief in his childhood homes, a thing of magic and fearsomeness; but his expanding perceptions could not countenance that belief. His hope for bettering human conditions had filled depths of being which might have responded to divine philosophy. Again his norm: "Somehow, we must ever build upon the concrete." Again his oft-repeated criticism rings in the ears of memory: *"Will it work—will you trust your life to it!"*

In a little book of Ernest Untermann's, "Science and Revolution," which Jack gave me to read at that time, I come upon a sentence underscored for my benefit: "My method of investigation is that of historical materialism."

It is also to be said that I unlearned much of my man that had been told and impressed upon me in the past, even by persons who should have known better or who did know better and cruelly misrepresented him. In fact, Jack forever claimed to nurse a small grievance that I should ever have been misled, no matter by whom, from my direct early conclusions upon him. I recall, however, in the old Piedmont days, that while reserving certain few uncomplimentary opinions, so ready was I to stand up to any one who made unjust remarks in his disfavor, that more than once I was accused of taking undue interest in the young celebrity.

To the exclusion of all else, I devoted myself to mastering the open book that he tried to render himself to me. Even the piano was silent except when I played for Jack, and the trips to Berkeley with my music roll became less frequent and eventually ceased, I will say to his unqualified disapproval. (He never could entertain the idea, in the long years of our brimming life, why I could not give more time to music, since he too loved it so.) I learned the eloquence of his tongue; the fine arrogance of his certitudes; convictions I came to respect for their broad wisdom; and I knew, too, and richly, the eloquence of his silences in the starry moments that come to those who loved as we loved, and, loving, understand mutely. More than once, Jack has broken a comprehending pause, or even interrupted speech to say to me the dearest and finest of all his salutations in my thrilling ears:

"My kin—my very own Twin Brother!"

One thing, in that earlier association with Jack, was almost uncanny: he never seemed to fail of my high expectation. Tremulous, I all but looked for him to fail of making good, to my ideal, in this or that small, fine particular. But in vain: usually he surpassed the tentative demand I made upon his quality. His own failings he had, to be sure; but they were not those ordinarily suspected of lesser men.

The frankness which we continued to practise and exalt, made of our mateship, through thick and thin, a gorgeous achievement.

So I walked softly that spring and summer and fall, dedicated to discern with my own soul's best all of him that was possible, that I might enlarge and fix this kinship forever and forever. Upon one star I was intent: Never must our love and its expression sink into commonplace, but it must be kept from out "the ruck of casual and transitory things." And this was Jack's answer:

"Commonplaceness shall have no part with us unless I myself should become commonplace; and I think that can never be."

And Jack London learned his woman, playing her game as she tried to play his. With his broad sympathies, to his own peculiar interests he subjoined mine; and I, in return, widened my focus to include hobbies for which I had theretofore had no caring, thus creating fresh interests for my own sphere. Jack, for example, loved keenly a good card game. I had little use for cards; but I applied myself, to the end that before long I could play a fair game of whist, or cribbage, or pinochle. And when Jack found that certain stern methods of instruction distressed and stood in the way of quick absorption on my part, in all gentleness he went right-about in his lifelong tactics, exhibiting due appreciation of the harmony that had come to prevail in his life. He had until then rather prided himself upon an ability to shake knowledge into others, and I credited him with altering his way to favor me. He told me of how he had once, in half an hour, taught a rather *moronic* young girl to tell time by the clock—all others having failed. "But that's no reason," I laughingly contended, "that you can teach me whist by the same rules!"

With regard to our hard work together, and making toward a co-existing love and comradeship, I said: "We can't fail, because everything we do is compensatory life and living. His reply was: "So try to enjoy the fight for its own sake!"

Critics then as now were prone to dispatch the subject of Jack London's personality with words like "primitive," "uncouth," "brutal." He saw the primitiveness in all life, in himself—as he saw everything else, and made all things come under the empery of his thought and written language; but he did not live primitiveness, inasmuch as he was delicate, complex, withal simple in the final analyses of him. The chastity of the last analysis is like the chastity of his art that so often showed the last least perfection of chiseling. Robustness of body and mind offset, almost contradicted, the sensitiveness to impressions, that reaction to beauty of every sort—though particularly intellectual beauty—and to sympathy from others in his mood, his aims; and his shrinking from hurt, although only from the very, very few. Yet in himself, in his actions, in his work, there existed a regnant overtone, a cogency. Again I say: there was no paradox in him. Beleaguered ever with the thousand-thousand connotations, factors, in the chaos he did not falter, but somehow achieved unity, and a great rhythm. He knew himself; and it was a day of rejoicing when one departed guest, Everett Lloyd, sent him Weininger's "Sex and Character," with the author's definition of a genius: "A genius is he who is conscious of most, and of that most acutely."

Jack's writing, his thousand words a day, was done in a little "work-room" established in the two-room cottage, quite without any of that work-fever often necessary to writers. And whensoever art conflicted with substance, he invariably maintained:

"I will sacrifice form *every time,* when it boils down to a final question of choice between form and matter. The thought is the thing."

As some one has said, "He cared little for writing and a great deal for what he was writing about."

Here is further expression of his unrelenting realism, "brass-tack" reality—although it seems to me, all having been said, that his materialism incarnated his idealism, and his idealism consecrated and transfigured his materialism:

"I no more believe in Art for Art's sake theory than I believe that a human and humane motive justifies the inartistic telling of a story. I believe there are saints in slime as well as saints in heaven, and it depends how the slime saints are treated—upon their environment—as to whether they will ever leave the slime or not. People find fault with me for my 'disgusting realism.' Life is full of disgusting realism. I know men and women as they are—millions of them yet in the slime state. But I am an evolutionist, therefore a broad optimist, hence my love for the human (in the slime though he be) comes from my knowing him as he is and seeing the divine possibilities ahead of him. That's the whole motive of my 'White Fang.' Every atom of organic life is plastic. The finest specimens now in existence were once all pulpy infants capable of being molded this way or that. Let the pressure be one way and we have atavism—the reversion to the wild; the other the domestication, civilization. I have always been impressed with the awful plasticity of life and 1 feel that I can never lay enough stress upon the marvelous power and influence of environment.

"No work in the world is so absorbing to me as the people of the world. I care more for personalities than for work or art."

And he always stuck to it that Herbert Spencer's "Philosophy of Style" helped him more in his youth, than any other book—save Ouida's "Signa," his initial impetus—to success in literature. "It taught me," he said, "the subtle and manifold operations necessary to transmute thought, beauty, sensation and emotion into black symbols on white paper; which symbols through the reader's eye, were taken into his brain, and by his brain transmuted into thought, beauty, sensation and emotion that fairly corresponded with mine. Among other things, this taught me to *know* the brain of my reader, in order to select the symbols that would compel his brain to realize my thought, or vision, or emotion. Also, I learned that the right symbols were the ones that would require the expenditure of the minimum of my reader's brain energy, leaving the maximum of his brain energy to realize and enjoy the content of my mind, as conveyed to his mind." But "In my grownup years," he surveyed, "the writers who have influenced me most are Karl Marx in a particular, and Spencer in a general, way."

So never was I able to wring from him any worship of art for art's sake, although he strove for art with every well-selected instrument of his chosen calling; attained art, high art at times; and, being a potential Teacher, he could explain the means of it—this because he knew so exactly how he produced his effects.

"You're the genius of us two," he flabbergasted me one day when I, who never knew how I did the very few things I did well, had excelled perhaps in a dive, or a passage in music, or the revamping of some sentence that had eluded his own skill. "You don't know at all how you do things,

you see," he went on, "You just do them. And sometimes
you fall down and cannot do them again. Now that's genius,
or of the nature of genius. Take George Sterling; hand
him a problem of almost any sort, something he had probably never thought of before, certainly never studied. And
ten to one in a short time he will have given a masterly
solution. That's genius—big genius. No, there's no genius
in mine—unless it's the Weininger kind. I'm too practical
—that's why I'm a good teacher. Now you, my dear," in
candidness he offset some of his praise, "make a rotten
teacher! For instance, that riding lesson to-day,—you ride
as if you had ridden into the world in the first place,—but
I'm damned if you can show me how to 'post' on a trot as
you do!"

The pleasurable course of our companionship had its
normal interruptions. I had to become familiar with his
man humors. But he never moped, and seldom was taci-
turn. And his immoderate smoking was a trial; but after
once broaching the subject and finding it a tender one with
him, I dropped all reference to the matter. Although
he admired frankness, courage, the pettish side that women
know of the biggest men where their personal comforts are
in question, prevented my courage from demanding what I
had confidently hoped for. I should have known better;
but then, I was learning. At no time did I ever hear him
advise against smoking; yet he promised his nephew, Irving
Shepard, a thousand dollars if he would refrain from
smoking until he was twenty-one. From our conversation
on smoking, I gathered that his habit was a rather negligible
detail in comparison with the thousand and one larger
issues that occupied his mind. How shall I say? . . .
that this one habit, a mere habit, which required none of his
conscious attention, should not be too seriously considered
by him or others. Also, Jack seemed of a mind that the
nerve-strain of refraining offset any advantage that might
be derived from abstinence from cigarettes.

Long hot afternoons of typewriter dictation under the trees sometimes got on our mutual touchy nerves, and we became cognizant of still more of each other's caprices. Or suddenly, not yet versed in his "brass-tack" reasoning, his "arithmetic," I might unwittingly start disputes in which I had no chance against the assault of his logic, and would struggle with nerves that urged me to weep in sheer feminine bafflement, hating myself the more heartily. But always before me rose an honest warning with which Jack had forearmed us both previously to his coming:

"One thing I want to tell you for your own good and our happiness together. I do not think you are a hysterical woman. But don't ever have hysterics with me. You may think I'm hard. Maybe I am; but very earliest in my environment, in the very molding of the tender thing I was, I came to recoil from hysteria—all the bestiality of uncontrol and its phenomena. In my manhood I have seen tears and hysteria, and false fainting spells, all the unlovely futility of that sort of thing that gets a woman less than nothing from me. So never, never, I pray, if you love me, show yourself hysterical. I promise you I shall be cold, hard, even curious. And I will admit, in your case, that I should be hurt as well. But remember, always, this coldness is not deliberate of me: it's become second nature—a warp. I cannot help shrinking from tantrums as from unforgotten blows. . . . Once, when I was about three (and this is burned into me with a hot iron), flower in hand for a gift, I was brushed aside, kicked over, by an angry, rebellious woman striding on her ego-maniacal way. Well, I made an unhappy mouth and went on my own puzzled, dazed path, dimly wounded, non-understanding. And that woman I believed the most wonderful woman in the world, for she had said so herself. So, this and other hysterical scenes have seared me, and I cannot help myself."

It is a privilege to serve under a great captain; and I sat at his feet and endeavored with all my womanhood to come up to his fine, sane standard of companionship, the thing he had missed even with men, it would seem. His free confidence and his Grand Passion were my guerdon. And there blossomed in him a new and wonderful patience that his older friends could hardly credit—patience in the little things that, handled rightly, or ignored, make for the day's harmony. And I hastened to discount his harshness in argument, in order to partake of the kernel, realizing that when he called a spade a spade, it was a battle against artificiality, toward soundness of thought and speech upon vital truths—or vital lies.

A woman whom he greatly admired had acquired Christian Science and wanted to argue upon it with Jack. With her enunciated premise, I saw Jack's blood begin to rise: "Can no-being be?" she shot at him, and sat back waiting his verdict. Although they had it hammer and tongs for hours, they actually never got beyond the premise. Jack refused to consider such a posit—his scientific mind revolted from it and the two failed to come together on even the definition of words, without which there could be no reasoning. For days he went about muttering, "Can no-being be! Can no-being be!—What do you *think* of it!"

But inasmuch as his arguing was impersonal, I think the following letter to Blanche Partington, written in 1911, after a warm discussion upon Christian Science generally and Christ's Temptation in the Wilderness in particular, is of value as an illustration:

"Dear Blanche:—

"Bless you for taking me just as I am, and for not implying one iota more to me than what I stand for.

"I am, as you must have divined ere this, a fool truthseeker with a nerve of logic exposed and raw and screaming. Perhaps, it is my particular form of insanity.

"I grope in the mud of common facts. I fight like a wolf and a hyena. And I don't mean a bit more, or less, than I say. That is, I am wholly concerned with the problem I am wildly discussing for the moment.

"The problem of the 'language of the tribe,' I fear me, is more

profound than you apprehend—also more disconcerting than you
may imagine for the ones who attempt to talk in the lingo of two
different worlds at one and the same time.

> "Affectionately thine,
>
> "Jack London."

Sometimes, when he had been shockingly literal in language of interpretation in one field or another, with blazing unrepentant eyes he would lash out:

"Am I right? You don't answer! Am I right? If not,
show me where I am wrong. I must be shown!"

The intense effort required to "show" where I thought
him wrong would keep poor me on tiptoe morning, noon and
night—more especially since I nearly always had to own
to myself and finally to him that he was right. Slowly I
commenced to lean upon his judgment, for time and again
I found he could not fail me. In the beginning I have in
sheer exhaustion been guilty, though very rarely, of the
unworthy ruse of giving in when I was not convinced. But
let him suspect the attempted deceit, and the dawning light
in his face fell into dark disapprobation. So I came to
face every issue with him squarely, no matter what the
price in time, inconvenience, nerves, everything.

As if in reassurance, he indited in my copy of "War of
the Classes":

"Dear Mate:

"Just to tell you that you are more Mate than ever, and that
the years to come are bound to see us very happy.

> "Mate."

This is not a wail—oh, quite the opposite. The education to me was an inestimable treasure. It insured a teem-
ing intellectual life for all my days on earth. Jack so loved,
and avowedly, to jar people out of their narrow ruts and
their preconceived notions about themselves. The insincere
shrinking of smug souls from the onset of argument
was sustenance to his missionary mind. He would make

them uncomfortable to sleep with their niggling little petty viewpoints, he would. I can see the flags of battle in his eyes, hark again to the old war-note strike in his fresh young voice. And when he had reduced them to powder without a spark left in it, he was delicious, irresistible, in his expression of contrition:

"Don't mind my harshness," he would plead. "I always raise my voice and talk with my hands; I can't help it.—But don't you see? Don't you see," more often than not he would come back. "Tell me, *am* I right or wrong? I beg you to show me where I am wrong." It was his intrepid way of expressing the abounding life and thought that were in him. On sentry-go at the gates of observation and conscience, he was the Apostle of the Truth if ever there was one.

Luckless was the victim who could not benefit by the brusk tonic of his argument; and indeed, it was a tonic to himself, until the years when he grew too weary with the hopelessness of leavening the inert mass of humanity. H. G. Wells's definition of the average mind—"A projection of inherent imperfections"—would have suited Jack.

He was an undisappointing wonder to us all. Despite his boredom with small minds, one would see him completely possessed, enthralled, by the simple goodness of some one in the humblest walk of life. There were in the neighborhood certain characters who had fallen into ways of hopelessness; and Jack's manly tenderness, always augmented by an unostentatious hand in his pocket, was a speechless pleasure to me, one to emulate for his sweet sake. Then there would be his unbounded appreciation of some tiny farm where perhaps a by-gone workman of Jack's with wife and child, lived happily with one cow, one horse, a few chickens. Delight shone all over him if he detected an idea of his own which had been incorporated into the other's agricultural equipment.

One shining example of that manly kindness I shall never forget: Once, at sea on a great square-rigger, the skipper, probably from illness that rendered him otherwise than his usual self, issued an order that all but piled us upon a famous "graveyard of ships." But Jack, jealous of a good seaman's reputation, protected the captain's blunder from the eyes of the world.

He cared almost not at all, except as it might affect his market, or his authority, for public opinion of himself or his books. But I came to find him simply, touchingly sensitive to approval from the exceeding few whom he loved, and another exceeding few whose discrimination he revered.

It is beyond hand of mine to draw with strong and supple strokes a convincing picture of this protean man-boy. To me he stands out simple enough in all his complexity; yet I can scarcely hope to leave this impression with the reader— so numberless were the factors in the sum of his personality. The greatest, perhaps, of all ingredients in his make-up, was the surpassing lovableness that made his very deficiencies appear loveworthy. No matter what the irritability of mental stress from whatsoever source, appeal to him with love and desire of understanding, and the world was yours could he give it to you.

Needing immediate cash, Jack delayed beginning "White Fang," and the young master of the short story went to work spilling upon tales like "Brown Wolf" the warmth and color of rural California that had got into his pounding blood; "Planchette"—the material for this last was founded upon an incident that had once come under my observation, and I passed it on to him; and presently, requiring the frozen spaces once more for scenes of other motifs, he wrote "The Sun Dog Trail," "A Day's Lodging," "Love of Life," and "The Unexpected"—all these to be found in "Moon Face" and "Love of Life" collections. In a letter to me during absence in the city, answering my query if his description of death were founded upon his own late bout with chloroform, he wrote:

"Yes—the death lines of 'All Gold Canyon' came from my experience with the 'little death in life,' 'the drunken dark,' 'the sweet thick mystery of chloroform,'—you remember Henley's 'Hospital Sketches.'"

Meantime "The Sea Wolf" held sway among the "best sellers," and was much discussed. Reviewers especially girded at the details of Humphrey van Weyden's lovemaking to Maud. "*I* don't think it's silly," Jack considered. "I think it is very natural and sweet. It's the way I make love, and I don't think I am silly!" As for the main motif, I find this:

"I want to make a tale so plain that he who runs may read, and then there is the underlying psychological motif. In 'The Sea Wolf' there was, of course, the superficial descriptive story, while the underlying tendency was to prove that the superman cannot be successful in modern life. The superman is anti-social in his tendencies, and in these days of our complex society and sociology he cannot be successful in his hostile aloofness. Hence the unpopularity of the financial supermen like Rockefeller; he acts like an irritant in the social body."

"Tales of the Fish Patrol" was appearing serially in *Youths' Companion,* and the critics worried over what they dared commit themselves to about "The War of the Classes" group of articles. Mostly, of course, it was severely slated for its radicalism, as the young evangel of economics had naturally forecast.

Better than all other accomplishment, the boy was so happy, gone the Long Sickness, and now living a new manner of life. It was the first time he had ever "let himself go for long," to relax and rest in the assurance of an atmosphere of eager comprehension. He came to realize the value and practice of the *little thing* that offsets the strain of the big thing. To saddle his horse leisurely, to direct its lesser intelligence; to play with Brown Wolf and delve into that reticent comrade's brain-processes; to see that a hammock was properly swung down the mossy stream-side under the maples and alders—oh, no, he did not hang it himself, but "bossed" while Manyoungi did the work. Aside from learning to saddle and harness horses, he was in the main faithful in his vow never again to work with his hands. The only exception I recall was when he became interested in cultivating French mushrooms. Spawn was ordered from the east, and he made the bed down by the Graham Creek near where he had once written on "The Sea Wolf," planted and tended and reaped, to the astonishment of all who knew him.

One peculiarity I never could fathom. Despite the small-ness of his hands, the taper fingers and delicacy of their touch, he was all thumbs when it came to manipulating small objects—say rigging up fishing gear, buttoning or hooking a garment, tending his stylographic ink-pencils. He might easily have been the original model of the humorists' exasperated husband playing maid to his wife's back-buttoned raiment. He did it willingly enough when no one else was about, but with much unsaintly verbiage of which he gave due heralding. Yet with this clumsiness which was a fount of speculation to Jack, he was able to pride himself that he never destroyed anything—this all the more remarkable when taking into account that he invariably "talked with his hands." Once, waving his arms at table, I saw him sweep a "student" lamp clear, which he caught before it could reach the floor; but he never broke a dish.

Here he gives me proof of my guerdon, written in the fly-leaf of "The Game," which came to Glen Ellen in June:

"Dear Mate:

"Whose voice and touch are quick to soothe, and who, with a firm hand, has helped me to emerge from my 'long sickness' so that I might look upon the world again clear-eyed.

"From your Mate."

And in "John Barleycorn," eight years later:

"Dear Mate-Woman:

"You know. You have helped me bury the Long Sickness and the White Logic.

"Your Mate-Man,
"Jack London."

We rode all over the Valley, and explored the sylvan mazes of its embracing ranges and the intricacies of little hills with their little vales, that to the north divide the valley proper. And we visited the hot-springs resorts southerly in the valley, Agua Caliente and Boyes, for the tepid swimming tanks. Once or twice we met Captain H. E. Boyes and Mrs. Boyes, who asked us into their quaint English cottage; and I remember that the Captain showed Jack a letter received from Rudyard Kipling, asking if he had run across Jack London around Sonoma, and inclosing a copy of "Mainly About People" containing a flattering criticism of Jack's work.

We boxed, we swam, we did everything under the sun except walk. Jack never walked any distance save when there was no other way to progress. I was in entire accord with this, as with a thousand and one other mutual preferences. I have seen him deprive himself of a pleasure, if walking was the means of getting at it. "You're the only woman I ever walked far to keep an engagement with," he told me; then spoiled the pretty compliment by adding mischievously, "but I rode most of the way on my bicycle—that night, you remember? when I got arrested for speeding inside Oakland's city limits!"

Those who regarded Jack London as physically powerful were quite right; but they would be astonished to find
that his big, shapely muscles of arm and shoulder and leg,
equal to any emergency whether from momentary call or of
endurance, were not of the stone-hard variety, even under
tension. Why, I, "small, tender woman," as he liked to
say, could flex a firmer bicep than Jack's, to his eternal
amusement. But we were as alike as some twins in many
characteristics—particularly our supersensitive flesh. I
had always been ashamed that in spite of years of horseback riding, let me be away from the saddle for a month or
even less, and the first ride would lame my muscles. To my
surprise Jack, who became an enthusiastic and excellent
horseman, showed the identical weakness to the end of his
life.

As the weeks warmed into summer, campers flocked to
Wake Robin, and the swimming pool in Sonoma Creek, below the Fish Ranch's banks, was a place of wild romping
every afternoon. Jack taught the young folk to swim and
dive, and to live without breathing during exciting tournaments of under-water tag, or searching for hidden objects.
Certain shiny white door-knobs and iron rings that were
never retrieved, must still be implanted in the bottom of
the almost unrecognizable old pool beneath the willows,
or else long since have traveled down the valley to the
Bay.

There were madder frolics on the sandy beach at the
northern edge of the bathing hole, and no child so boisterous or enthusiastic or resourceful as Jack, "joyously noisy
with life's arrogance." He trained them to box and to
wrestle, and all, instructor and pupils, took on their varying gilds of sun-bronze from the ardent California sky that
tanned the whole land to warm russet.

I am suddenly aware of the fact that much as Jack
shared his afternoons in sport with the vacation troops of
campers, many as were the health-giving things of flesh

and spirit which he taught them, not one learned from him in the sport of killing. Nor can I remember him ever going out hunting in this period. The only times I saw firearms in his hands were at intervals when we all practised shooting with rifle and revolver at a target tacked against the end of an ancient ruined dam across the Sonoma. Once, years afterward, in southwesern Oregon, Jack was taken bear-hunting in the mountains. When he returned to the ranch-house he said:

"Mate, these good men don't know what to make of me. They offered me what the average hunting man would give a year of his life to have—the chance of getting a bear. As it happened, we did not see any bear; but coming into a clearing, there stood the most gorgeous antlered buck you ever want to see, on a little ridge, silhouetted against the sunset. The men whispered to me that now was my chance. They were fairly trembling with anxiety for fear I might miss such a perfect shot. And I didn't even raise my gun. I just couldn't shoot that great, glorious wild thing that had no show against the long arm of my rifle."

So the children at Wake Robin—how little a child will miss—resurrected the old ditty of two summers gone, about "The kindest friend the rabbits ever knew," and loved their big-hearted play-friend the more.

One small Oakland shaver, badly out of sorts with his maternal parent, one afternoon began "shying" pebbles at all and sundry. After every one else had gone to supper, Jack excepted, the little fellow sullenly turned his jaundiced attention to the one live mark remaining—friend or foe it mattered not. Jack admonished him to stop, but instead he selected larger missiles and went on firing them. Furious because Jack laughingly dodged them all, the mite jumped up and down in baffled wrath and shrieked: "You hoodlum! You hoodlum!"

"Now, I wonder," Jack reflected through a cloud of

cigarette smoke after supper, "Where he heard me called a hoodlum?"

Again recurring to Jack's alleged brutality, I smile to think how considerate he usually was. In all the rough-and-tumble play with the children and often young folk of maturer growth, any one who was hurt by him quickly smothered the involuntary "ouch" because all knew it was unintentional.

With the girls and women—I speak from long experience. Yes, I have been hurt—one does not box for cool relaxation, but for the zest of rousing the good red blood and setting it free to race through sluggish veins to clear lungs and brain and give one a new lease on life. To Jack, who loved gameness above all virtues, it was his proudest boast that on two or three occasions gore had been drawn from one or the other of our respective features; but it was of his own undoing he was vainest, because "the Kid-woman squared her valiant little shoulders and stood up with her eyes wide open and unafraid and delivered and took a good straight left."

The point I am leading to is this: I never was even jarred in any part of my feminine anatomy that Jack knew was taboo. Allowing that a woman's head, neck and shoulders are about all it is permissible for her opponent to assail, Jack, with greater surface to cover from her quick gloves, worked out and benefitted immeasurably by a system of defense that was my despair and that few men could win through.

About the water hole, not one playfellow but would gladly drop the strenuous fun to listen to Jack read aloud; and sometimes at special urging from the charmed ring, he would with secret gratification respond to a request for some story of his own making. Joshua Slocum's "Voyage of the *Spray*" came in for its turn, and suddenly, one day, Jack laid down the book and said to Uncle Roscoe Eames:

"If Slocum could do it alone in a thirty-five-foot sloop,

with an old tin clock for chronometer, why couldn't we do it in a ten-foot-longer boat with better equipment and more company?"

Uncle Roscoe, devoted yachtsman all his life, and to all appearance as devoted as ever at nearly sixty, beamed with interest. The two fell with vim to comparing models of craft, their audience open-mouthed at the proposition. All at once Jack turned to me, and I am sure there was no misgiving in his heart:

"What do *you* say, Charmian?—suppose five years from now, after we're married and have built our house somewhere, we start on a voyage around the world in a forty-five foot yacht. It'll take a good while to build her, and we've got a lot of other things to do besides."

"I'm with you, every foot of the way," I coincided, "but why wait five years? Why not begin construction in the spring and let the house wait? No use putting up a home and running right away and leaving it! I love a boat, you love a boat; let's call the boat our house until we get ready to stay a little while in one place. We'll never be any younger, nor want to go any more keenly than right now.—You know," I struck home, "you're always reminding me that we are dying, cell by cell, every minute of our lives!"

"Hoist by my own petard," Jack growled facetiously, but inwardly approving.

This was the inception of the *Snark* voyage idea, most wonderful of all our glittering rosary of adventurings.

Aside from the campers, who did not invade his sanctuary, Jack saw almost no visitors. "One," he told a reporter, "was a Russian Revolutionist; the other I avoided!" We were swinging in his hammock at the far end of "Jack's House" from the road, when we glimpsed the latter unannounced and unwelcome figure on the pathway from my Aunt's home. Undetected, we slipped from the hammock, and kept still invisible as we soft-padded around the cottage, always keeping on the opposite side from the searching caller, who shortly went away. "I'm going to put up two signs on my entrances," Jack giggled. "On the front door will be read:

NO ADMISSION EXCEPT ON BUSINESS;
NO BUSINESS TRANSACTED HERE.

On the back:

PLEASE DO NOT ENTER WITHOUT
KNOCKING. PLEASE DO NOT KNOCK."

He was as good as his word. I lettered the legends, and Manyoungi nailed them up, to the scandal of the neighbors. But this summer was the one and only period of inhospitality of any length in Jack's whole life—an instance when he really wanted to be let alone—a necessity in his development at that phase. A few months later, in Boston, he gave this out to one of the papers:

"No, I do not care for society—much. I haven't the time. And besides, society and I disagree as to how I should dress, and as to how I should do a great many other things. I haven't time for pink teas, nor for pink souls. I find that I can get along now less vexatiously and more happily without very much personal dealing with what I may call general humanity. Yet I am not a hermit; I have simply reduced my visiting list."

Society always had him at bay about his clothing. Once he wrote: "I have been *real*, and did not cheat reality any step of the way, even in so microscopically small, and comically ludicrous, a detail as the wearing of a starched collar when it would have hurt my neck had I worn it." How he would have bidden to his heart that "Shaw of Tailors," H. Dennis Bradley of London Town, who wishes, amidst other current post-bellum reconstruction, a revolution in the matter of starch: "If starch is a food," he adjures, "for goodness' sake eat it; do not plaster it on your bosom and bend it round your neck. The war has taught the value of soft silken shirts and collars; and we shall not return to the Prussianism and the Militarism of the blind, unreasoning 'boiled' shirt without a murmur.'"

Now and again Jack tore himself from his happy valley, to lend his voice to the Cause. One of these occasions was on May 22, when he lectured at Maple Hall, at Fourteenth and Webster Streets, Oakland. In the same month we two rode one day to Santa Rosa, to call upon Luther Burbank, who was an old friend of my family. On August 22, together he and I traveled to San Francisco to see the presentation of a one-act play done by Miss Lee Bascom, "The Great Interrogation," based upon Jack's "Story of Jees Uck," from Faith of Men collection .

Jack, as collaborator, was ferreted out from where we had made ourselves as small as possible in the Alcazar's gallery, and appeared before the curtain with Miss Bascom, to whom he gallantly attributed whatever excellence the pleasing drama possessed.

About this time a dramatization of "The Sea Wolf," which was unintentionally farcical in the extreme, was put on at an Oakland playhouse. Catering to the finicky theater-goer, the playwright had introduced a chaperone, who evidently called for company in the shape of an ingenue. This young person was portrayed by no other than the winsome Ola Humphrey, of Oakland, whom later we were to know in Sydney, Australia, as a leading woman, and still in the future as the Princess Ibrahim Hassan.

As in the Alcazar, Jack chose the most inconspicuous position from which to view what had been done to theme of his. On the present occasion he remained undiscovered, and was able to shed his tears of mirth on either shoulder he desired, Sterling's or mine, when the shrieking melodrama became too much for his control. "O Gawd! O Gawd!" he mimicked the *Ghost's* cook, Muggridge; and

"If they *should* hunt me out and get me on the stage, what could I say but 'O Gawd! O Gawd!'" The unfortunate Van Weyden, if I remember aright, chose to wear, from rise to fall of curtain, a well polished pair of tan shoes for which the rigors of the salt sea had no terrors.

On September 9, Jack went to Colma, as one of a constellation of *The Examiner's* star writers, to do the Britt-Nelson prizefight. It was in the course of this write-up he coined another catch-phrase that went into the language of the country, as "the call of the wild," "the white silence," and even "the game" had become almost household words. This time it was "the abysmal brute," to which certain pugilists took exception until they came to realize the author's meaning—the life that refuses to quit and lie down even after consciousness has ceased.

"By 'abysmal brute,'" Jack would extemporize, "I mean the basic life deeper than the brain and the intellect in living things. Intelligence rests upon it; and when intelligence goes, it still remains. The abysmal brute life," he illustrated, "that causes the heart of a gutted dog-fish to beat in one's hand—you've seen them do that when we were fishing off the Key Route pier," I was reminded. "Or the beak of a slain turtle to close and bite off a man's finger; it's the life force that makes a fighter go on fighting even though he is past all direction from his intelligence." So enamored was he of his own phrase that eight years afterward he used it for title of another prize-fight novel.

In addition to his regular work, Jack would find time to review a book, as for instance "The Long Day," which critique occupied a page in an October *Examiner;* or to contribute an article, like "The Walking Delegate," in the May 28th issue of the same paper.

It was in August of this year that he sent to *Collier's Weekly* the article entitled "Revolution," based upon the lecture. He had already sent it to *The Cosmopolitan,* but owing to some disagreement upon the price had withdrawn the manuscript. This article was published in London in the *Contemporary Review*. Jack's letter to the Editor of *Collier's* I give below:

"I am sending you herewith an article that may strike you as a regular firebrand; but I ask you to carry into the reading of it one idea, namely, that the whole article is a statement of *fact*. There is no theory about it. I state the facts and the figures of the revolution. I state how many revolutionists there are, why they are revolutionists, and their views—all of which are facts.

"It seems to me that this article would be especially apposite just now, following upon the wholesale exposures of graft and rottenness in the high places, which have of late filled all the magazines and newspapers. It is the other side of the shield. It is another way of looking at the question, and half a million of voters are looking at it in this way in the United States. And it might be interesting to the capitalists to see thus depicted this great antagonistic force which they, by their present graft and rottenness, are not doing anything to fend off. But rather are they encouraging the growth of this antagonistic force by their own culpable mismanagement of society.

"Of course, should you find it in your way to publish this article, it would be very well to preface it with an editorial note to the effect that it is a statement of the situation by an avowed and militant socialist; and of course you would be quite welcome to criticize the whole article in any way you saw fit."

All those bright, vitalizing months, there was growing in his bosom a seed sown two years earlier when he had come to love Sonoma Valley. "The Valley of the Moon," he called it, having unearthed the fact that Sonoma stood for "moon" in the early Indian tongue of the locality. I have since heard Sonoma defined as "seven moons," because, driving in the crescent of the valley, one may see seven risings of the orb behind the waving contours of the summits.

His eyes roved over the forested mountainside, and yearning heightened to make some part of it his own, for home when we should be man and wife—his very own while life should last. But it appeared not to be for sale. One prospect above all others filled our eyes whenever we rode side by side up a certain old private road—three inexpressibly romantic knolls crowned with fir and redwood, rosy-limbed, blossom-perfumed madroño, and scented tapers of the buckeye—wooded islets rising out of a deep, tossing sea of tree-tops. And one day a neighbor said:

"Why, those knolls there belong to a section of over a hundred acres owned by Robert P. Hill down at Eldridge, yonder, the next station below Glen Ellen. Go and see him, and I bet he'll sell it to you. I'm sure I heard it could be bought."

In no time at all, Jack was possessor of one hundred and twenty-nine acres of the most idyllic spot we were ever to behold—later to be glorified in his novel "Burning Daylight." Its irregular diamond-shape was bounded by the magnificently wooded gorge of old Asbury Creek to the southeast, and the whole sweet domain was wilderness of every sort of Californian timber and shrubbery, save some forty acres of cleared land that had once yielded wine-grapes and now waved with grain.

Jack paid $7000.00 for the property, which turned out to be a portion of the original grant of some two hundred square miles from the Mexican Government to General Vallejo. Mr. and Mrs. Hill declare to this day that they fear Jack could probably have beaten their figure if he had stood out. But there is another aspect to the happening. Jack, alas, had no chance; he accused me of precluding any such move on his side, by any unthinking ravings over the land in question. And I meekly refrained from protesting when he excluded me from all business sessions thereafter.

Mrs. Hill, who was President of the California Woman's Federation of Clubs, amongst other engaging customs displayed the one of welcoming a guest with both her hands clasping the other's one. And after a little acquaintance with our new friends, I noticed that Jack adopted the gracious habit with his own guests—quite unknowingly, I am sure, for he was not addicted to copying manners. This reminds me that when I first met Jack London, it was with surprise I noted that he shook hands rather limply. It must have been a reminiscence of childhood diffidence; it could not be coldness, for he radiated warmth and sincerity from head to foot. Later, I had dared tell him of my be-puzzlement, and found that he had no idea his clasp was not a hearty one. He set about remedying the lack of firmness. Looking through his 1905 clipping book, I come upon this from an interviewer in an Iowa town where Jack had lectured:

"The words and hearty clasp were with boy-like frankness, a boy's greeting to another boy."

We called it our Land of Dear Delight, but, to the world, simply The Ranch. What Jack thought of it, and his enthusiasm, taking the place of his old unrest, in all the simplest details of his new farm, is indicated in his letters to George Sterling and Cloudesley Johns. To George he wrote:

"I have long since given over my automobile scheme; it was too damned expensive on the face of it, and I have long since decided to buy land in the woods, somewhere, and build. . . . For over a year, I have been planning this home proposition, and now I am just beginning to see my way clear to it. I am really going to throw out an anchor so big and so heavy that all hell could never get it up again. In fact, it's going to be a prodigious, ponderous sort of an anchor."

What the neighbors thought of the transaction, he words in "The Iron Heel:"

"Once a writer friend of mine had owned the ranch. . . . He had bought the ranch for beauty, and paid a round price for it, much to the disgust of the local farmers. He used to tell with great glee how they were wont to shake their heads mournfully at the price, to accomplish ponderously a bit of mental arithmetic, and then to say, 'But you can't make six per cent on it.' "

"Jack London,
"Glen Ellen,
"Sonoma Co., Cal.,
"June 7, 1905.

"Dear Cloudesley:

"Yea, verily, gorgeous plans. I have just blown myself for 129 acres of land. I'll not attempt to describe. It's beyond me.

"Also, I have just bought several horses, a colt, a cow, a calf, a plow, harrow, wagon, buggy, etc., to say nothing of chickens, turkeys, pigeons, etc., etc. All this last part was unexpected, and has left me flat broke. . . . I've taken all the money I could get from Macmillan to pay for the land, and haven't any now even to build a barn with, much less a house.

"Haven't started 'White Fang' yet. Am writing some short stories in order to get hold of some immediate cash."

And this fragment from his next, dated July 6, 1905:

"As regards the ranch—I figure the vegetables, firewood, milk, eggs, chickens, etc., procured by the hired man will come pretty close to paying the hired man's wages. The 40 acres of cleared ground (hay) I can always have farmed on shares. The other fellow furnishes all the work, seed, and care, while I furnish the land. He gets ⅔ of crop of hay. I get ⅓—about 25 or 30 tons for my share.

"I'm going swimming. I take a book along, and read and swim, turn and turn about, until 6 P.M. It is now 1 P.M.

"Wolf."

"August 30, 1905.

"Dear Cloudesley:

". . . By the way, *Collier's* has accepted 'Revolution.' What d'ye think o' that? Robert J. Collier wrote the letter of acceptance himself, saying: That he was going to publish my fire-brand as a piece of literature, even if it did lose him several hundred thousand of his capitalistic subscribers. Also, wanting to know how much I asked for the article, he said, 'Don't penalize me too heavily for my nerve in publishing it.'

"I am racing along with 'White Fang.' Have got about 45,000 words done, and hope to finish it inside the next four weeks, when I pull East on the lecturing-trip.

"Have you read Jimmy Britt's review of 'The Game'? It is all right!

"Say, read 'The Divine Fire,' by May Sinclair, and then get down in the dust at her feet. She is a master.

Of all books of fiction we read at this period, "The Divine Fire" and Eden Phillpotts's "The Secret Woman" made the deepest mark upon us both.

When laying foundation for a novel, Jack would isolate himself for the forenoon, in a hilly manzanita grove adjoining the Wake Robin acres—the "wine-wooded manzanita" he named it in "All Gold Canyon." But for all short work he made his notes at a table in the redwood-paneled room where he worked and slept. He liked music while he composed, and was never so content as when open windows brought my practising to him from the other house.

One day, returning from San Francisco, he said: "We've got to have a phonograph!" "Awful!" I countered. "You don't know what you're saying," he reproved in sparkling tone. "I've been listening for hours to the most wonderful records, and there's a man down in Glen Ellen who has an agency, and we're to come down to-night and hear the thing. No—don't say a word—you'll go perfectly crazy over it!"

I did; and a Victor came to stay at Wake Robin, subsequently sailing with us to the South Seas with one hundred and fifty records presented by the manufacturers. This music Jack also liked while he worked, so long as he could not distinguish the words of songs, which would distract his attention from the words he was juggling with.

At that time he cared far more for orchestral than for

vocal harmonies, especially the Wagnerian operas. In the latter, as well as in quite a repertory of other operatic work, he had been well coached by his friend Blanche Partington, musical and dramatic critic on the *San Francisco Call* for seven years, who had taken him with her to many performances. I, on the other hand, favored the voice records above the instrumental. After several years, as one manifestation of his searching into the human, Jack leaned more and more to the voice, until he seldom put on the orchestral disks.

"Sept. 4, 1905.

"Dear Cloudesley:

"So you're going to begin writing for money! Forgive me for rubbing it in. You've changed since several years ago when you place A R T first and dollars afterward. You didn't quite sympathize with me in those days.

"After all, there's nothing like life; and I, for one, have always stood, and shall always stand, for the exalting of the life that is in me over Art, or any other extraneous thing.

"Wolf."

George Serling had affectionately dubbed him "The Wolf," or "The Fierce Wolf," or "The Shaggy Wolf." In the last month of Jack London's life, he gave me an exquisite tiny wrist-watch. "And what shall I have engraved on it?" I asked. "Oh, 'Mate from Wolf,' I guess," he replied. And I: "The same as when we exchanged engagement watches?" "Why, yes, if you don't mind," he admitted. "I have sometimes wished you would call me 'Wolf' more often."

"I wish I had called you 'Wolf,' then," I said remorsefully, "since you would have liked it. But it seemed preciously George's name for you, and that is why I seldom used it." The wee Swiss timepiece was lettered accordingly, this after his light had gone out forever, for I had not been again in town.

Jack was generous about helping his friends out in

time of need, but the following, to one of them in October, shows how closely he was running, and again mentions his intended lecturing trip:

"To buy the ranch and build barn, I had to get heavy advances from my publishers. I had already overdrawn so heavily, that they asked me, and in common decency I agreed, to pay interest on these new advances made.

"At present moment my check book shows $207.83 to my credit at the bank. It is the first of the month and I have no end of bills awaiting me, prominent among which are: (Here follows list of payments to his own mother, his children's mother, his rent, tools for the Ranch, and some smaller bills.)

"Now, I have to pay my own expenses East. Lecture Bureau afterward reimburses me. I haven't a cent coming to me from any source, and must borrow this money in Oakland. Also, in November I must meet between seven and eight hundred dollars insurance. My mother wants me to increase her monthly allowance. So does B. I have just paid hospital bills of over $100.00 for one of my sisters. Another member of the family, whom I cannot refuse, has warned me that as soon as I arrive in Oakland he wants to make a proposition to me. I know what that means.

"And I have promised $30.00 to pay printing of appeal to Supreme Court of Joe King, a poor devil in Co. Jail with 50 yrs. sentence hanging over him and who is being railroaded.

"And so on, and so on, and so on—Oh, and a bill for over $45.00 to the hay press. So you see that I am not only sailing close to the wind but that I am dead into it and my sails flapping."

"I'm always in debt," Jack said to Ashton Stevens, who interviewed him for *The Examiner*. "Look at that hand! See where the light comes through the fingers! That hand leaks. It was explained to me by the Korean boy that took me through Manchuria. All I'd like to do is to be able to get enough money ahead to loaf for a year—that's my little dream."

"And buy some dress shirts and evening clothes?" Mr. Stevens slyly baited.

"Oh, I have them," Jack grinned; "I've got them. But

I'm willing to put 'em on only when I can't get in without them. I loathe the things, but if the worst comes to the worst I've got 'em; I insist I've got 'em.''

"Then your dream of rest realized wouldn't be all purple teas?"

"Indeed it would not. At Glen Ellen I've got a farm, and I'm going to build a house and a lot of things; it'll take me about two years to make improvements and settle down. And then I'm going to build a forty-foot sea-going yacht and with two or three others cruise around the world. We'll be our own crew and cook and everything else, and the first port will be twenty-one hundred miles from San Francisco—Honolulu. Thence on and on. Maybe I'll realize on that trip some of my dream of rest."

In the months before he came to Glen Ellen that year, he would ask musical friends for "The Garden of Sleep," a song by Clement Scott and Isidore de Lara, and for "Sing Me to Sleep," by Clifton Bingham and Edwin Green. As time went on, he called upon me less and less for these restful melodies. When they had at length served his need, in characteristic manner of not looking backward, he was through with the songs.

Concerning the world voyage, he wrote to Anna Strunsky:

"You remember the *Spray* in which you sailed with me one day? Well, this new boat will be six or seven feet longer than the *Spray*, and I am going to sail her around the world, writing as I go. Expect to be gone on trip four or five years—around the Horn, Cape of Good Hope, Europe, Asia, Africa, South America, Australia, and everywhere else."

Jack's "dream of rest" had more than once, in my hearing, been associated with death itself. Never was he so happy, he who at the same time so exalted life, that he could not descant upon the repose of death. One of my earliest memories of him is such a remark as this:

"To me the idea of death is sweet. Think of it—to lie down and go into the dark out of all the struggle and pain of living—to go to sleep and rest, always to be resting. Oh, I do not want to die now—I'd fight like the devil to keep alive. . . . But when I come to die, it will be smiling at death, I promise you."

Early in our married life I entreated:

"Don't, don't plan so many great things that you will always have to slave for the means. Make your money and 'loaf' for a while." But in all the years we were together, the day of living rest fled before him. His vast plannings widened as widened his fund of knowledge—there was no horizon at any point of his compass. So I came to give up, and coöperate with him wherever his ambition chose to express itself.

Yes, Jack was always in debt; but never to the point of failing to see his way out. Which, after all, is merely good business. He was aware of his augmenting earning power; but timid ones lacking his vision refrained from depending upon him because their prognosis was that he would fail through poor judgment. And yet, after his death, as many as depended upon him in lifetime are still cared for by his foresight—even more than those. Any one who gave voice to the opinion that Jack London was a poor business man was a source of irritation to him, such was his realization his own efficiency.

CHAPTER XXVII

SECOND MARRIAGE; LECTURE TRIP; BOSTON

1905-1906

IT is of record, in the files of every American newspaper, that the final decree in the Jack London divorce was granted on November 18, 1905—this after a separation of two and a half years between the parties thereto. Jack had once said to me:

"If a divorce had not been allowed me, I would not have given you up—that would be unthinkable. We would have gone somewhere, if you would, and I think you would—on the other side of the world, and dignifiedly lived out our lives, 'on the square, like a true married pair.'"

But this was thought of by him only as an extreme. For, as in most considerations, Jack supported law, holding that society rested upon monogamy; though that all-round mind of his as firmly stood behind his biology with regard to man's polygamous place in the animal kingdom. "And anyway, our love and mateship is of the stamp that bonds cannot tire, thank God," he would rejoin. Then, in a note: "We will respect the world and the way of the world."

Once, out of a spell of despondency before he came to Glen Ellen, Jack wrote me a letter which I give below, so that all may have access to the solid foundation upon which reason stood, upholding romantic love:

"Dear, dear Woman:

"Somehow, you have been very much in my thoughts these last few days, and in inexpressible ways you are dearer to me.

"I will not speak of the mind-qualities, the soul-qualities—for somehow, in these, in ways beyond my speech and thought, you have suddenly loomed colossal in comparison with the ruck of women.

"Oh, believe me, in these last several days I have been doing some thinking, some comparing—and I have been made aware, not merely of pride, and greater pride, in you, but of delight in you. Dear, dear Woman, Wednesday night, how I delighted in you, for instance! Of course, I liked the look of you; but outside of that, I delighted—and not so much in what you said or did, as in what you did not say or do. You, just you—with strength and surety, and power to hold me to you for that old peace and rest which you have always had for me. I am more confident now than a year ago that we shall be happy together. I am *rationally confident*.

"God! and you have grit! I love you for it. You are my comrade for it. And I mean the grit of the soul.

"And the lesser grit—you have it, too. I think of you swimming, and jumping, and diving, and my arms go out to the dear, sensitive, gritty body of yours, as my arms go out to the gritty soul of you within that body.

"My first thought in the morning is of you, my last thought at night. My arms are about you, and I kiss you with my soul.

"Your Own Man."

But he was also the mad lover, gloriously, boundlessly so. As witness this, written three weeks before our wedding, after he had gone East:

"Blessed Mate:

"I do not think that I have yet parted with you, so full am I, heart and soul, with the vision of you.

"Standards are nothing, judgments are nothing; I need not reason about you except in the simplest way, and that way is that you mean *everything* to me and are more to me than any woman I have ever known.

"Your own man,
"The Wolf."

Editors have repeatedly approached me on the subject of publishing Jack London's letters to myself. All arguments were barren of result, save one: that Jack London's love nature is little known or reckoned with in the average estimate of him; or, worse, misunderstood. This slant of argument of course had not been unthought of by me. And because no just study of the man can otherwise be made, I present, throughout this book, the letters I have chosen from the uncounted ones in my possession. Below I quote the very first in which he mentions his regard, something that had theretofore been undreamed of by me. We had been discussing something about my own make-up which he said had always eluded him—and I had gathered that it was not especially complimentary. My curiosity being aroused, I wrote and asked him if he could not definitely word his feeling. Here is the reply:

"I see that what I spoke of worries you. It would worry me equally, I am sure, did it come from a friend. But the very point of it was that I did not know what it was. If I had, I should not have brought it up. If you will recollect, it was one of the lesser puzzles of your make-up to which I merely casually referred. None of your guesses hits it: I have seen and measured your 'inordinate fondness' for pretty things and for the correct thing. These are logical and consistent in you, and the fact that they are arouses nothing but satisfaction in me. I referred to something I did not know, something I felt as I felt the vision of you crying in the grass. Perhaps I used the word 'conventionality' for lack of adequate expression, for the same reason that I spoke from lack of comprehension. A something felt of something no more than potential in you and of which I had seen no evidences. If you fail to follow me I am indeed lost, for I have strained to give definite utterance to a thing remote and obscure.

"You speak of frankness. I passionately desire it, but have come to shrink from the pain of intimacies which bring the greater frankness forth. Superficial frankness is comparatively easy, but one must pay for stripping off the dry husks of clothing, the self-conventions which masque the soul, and for standing out naked in the eyes of one who sees. I have paid, and like a child who has been burned by fire, I shrink from paying too often. You surely have known such franknesses and the penalties you paid. When I found heart's desire speaking clamorously to you, I turned my eyes away and strove to go on with my superficial self, talking, I know not what. And I did it consciously—partly so, perhaps—and I did it automatically, instinctively. Memories of old pains, incoherent hurts, a welter of remembrances, compelled me to close the mouth whereby my inner self was shouting at you a summons bound to give hurt and to bring hurt in return.

"I wonder if I make you understand. You see, in the objective facts of my life I have always been frankness personified. That I tramped or begged or festered in jail or slum meant nothing by the telling. But over the lips of my inner self I had long since put a seal—a seal indeed rarely broken, in moments when one caught fleeting glimpses of the hermit who lived inside. How can I begin to explain? . . . My child life was uncongenial. There was little responsive around me. I learned reticence, an inner reticence. I went into the world early, and I adventured among different classes. A newcomer in any class, I naturally was reticent concerning my real self, which such a class could not understand, while I was superficially loquacious in order to make my entry into such a class popular and successful. And so it went, from class to class, from clique to clique. No intimacies, a continuous hardening, a superficial loquacity so clever, and an inner reticence so secret, that the one was taken for the real, and the other never dreamed of.

"Ask people who know me to-day, what I am. A rough, savage fellow, they will say, who likes prizefights and brutalities, who has a clever turn of pen, a charlatan's smattering of art, and the inevitable deficiencies of the untrained, unrefined, self-made man which he strives with a fair measure of success to hide beneath an attitude of roughness and unconventionality. Do I endeavor to unconvince them? It's so much easier to leave their convictions alone.

"And now the threads of my tangled discourse draw together. I have experienced the greater frankness, several times, under provocation, with a man or two, and a woman or two, and the occasions have been great joy-givers, as they have also been great sorrow-givers. I do not wish they had never happened, but I recoil unconsciously from their happening again. It is so much easier to live placidly and complacently. Of course, to live placidly and complacently is not to live at all, but still, between prizefights and kites and one thing and another I manage to fool my inner self pretty well. Poor inner self! I wonder if it will atrophy, dry up some day and blow away.

"This is the first serious talk I have had about myself for a weary while. I hope my flood of speech has not bored you.

"When may I see you?"

When, so shortly afterward, we had discovered, almost as with love-at-first-sight, the great glory that was rising in us, this was his next message—a burst of sunshine after dark days:

"I am dumb this morning. I do not think. I do not think at all. Talk of analysis! I should have to get a year or so between me and the last of you in order to generalize, in order to answer the everlasting query: '*What is it all about?*'

"What IS it all about? I do not know. I know only that I am off my feet and drifting with the tide; drifting and singing, but it is a flood tide and the song a pæan.

"Younger? I am twenty years younger. So young that I am too lazy to work. I am lying here in the hammock thinking dreamily of you. No, I am not lazy at all. I am doing no work because I am incapable of doing it. Wherever I look I see you. I close my eyes and hear you, and still see you. I try to gather my thoughts together and I think—You. But it is not a thought— it is a picture of you, a vision—a something as objective and real as when I used to see you crying in the grass.

"An hour has passed since I wrote the last word. I am still in the hammock, and what I have written is the history of that hour, as it is of all the other hours.

"Well, they are good hours. Though I never saw you again, the memory of them would be sweet. To have lived them, here in the hammock, is to have lived well and high."

And again: "This I know—that you will come to me, some time, some where. It is inevitable. The hour is already too big to become anything less than the biggest. We cannot fail, diminish, fall back into night with the dawn thus in our eyes.

For it is no false dawn. Our eyes are dazzled with it, and our souls.
We know not what, and yet WE KNOW. The life that is in us
knows. It is crying out, and we cannot close our ears to its cry.
It is reaching out yearning arms that know the truth and secret
of living as we, apart from it and striving to reason it, do not
know. O my dear, we give and live, we withhold and die.

"You may laugh and protest, but you ARE big. A thousand
things prove it to me—to me who never needed the proof. I knew—
knew from the first. I, who have felt and sounded my way through
life like some mariner on a fog-bound coast, have never felt nor
sounded when with you. I knew you from the first, knew you and
accepted you. This is why, when the time for speech came, there
was no need for speech.

"I do not know if I shall see you to-night, and, such is the
certitude of our tangled destiny, I hardly think I care. Did I
doubt, it would be different. But it must be so, I know, not
sooner or later, but soon. It is the will of your life and mine that
it shall be so, and we are not so weak that we cannot keep faith with
the truth and the best that is in us.

"You are more kin to me than any woman I have ever known."

The next letter gives a deathless picturing of Jack London's loneliness of old and his new-found happiness:

"Do you know a happy moment you have given me—a wonderful moment? When you sat looking into my eyes and repeated to
me: 'You are more kin to me than any woman I have ever known.'
That those words should have shaped to you the one really great
thought in the letter, the thought most vital to me and to my love
for you, stamped our kinship irrevocably. Surely we are very One,
you and I!

"Shall I tell you a dream of my boyhood and manhood?—a
dream which in my rashness I thought had dreamed itself out and
beyond all chance of realization? Let me. I do not know, now,
what my other loves have been, how much of depth and worth
there were in them; but this I know, and knew then, and know
always—that there was a something greater I yearned after, a something that beat upon my imagination with a great glowing light
and made those woman-loves wan things and pale, oh so pitiably
wan and pale!

"I have held a woman in my arms who loved me and whom I loved, and in that love-moment have told her, as one will tell a dead dream, of this great thing I had looked for, looked for vainly, and the quest of which I had at last abandoned. And the woman grew passionately angry, and I should have wondered had I not known how pale and weak it made all of her that she could ever give me.

"For I had dreamed of the great Man-Comrade. I, who have been comrades with many men, and a good comrade I believe, have never had a comrade at all, and in the deeper significance of it have never been able to be the comrade I was capable of being. Always it was here this one failed, and there that one failed until all failed. And then, one day, like Omar, 'clear-eyed I looked, and laughed, and sought no more.' It was plain that it was not possible. I could never hope to find that comradeship, that closeness, that sympathy and understanding, whereby the man and I might merge and become one in understanding and sympathy for love and life.

"How can I say what I mean? This man should be so much one with me that we could never misunderstand. He should love the flesh, as he should the spirit, honoring and loving each and giving each its due. There should be in him both fact and fancy. He should be practical insofar as the mechanics of life were concerned; and fanciful, imaginative, sentimental where the thrill of life was concerned. He should be delicate and tender, brave and game; sensitive as he pleased in the soul of him, and in the body of him unfearing and unwitting of pain. He should be warm with the glow of great adventure, unafraid of the harshnesses of life and its evils, and knowing all its harshness and evil.

"Do you see, my dear one, the man I am trying to picture for you?—an all-around man, who could weep over a strain of music, a bit of verse, and who could grapple with the fiercest life and fight good-naturedly or like a fiend as the case might be. . . . the man who could live at the same time in the realms of fancy and of fact; who, knowing the frailties and weaknesses of life, could look with frank fearless eyes upon them; a man who had no smallnesses or meannesses, who could sin greatly, perhaps, but who could as greatly forgive.

"I spend myself in verbiage, trying to express in a moment or two, on a sheet of paper, what I have been years and years a-dreaming.

"As I say, I abandoned the dream of the great Man-Comrade who was to live Youth with me, perpetual Youth with me, down to the grave. And then You came, after your trip abroad, into my life. Before that I had met you quite perfunctorily, a couple of times, and liked you. But after that we met in fellowship, though somewhat distant and not so very frequently, and I liked you more and more. It was not long before I began to find in you the something all-around that I had failed to find in any man; began to grow aware of that kinship that was comradeship, and to wish you were a man. And there was a loneliness about you that appealed to me. This, perhaps, by some unconscious cerebration, may have given rise to my vision of you in the grass.

"And then, by the time I was convinced of the possibility of a great comradeship between us, and of the futility of attempting to realize it, something else began to creep in—the woman in you twining around my heart. It was inevitable. But the wonder of it is that in a woman I should find, not only the comradeship and kinship I had sought in men alone, but the great woman-love as well; and this woman is YOU, YOU!"

Let himself say what Love meant to him:

"Once you strove to write me a love letter—with tolerable success. But you have now written me a love letter. When it came this morning, and I read it, I was mad—mad with sheer joy and desire. The bonds tighten, my love; we grow closer and closer. Ah, God. You are so close to me now, so dear, so dear. You are in my thought all the time. I am swimming, and as I poise for a dive, I pause a fleeting second to think of you. No matter what I do, now, I make the little pause and think of you. I do it when I am working, when I am reading, when people are talking to me. At all times it is you, you, you.

"Love? I thought I was capable of a great love, as one will think, you know. But I never dreamed so great a love as this. I have stood on my own feet all the years of my life, was independent, self-sufficient. Men and women were pleasant, of course, but they were not necessary. I could get along without them. I could not conceive a time when I could not get along without them. But the time has come. Without you I am nowhere, nothing, You

are the breath of life in my nostrils. Without you, and without
hope of having you, I should surely die. Oh, woman, woman, how
I do love you.

"I have no doubt, now, of your love for me. You do love me,
must love, or life is false as hell and there is no sanity in anything.
But I do not measure your love thus. I just *know* you love me.

"I write this while people wait; and I kiss you thus, and thus,
on the lips, and hair, and brow—thus, and thus."

Before even dreaming of coming into the country to
live, Jack had pledged himself to lecture in the east and middle west. He had never really enjoyed public speaking,
but was bent upon hunting a protracted session of it—a first
and last tour. Moreover, and very important, here was opportunity to spread propaganda for the Cause, and it was
stipulated with the Lyceum Bureau that he should be at
liberty to expound Socialism wherever and whenever it
did not conflict with his regular dates.

As our Indian Summer drew on, however, more and
more he fretted that he must pull up stakes and tear himself from the happy camp that had wrought so marvelously
upon him. But the third week in October saw him on his
strenuous way, having demanded expenses for two, that
Manyoungi might relieve him of all distracting personal
details. My face laughed into his from the inside cover
of that thin gold watch I had given him; and one unforgotten item of luggage was an exquisite miniature of his two
little girls which he had had painted by Miss Wishaar
months before.

Shortly after his departure, I, too, did some packing—
of a simple trousseau in the pretty bureau-trunk Jack had
presented me. This trunk was the result of one of his ad-
vertisement-answering hazards, as was one of the early
models of wardrobe-trunk. The latter was so tall that,
after expending more than its original cost in excess-length
charges, he had the thing cut down to regulation size.

In Newton, Iowa, I visited my friend Mrs. Will Mc-

Murray, for a November 25 lecture had been scheduled for the college town of Grinnell, but a short distance from Newton; and it was our intention to be married at the McMurrays' and spend with them an idle week occurring in the tour. But the lecturer, fulfilling an engagement with the People's Institute in Elyria, Ohio, upon receiving a telegram from California that he was entirely free, decided on the spur of the moment not to delay until the Grinnell date.

On the eve of the 19th, I had his wire in hand for me to be in Chicago the next night, since he was to pass through on the way to lecture in Wisconsin. Being Sunday, he was obliged to arrange a special license with the County Clerk of Cook County. And when in obedience to his summons I stepped off my train in the Windy City at nine of the evening, three hours behind-time, a very weary but happily patient bridegroom elect was pacing the station pavement. In his pocket was the license, in mine my mother's weddingring; and at the curb waited two hansom cabs, one containing an interested and beaming Manyoungi, who wanted to see an American wedding.

The informal suddenness and speed of this termination to our courtship savored of the age of chivalry, when knighterrant with doughty right arm slung his lady love across the saddle bow on a foaming black charger. Let none say that ours was less romantic. What mattered it that our vows were spoken in a civil ceremony! After Notary Public J. J. Grant had made us one, we drove to the old Victoria Hotel where Jack interlined 'Mrs. Jack London" between his and Manyoungi's signatures registered the previous day. I meanwhile, by another entrance, slipped upstairs.

No one connected intimately with this "most advertised writer in America" could hope to escape the more or less notorious consequences. By me it had to be regarded as part of the game, if I were to observe my responsibilities. Therefore my philosophy of life had fortified me against the worst. Before Jack could procure his key, he was way-laid by three newspapermen—but they chanced to be merely in search of items about his trip and his books. But a fourth had discovered the hardly-dry interpolation on the register, and hovered anxiously about the quartette to learn if he was the only sleuth who had made the find. Jack sensed the situation, and presently excused himself and ran upstairs. In three minutes the four reporters were at our door, imploring an interview. Reënforcements began to arrive, and into the small hours besieged by knocks, notes, telegrams, cards, telephone calls from the hotel office—streams of entreaties in every guise flowing under the door and over wire and transom. To all of which my husband remained deaf and dumb, for he must scrupulously redeem his promise made months before, to give the Hearst papers the "scoop" in return for their discretion. This he had done on Saturday, and the *Chicago American* city editor, Mr. Harstone, was instrumental in obtaining the special license; also, with a reporter, Mr. Harstone had served as witness to the ceremony.

The appeal which came nearest to stirring Jack was the whispered and written: "Come on through with the news, old man—be merciful; we've *got* to get it. You're a newspaperman yourself, you know. Come across and help us out."

When the *Chicago American* had appeared Monday morning with the heavily leaded item, the disappointed dailies sent representatives to call upon the bride and groom; and I must take occasion to congratulate those gentlemen upon the good-natured courtesy which cloaked their chagrin. Nevertheless, the end was not yet. Vengeance was theirs. On Tuesday morning, coming back into Chicago from Geneva Falls, Wisconsin, on the business-men's train, we had slipped into a rearmost seat. What was our horror to behold, upthrust before the greedy eyes of "commuters" the entire length of the car, full-page photographs of ourselves with large headlines announcing Jack London's marriage "Invalid."

"What the hell!" spluttered Jack, laughing in spite of himself. "The other sheets are getting even. We're in for it!" and thereupon delivered himself: "A fellow's got to pay through the nose for being loyal to his own crowd!" They won't stop to consider that I'd have done the same for them, if most of my newspaper work had been for them!"

The "other sheets" had merely endeavored to tangle the divorce laws of California and Illinois; but a noted Judge pronounced all straight. The *Chicago American* gave due space to the refutation, and we went on our path rejoicing. But for weeks we could not pick up a paper, great or small, that did not contain publicity of one sort or another concerning the most advertised writer in America—whether reviews of his books, of our marriage, of the lectures, the round-the-world yacht voyage, the Ranch, and what not.

Jack maintained to all interviewers, "If my marriage is not legal in Illinois, I shall re-marry my wife in every state in the Union!"

A comical thing happened in California, when one of Jack's little-girl swimming pupils hurriedly scanned the title, "Jack London's Marriage Invalid." Hastening to her mother, in accents of distress she cried:

"Oh, mama, mama, how awful! Mr. London did not marry Miss Kittredge after all! This paper says he's married an *invalid!*"

One day, from Lynette McMurray's parlor, there issued Jack's irrepressible snicker, increasing to a wild call for me:

"Oh, I've got you now, Mate Woman! You can never look me in the face again after you hear this!" And proceeded to read aloud a libelous squib from a Washington, Iowa, weekly paper. It was to the effect that the "ugly-faced girl from California, so ugly that the children on the streets of Newton ran screaming to their mothers when-

ever she passed by, had married Jack London. That it
was reported the pair were soon to go to sea in a small boat,
to be gone for years. That it would be a mercy to everybody
if they were drowned at sea and *never* came back."

"You think I'm making it up, don't you!" Jack read
my scornful face. "But here—look at it!—why, the old
sour-ball—the wretched old slob! I wonder what he'd
had for breakfast!"

But it was I who first happened upon a reference to Jack
London as being possessed of a "bilaterally asymetrical
countenance," and it may correctly be assumed that I
pressed the same home with all dispatch.

"I'm NOT bilaterally asymetrical, though," indignantly
he defended; "and anyway, I don't know what bilaterally
asymetrical means. Take a look at me," studying himself
in my hand-mirror. "I'd say my features are fairly
straight . . . The man that said bilaterally asymetrical was
looking for a chance to work off the expression!"

The time Jack was really sorry for his wife was in
1909, in Hobart, Tasmania, when another reporter with
something funny to work off, wrote: "Jack London's
speech is as that of an American with an Oxford education;
but as for Mrs. London, hers is Americanese, undefiled, and
unfiled." What irritated Jack in this instance was: "But
you didn't open your head; and the man scarcely saw you,
there in the dark of the carriage!"

From November 26 until December 7, on which latter
day Jack spoke at Bowdoin College, Brunswick, Maine, we
shared the journey, and a unique one it was for me. Seldom
was I so tired from travel that I missed a lecture, whether
upon Socialism, or his experiences as tramp, Klondiker,
War Correspondent, Sailor, or Writer. I never wearied
of seeing Jack step out upon stage or platform, with that
modest-seeming, almost bashful boyishness which so
charmed his audiences, and yet which so quickly, when he

raised his splendid head and launched into any serious theme, changed to the imperiousness of certitude. Once, well appreciative though I was of his beauty in this one of his myriad phases, I remonstrated:

"I wonder if you realize how forbidding you look when you walk out of the wings. Your expression is positively haughty!—as if you considered your audience mere dust under your feet!"

He laughed outright.

"Why, I don't feel that way at all, of course. Don't forget—I'm making up my mind what I'm going to say, and really not thinking of my hearers—busy with my thought. And then, too," he figured it out, "it may be a left-over of the system by which I first overcame stage-fright. It was something like this: I've got something to say. I've got to say it. I'm going to say it the best way I can, even if it's not oratory. If I try to make a good speech and fail—well, I shall have failed, that's all. I very soon had decided not to take too seriously any failure to speak graciously. What of it? I said. I won't be the only one; others have fallen down and why should I be proud! And anyway, diffidence arises from conceit, I don't care who disagrees with me . . . So remember, Mate, when I assume what you are pleased to call my imperial pose, it is done quite unconsciously, being an outgrowth of my early search after a shield for backwardness. I am not consciously thinking of myself at all; I am busy with my thought and the imminent business of putting my thought in the best way possible."

At the next lecture, when he moved out upon the boards he looked over at my box, his face breaking into that unstudied morning smile that wrought lovers out of enemies, and a little rustle passed through the house as if wings were ruffling and stretching. But in a flash the smile had fled behind the lordly mask of his concentration, and I knew I had ceased to exist for him.

But never, in any presentment of himself, was he so

splendid, so noble, as when, with starry eyes, he flamed out the vision of his conversion to the only religion he was ever to know: "All about me were nobleness of purpose and heroism and effort, and my days were sunshine and star-shine, all fire and dew, with before my eyes, ever burning and blazing, the Holy Grail, Christ's Own Grail, the warm, human, long-suffering and maltreated but to be rescued and saved at the last."

Jack swore he was getting enough train-travel to last all his life, and loathed it ever after. But very merrily, whether in Pullman or jerky day-coach, we put in hours that might otherwise have been irksome, reading aloud, playing casino and cribbage, writing letters, and altogether enjoying our companionship. Moreover, and blessed assurance of its continuance undimmed, we respected each other's solitude and independence—Jack at intervals spending hours in the smoker, listening profitably to the conversation of his own sex, or napping to make up for broken nights of travel. The all-around "good time" we invariably found together is best pointed by an incident several years later, when we were returning home from South America by way of the Gulf and New Orleans. As usual, we were bound up in each other and the interest of our occupations, at cards, sharing in books, the scenery, or in speculation upon the passengers. During one of Jack's absences, I was resting with closed eyes, when a beautiful matron in the section ahead, whom we had noticed with two younger women, came and sat beside me:

"I hope you'll not think me too rude," she opened, "but I want to ask a very personal question. Are you really Mrs. Jack London?"

There was such entire absence of offense in her eager, frank address that I could only laugh delightedly while assuring her this bliss had been mine for four years. But again she pressed:

"Are you *really* she?" and before I could protest in surprise, she hurried on, "My daughters and I have been discussing you two with the greatest curiosity, and said we were sure there must be some mistake—the thing is incredible; married people don't act as you do. *Never* have we seen a married couple, except possibly on their honeymoon, have such a good time together!"

All I could do, in return, was to assure her that we *were* on our honeymoon.

From Brunswick, where Jack averred to President Hyde that if his college days could come again he would attend Bowdoin, we filled another lecture-blank week with my father's people in Ellsworth and Mt. Desert Island, Maine. A day here, a day there, in the dear homesteads that had once been my homes for a long free year, we spent with this and that aunt or cousin—solid hearts of the very granite of old "State o' Maine," with their own glow and sparkle that renders them instantly aware of sham of any kind. One and all they pronounced the captivating boy I had wedded, with his irradiation of sweetness and sympathy and the open boyish face and heart of him, "Just *one of us!*" and called him their own forever and ever. Jack in turn dubbed them "salt of the earth," and gave them of his best.

Around Bar Harbor ("Somesville"), West Eden and Northeast Harbor, in an ideal "Down East" winter, we drove over the snow-packed, glinting roads that skirt the toothed coast of this isle of seafarers. Oddly enough to those who think of Jack London in terms of icy Alaska with its white ways of transportation, Jack had never before driven in a sleigh. So varied had been his adventures, that it was a prize of life for me to participate with him in an unknown one. Smothered to the ears in a borrowed coon-coat, head and hands snug in sealskin cap and gloves he had bought in Boston, he took keen interest in managing a span of spirited blacks harnessed to a smart "cutter," their red-flaring nostrils tossing white plumes of steam in the crackling, sun-gilt air.

Again in Boston, we became the guests of Mr. and Mrs. Frank Merritt Sheldon, in their handsome colonial home at Newton—with whom I had gone to Europe. Jack's advent must.have been an illuminating if not disturbing one to them, for many and ofttimes weird characters found their way up the driveway to the pillared portico of the lofty white house on a hillock. And of course newspapermen came and went. One of those my husband hoped to meet again some time, preferably in a dark alley where a nose might be tweaked unseen by the police; for, in reply to this man's question as to how it seemed to be the wife of a celebrity, he had made me deliver the ecstatic cry, "It's just grand!"

It was nothing unusual for some inebriated derelict to press the button upon the stroke of midnight; and once an indubitably insane crank perturbed the early hours and the housemaid. But our host and hostess were ideal, sparing no pains to place their home and themselves at their guests' disposal in every finest sense and detail, and apparently enjoying it all thoroughly.

Jack was driven nearly to the limit of endurance in the week before the twenty-seventh, when, with a holiday month in store, we sailed for Jamaica. Boston cameras pictured him hollow-eyed; but be he driven or not driven, I came to learn that he was wont to look other than his fresh, virile self whenever cities laid clutch upon him. Never did he thrive in a great metropolis.

In Tremont Temple, and in historic Faneuil Hall, under the noted Gilbert Stuart of the Father of His Country, to packed audiences Jack London sent forth his voice for the Cause. In the latter auditorium, that sweet and unvanquished fighter, "Mother Jones," marched up the central aisle to the rostrum, and greeted the young protagonist

of her holy mission with a sounding kiss on either cheek.
He spoke also at Socialist Headquarters.

The Intercollegiate Socialist Society had been organized
for a month or two, and the Harvard members got together
and saw to it that the first President, Jack London, should
be heard in Harvard Union.

Aside from Mrs. Sheldon, myself, and one or two others,
there were no women present in Harvard Union that night.
We sat with Frank Sheldon and Gelett Burgess in a tiny
gallery hung upon the rear wall of the high hall. A thrilling sight it was, that throng of collegians, not only those
crowded both seated and standing on the floor below, but
the scores hanging by their eyebrows to window case-
ments, welcoming Jack with round upon round of ringing
shouts and cheers—an ovation, the papers did not hesitate
to call it.

He gave them, unsparingly, all and more than they had
bargained for, straight from the shoulder, jolting "Revolution" into them. Once, when a statement of starvation
facts, concerning the Chicago slums, was so awful as to
strike a number of the chesty young bloods as a bit melo-
dramatic, a laugh started. Jack's face set like a vise, and
he hung over the edge of the platform, a challenge to their
better part flaming from black-blue eyes and ready, merci-
less tongue. Be it said that the response was instantaneous
and whole-hearted, the house rising as one man and echoing
to the applause until I, for one onlooker, choked and filled
with emotion at the human fellowship of it. At the close
of the lecture, Jack and Mr. Sheldon were carried off to the
fraternity houses and royally entertained the rest of the
night.

One afternoon, at the request of the *Boston American*,
Jack attended and wrote up a performance of the Holy
Jumpers, whose breezy antics, I dare opine, he did not re-
gard as any more outlandish than certain metaphysical

gymnastics he wotted of—and thought them far more whole-somely cheerful.

Still another afternoon, we put in three breathless hours in Thomas W. Lawson's private office at Young's Hotel, entirely absorbed (in a room peopled with replicas of elephants of every size, breed, and composition), in that brilliant and energetic gentleman's proposed "cure" for the ills and shams of modern society. Be it known, that the assertive and vehement conversationalist Jack London was also a prince of listeners. His was the perfection of attention to any speaker who was worth while. True, he seldom squandered precious time upon one who was not, but would proceed to harry unrelentingly until he had routed the other; after which he would try to make up in various ways for his aggressiveness.

One of our most interesting acquaintances in Boston was Dr. George W. Galvin, staunch Socialist and clever surgeon; and one day he arranged to take us through the Massachus-etts General Hospital. Once inside, would we care to see an operation? Dr. Richardson was in the theater and about to remove an appendix. While my lips formed Yes, swiftly I roved my adventurously promising career beside the bright comet I had taken unto myself for better or worse, a future wherein I might be required to reckon with singu-lar emergencies in war or travel by sea and land. I must never fail my man who despised a coward beneath all things under the sun. Here was chance for a certain kind of prepa-ration. Nerves I confessed in abundance: had I *nerve* also?

And so, curious concomitant of a honeymoon, I wit-nessed the masterly elimination of an appendix from a patient who bore startling facial resemblance to my own husband; thence to a second operating theater where we were present at the sanguinary trepanning, for tumor of the brain, of a woman's skull—"a Sea-Wolf operation, eh!" Dr. Galvin chuckled.

Through all of which, placing myself in a rigidly scientific frame of mind, I emerged with flying colors, to Jack's congratulation. Two months later, never having viewed a corpse in my life, except when too young to remember, I was introduced to such for the first time—when they ushered me into the dissecting chamber of the University of Chicago, where some dozen or so cadavers stiffly bade greeting to my unaccustomed gaze. These two trials, trials in a number of senses, reënforced by a day among the bleeding horrors of the stockyards in the same City, graduated Jack London's wife forever out of apprehension as to similar tests that might overtake her.

CHAPTER XXVIII

JAMAICA, CUBA, FLORIDA, NEW YORK CITY

30th Year

THE *Admiral Farragut*, in ballast, rode high and rolled prodigiously. Our cabin, well aft, suffered the full wallowing effect of the vessel's "sitting down in the sea-hollows," and I, for the first time in adult life, fell violently sick. Great mortification was mine, before a sailor husband, who eyed me with surprise and some misgiving, looking to our aqueous future. But on the third day out, he sat him down in the stateroom and regarded me, with eyes in which there was the pleasure of a discovery:

"I've been learning something about myself, and I may say about you," he launched forth. "I never thought I had it in me to feel any accession of tenderness toward a sea-sick woman! But somehow, I seem to love you more than ever before—I don't know why, unless because each new environment, whatever it may be, seems to make you still dearer to me."

Inside the month, crossing in a dirty little Spanish steamer from Jamaica to Cuba, to our mutual astonishment, Jack himself went to pieces. A slight shock precipitated the attack. Only one steamer chair being visible, we had appropriated it; and in a heavy surge the flimsy thing collapsed. A moment's pause, and Jack picked himself up and walked aft without a word. He did not return. Inquisitive, I went to investigate, and halted petrified to behold my hardened tar, hanging, green-pallid and audible, over the stern-rail, thoroughly seasick for the initial time in his nautical history. And in the years to come, he accepted a recurrence as a matter of course in rough weather. He likened the phenomenon of mal de mer to our native poison-oak—catch it just once, and immunity is a lost blessing. In passing, I must state that Jack continued immune to that irritating scourge of California, poison-oak.

The *Admiral Farragut* docked at Port Antonio, Jamaica, on New Year's morning, 1906. In the harbor was anchored the Howard Gould yacht, and at the Hotel Titchfield we made the acquaintance of Ella Wheeler Wilcox (whom Jack had championed so valiantly of old to the Lily Maid), and her husband, Robert.

In the afternoon I had my first revel in milk-warm, tropical waters, coral-girt, and we made sport for our party by diving for coins and practising life-saving as we had done in Wake Robin pool. The next day was spent in the saddle. Our mounts were spindly, blood-bay race-horses, and Jack's never for a moment let out of our minds the fact that he had been first under the wire in the previous day's races. But we saw the more, by our involuntary speed, of the British-neat island paradise, exploring the town itself, a pineapple plantation, and the romantic hill-stronghold of Moortown, still inhabited by the maroons—descendants of Spanish slaves.

The sharpest impressions carried away of that journey, in our first foreign clime together, were of the buxom, broad-smiling, broad-hipped negro wenches, basket-on-head, met on the dustless mountain roads that were in reality fern-hedged boulevards; the spiritual featured Hindoo women, weighed with their family wealth of silver adornment, specimens of which we purchased; the foolish luncheon out of queer, tempting tins, accompanied by English "biscuits," consumed while we dangled blissful heels from the counter of a little wayside store with a superb sea-view leagues below, the ebony proprietor and his indolent friends loafing genially about. But clearest of all remained the raffish spectacle, at Moortown, of a home-made merry-go-round. It was weather-grayed, witchy, rickety, and ridden by grinning black natives to a rhythmic chant from their own throats that affected us strangely—as if by some potent incantation dragging into the sunlight of civilization the most abysmal of racial reticences. It bestirred that mental unease which sometimes overtakes one who listens over-long to the primitive, disturbing call of modern "jazz" orchestration.

Leaving Port Antonio on the third day, by train for Buff Bay, we were there met by a dusky guide with horses, we having chosen this route across the green, fern-forested mountains to Kingston. It was all "unspeakably beautiful," I read in a pocket diary. We lunched and siesta'd at Cedarhurst, an English plantation, where Barbara Francis brewed incomparable coffee from beans which, by a true lady of the land, are roasted to a crisp for each meal. Three large cupfuls, black and strong, I, Jack's "insomniast," dared to tuck away; and three long hours afterwards, I, the insomniast, slumbered peacefully. "Why, *our* coffee *cures* insomnia," crooned Barbara Francis, as she snuggled me into a downy four-poster from "Home." "It's the way we roast it and percolate it, I fancy—besides being the best coffee in the world to begin with!"

Her husband led us about the plantation before we swung again into our saddles for the next lap, and Jack, irresistibly enthusiastic, made it very plain to me how coffee must be served on the Ranch when we should go to housekeeping.

Out we fared into a sunset of tropically crude blue and copper and rose, slipping through swift twilight into starlit blue dark. Trustingly behind the mellow-throated guide our sure-footed little beasts dropped steeply down a fragrant trail, lighted fitfully by darting fireflies, into Chester Vale. Here, at Sedgwick's, the very picture of an ancient, rambling English country home, we spent the night. "You couldn't pack a Broadwood half a mile," Jack quoted, coming beside me where I was examining my first Broadwood pianoforte. "Try it, do." But the stately relic answered back in tones probably such as Kipling's Broadwood might have rendered up had it been "packed" to the humid river region he rimed with "mile."

In the dewy, singing morning, it was boots and saddles over the Blue Ridge Range—through Hardware Gap, Silver Hill Gap, Greenwich, Newcastle Barracks, Gordontown, sometimes in lanes and driveways made especially beautiful by tree-ferns and crimson hibiscus blossoming tree-high, and into Kingston by the sea. Here at the Park Lodge Hotel, our first caller was Ben Tillett, M. P. and labor leader, he and Jack of course being known to each other.

Ah, it was so softly exciting, so wondrous, seeing the world together, all the glamorousness enhanced by that lovely old hostelry with its long French windows that let in the scented tropic air. My husband, who had pleasured exceedingly in my wintry Boston shopping for "flimsies" to be donned in the warmer latitudes, now had the satisfaction of seeing the light apparel in use—then, as always in the future, appreciative and critical of every detail of my wardrobe. Nothing would do but he must take me curio-seeking in quaint shops, more particularly for a bejeweled, flexible silver girdle of Hindoo origin, and snaky bracelets to match.

Only one incident arose to mar the holiday perfection. It was on the very night of arrival that I came abruptly upon the stone wall of one of Jack's self-styled "disgusts." In review, I cannot place the cause—perhaps it was some hitch on Manyoungi's part regarding the luggage, or Jack's dinner-clothes; at least, I saw no large concern back of his silent anger, unless . . . unless, indeed, some trifle had connected his memory with some unhappy occurrence in his past. But it was black, that mood, from whatever deeps it rose; and ruthlessly he sent me, alone, to the viny bower that was the hotel's dining-hall, in a court of flowers that screened the musicians, to keep an engagement we both had made with a fellow traveler from Boston.

Puzzled and hurt I was, but held my peace, and made smooth wifely excuses for a severe headache that was not altogether an untruth. In the morning Jack woke his sunniest, save for a wordless penitence that looked out of eyes which went so darkly-blue under a generous emotion.

It was ages before the matter ever came up between us. But although we spoke of it, I never made sure of the underlying impulsion that had sent him agley. It was not the only instance of its kind, but I came timely to sense the causes, and avert them wherever in my power. Yet I hasten to undo any impression I may have given that in our lives such "spells" were the order of the day. On the contrary, months and years might elapse during which no trace of the old blues intervened; and, in this connection, I am reminded of the gradual disappearance, after our marriage, of certain terrible headaches to which he had been subject. This was, I think, largely due to his seeking more adequate sleep.

The Spanish steamer aforementioned, the *Oteri*, landed us in Santiago de Cuba on the 6th, where, from the Hotel del Alba, we drove about the city and to San Juan Hill, and strolled lace-hunting in cool little shops. And Jack bought some lovely fans to gratify my slight Spanish streak, which I called up to play its part in its own congenial habitat. A dinner which we enjoyed in the Café Venus, guests of a charming gentleman who was living out what of life was still vouchsafed by one remaining lung, was always a colorful memory to Jack, who incorporated it somewhere in his fiction. I, in a soft rosy gown, swaying languidly my spangled, pearl-handled fan to the lilt of a plaza band in the lazy warm airs under the palms, wondered if anything to come in our wanderings could approach the romance that was here.

After the final act at a theater, when the pretty victoria had left us at the hotel, we ascended to our vaulted chamber and drifted out upon a balcony railed in fretted gilt iron, and lounged a restful hour, shamelessly gazing into luxurious Spanish interiors and balconies across the narrow street, where señoras and señoritas entertained in their courtly manner. I am certain that Jack reveled in that night; but more certain am I that some seven-eighths of his content was vested in that of his bride, to whom every moment was as a pearl of price and as such abides.

Jack, his manhood revolting at the brazen falsity of a cab-driver who delivered us at the railroad station, became the nucleus of a gesticulating and to all appearances not harmless mob. As the moment of departure neared, he called to me to go aboard with Manyoungi. Only the fact that Jack had tickets and money in his possession restrained him from going to jail at the last instant rather than abase his Anglo-Saxon pride before the impudent half-breeds. As it was, mad as a hatter, he paid for an extra passenger who existed solely in the crafty imagination of the cab-man, and boarded the train after it was in motion. There was some consolation, however, when in Havana the same ruse was tried, and the American Consul, himself a Spaniard, to whom Jack appealed, in short order sent to the right-about a much-cowed coachman who had sworn by the Virgin to *two* extra fares!

The rich country across which we sped that golden day, and an Egyptian sunset athwart little hills for all the world so like pyramids that one's eyes went questing through the rose and yellow and lilac for a Sphinx, all wrought upon Jack's creative faculties. He withdrew into himself at intervals, to make notes for a novel which I now realize never was written—"The Flight of the Duchess."

In the Spanish city of Havana, with its dream-tinted palaces, instead of putting up at a hotel, we found cool gray rooms in a flower-girt patio at Consolado and Neptune Streets. Of course, we did and saw everything there was to do and see in so short a sojourn: a launch trip around the twisted wreck of the *Maine;* visits to Moro Castle and Cabañas Fort, and to the swimming baths of hewn coral; and we drowned our souls in the fairy coloring of the isle and the waters of the Gulf. Notable amid our entertainment was a sportive evening watching the Basque game of *Jai Alai,* followed by a gorgeous banquet in the famous Hotel Miramar, originally built by a rich American for the pleasure of his guests.

A book in itself would be required to relate an afternoon we spent in the lazar-house—an experience that for all time interested us in the tragedy of the leper.

"We hated to leave Havana," says my red booklet, "but all the world's before us!"

The steamer *Halifax* set us down at Key West, where we transferred to the *Shinnecock* for Miami. Jack, who from his omniverous reading knew considerable about almost everything under the sky, was curious to hook a few of the six hundred-odd varieties of fish reputed to swim in Miami waters. "Just think, Mate," he said to me, "one-fifth of the entire fauna of the American Continent, north of Panama, inhabit this part of the coast." Boating, angling for edible fish and hooking outlandish finny shapes, driving in the Everglades, calling at the alligator and crocodile farm, and shopping for curios and snake-skins, filled the Miami visit. Next we stopped at Daytona Beach, where from the Hotel Clarendon we branched out on automobile trips over the beautiful stretches of sand, fished off the long pier, and took a day's launch-exploration up the tropical Tomoka River.

Jack had been drooping, dull and listless, for a day or

two. On the return cruise he became rapidly worse, so that I was up all night with him, and in the morning sent numerous telegrams delaying New York appointments.

No doctor would he let me summon, "Because I simply *can't* be laid up long, with New York and the rest of the lecture schedule to be lived up to," he demurred. "Besides, it's only grippe—I know the symptoms; and I also know myself and my recuperative abilities better than any doctor."

I sat by his bedside reading aloud and running to the window whenever a racing car whizzed past, while the patient grumbled and groaned with splitting head: "And I came to this damned place mainly to see those cars at practice; and now look at me!"

The next I knew, glancing up from a totally unemotional page of Shaw's "The Irrational Knot," was that Jack was weeping copiously, the tears coursing down his hot cheeks. Much perturbed, I yet failed to wring from him any explanation. But I was to learn through painful experience that very night, for I was struck down by the identical malady and myself fell emotional to a degree upon the mildest provocation.

Manyoungi, fortunately, remained untouched by the sickness, and nobly nursed the pair of us, sending further telegrams that moved ever ahead our New York arrival. Crawling in to Jack from my room, he received me with feeble arms and trembling voice:

"Mate Woman, I know I shall love you always!" and we both cried sumptuously over the sentiment. And how we laughed in memory of our mawkishness, once the attack of *dengue*, or "boo-hoo" fever, which it proved to be, was a thing of the past.

As soon as we were slightly better, we took a drawing-room for New York, stopping over at Jacksonville for an afternoon in which to totter around the Ostrich Farm.

The foregoing is by way of preparing the reader for receiving into New York City a white, hollow-eyed, very miserable Jack London, burdened with an almost insupportable number of engagements to fulfil in half the days he had originally alloted them. The first was a socialist meeting in Grand Central Palace, his lecture advertised for eight p. m., and our belated train gave him scant leeway. In no wise aided by the fact that I had to go to bed, too blind with pain in head and muscles to lend cheer by word or smile, Jack, ill, travel-worn, dinnerless, got into his black suit and somehow carried off the occasion. His audience, a mixed one, totaled nearly four thousand.

More than once Jack had forewarned me, in similar strain to his remarks in the Johns Letters, of the baleful influence exercised upon him by this mighty man-trap, New York City. Even so, that early, I was inclined to discount the mental factor, laying his condition mainly at the door of fever and social over-strain. But I was forced to change my mind. His own diagnosis was that his experience with the City, first from the viewpoint of tramp and beggar, and afterward from that of successful author at whom "publishers were trying to throw money in the form of advances on unperformed work," seemed to have unbalanced his preceptions and sent him reasoning in a circle like that of certain young German philosophers.

"It's all a madness," he would gird. " 'Why should anybody do anything?' is my continual thought when I am in New York. I am being shaved: I look up into the face of the man who is using the razor on me, and wonder why he doesn't cut my throat with it. I stare with amazement at the elevator-boy in the hotel, that he doesn't throw everything to the winds and let loose in one hell of a smash-up, just for the whimsey of it!"

At the opera, he brooded and made notes. If the music reached him at all, it was not as music, but as an urge toward other thoughts and speculations. "Music! It is a *drug*," said he. "I have asked several men and women for a definition of music. George Sterling comes the nearest to satisfying—a *drug*. It sets me dreaming like a hasheesh-eater."

We sat at the Winter Garden. He filled the evening agonizing mentally over the probable careers, in the theatrical shambles, of the chorus girls, beautiful mere children that they were, flown like moths to the bright lights that were consuming them.

We supped at the Revolutionists' Club, and afterward inspected a mile or so of the Ghetto, peering into the unventilated gloom of "inside rooms," at the sullen pasty faces of the inmates. Jack moved about, either silently, as if playing his part in a nightmare, or arguing strenuously as if against time.

Up-town or down-town, it seemed as if all normal spontaneity had fled from him, and I could but exist in hope that the man, who was as though a thousand-thousand leagues apart from me, might one day come suddenly to his own again, to the healthy, vital boy that was himself.

After one reception that was given in our honor, when a newspaperwoman had seized the occasion to poke a little fun at the bride's obvious devotion, Jack sneered with mirthless laugh: "What did you expect?—Any natural human appreciation of anything natural and human, in New York?"

It was about this time that *The Cosmopolitan Magazine* had issued a challenge to a few of America's thinking writers, to contribute articles on the theme "What Life Means to Me." Jack had not yet found leisure in which even to ponder what he should say; but a conversation with Edwin Markham stirred him to action:

"How are *you* going about it?" asked the white-maned poet, his splendid dark eyes bent upon the younger man.

"Damned 'f I know!" smiled Jack. "How are *you?*"

Followed a discussion, Mr. Markham appreciating

Jack's uncompromising socialist approach to the subject, but doubtful of its expediency as regarded the magazine editors.

But when the Jack London production appeared in *The Cosmopolitan,* it was without editorial blue elision, "Which is why I like to work for Hearst," Jack repeated an oft-voiced opinion. "Writers for Hearst, special writers like myself, are paid well for expanding their own untrammeled views." (Once he expatiated: "Why, when I returned from Manchuria and presented my expense account, the *Examiner* editor said, 'For God's sake, London, do itemize this a little before I send it in!' I did this, and the unquestioned total was remitted in due course." So meticulously, indeed, had *The Examiner* observed the details of Jack's war correspondence, that he had been greatly entertained, upon his return, to notice that wherever he had queried his own spelling, the "(Spl?)" with which he had preceded the word was left untampered!)

In Jack London's "What Life Means to Me" (final article in book entitled "Revolution"), one reads what is perhaps his most impassioned committal of himself as a rebel toward the shames and uncleannesses of the capitalist system. Here he dedicates himself to what he sees as his Holy Grail, to "the one clean, noble and alive" thing worth working for—George Sterling's definition of Socialism. In the essay Jack hints at some of his experiences, east and west, more than one of them in the immediate past of his lecturing tour, and what he learned therein concerning the women and men of the "tottering edifice" of the upper crust of Society. His challenge is flung to that thin and cracking upper crust as he saw it: "with all its rotten life and unburied dead, its monstrous selfishness and sodden materialism."

The only break in the New York days was when Jack went to New Haven to give the "Revolution" lecture at

Yale University, under title of "The Coming Crisis." To my everlasting regret I was too weak to accompany him. He was invited to speak by the author of that exquisite, human Irish idyl, "My Lady of the Chimney Corner," Reverend Alexander Irvine, who represented the state committee and the New Haven Local. Jack cut out several less important affairs, and gave to Connecticut January 26. No theater nor hall being available, the Socialists, including members of the Intercollegiate Society, had held an informal Smoker in an ivied tower in Vanderbilt Hall of the august college, and hatched the critical scheme of getting the Faculty interested in bidding Jack London, famous young litterateur, to grace Woolsey Hall, Yale's million-dollar white marble memorial.

Dr. Irvine commissioned an astute, socialistically-bent student to take the matter up, first, with an officer of Yale Union, a debating society. The seed fell on fertile ground. "The officer of the Yale Union," says Dr. Irvine, in a delightful illustrated brochure which he afterward compiled, "was a youth of exceeding great callowness.

" 'They say he's socialistically inclined, Doctor,' he said.

" 'Rather,' I replied.

" 'Well,' he said, 'I suppose we'll have to take our chances.' "

Dr. Irvine guaranteed the hall rent, advertising, and so forth, provided an admission fee of ten cents might be charged, which was agreed upon.

It really was a shame, what these graceless free-thinkers put over upon President Hadley. One of the leading Professors, although apprehensive of Jack's "radical tendencies," was yet reasonable: "Yale is a University," enounced he, "and not a monastery. Besides, Jack London is one of the most distinguished men in the world."

Dr. Irvine tells: "A few hours after it was decided that we could have Woolsey Hall the advertising began. The factories and shops were bombarded with dodgers. Every tree on the' campus bore the mysterious inscription: 'Jack London at Woolsey Hall.' Comrade Dellfant painted a poster which gripped men by the eyes. In it Comrade London appears in a red sweater and in the background the lurid glare of a great conflagration. . . . On the morning of the 26th Yale—official and unofficial—awoke as if she had been dreaming. She rubbed her eyes and again scanned the trees and the billboards. Then the officers of the Yale Union were run down. They had previously run each other down. Explanations were in order all around. Several of the Yale Union boys—in pugilistic parlance—lost their little goats. They were scared good and stiff. Several Yale Dons got exceedingly chesty over the affair. But the New Yale took a hand, and Professors Kent and Phelps counseled a square deal and fair play. One student, in sympathy with the meeting, said: ''Yale Union and many of the Faculty are sweating under the collar for fear London *might* say something socialistic.' ''

But it was definitely settled that the lecture could not be called off and the only thing was to make the best of it. ''When we arrived on the scene,'' Dr. Irvine refers to Jack and himself, ''the boys still believed that any reference to Socialism would be merely incidental.'' Jack's friend, by the way, in his spirited account attires the speaker, with marked respect, in a white *flannel* shirt! Friends and enemies alike insisted upon his wearing flannel!

The crowd that packed Woolsey Hall represented every social phase of New Haven and its suburbs—a hundred professors and ten times as many students; many hundreds of workingmen; many hundreds of citizens; many hundreds of Socialists. ''But,'' the humorous Irish divine remarks, ''the Socialists were so overwhelmed by the bourgeois atmosphere that there was not the slightest attempt to applaud during the entire length of the lecture.'' And the Socialist ''bouncers'' who had been surreptitiously stationed throughout the big audience, in reserve for possible ructions, held their idle hands.

"For over two hours the audience gave the lecturer a respectful hearing. A woman—a lady—went out swearing. A few students tried hard to sneer, but succeeded rather indifferently. Jack London gripped them by the intellect and held them to the close. Following the lecture, Comrade London was invited to a student's room—one of the largest —and there he answered questions until midnight. As the clock struck twelve a member of the Yale Union came to me and asked me seriously if I thought there was any hope of keeping London for a week! 'We can fit him up here,' he said, 'in fine shape.'

"There was a second conference at Mory's and some tired intellects were handled rather roughly by the guests· of the evening—but the students clung to him and escorted him in the we sma' hours up Chapel Street toward the Socialist parsonage where another reception was awaiting him.

"A Professor of Yale," Dr. Irvine concludes, "told me a few days after the lecture that it was the greatest intellectual stimulus Yale had had in many years, and he sincerely hoped that London would return and expound the Socialist program in the same hall."

Jack had been advised beforehand as to certain faulty acoustics in the beautiful auditorium. That he lent no deaf ear may be judged from one of the newspapers, which also gives a hint upon his platform personality at that time:

". . . he walked to the edge of the stage and began to speak in a clear voice, which reached easily to the farthest corner of the hall. He used scarcely any gestures, and rarely raised his voice even to emphasize a point. His emphasis he got by reiteration."

As for his countenance, in a photograph taken with

Dr. Irvine, there can be noticed the strange, haggard look he wore during that period.

His immediate treatment by the New Haven dailies was one of leniency, not lacking the dignity of at least trying to quote him verbatim. He was not flattered by the portrait they published, since it was of some one else, youthfully apostolic in appearance, arrayed quite differently from Jack's reputed "white flannel shirt."

While the local press was minded to be indulgent and the University as little unduly excited as had been Harvard in its turn, the trustees of Derby Neck Library, in the same State, rose in a denunciatory body and repudiated, to all intents and purposes forever, the entire works of Jack London. Further misquoting his "to hell with the constitution" pronouncement, those opinion creators exhorted the public, in no uncertain terms, likewise to spurn all periodicals containing Jack's stories.

It had happened that Mr. Melville E. Stone, general manager of the Associated Press, spoke in New Haven upon the same evening with Jack London. But whenever asked, by sympathizers, regarding the policy of the Derby Neckers, if he thought Mr. Stone's presence had anything to do with the deluge of adverse newspaper notoriety which followed, Jack invariably insisted: "Not in the least. I am personally convinced that Mr. Stone had nothing to do with it."

But it was ludicrous how the tune of the press changed from "the brilliant young author" to criticisms such as, "pathologically he is a neurasthenic," or it disposed of him lightly as "that socialist sensation-monger who calls himself Jack London." It is noteworthy, however, that his mother's home town, Massillon, Ohio, supported an editor with a sense of proportion, for he naïvely propounded, in *The Morning Gleaner,* "Must a novelist necessarily admire the Constitution?"

The truth is, that the wide controversy as to blacklisting Jack's books caused an alarming slump in sales for some time to come. He, who always maintained his unfitness for physical martyrdom: "I'd tell *anything* under torture!"—thus sacrificed unflinchingly for his beliefs, martyred his brain faculties in the cause of Truth.

About the nearest the capitalist editors leaned toward championing him, or at least reacting to the high-handed imposition of arbitrary standards upon readers of Derby Neck or other communities, was when they voiced something of President Wheeler's earlier sentiments as to the unlidding of highly explosive propaganda.

Came the ninth and last day that parted us from our western trek. Whisked from a luncheon of celebrities to the Twentieth Century Limited, we were settled in our section and the car gliding homeward, when Jack, suddenly, with a sigh, nodded his curly head and as suddenly fell asleep. All strain was erased from his features—it was the face of a dreaming child that slipped into the hollow of my shoulder, ordained from aforetime. When he awoke, and consciousness had focused in his eyes, they looked up into mine with a matter-of-course recognition of content. Upon his tongue was speech of home—and how were the dear Brown Wolf, and that rabbity little bay mare, Fleet, which the young Allens had sold us along with other farm perquisites when they vacated the old house on the Hill place?

It was preciously similar to the way he had emerged from his thrall on that epochal spring day in Nunn's Canyon. And I was to learn, whensoever great Gotham claimed its price and prize of his unresting heart and brain, that I must deal with another personality than the wonted Jack London.

CHAPTER XXIX

CHICAGO; RETURN TO OAKLAND, GLEN ELLEN; EARTHQUAKE

1906

CHICAGO, noises and drafts and sifting soot and all, seemed to reach to us east-worn travelers like home and peace, despite the rushing stop-over that had been charted.

On Sunday, January 28, Jack lectured to the Socialists at the West Side Auditorium, introduced by A. M. Simons, editor of the *International Socialist Review*. Standing-room only, and that all taken, was the situation long before Jack had risen to speak.

On Monday he repeated "The Social Revolution" at the University of Chicago, and the Socialists were more than ever elate that the "magnificent lecture of Comrade London" should be staged in the "intellectual stronghold of Standard Oil." Kent Hall, which had been opened to the Sociological Club, was incapable of holding the mob bent upon seeing and hearing its famous mouth-piece, to say nothing of the students themselves and a horde of citizens.

It was a fine sight to me, the hundreds overflowing on to the stage itself, sidewalks jammed outside, and more coming every second. Things were growing tense. The dissatisfied murmur of the many denied admission floated into the packed playhouse. Then an usher climbed before the footlights and announced that the meeting would adjourn to Mandel Hall—Mandel Hall! the auditorium consecrated to the most dress-parade functions of the great University, and even known to have been refused to the minor colleges for their commencement exercises.

112

The galleries had been barred; but when the throng had swept aside the helpless ushers and occupied every foot of space, seat and aisle, fear of infringing fire regulations caused the galleries to be thrown open.

The dailies of Chicago, still smarting under the suppressed wedding news, as well as from Jack's late attacks, from the Atlantic Coast, upon her sweat-shop atrocities, naturally let him have the broadside of their ridicule and enmity. But somehow, so fond were we of the city, it failed to offend.

Before we said good-by, Mr. Simons and his attractive and learned wife had us to the University dissecting rooms aforementioned, as well as to the Armour and Swift stock-yards and slaughtering plants. And while we were on the trail of unpleasant but instructive sights of the world in which we live, we spent a night going through one section of Chicago's "red-light" district.

Our last sight-seeing, ere we left on the 31st for St. Paul, was of Hull House, where we made the acquaintance of Miss Jane Addams. It was a treat to listen to a discussion between Miss Addams and Jack London—each approaching the same heartfelt problems from widely divergent angles.

"Well," Jack observed, stretching himself in the Pullman, "the Little Woman has added a number of strange experiences to her life. And you don't know," he broke out, "you can't guess, what it means to me, to have you by my side everywhere, in everything I do and see. I am not lonely any more. Wherever I go,—at least, wherever it is possible for me to take you, I want you with me—I want you to know the world as I know it, the good and the bad of it. It means the world to me that you don't flinch from any of it, so far as I can see.—In fact," his tone went grave and his brow severe, before breaking into laughing speech, "the way that you, shameless women that you are, tenderly raised a vegetarian, put away that hearty lunch after seeing animals slaughtered all forenoon, worries me about your immortal soul!"

"But you will kindly remember," I came back, "that I confined my depredations solely to bivalves and prawns!"

In the little diary of that day's ride I find: "Jack says we two are living in a Land of Love, wherever we are." There is less tender notation to the effect that I was sorely beaten at both casino and cribbage; also mention of our finishing Turgenev's "On the Eve" and beginning Gissing's "The Unclassed," reading aloud, turn about.

At St. Paul, Jack lectured for the Lyceum Bureau. We visited the handsome State Capitol, fashioned throughout, marbles and all, from native American materials. We sat through an exciting wrestling match in the Armory. And nothing would do but Jack must take part in an impromptu "curling" tournament. It was with keen enjoyment he drove the heavy but elusive disks over the constantly swept ice-rink, and the very picture of a Scotch laddie was he, in borrowed tam o'shanter and woolen plaid. We heard later, much to his amusement, that the driver of the automobile that returned us over the hard snow to the hotel, had been arrested for speeding!

Grand Forks, North Dakota, was the next jump, where we were entertained by President Merrifield of the State University, and in this city on February 3 were given Jack's two final lectures. The "first and last tour," so far as the speaking end of it was concerned, had terminated—untimely, for Jack was tired and ill from the long siege, and had crossed off a number from the itinerary. On the train he wrote Cloudesley Johns:

"I called off the Mills [B. Fay Mills, The Evangelist] debate because he requested me to, and because the only alternative was a refined and sublimated statement that had nothing in it to debate about. Have been miserably sick, and have cancelled a whole string of lectures, including all California lectures. I sent you a wire canceling Owen debate. . . . I won't get down to Los Angeles this spring."

The remainder of the journey was without special event, except that our train was delayed above beautiful Dunsmuir, in California, by a freight wreck ahead in a canyon. The passengers made a picnic of it, wandering about the adjacent country; and we twain, being immersed in Selma Lagerlof's "Gosta Berling," reclined upon a grassy slope and read to each other. I think it will be seen, by now, why Jack and I were never bored, no matter how long nor uninteresting, in the estimate of some mortals, our traverse. Life was not long enough in which to read the books we desired, to do the work laid out, to talk of the myriad things suggested by other myriad things; nor to love.

At three o'clock, the last but one morning before we reached Oakland, Jack woke me in my berth. Disturbing my rest being a tacit taboo, I was startled; but his instant whisper, shaken with eagerness, reassured: "Throw on your kimono and come out on the platform with me. I want to show you something—you've got to see it!"

It was indeed "something"—great Shasta, upthrust 14,000 feet, snow-crowned, into the moonlit, night-blue dome of the sky; and the Lassen Buttes, stark and flat in the beams of a setting moon, like peaks cut from heavy dull-gold cardboard. Eight years thereafter, in Mexico, when General Funston remarked that he had read in "El Imparcial's" telegraphic column that Mt. Lassen was in eruption, my mind flew back to that hour before dawn when Jack and I, so airily clad, arm-in-arm on the lurching vestibule platform, gazed out upon the fairy scene, and spoke in hushed tones.

The Oakland reporters flocked to Jack upon his return, and to their queries he repeated that if his marriage had proved invalid in Illinois, he would have remarried in every state in the Union. Referring to some misreport about himself, I find this from the *Oakland Herald*:

"Yes, that was another case of being the victim of reporters' readjustment of facts. Oh, I know I have been a newspaperman myself—thereby perhaps I know so well how impossible it is for reporters to avoid perverting facts. Oh, heavens, no! I am not trying to demonstrate that reporters are natural-born liars, and yet. . . .

"Why, do you know, while I was in Chicago the other day, I had two reporters struggle with my immortal soul for hours trying to get me to say that I am a believer in free love—which I am not at all. They struggled nobly, but I stood firm to the argument that the family group is the very hub of things.

"But then I rather enjoy this misrepresentation. It is amusing; and besides you know, it's fine advertising! And I don't take myself seriously, so can take all that's said about me as a joke, for I always try to laugh at the inevitable."

Jack had concluded to cease paying rent in Oakland; and shortly after our arrival, as man and wife, at the little flat in Telegraph Avenue, we set about finding a suitable house for his mother and Johnnie, as well as Mammy Jennie. One was purchased on Twenty-Seventh Street, Jack's ultimate decision influenced by the handsome woods of its interior finishing, for he was fond of good lumber. One room in the upper story we reserved for town headquarters.

By mid-month we were on the way to our true home, and were met at the Glen Ellen station by Werner Wiget, who had long since changed his abode from the Fish Ranch to the farm-house up the mountain, where now he was in charge, under my Aunt's supervision in Jack's absence.

"Jack's House," at Wake Robin, as it has ever since been known, served as formerly for writing quarters and Manyoungi's sleeping place. Other living rooms, added to

Wake Robin Lodge proper, and spoken of as the Annex, were in readiness for our use, and a neat and comely neighbor, Mrs. Grace Parrent, who wanted to swell her own family exchecquer for some special purpose, had engaged to cook and ply her deft French needle in preparing me for the round-world voyage.

It was a sort of sublimated camping. Our winter table was set in a corner of the spotless kitchen that was odorous of new pine; and later on, when spring's caprices had quieted, the table was removed out under the laurels at the brookside, where our crocked butter and cream cooled in the ripples. Mrs. Parrent's excellent repasts were enjoyed to the music of tuneful Korean treebells that Man-youngi knew well how to place to advantage among the bays and oaks. Jack and I had discovered many tastes in common, even to a fondness for olive oil as a culinary lubricator. in preference to the animal fats. He had acquired his among the Greek fishermen, I in my Aunt's vegetarian household.

Jack was not yet looking quite himself, the sunken shadows still lurking about his eyes; and a marked decrease in weight was noticeable. I was aware of an almost painful relief in that he was once more out of the turmoil of urban life and immersed in laying plans for the summer's work and play, the building of his deep-sea boat, and the modest improvement of the ''Blessed Ranch,'' as he lovingly referred to it. Consequently, it was with positive alarm that I regarded the managing editor of a large eastern monthly, who arrived from New York two days after our return to Wake Robin, his mission to induce Jack immediately to re-cross the continent, for the purpose of making a first-hand study of the southern cotton-mills in relation to child-labor.

Caring—perhaps sinfully, who shall say?—more for the imminent welfare of this man of mine than for all the serfs of all ages, I sat at the interview silently exerting every fiber of me against his going. I was certain, from observation of his internal restlessness, that if he went back into the cities so soon, there might be dire consequences. Reasoning back to his state antedating the summer of 1905, I knew he had had enough, for the time being.

The editor was plainly anxious not to find his journey in vain. Eloquently he pleaded. Jack pondered with troubled eyes, and would not give answer until he and I had talked it over. He wanted to do the thing; his conscience pressed him to do it. And though he recognized as well as I the need in which he stood of freedom from what he had only just escaped, he would not have *shirked* even if his actual life had depended upon it. But balanced against this new work was the work he had already pledged, together with other responsibilities; and there came to aid his ultimatum a slight misstep of the editor, who let drop that if Jack did not undertake the commission, another man, only a little less noted—Socialist—was in view. "Let the other fellow have a chance," often a slogan of Jack London's, was the outweighing grain in the scales.

Jack knew, and why, though I said little and tried not to look too much, that I was dead-set against his going. I never learned precisely what he thought of my attitude —whether he blamed me for being instrumental, by mere woman-mothering possessiveness and solicitude, in withholding him from a duty, or was glad I agreed that he stay west for a while. If there resided in his mind any unflattering criticism, it died with him. It may be that something restrained me from asking; and joy in his augmented well-being—always my religious care—took the place of morbid self-examination. Before I desert the subject, let it be said that the second-choice of author and investigator did a splendid piece of work—"Better than I could have done it, by far!" Jack enunciated his satisfaction; hence the ultimate good was served. Furthermore, one of Jack's finest bits of writing, after our return, was a story of the making of a hobo by the process of cotton-mill child-slavery. This was "The Apostate," which, following serial publication, came to have wide circulation in pamphlet form through a Socialist publishing house in Chicago. (The book "Revolution" contains this tale.)

How more than busy we were! Aside from regular writing, which was soon resumed, Jack, with eye to home-building, ordered fruit-trees of all descriptions suitable to the latitude, and seventy-odd varieties of table-grapes —orchard and vineyard to be planted upon an amphi-theater behind a half-circle we had chosen for the house-site. Johannes Reimers tendered the benefit of his pro-fessional advice about the trees and vines, and ordered for us a hedge of Japanese hawthorne to flourish between or-chard and house-space, which in time grew into a glory of orange and red berries alternating with a season of white blossoming. The plot was on the lip of a deep wooded ravine which was the Ranch's southern boundary, ancient redwood and spruce, lightning-riven and eagle-nested, accenting the less majestic growth. We never wearied of riding Belle and Ban to the spot, in our minds' eyes the vision of a rugged stone house that was to rise like an indigenous growth from the grassy semi-circle.

While occupied upon two Alaskan tales, "A Day's Lodging" and "The Wit of Porportuk" (bound in "Love of Life" and "Lost Face"), Jack arranged the manuscripts for two short-story volumes, "Moon Face" and "Love of Life," published in 1906 and 1907 respectively. Next, Upton Sinclair's "The Jungle" was reviewed. Jack, who apositely dubbed it "The 'Uncle Tom's Cabin' of Wage-Slavery," sadly observed thereafter that the most conspic-uous result of this expose of labor conditions in the stock-yards was only to make the public more careful what it put into its stomach.

While he was working on another story, "When God

Laughs,'' a letter was received from Mr. E. H. Sothern, asking him to write a socialistic play for himself and Miss Julia Marlowe; but nothing ever came of this.

Before starting upon a new novel, ''Before Adam,'' Jack had, in addition to the above-noted short work, completed an article, ''The Somnambulists'' (in ''Revolution''), also the stories ''Created He Them'' and ''Just Meat'' (both in ''When God Laughs'' collection), and ''Finis'' (in ''The Turtles of Tasman.'') Then, by way of relaxation and practice on drama form, he did a curtain-raiser from his story ''The Wicked Woman''—this flick of drama going into the volume ''The Human Drift,'' brought out posthumously.

During March, he visited Oakland to deliver a Socialist lecture at Dietz Opera House. Following this event, Jack London was talked of for Socialist Governor at the next elections. While in Oakland, we selected a two-seated rig and a runabout. Jack had set his heart upon a buckboard, such as one in which his neighbor, Judge Carroll Cook, used to meet friends at the railroad station. But we were in urgent need of a vehicle for the same purpose, and snapped up the neat uncovered wagon with yellow wheels, looking forward to a buckboard later on. Jack never acquired that buckboard. Instead, when the Napa Winships went in for gasolene, we bought out their other rolling stock, which came to serve all purposes.

Mrs. Louise Clark, a neighbor, sold us the horse Selim, a black handful of abounding energy. Jack, in the process of subduing Selim and the silly Fleet to gentle uses, waxed in soft-spoken patience unbelievable to his old pals who came to look on. We took much interest, also, in forming different spans with our four light horses, harnessed to the new four wheelers.

And oh, yes—the good Brown Wolf, tiny pointed ears flattened ingratiatingly back into his russet ruff, and long pink tongue lolling dumb delight and pride, presented us to a new family of puppies. One of these went to Jack's children. "I don't think much of the rest," he ruefully surveyed them and their mongrel if excellent mother; so we kept none of the litter.

Presently the astounding booksmith had begun his atavistic "Before Adam," which came out in *Everybody's Magazine*. Upon its publication a hue and cry went up, originating in a men's club, to the effect that Jack London had plagiarized Stanley Waterloo's "The Story of Ab." Be it said, however, that Mr. Waterloo did not start the trouble. Jack was frank to admit that "The Story of Ab" had been one of his sources of material. "But Waterloo was not scientific," he stoutly defended, "and I have made a scientific book out of my re-creation on the subject." So correct was his assumption, that "Before Adam" went into the universities of the United States as a text-book in Anthropology. To George Sterling, in June, he wrote:

"Have just expressed you MS of 'Before Adam.' It's just a skit, ridiculously true, preposterously real. Jump on it."

England, even that early, in the character of Red Eye saw a "cryptic reference to the German Emperor."

Jack, who derived material from every available source and especially from the newspapers as representing life, was eternally dogged at the heels by small men at home and abroad who charged plagiarism—these having little commerce with one, more generous, who said, "If I could by hook or crook write anything worth Jack London's copying, I should consider it a privilege." As for Jack, he did not try to boycott those who benefited by his creations. Rather was he pleased that he had been first!

That year of 1906, sketchy as was our domestic menage, many visitors came to the Lodge annex, and Auntie let us spill over into the main house. Among the names in my journal I come upon our good friends the Granville-Shueys

—Dr. Shuey was custodian of the welfare of Jack London's troublesome teeth to the end of the patient's life; Mr. Bamford; I. M. Griffin, the artist, a number of whose canvases, painted in the neighborhood, Jack purchased; Henry Meade Bland, of San José, at all times one of Jack's most tireless biographers; Felix Peano, sculptor, in whose house, La Capriccioso, Jack had once lived; young Roy Nash, of whom "The People of the Abyss" had made a Socialist; Ernest Untermann, author, and translator of Karl Marx; the George Sterlings; different members of the talented family of Partingtons; George Wharton James, who charmed with his social qualities and music, and later published most readable articles upon his visit; Elwyn Hoffman, poet; Herman Whitaker; Xavier Martinez, artist and prince of bohemians—"Sometimes I think," Jack once remarked, "that George Sterling and 'Marty' are the realest bohemians I have ever known!"; Maud Younger, settlement worker and philanthropist; and a long list beside.

Our amusements consisted in exploring, alone or with our guests, the infinite variety of the one hundred and twenty-nine acres of Jack's "Beauty Ranch"; driving or riding to points in the valley—say Cooper's Grove, a stately group of redwoods; or to Hooker's Falls across in the eastern range; or to Santa Rosa, as when we drove Professor Edgar Larkin, of Mt. Lowe Observatory, to call upon Luther Burbank; or to the valley resorts to swim, for a change from Sonoma Creek, in the warm mineral tanks.

During the Moyer-Haywood trouble in Idaho, Jack was urger by *The Examiner* to go there and report proceedings in his own way; but he was too involved at home to spare the time. Nevertheless, he managed to sandwich in a rousing article, which was printed by the *Socialist Voice,* of Oakland.

All of which reads like the crowded year it was; yet it is but a sample of eleven surpassingly full years we were to live out together. In addition to what I have set down, Jack read numberless books of all sizes and titles, and we still found opportunity to share, aloud, H. G. Wells, de Maupassant, Gertrude Atherton, Sudermann, Phillpotts, Saleeby, Herbert Spencer, and countless others, including plays—among them Bernard Shaw's, Clyde Fitch's, Ibsen's; and, above all, endless poetry. It is a curious jumble, I know; but Jack read rapaciously—both of the meatiest and the trashiest. He must know "what the other fellow is doing."

One day, he received a letter from a bank in Billings, Montana, informing him that two checks bearing his signature had been returned from Chicago marked "No Funds." It was an instance of the "doubles" who were fast coming into being. The nearest Jack had ever been to Billings was when, a few months previous, we had passed through on our westward way. Jack promptly forwarded to the bank his photograph and signature, and also an outside cover of the current *Everybody's Magazine,* on which under a sort of "footprints-on-the-sands-of-time" illustration for "Before Adam" his autograph was reproduced. The Bank was finally convinced; but from all accounts the imposter had closely resembled Jack London, and the handwriting was not dissimilar.

This was, I think, the only time a "double" passed worthless checks; but several others worked the country in capacities more or less injurious to the original. One of them stirred up revolution in Mexico, long before 1914, at which time Jack London paid his first and last visit to that restless republic, as war correspondent with General Funston. Another winnowed Oklahoma and adjoining territory, and the celebrated "101 Ranch," for all they were worth in board and lodging and information. Still others led girls astray, and many the piteous letters, addressed to places where Jack had never set foot, or when the pair of us were on the other side of the world, begging restitution for anything from stolen virtue to diamonds. Jack tried to get in touch with these floating impersonators, promising safe departure if they would only come to the Ranch and entertain him with their methods. But even when his letters never returned, there were no replies. While we were honeymooning in Cuba, according to one side of a correspondence that came into Jack's possession, a spurious J. L. was carrying on an affair with a mother of several children in Sacramento, California.

On April 18, 1906, there came, in a sense, the "shock of our lives." One need hardly mention that it was the Great Earthquake, which, most notable of consequences, destroyed the "modern imperial city" of San Francisco as no other modern imperial city has been destroyed. If it had not been for this stunning disaster to the larger place, the ruin of our county seat, Santa Rosa, in which many lives were crushed out, would have commanded the attention and sympathy of the world. As it was, refugees from the Bay metropolis began presently to straggle up-country, only to find the pretty town prone in a scarcely laid dust of brick and mortar and ashes.

Jack's nocturnal habits of reading, writing, smoking, and coughing, or sudden shifts of posture (he could not move his smallest finger without springing alive from head to foot), not being exactly a remedy for my insomnia, we ordinarily occupied beds as far apart as possible. A few minutes before five, on the morning of the 18th, upstairs at Wake Robin, my eyes flew open inexplicably, and I wondered what had stirred me so early. I curled down for a morning nap, when suddenly the earth began to heave, with a sickening onrush of motion for an eternity of seconds. An abrupt pause, and then it seemed as if some great force laid hold of the globe and shook it like a Gargantuan rat. It was the longest half-minute I ever lived through.

Now, I am free to confess, I do not like earthquakes. Never, child and woman, had I liked earthquakes. But my mind had been made up long since that while I wasted time being afraid of them, less terrified or at any rate more observant persons were able to take in phenomena which I had missed. And, so help me, when the April 18 quake got under way, and though very lonely in the conviction that my end was approaching in leaps and bounds, I lay quite still, watching the tree-tops thrash crazily, as if all the winds of all quarters were at loggerheads. The sharp undulation stopping, Jack and I met our guests, Mr. and Mrs. Reimers, in the living-room, and we all had the same tale to relate—of watching, from our pillows, the possessed antics of the trees; only, all but myself had had a view of the trunks rather than the tops.

When Jack and I ran over to the barn still rented at the Fish Ranch, we found our saddle animals had broken their halters and were still quivering and skittish. Willie, the chore-boy, said the huge madroño tree near by had lain down on the ground and got up again—which was less lurid than many impressions to which we listened that weird day.

In half an hour after the shock, we were in our saddles, riding to the Ranch, from which height could be distinguished a mighty column of smoke in the direction of San Francisco, and another northward where lies Santa Rosa. In the immediate foreground at our feet a prodigious dust obscured the buildings of the State Home for the Feeble-minded.

"Why, Mate Woman," Jack cried, his eyes big with surmise, "I shouldn't wonder if San Francisco had sunk. That was some earthquake. We don't know but the Atlantic may be washing up at the feet of the Rocky Mountains!"

Our beautiful barn—the shake had disrupted its nearly finished two-foot-thick stone walls, and to our horror revealed that the rascally Italian contractor from Sonoma, despite reasonable overseeing, had succeeded in rearing mere shells of rock, filling in between with debris of the flimsiest. Jack's face was a study.

"Jerry-built," he murmured, hurt in his voice, "and I told him the solid, honest thing I wanted—and did not question his price. What have I done to him, or anybody, that he should do this thing?"

He turned his back upon the swindle, for there were other things to see; and I could almost vouch that his wrecked property did not enter his head for the next several days—any more than he would bother about a worrisome letter or problem until the moment came to dispose of it.

"And anyway," he dismissed the subject as we turned down-mountain, "it's lucky the heavy tile roof wasn't already placed, and some poor devil sleeping under it!"

One day, weeks afterward, the Italian had the ill-considered "nerve" to call at "Jack's House." I remember that we were showing the work-room to the Winships. At the knock, Jack turned and recognized the contractor. Facing back to me, he said in a low, vibrating tone: "Mate, will you attend to him?—send him away, as quickly as possible?" Never fear that I did not do that same. Once outside, I said to the man: "You must get out of here *quick!*" And when he started to whine a remonstrance, I repeated, with glance over-shoulder: "Quick! Get out! And don't ever come back!"

Back to breakfast, after reconnoitering the neighborhood as far as the State Home, where, through the perfect discipline, no lives had been sacrificed, we prepared to board the first train to Santa Rosa, hoping to find another to San Francisco in the afternoon. And the trains ran, though not on time, what of twisted rails and litter of fallen water-tanks along the roadway. Reports of the Great Fire and broken water-mains in San Francisco made us long to be in at the incredible disaster, so long as it had to be.

With no luggage except our smallest hand-bag, which

we left with the restaurant cashier of the last ferry-boat permitted to land passengers that night, we started afoot up old Broadway, and all night roamed the city of hills, prey to feelings that cannot be described. That night proved our closest to realizing a dream that came now and again to Jack in sleep, that he and I were in at the finish of all things—standing or moving hand in hand through chaos to its brink, looking upon the rest of mankind in the process of dissolution.

Having located relatives I knew had been overtaken, and found them unharmed, Jack and I were free to follow our own will.

"And I'll never write about this for anybody," he declared, as we looked our last upon one or another familiar haunt, soon to be obliterated by the ravaging flames that drove us ever westward to safer points, on and on, in our ears the muffled detonations of dynamite, as one proud commercial palace after another sank on its steel knees, in the desperate attempt of the city fathers to stay the wholesale conflagration. And no water.

"No," Jack reiterated. "I'll never write a word about it. What use trying? One could only string big words together, and curse the futility of them."

One impinging picture of those fearful hours was where two mounted officers, alone of all the population, sat their high-crested horses at Kearney and Market Streets, equestrian statues facing the oncoming flames along Kearney. Hours earlier, we had walked here, two of many; but now the district was abandoned to destruction that could not be retarded.

In my eyes there abides the face of a stricken man, perhaps a fireman, whom we saw carried into a lofty doorway in Union Square. His back had been broken, and as the stretcher bore him past, out of a handsome, ashen young face, the dreadful darkening eyes looked right into mine. All the world was crashing about him and he, a broken thing, with death awaiting him inside the granite portals, gazed upon the last woman of his race that he was ever to see. Jack, with tender hand, drew me away.

Oh, the supreme ruth of desolation and pain, that night of fire and devastation! Yet the miracle persists, that one saw nothing but cheerful courtesy of one human to another. And I was to learn more of my mate's cool judgment in crises. Now and again it seemed as if we would surely be trapped in some square, where the fourth side had started to burn. But he had always, and accurately, sensed and chosen the moment and the way out, when we should have seen all we could risk.

Toward morning, finding ourselves in the entryway of a corner house on "Nob Hill" very near the partially-erected and already-ignited Hotel Fairmont, Jack fell into a doze; but I was unable to still the tingling of heart and nerves long enough to drop off even from exhaustion. Presently a man mounted the steps and inserted a key in the lock. Seeing Jack and myself on the top tread—he had had to pick his way through a cluster of Italians and China-men on the lower ones—something impelled him to invite us in. It was a luxurious interior, containing the treasures of years. His name was Perine, the man said, and he did not learn ours. Suddenly, midway of showing us about, he asked me to try the piano, and laid bare the keys. I hesi-tated—it seemed almost a cruel thing to do, with anni-hilation of his home so very near. But Jack's whispered "Do it for him—it's the last time he'll ever hear it," sent me to the instrument. The first few touches were enough and too much for Mr. Perine, however, and he made a restraining gesture. If he ever reads this book, I want him to know that none in poor racked San Francisco that week was more sorry for him than we.

We must have tramped forty miles that night. Jack's feet blistered, my ankles were become almost useless, when next day we sat on a convenient garbage can at Seventh and Broadway, Oakland, waiting for a street car out Telegraph Avenue. A pretty young woman accosted the dilapidated pair we made, with information that food and shelter would be supplied us refugees at such-and-such address, and laughed pleasedly when we thanked her and said we had an uninjured place of our own. Oakland had suffered comparatively little from the quake, and there were few fires. Jack of course had ascertained, before we went to San Francisco, that his mother and his children were safe and sound, with roofs over their heads.

In Glen Ellen once more, we were met with frantic telegrams from *Collier's Weekly,* asking for twenty-five hundred words, by wire, descriptive of San Francisco. Jack, still averse to undertake the compressing of his impressions, or, as he had said, writing at all on the subject, yet considered his now aggravated money-need, with the yacht and barn-rebuilding in view. And *Collier's* had offered him twenty-five cents a word—by far the best figure he had yet received. It was, I may as well note here, the highest he ever obtained.

Shaking his bonny shoulders free of all else, that very day he jumped into the twenty-five hundred word article. Hot from his hand I snatched the scribbled sheets, and swiftly typed them. Our team-work soon delivered the story over the wires, and "just for luck" Jack mailed the manuscript simultaneously. Followed wild daily messages from *Collier's* for a week to come: "Why doesn't your story arrive?" "Must have your story immediately," and, latest, "Holding presses at enormous expense. What is the matter? Must have story for May Fifth number."

It seems that the telegraph companies were able to get service through to the Pacific Coast, but not the reverse. The posted manuscript was received in the nick of time, while the wired one straggled along subsequently to the other's appearance in the May 5th issue.

Jack, it is only fair to record, entertained the poorest opinion of his description. "It's the best stagger I can make at an impossible thing," is the way he put it. And here is an excerpt from a letter to George Sterling, dated May 31:

"Hopper's article in *Everybody's* is great. Best story of the Quake I've seen. My congratulations to him."

Fifteen days after the Earthquake, we treated ourselves to a two-weeks' holiday. Jack bestrode Ban. Belle, occupied with maternal prospects, I passed by in favor of the rabbity Fleet. Hatless, with toilet accessories and reading matter stowed in saddle-bags behind our Australian saddles, we set out northerly to see what the quake had wreaked upon rural California. At this and that resort, we would feel one or another of the many lighter temblors that followed the big shake, marking the subsidence of the "Fault" that is supposed to enter from the sea-bed at Fort Bragg, and zigzag southeasterly across the State.

Jack, his rumpled poll sun-burned yellow, was a brave and lovesome sight on his merry steed, whose burnished chestnut coat threw out lilac gleams as the satiny muscles moved in the sunlight. The rider threw himself with vim into our little adventure. He was never tired exploring with me the nooks of Sonoma County, where Belle and I had been familiar figures before he came to dwell with us. And we always found so many common topics to discuss, and parallels in our lives. Why, old man Tarwater, immortalized in one of the very last stories Jack ever wrote ("Like Argus of the Olden Times," published in 1919 in volume entitled "The Red One"), had been the subject of one of my Aunt's newspaper articles. I had accompanied her, years before Jack met Tarwater in Klondike, on a pilgrimage to his mountain cabin, and sketched that abode and himself for an illustration. And there were our teachers in Oakland, Mrs. Harriet J. Lee and her daughter Elsie—we had both sat under these charming women, Jack in High School, and I in Sunday school at Plymouth Avenue Church on Thirty-fourth Street. It was deliciously preposterous, this lining up of our mutual experiences.

Not a tap of work did we perform on this real vacation. There is ample material in my brain for a readable book, in that idyllic journey through one of California's most attractive regions, unadvertised and undreamed to the casual tourist. Although I may not relate the details, still, for the guidance of any whose interest in Jack London's mazy trail might lead them into these western fastnesses of great beauty and geological interest, I present the route our nimble horses bore us:

From Glen Ellen, by Rincon Valley road, through Petrified Forest, to Calistoga, in Napa Valley. Calistoga to The Geysers. Thence to Lakeport, on Clear Lake—a little Geneva—by way of Highland Springs. We sailed on Clear Lake.

Lakeport to Ukiah, via Laurel Dell, Blue Lakes. Ukiah to Willitts. Through grandeurs of mountain and redwood forest, to logging camp "Alpine." Thence to Fort Bragg, on the Coast.

From Fort Bragg, down the coast, sleeping at lumber villages. Navarro, Albion, Greenwood. Thence to Boonville, with luncheon at Philo. Philo to Cloverdale; thence to Burke's Sanitarium. Thence to Santa Rosa, and on down to Glen Ellen.

Jack, consciously or unconsciously, had studied the brain-processes of animals since the days of his little dog Rollo in Oakland. On this long ride, the difference, which is all the difference in the world, which he noticed between Fleet and Ban on our return, was that one was tired and showed it, and the other, Thoroughbred, keyed to the utter-most step, was tired and did not know it. But when Jack, after unsaddling, had placed an extra large measure of oats before the splendid creature, the velvet nozzle went down with a great, blowing sigh. Brown Wolf, wriggling prodigiously, came to bury dumb, eloquent head between his idolized master's knees, after which, with a shake of rolling fur hide, he went to poke his nose into Ban's fodder, taking a generous mouthful, to our astonishment and the horse's snorting disapproval. Then, our fingers interlaced, we two dusty wayfarers trudged across to Wake Robin, happier and richer by another united experience.

Near the end of the month, during our absence of two days in Oakland to attend a rousing Ruskin Club dinner in Jack's honor, Willie one night left Ban out in the Fish Ranch pasture, where he became entangled in a loose strand of that accursed invention, barbed wire, which had eluded our vigilance. Hour upon hour, the poor, helpless thing sawed one of his beautiful, fleet hind legs to the bone. It was a sad homecoming to us, and in consultation beside our drooping, ruined pet we decided he must die. Jack said, his eyes dark with sorrow:

"Wiget, I'll do it if I have to; but I don't want to. If you don't mind too much . . ." And Wiget had to avert his face as he replied: "I'll do it for you folks."

In a hammock at the Lodge we sat knowing we could not fail to hear the shot that would be the ending of our willing and beloved friend. Jack had carefully instructed his man to deposit the charge in the middle of the forehead, where cross-lines drawn from ears to eyes would intersect. When the sound of the shot rang across the waiting stillness, we wept unrestrained and unabashed in each other's arms. All I could think of to solace Jack was to offer him the gift of my own new filly, Sonoma Maid, granddaughter of the great Morella, which Belle, in the fullness of her time and in our absence, had presented to me.

I remember, once, on a steamer voyage, that a fine horse injured during a rough night had to be killed. A lamentable botch was made of the execution, and I never saw Jack London worse upset than he was over the reports of the animal's inexcusably hard death. "If they'd only learn how to do a thing like that in the right way!" he exclaimed, thrashing about in his chair in a manner he had when suffering mentally.

A preverted order of humaneness, often displayed by unthinking persons, always came in for harsh language from Jack. "Men who brag of being too tender-hearted to kill an aged and suffering animal, or a hopelessly-wounded or sick one," he would rave,"—I don't know anything too bad for them. Why don't people *think!*" And again: "The only way to kill a cat is to chop off its head," he preached. "Death is instantaneous, when the spinal cord is severed. Drowning, and suffocation by chloroform, are two of the cruelest methods you can use on a cat. The other way means instantaneous death, with no terrors of strangulation. Some people think I'm brutal to advise this, but the thing is self-evident—oh, what's the use!" he would surrender in disgust. In illustration of indirect brutality, he told me of something he had done during a short camping expedition, in 1904, with "The Crowd," on the deserted Kendall Ranch in Grizzly Canyon, near Moraga Valley.

The last tenants had left some time previously, and were too sensitive and kind-hearted to lay away the family dog, a large collie, I think Jack said, who was tottering, from starvation, too old to hunt for himself. "Nobody else wanted the job of shooting him," Jack went on, "and it was up to me. You know how I *love* to kill things," he interpolated with a wry mouth. "I got the shotgun ready, and went toward that poor dog, and he crouched when he saw me coming. *God!* no one will ever know how I shrank from that self-imposed task. That dog *knew*—his poor old eyes looked straight into mine and did not waver—but the knowledge of death was in them. He'd been out with a gun too much in his life not to know what it meant when one was aimed at a living creature. . . . Oh, yes, I got it done—first charge . . . He never moved after he dropped.''

Jack was capable of such adorable ways. One afternoon, that summer of 1906, he and I, with Manyoungi's help were sorting over old possessions, making ready long in advance for our voyage. The Korean came upon my old French doll, an adult-appearing, jointed model with six inches of ''real'' hair. Lifting it tenderly, reverence in his handsome olive face, the boy carried it to Jack, who was talking to himself amidst a tumbled mountain of dusty books—he invariably talked and hummed when doing work of this kind or filing letters. And Jack, with a dewy look in his great eyes, held out both grimy hands for the relic, and kissed it! The act was devoid of affectation —just a spontaneous expression of all the complication of his love. ''The little woman's doll!'' was all he said, returning to his work with an odd smile deepening the ''pictured corners'' of his mouth. . . . Once, ''after long grief and pain,'' in rare abandon he had pressed those lips to the hem of my garment.

Even from so brief an absence as the riding jaunt, our duties had piled up, and we were rushing all hours except for the swimming, rides to the Ranch, the campfire gatherings, moonlight romps and games, with boxing, fencing, kiting, and what not, in the camps of the Connings, the Selbys, the Brecks, the Reynolds, and my own summering families.

Blowing soap-bubbles was popular for a time, and certain long-stemmed Korean pipes, among Jack's ''loot'' from the orient, came into novel requisition. There were debates of evenings in the Lodge, to which the older campers were invited, in which the materialist monist, Jack London, was somewhat unwillingly pitted against Mr. Edward B.

Payne, a far older man whom Jack styled "metaphysician." I should have said attempted debate, for the same familiar stumbling-block was encountered that had disrupted earlier discussions whenever Jack and the metaphysicians locked horns: Jack could not and would not accept the premise offered; and after several futile efforts of the instigators of the meetings, to ease him surreptitiously over the first stages of the argument, the debates were discontinued.

"Edward's got a beautiful mind, and he's the most logical rhetorician I ever met in my whole life," Jack would defend himself; "but when, in his reasoning, he comes to the enchanted bridge he has tried to build, on which I am supposed to reject my solid foundation and step across to his metaphysical one, I revolt." Martin Luther's "Here I stand. I can do no otherwise, so help me God! Amen!" was no less firm than Jack London's "I can't help it. I am so made. I can't see it any other way. I've got to keep my feet on the concrete."

I have seen him quite white with distress that he had to spoil a party by depriving guests of the spectacle of himself routed from his materialistic terra firma and driven upon the impalpable ground of the metaphysicians with their, to him, "colossal evasions of mundane interpretations," as our friend Mary Wilshire puts it. "Each of you," he said, "goes into his own consciousness to explain anything and everything." Again, "The metaphysician explains the universe by himself, the scientist explains himself by the universe." Jack believed that the keenest and most irresistible impulses toward self-preservation are shown by what he termed metaphysicians. "Take the earthquake, for instance," he would rail. "You and I, and an infidel artist, remained in our beds until well after the shock. And when we emerged, where did we find the metaphysicians of the household?—Out of doors, in unseemly attire, and unable to tell how they got there, but, from circumstantial evidence, having arrived on the un-stable earth by way of a first-story window!"

There were swimming visits exchanged that year with our neighbors the Rudolf Spreckelses and a bevy of Mrs. Spreckels's sisters, the Misses Joliffe; and once we went to to Napa to see the Winships. But Jack, as a rule, was not fond of visiting, and occasionally was heard to remark that the Winships and the Sterlings were practically the only friends to whose houses he went, and these at wide intervals. He preferred, in short, to entertain rather than to be enter-tained.

At times, but rarely, he would treat himself to a holiday, perhaps to read aloud a book that had claimed him for the moment, or to take some special jaunt. But the fingers of one hand could easily tally the days when he failed to deliver ten pages of hand-written manuscript to my type-writer desk. It was my custom to have his previous day's instalment, typed and words counted, in readiness upon his table by nine. He loved to read me his morn-ing's work—and even in the writing of it, if I happened to pass by, would interrupt himself to let me share what he had done. The first writing day, in all our days, that this did not happen, was the first day upon which he wrote no more.

Evidently this life of closely-wedged activities was quite to my taste, for at the end of one date's diary-items I see: "Happy as an angel!" This may, however, have been when I had won from Jack some praise or especial appre-ciation; but he was wont ruefully to utter that my finest heights of bliss were attained when I had beaten him at cards (which was seldom enough to justify chortling), or won a bet upon the weather ranging anywhere from ten cents to ten dollars.

Another and sweeter source of happiness to me would be when I had played an hour for him while he sat or reclined, one hand over his eyes, dreaming upon a couch in Auntie's cool living-room. The music he then oftenest asked for was Arthur Foote's Rubaiyat Suite, and much of Macdowell— "The Eagle" and "Sea Pieces" remaining favorites. His disposition those days was almost always equable, and I learned to circumvent the blues he had once forewarned he might be subject to upon the day of completing a long manuscript. On June 7, he laid down his ink-pencil for the last time on "Before Adam," first writing in my count of 40,863 words. But there was little or no depression to follow. I had seen to that, by planning a string of overlapping engagements for the day, which left him no moment for relaxing until sleep-time was at hand. Oh, no—never did I cheat myself into believing that he did not see through my machinations; rather, did he coöperate—but no word jarred the moment's harmony.

Have I mentioned that he was fond of ordering advertised articles? "And if one out of ten proves a real find, I am repaid for my time and money!" was his argument. Many were the packages, great and small, that enlivened our morning mail during preparation for the small-boat voyage; for whether emanating from "ad" or catalogue, Jack meant to leave nothing behind that would contribute to the venture's success. Fishing tackle of the most alluring; numberless strings of beads, and loose beads by the gross, of all sizes and hues to gladden savage hearts that beat under the Southern Cross; gay neckerchiefs and calicoes and ribbons —nothing was omitted. And the fun we, like veriest children, had opening our "Christmas packages" from day to day, can best be imagined.

Early in our comradeship I had noted Jack's habit of looking ahead, not back. "Leave retrospect to old men and women. The world is all before me now," was his pose toward the dead past. While this remained a characteristic, the general normal happiness of his new environment rendered him less averse to dwelling upon his yesterdays. As our united yesterdays lengthened in our shadow, he became as fondly addicted as I to reminiscence of them.

Before me, as I write with his own pen, lies a clipping referring to "The Iron Heel," which begins: "In one of Jack London's less important works, there was a description of a pitched battle in Chicago, in the near future, by way of quelling what would now be called a Bolshevist revolution." And the commentator adds: "Now the battle is going on in Berlin." Beside the clipping reposes a letter to me from a sociologist, from which I quote as refutation of the other's phrase, "less important works":

"The earlier portion of the book is the most impressive, the most unanswerable impeachment of the capitalist system to be found in all the voluminous sociological literature of our times."

And I feel free to quote Mr. George P. Brett, President of The Macmillan Company, who published the book:

"I consider 'The Iron Heel' the greatest compendium of Socialism ever written."

From week to week, in these stirring days of reconstruction following the World War, there come to me, alone upon Jack London's mountainside, appreciations from all classes concerning "The Iron Heel," once hated and derided and feared by the factions most opposed to one another. Jack had gone to work upon it that midsummer of 1906, placing some of its scenes round-about "the sweet land" in which he had elected to dwell. When the manuscript later failed to find place in any paying magazine, and saw book-covers, in 1907 during the "panic," mainly because the publishers held a blanket contract bearing Jack London's sprawling signature, the poor author said regretfully one day in Hawaii:

"I thought it would be timely, that book; but they're all afraid of it, Mate Woman." He pointed to letters just received from the States: "See: the socialists, even my own crowd, have thrown me down—they decry it as a lugubrious prophecy; and the other camp, of course, revile it as they revile everything socialistic they possibly can of mine.

"But," he broke in heatedly upon his reverie, "I *didn't* write the thing as a prophecy at all. I really don't think these things are going to happen in the United States. I believe the increasing socialist vote will prevent—hope for it, anyhow. But I will say that I sent out, in 'The Iron Heel,' a warning of what I think *might* happen if they don't look to their votes. That's all."

In the copy he gave me is written: "We that have been what we've been. . . . We that have seen what we've seen—we may not see these particular things come to pass, but certain it is that we shall see big things of some sort come to pass."

In the light of present events, the story would seem to have been more than roughly prophetic; and the end, mayhap, is not yet.

The phrase "well-balanced radicals" came to be a pet aversion of Jack's for the rest of his life. For, outside of the capitalist class, it was the self-named "well-balanced radicals," who would have none of his "Iron Heel."

Yet it was one of these, after Jack London's death, who wrote me: "The earlier portion of the book is the most impressive, the most unanswerable impeachment of the capitalist system to be found in all the voluminous sociological literature of our times. I have read many severe criticisms of capitalist procedure, but this cuts deeper and cleaner than they all."

"The Iron Heel," once finished and started on its round of the magazines, Jack's next contemplated book was a group of tramping episodes, brought out serially as "My Life in the Underworld," and, in book-form, "The Road."

Two paragraphs from Jack's letters to George Sterling,

of dates February 17, 1908, and March 3, 1909, throw illumination upon his open attitude toward his past:

"I can't get a line on why you wish I hadn't written 'The Road,'" he challenges. "It is all true. It is what I am, what I have done, and it is part of the process by which I have become. Is it a lingering taint of the bourgeois in you that makes you object? Is it because of my shamelessness? For having done things in which I saw or see no shame? Do tell me."

And this:

"Your point about 'The Road,' namely that it 'gave the mob a mop to bang' me with. What of it? I don't care for the mob. It can't hurt me. One word of censure or disapproval from you would hurt me a few million myriads of billions times more than all the sum total the mob would inflict on me in one hundred and forty-seven lifetimes. I thank the Lord I don't live for the mob."

This seems the place to point Jack's intolerance of restricted or anachronistic vision, by quoting further from letters to Sterling. The latter sat between the horns of a dilemma with regard to his two closest friends—Jack London and Ambrose Bierce, who were as far apart as the poles in their philosophies. Because Jack had experienced certain phases of living which were untenable to the satirist's niceties, the latter seemed entirely to discount the younger author as one entitled to consideration in the brotherhood of polite society. In short, after he had read "The Road," Mr. Bierce was emphatic in his opinion concerning what summary disposal should be made of Jack. But Jack, with a generosity and lack of bitterness which would have well become the elder man, wrote Sterling:

"For heaven's sake don't you quarrel with Ambrose about me. He's too splendid a man to be diminished because he has lacked access to a later generation of science. He crystallized before you and I were born, and it is too magnificent a crystallization to quarrel with."

Earlier letters to Sterling amplify Jack's contention, and his own up-to-the-mark step with the marching world:

"If Hillquit and Hunter didn't put it all over Bierce—I'll quit thinking at all. Bierce's clever pessimism was nowhere against their science. He proved himself rudderless, compassless, and chartless. Bierce doesn't shine in a face to face battle with socialists. He's beat at long range slinging ink. He was groggy at the drop of the hat, and before they got done with him was looking anxiously around and wondering why the gong didn't ring. All he did was to back and fill and potter around, dogmatize and contradict himself. When they cornered him, he went off on another tack, wherefore they'd overtake him and lambaste him again. Bierce, with biological and sociological concepts that crystallized in the fervant heat of pessimism a generation ago, was—well, pathetic. And more pathetic still, he doesn't know it."

"I wouldn't care to lock horns with Bierce," is a later reference. "He stopped growing a generation ago. Of course, he keeps up with the newspapers, but his criteria crystallized 30 odd years ago. Had he been born a generation later he'd have been a socialist, and, more likely, an anarchist. He never reads books that aren't something like a hundred years old, and he glories in the fact!"

The latest remarks I find, in the same correspondence, are these written from Hilo, Hawaii, in July of 1907:

"The quotes from Ambrose were great. What a pen he wields. Too bad he hasn't a better philosophic foundation."

CHAPTER XXX

SNARK VOYAGE

End 1906; 1907-8-9

THE Great Earthquake proved very expensive to Jack London. Primarily because of it, the yacht-building, which he had calculated would cost seven thousand dollars, or at most ten, incredibly squandered some thirty thousand. The iron keel was to have been run on the very evening of the Earthquake, April 18. Following that event (which we of California are averse to term an "Act of God," much less one of a beneficent Providence), what Jack should have done, too late he came to see, was to look around for a ready-built hull. At almost any time before the World War, fine deep-water yachts could be picked up on the Atlantic seaboard at a tithe of their original cost. In future years, after the abandonment of our voyage, Jack pored over many a blue-print received from agents in the east, of well-appointed vessels that could be had for mere songs.

No man born of woman could forecast the insurmountable anarchy that the post-quake and fire-havoc wrought in building conditions. I shall leave it to the reader to guess at the inwardness of our spirit-trial, so lightly sketched in the first article ("The Inconceivable and Monstrous") of the nineteen, including Foreward and Backword, that compose Jack London's "The Cruise of the Snark." This collection relates, in more or less disconnected fashion, a few of the main happenings and observations incident to the cruise. My own book, I wish to mention here, "The Log of the Snark," also published by The Macmillan Company, gives, as its name implies, the consecutive

142

journal from the day before we sailed from San Francisco until we returned to California. There is one exception to the foregoing statement. My two-years' diary being too protracted for one volume, the five-months' experiences ashore in the Hawaiian Islands, together with the general details of our 1915 and 1916 visits, form a bulky book by themselves, which also appears under the Macmillan imprint. This volume I have revised and brought up to date for a new edition in 1921. Jack, aside from his incomplete *Snark* record, as above, devoted himself to fiction, which I name below, inspired by the Pacific and its enchanting isles, irrespective of other books in which incidents from his South Sea lore appear, such as "Michael Brother of Jerry," "Martin Eden," "The Red One," and others. Here are the strictly tropical ones:

"Adventure," novel, 1911.

"South Sea Tales," 1911.

"The House of Pride," 1912.

"A Son of the Sun," 1912.

"Jerry of the Islands," 1918.

The opening adjuration in "The Inconceivable and Monstrous" sounds the note adhered to by Jack throughout the construction and manning of the little ship that was, we fondly believed, to be our home for indefinite years of adventure. "Spare no expense" was the slogan he impressed upon his lieutenant, Roscoe. And no matter what exasperation followed, "gipsy heart to gipsy heart," undaunted Jack and I traced our route upon a sizable world-globe bought for our future library.

In the end, allowing for all the heartbreaking wastage and plain graft that sent the yacht, half a year late, an unfinished, internal wreck upon the high seas to Honolulu, still was she, with her sturdy sticks and her ribs of oak, pronounced by that master-small-boat-sailor, Jack London, the strongest vessel of her proportions ever launched—

"Stronger, even, I tell you," he held, "than the *Goya,* that made the Northwest Passage."

Be it known, once and for all, this point having been airily misrepresented for years, that every human being of the *Snark's* complement of seven, except Jack London and myself, who worked to pay them—every soul, I say, was drawing a salary for work performed or unperformed during that crazy traverse of 2200 miles to Honolulu. From every class of society over the wide world we thought to circumnavigate—doctors, lawyers, beggarmen, chiefs, thieves, multimillionaires, sailors single and in crews, poets, historians, geologists, painters, doctors of divinity—in short, men, women and children of every color and occupation, wrote or telegraphed or paid us calls, imploring to sail on any terms, or none. They even appealed for the privilege of paying lavishly for the privilege. One there was who wrote: "I can assure you that I am eminently respectable, but find other respectable people tiresome." Since he expressed an overwhelming desire to be of our party, we could not but wonder exactly what he meant!

But Jack was no fool. Whosoever joined the *Snark* should do so upon a stated salary, and there could be no recriminations. Inconceivably and monstrously, there were recriminations, despite the precautionary measures. When all but one of our first company returned to San Francisco before we had left Hawaii for the equator, the mendacious papers flashed reports that there had been violence following disagreements during the first lap of the cruise. Jack London his own Sea Wolf, was the implication, of course; and what could Jack do but grind his teeth, and then laugh: "They can all go to blazes! You and I know better; and what really counts is you and me!"

Disagreements there had been—but I employ the wrong word; for it was an agreement, quietly arrived at between Jack and his sailing master before Honolulu was sighted, that the latter should go home at his leisure from that port.

A younger member of the party decided to return to college; while our Japanese cabin boy, Tochigi, failed to conquer an incorrigible seasickness. So these two, also, went back to California.

It all boils down to the fact, well-established in Jack's mind and my own from our incredulous observations of lack of discipline and neglect of property—"appalled and bewildered" my diary states our emotions—that those who deserted the *Snark* merely discovered they had been mistaken in thinking sea-adventure was what their natures craved. The details of certain unfairness to Jack that were so blindly practised, I omit. However inclined to garrulousness I may be on Jack's behalf, I do want to be fair enough to all of them in their blindness, largely to lay the blame, as already hinted, to the chaotic circumstances under which the boat was built. This, in the last analysis, had worn out the patience, the grit, and the indubitably feeble adventure-lust that had been the reason for their engaging in the enterprise.

I think the difference between them and ourselves was that Jack and I knew what we wanted, and in unison overtook it in spite of colossal odds from all sides; while the others simply had mistaken their desires. The secret of finding our rainbows' ends always, I am sure, lay first and last in our knowledge of what we wanted. The longest search never palled, because the search was an end in itself. Of one of our men, who had failed to fill even the berth of a preceding failure, Jack said: "He caught a glimpse, in some metallic, cog-like way, of the spirit of Adventure, and he thought to woo her—Adventure, who must be served whole-souled and single-hearted and with the long patience that is so terrible that very few are capable of it."

But I am ahead of my narrative:

Early in the year, with the framework of the yacht just begun, Jack had written to a magazine the letter given below, outlining the purposed voyage and offering a chance at the story of the cruise.

Here let me remark that a leading reason for the inclusion of this correspondence is to emphasize the exact proposition which Jack London made. This, in turn, because, following his death, one journalist, in an otherwise gracious and well-meaning article, created, unintentionally I wish to believe, a misapprehension in the minds of his many readers as to happenings in connection with the arrangement for the boat-articles. During a call with which this writer honored the Jack London Ranch after Jack's passing, I threatened that I should, in all friendliness, go after him in the open when I should write this book; and he, with entire good-nature, gave me his blessing to "go to it and do the worst."

Here is the opening letter. The italics are mine, guided by marginal markings of Jack's:

"Feb. 18/06.

"Dear ———:

"The keel is laid. The boat is to be 45 feet long. It would have been a little bit shorter had I not found it impossible to squeeze in a bathroom otherwise. I sail in October. Hawaii is the first port of call; and from there we shall wander through the South Seas, Samoa, Tasmania, New Zealand, Australia, New Guinea, and up through the Philippines to Japan. Then Korea and China, and on down to India, Red Sea, Mediterranean, Black Sea and Baltic, and on across the Atlantic to New York, and then around the Horn to San Francisco. . . . I shall certainly put in a winter in St. Petersburg, and the chances are that I shall go up the Danube from the Black Sea to Vienna, and there isn't a European country in which I shall not spend from one to several months. This leisurely fashion will obtain throughout the whole trip. I shall not be in a rush; in fact, I calculate seven (7) years at least will be taken up by the trip.

"This boat is to be sailed by one friend and myself. There

are no sailors. My wife accompanies me. Of course, I'll take a cook along, and a cabin boy; but these will be Asiatics, and will have no part in the sailorizing. [The ultimate personnel of the crew was rearranged.] The rig of the boat will be a compromise between a yawl and a schooner. It will be what is called the ketch-rig—the same rig that is used by the English fishing-boats on the Dogger Bank.

"Shall, however, have a small engine on board to be used only in case of emergency, such as in bad water among reefs and shoals, where a sudden calm in a fast current leaves a sailing-boat helpless. Also, this engine is to be used for another purpose. When I strike a country, say Egypt or France, I'll go up the Nile or the Seine by having the mast taken out, and under power of the engine. I shall do this a great deal in the different countries, travel inland and live on board the boat at the same time. There is no reason at all why I shouldn't in this fashion come up to Paris, and moor alongside the Latin Quarter, with a bow-line out to Notre Dame and a stern-line fast to the Morgue.

"Now to business. I shall be gone a long time on this trip. *No magazine can print all 1 have to write about it.* On the other hand, it cannot be imagined that 1 shall write 50,000 words on the whole seven years, and then quit. As it is, *the subject matter of the trip divides itself up so that there will be no clash whatever between any several publications that may be handling my stuff. For instance, here are three big natural, unconflicting divisions: news, industrial, and political articles on the various countries for newspapers; fiction; and finally, the trip itself.*

"Now the question arises, *if you take the trip itself* (which will be the cream), how much space will *The ——* be able to give me? In this connection I may state that *McClure's* and *Outing* are after me; and, as I am throwing my life, seven years of my time, my earning-power as a writer of fiction, *and a lot of money,* into the enterprise, it behooves me to keep a sharp lookout on how expenses, etc., are to be met. And one important factor in this connection that I must consider, is that of space.

"And while I am on this matter of space, I may as well say that it is granted, always, that I deliver the goods. Of course, if my articles turn out to be mushy and inane, why I should not expect any magazine to continue publishing them. I believe too much in fair play to be a good business man, and if my work be rotten, I'd be the last fellow in the world to bind any editor to publish it. On the other hand, I have a tremendous confidence, based upon all kinds of work I have already done, that I can deliver the goods. Anybody doubting this has but to read "The People of the Abyss" to find the graphic, reportorial way I have of handling things. . . .

"While on this matter of space, I may also state that it is not so much the point of how large the space is in a given number of magazine, but how long a time the story of the trip can run in the magazine."

Here he inserts a paragraph concerning his abilities to furnish good photographic illustrations. And he goes on:

". . . We expect lots of action, and my strong point as a writer is that I am a writer of action—see all my short stories, for instance. Another point is, that while I am a writer, I am also a sailor . . .; and a still further point is, that I am an acknowledged and successful writer of sea-matter; see 'The Sea Wolf,' 'The Cruise of the Dazzler,' and 'Stories of the Fish Patrol. . . .'

". . . Now comes the item of pay. In the first place, here is a traveler-correspondent, and traveler-correspondents are usually expensive, because their traveling expenses are paid by their employers. *But in my case I'd pay my own traveling expenses. I build my boat, I outfit my boat, and I run my boat.* . . . So, in whatever conclusion we arrive at, it must be stipulated that I receive in advance, in the course of the building of the boat, say $3000.00."

The editor stated his willingness to make the advance;

and Jack shot back, "All right. We sail October 1," ending the letter, "I'm going to turn out some crackerjack stuff on this trip!"

April 3, 1906, is the date of Jack's agreement to "furnish The ——— *Magazine* a series of exclusive articles *descriptive of my voyage in my sailboat,* which voyage is to extend, if possible, around the world." The number of contributions, he stipulated, was not to exceed ten unless more were ordered. Jack agreed to supply photographs.

Meanwhile, he had got under way a proposal to furnish land-articles, say upon domestic customs of native peoples, for a woman's magazine in the east—this in line with remarks which I have underscored in letter above quoted.

Came the Earthquake, and on May 16, he wrote: "You ask for my picture alongside the hull. There ain't no hull. The iron keel, wooden keel, and stem and a few ribs, are standing, and so they have been standing for some time. I have not been near the boat yet, and do not expect to go until it is practically finished. I am too busy." When the building had been resumed, Jack put my uncle, who had been for himself an enthusiastic boat-builder in his time, and was to be sailing-master, upon a salary to superintend the construction.

In July 1 find this from Jack to the first magazine:

"You will have to defer my opening article until the November number. I have finally succumbed to the California earthquake. I find it impossible to get a decent engine this side of New York, and the consequent delay throws me back a full month. I shall sail November 1, instead of October 1." Later he wrote: "This damned earthquake is just beginning to show up the delays it caused. There is scarcely a thing we want that we can buy in the local market." Then, "We are going to call her the *Snark,*" he announced his final choice of a name for the "beautiful elliptical stern." His reason was that he could think of no other name that suited, and his friends, with bright suggestions of "The Call of the Wild," "The Sea Wolf" and eke "The Game," had worn him out. He even put it as a threat to one and all, that if nothing less silly were forthcoming, *Snark* she should be—this snappy title being chosen from Lewis Carroll's "The Hunting of the Snark."

"I never thought about naming the boat after your magazine," he replied to the editor's suggestion. "The only objection to that name is, that boats, like horses and dogs, should have names of one syllable. Good, sharp, strong names, that can never be misheard. There's only one thing that would make me change the name *Snark* to that of your magazine, namely, the presentation of the *Snark* to me as an out-and-out present. She is costing me $10,000, and by golly, it would be worth $10,000 worth of advertising to the magazine. In return for such a present," (and I can hear Jack's titter as he dictated the outrage to me), "not only would I put up with the five-syllable name, but 'Magazine' to be appended. That would make eight syllables. Why, I'd even take subscriptions and advertisements for the magazine as I went along!"

In September the editor was succeeded by another, and I find an amusing item in his first letter to Jack: "The correction you ask to be made has been attended to and you may rest easy in the assurance that 'Roscoe' will not be misrepresented but will be placed in his true light as a 'follower of the science, though not the religion, of one Cyrus R. Teed.' " For our sailing-master, be it known, firmly believed in the Teed "cellular cosmogany," and that he was to experience the *Snark* voyage on the inner skin of the planet.

Glancing over these letters, I discover that Jack had raised his fiction rate to fifteen cents a word to the magazines, and his story, "Just Meat," (book published in "When God Laughs"), was being discussed on this basis.

There fell more trouble. The editors of the two magazines each tried to "grab the whole show" in their advance advertising of their totally different *Snark* material, and Jack, indignant with both for accusing him of bad faith, entirely clear in his own head and in his two unconflicting contracts, was made the sufferer. His retaliation is in plain and uncompromising terms. After treating the first editor to a few of his opinions of magazine offices, he quotes verbatim from his contract with the woman's magazine: "These articles are to be upon home life and social conditions in a broad sense of the term, etc., etc."

"Speaking now in connection with contents of foregoing paragraph," he enlarges, "I want to know what in hell you think 35,000 words will cover! Do you think 35,000 words will cover a tithe of the boat-trip itself, much less all the things I expect to do and see in the course of seven years! . . . Don't you think I've got a kick coming for the way you have advertised me as going around the world for *The* ———? . . . hell, everybody thinks you are building my boat for me, and paying all my expenses, and giving me a princely salary on top of it . . . 35,000 words at 10 cents a word means $3500.00 and the initial cost of my boat is running past the $12,000.00 mark, to say nothing of expenses of running said boat. . . . Those are the figures up to date, and they're still going up. San Francisco is mad. Prices have climbed out of sight. I pay $200 for a bit of iron work on the boat, that should cost $40.00. Everything is in this order. The outlook is now, that I shall not sail before January. Weeks go by without a tap of work being done on the boat. Can't get the men. All my stuff is coming from the east because the earthquake destroyed the local market; and freight is congested."

On November 1, 1906, Jack wrote again: "Yes, Mr. ——— [the new editor's predecessor] did write me upon the matter of 'distributing my cabbages in several baskets,' and I must confess that he got me rather hot in the collar, what of the sized-basket he had furnished me and thought would hold all my cabbages—the crop of seven years in a

35,000-word basket! I am inclosing you a copy of the letter
I sent him. . . . Since writing this, I wrote him another
calling the turn on him for doing just what Mr. —————— [the
editor of the woman's magazine] had done, namely, claim-
ing everything in sight so far as my seven-years' voyage is
concerned. Your periodical said that practically my total
output would go to it, concerning lands, people, etc., that I
would see. The mental processes of editors are beyond me.
I fought with Mr. —————— for 35,000 words, and couldn't
get it out of him.''

When the Christmas number of the magazine that was to
have the story of the voyage came out, containing the first
of his boat-articles, Jack let loose his ''long wolf-howl''
upon the liberties that had been taken with his copy. ''Any
tyro can cut a manuscript,'' he storms, ''and feel that he is a
co-creator with the author. But it's hell on the author.
Not one man in a million, including office-boys, is to be
found in the magazine office who is able properly to revise
by elimination the work of a professional author. And the
men in your office have certainly played ducks and drakes
with the exposition in the first half of my first boat-article.
. . . For instance, I have just finished the proofs of 'Just
Meat.' In one place I have my burglar say, 'I put the kibosh
on his time.' Some man in your office changed this to, 'I
put a crimp in his time.' In the first place, 'crimp' is in-
correct in such usage. In the second place, there is nothing
whatever in the connotation of 'kibosh' that would prevent
its appearing in the pages of your magazine. 'Kibosh' is
not vulgar, it is not obscene. Such action is wholly unwar-
ranted and gratitously officious. Did this co-creator of mine,
in your office, think that he knew what he was doing when
he made such a ridiculous substitution? And if he does
think so, why in the dickens doesn't he get in and do the
whole thing himself?

''In our contract,'' he grows hot and hotter, ''I take
your right of revision to consist in rejecting an article as

a whole or in eliminating objectionable phrases. Now I have no objection to that. I have no objection to your truckling to Mrs. Grundy, when, for instance, you cut out swear-words or change 'go to hell' to 'go to blazes.' That's the mere shell. In that sort of revision you can have full swing; but that is different matter from cutting the heart out of my work, such as you did in my first boat-article. You made my exposition look like thirty cents.

"I WEAVE my stuff; you can cut out a whole piece of it, but you can't cut out parts of it, and leave mutilated parts behind. Just think of it. Wading into my exposition and cutting out premises or proofs or anything else just to suit your length of an article, or the space, rather, that you see fit to give such article. [The editors were succeeding each other rapidly about this time, and Jack was quite in the dark as to whom, personally, he was addressing.] . . . "Don't you see my point?" he urges. "If the whole woven thing—event, narrative, description—is not suitable for your magazine, why cut it out—cut out the whole thing. I don't care. But I refuse to contemplate for one moment that there is any man in your office, or in the office of any magazine, capable of bettering my art, or the art of any other first-class professional writer.

"Now, I want to give warning right here: I won't stand for it. Before I stand for it, I'll throw over the whole proposition. If you dare to do this with my succeeding articles. . . . I'll not send you another line. By golly, you've got to give me a square deal in this matter. Do you think for one moment that I'll write my heart (my skilled, professional heart, if you please) into my work to have you fellows slaughtering it to suit your journalistic tastes? Either I'm going to write this set of articles, or you're going to write it, for know right here that I refuse definitely and flatly, to collaborate with you or with any one in your office.

"In order that this letter may not go astray," he winds

up, "1 am sending copies to each of the three men who, in my present hypothesis, I think may possibly be editor . . . And I want, at your earliest convenience, an assurance that the sort of mutilation I am complaining about, will not occur again."

After an unsatisfactory reply, Jack wrote: "Frankly, I'd like to call the whole thing off," following this with a still warmer letter than his former one, impressing upon the editor, "This is the first squabble I ever had in my life with a magazine. I hope it will be my last, but I'll make it hum while it lasts."

The upshot of the "squabble" was that the boat articles were actually called off, another serial, already under way, to be submitted at a still better rate. Jack was well pleased, and I was relieved for his sake, as the unsettled state of matters both with regard to his work and the exasperating *Snark* progress was very grilling to his nerves.

Another disappointment we had sustained was the loss of Manyoungi. For weeks, with true oriental indirection, he had set about making himself dispensable. The only motive, Jack convinced himself, was that the boy harbored a disinclination to visit the Seven Seas in an inconsequential shallop such as to him appeared the small *Snark* on her rickety ways at the shipyard. The heart of the sailor was not in his breast. His misbehavior, which had extended into every department of his service, culminated one evening in a very ludicrous manner. He had all day blatantly omitted his habitual address of "Master," substituting "Mr. London," or "Boss," with labored variations. His bold black eyes and studiedly nonchalant tongue advertised bid upon bid for discharge. And still new titles fell from his foolish lips, and still "Master" looked up when they became especially if unintentionally funny, and grinned at the silly boy, though one could note a peculiar absence of expression in Jack's gray eyes. For he was sad to lose Manyoungi, and in such undignified fashion—the perfect servant in so many capacities, of whom we were both personally fond into the bargain.

It was the custom each night, when we played our night-cap game of cards, for Manyoungi to ask what we would have to drink—grape-juice, or ginger-ale, lemonade, or beer. On this evening I was bending apprehensively over the cribbage-board, watching my opponent peg a shocking advantage, when an ominously quiet but impudent voice behind me asked:

"Will God have some beer?"

The only muscles I moved were in raising my eyes to Jack's face. I was braced for anything; words and tone were an invitation to wipe up the floor with Manyoungi's offending countenance. Jack went pale with surprise; but his sense of humor prevented him from thrashing the Korean, as man to man. He was not even angry, properly speaking, and I relaxed when, controlling the desire to laugh, he said composedly:

"I do not want anything at all from you, Manyoungi," and dealt another hand.

It meant the breaking of a new man to all the details of our complicated requirements, not only in relation to our present life, but to the prospective one upon the water. Tochigi, a poet-browed Japanese, later to become an ordained minister in the Episcopal clergy, came to fill the vacancy; and each day's lunch-table was a thing of artistic anticipation, for never did the same exquisite floral decoration appear twice.

Jack forever maintained that there never could be equaled Manyoungi's perfect "spirit of service" that animated his manifold accomplishments. "Why, that boy could make both Charmian and me ready in half an hour for Timbuctoo!" he would praise. And it was not far from the fact.

In a letter to Cloudesley Johns, written in September, is a lovely attestation of Jack London's inner contentment as regarded the voyage:

"Nay, I'll not come back in 18 months. Barring boat and financial shipwreck, shall be gone for at least seven years. Also, shall not 'come back young again.' I am long since 'young again.' You ought to see me, and you ought to have seen me all this year at Glen Ellen."

Curiously enough, eighteen months was practically the extent of our actual residence on the *Snark*, although we were absent twenty-seven months altogether.

In early November, hoping soon to weigh anchor, we moved to Oakland, with Mammy Jennie and Tochigi to keep house. That month, Jack wrote Cloudesley:

"Sorrier than the devil; but can't make Los Angeles before I sail. And when I sail, I'm going to hit the high places for mid ocean in order to learn navigation and learn the boat where I've plenty of room. No rockbound coast for me as a starter. A thousand miles of offing isn't any too good for me as a starter. . . . Dec. 15th is sailing date."

The first week in December saw the completion of "The Iron Heel," begun in August, and Jack bent his efforts upon the tramp series. That done, too restless to concentrate upon another long stretch, he wrote the stories: "Goliah" (in "Revolution"), "The Passing of Marcus O'Brien (in "Lost Face"), "The Unparalleled Invasion" (published in "The Strength of the Strong," and interesting in view of the alleged methods during the Great War), "The Enemy of All the World" and "The Dream of Debs" (both in "The Strength of the Strong"), and "A Curious Fragment" (in "When God Laughs").

For recreation, the living-room echoed to exciting contests in poker or hearts, among the players and onlookers being George Sterling, Henry Lafler, Carlton Bierce, Richard Partington, Rob Royce, Porter Garnett, Nora May French, and the Lily Maid, with a host of others. Upon one of these occasions, the first part of December, while we wives of "the boys" were entertaining ourselves at my newly acquired Steinway "B" grand, there arrived, from Kansas, in a drenching southeaster. Martin Johnson, who was destined to be the only unshaken unit in the *Snark's* crew. After partially drying himself, he sat in at the game of hearts.

There were Sunday foregatherings with what was left of the old "Crowd" in Piedmont; Rugby at the University of California, and concerts in its Greek Theater; plays and concerts at the Macdonough Theater or the Bishop Playhouse; gay dinner-parties at the Oakland Restaurants —The Forum, The Saddle Rock, and Pabst Café. Jack consumed many "ten-minute" wild ducks, canvasback, mallard, teal, washed down with his favorite wine, imported Liebfraumilch, in the tall opaline glasses he loved. For he, who "bothered" so little what he put in his stomach, was devoted to this type of game, excessively rare and accompanied by potatoes *au gratin;* and the fact that he had not missed the open season was somewhat of a solace for the almost insupportable delay in *Snark* affairs.

We made up frequent swimming parties for the Piedmont indoor tank; and once or twice, roved the town on rented saddlers, taking photographs of all that were left standing of Jack's many homes that had been. We boxed regularly at the house on Twenty-seventh Street, rather to the disapproval of Jack's mother, who remained silent until one day I drove my retreating opponent, beaten by his own mirth at my ferocity, into the dining-room door, cracking the redwood panel. Prizefights took Jack to the West Oakland Athletic Club, as before mentioned; and, when the *Snark,* after once breaking the inadequate ways, had been finally launched in San Francisco and brought to East Oakland for completion, there were steamed-mussel dinners aboard in the unfinished cabin.

I learned to ride a wheel, good horses being unobtainable, and also that I might participate with Jack in another of his old hobbies; so he bought me a "bike," and was loud in his boast that with three hours' practice I was able, without mishap, to ride clear to East Oakland to inspect progress on the yacht.

We took our work to Carmel-by-the-sea, and visited the Sterlings for a fortnight; and a journey in mid-winter was made into Nevada, to Tonopah and Goldfield—in which latter mining-town we were guests of Mr. and Mrs. January Jones, who showed us everything our time permitted, above the ground, and many hundreds of feet beneath the surface, by means of the precarious rim of an iron bucket. We returned to California by way of Rhyolite and Bullfrog, booming gold-centers, and had a never-to-be-forgotten glimpse into Death Valley; then Los Angeles, and home again. This trip was succeeded by one to Stanford University, where Jack lectured upon Socialism. We were met by three "clean, noble, and alive" students, Ferguson, Tuttle and Wentz. Jack was entertained by the Delta Upsilon Fraternity; and I by the Alpha Phi Sorority.

There was a Ruskin Club dinner on February 1, which Jack addressed upon the subject of "Incentive." Like a red scarf to a bull was to Jack the stock argument so often advanced, that without material gain there would be no incentive to good deeds. His speech, which I have in manuscript, is too long to quote entire; but the opening challenges are enough to indicate what follows:

"Does a child compete in a spelling match for material gain?

"Do the boys wrestling or racing in the schoolyard compete for material gain?

"Do sailors at sea volunteer to launch a boat in a mountainous sea to rescue shipwrecked strangers for material gain?

"Did Lincoln toil with his statecraft for material gain?

"Are you here to-night for material gain?

"Do the professors in all the universities toil for material gain?—you know their average salary is less than that of skilled laborers.

"Do the scientists in their laboratories work for material gain?

"Did men like Spencer, Darwin, Newton, work for material gain?

"Did the half million soldiers in the Civil War endure hardships, mangling, and violent death for the material gain of thirteen dollars per month?

"And is there any incentive of material gain in the love of mothers for their children in all the world?—and remember that the mothers constitute half of all the world.

"In short, have I not mentioned incentives, that are not alone higher than the incentive of material gain, but that dominate the incentive of material gain—and that also compel to action multitudes of people, in fact, all the people of the world?

"Can you not conceive that mere material gain, a once useful device for the development of the human, has not fulfilled its function and is ready to be cast aside into the scrap-heap of rudimentary organs and ideas, such as gills in the throat and belief in the divine right of kings?"

These latter months of waiting, Jack was up and down in his temperament, and more or less continually depressed. So much so, at intervals, that for once it was I who said to myself: "Thank heaven I don't have to live in a city always!" Even Oakland, suburb of the greater town across the Bay, had a bad effect upon him. But at last the trial-trip of the *Snark* was heralded for February 10, and upon the breathing swell, ten miles out to sea, the saucy, if grimy, little hull bore under sail and gasolene. Our spirits soared; and Jack, where we sat together in the bows for an hour, said to me:

"And we're going around the world together in her, you and I, Mate Woman. . . ."

He presented me with "The Cruise of the Dazzler," and in it wrote: "And soon we sail on our own cruise. 'The

Cruise of the Snark'—and we shall be mates around the whole round world.''

So loved we our adventure, that of mornings we often exchanged overnight dreams of boat and voyage. Then, unable, on account of further "inconceivable and monstrous" excuses, to get away until April, once we went home to Glen Ellen. Snow was on the mountain, and we rode to the top, Selim and Belle, pasture-fat, sniffing suspiciously at the white earth. And we heard, to our lasting sorrow, how Brown Wolf, whose prophetic eyes and ways had wrung our hearts while preparations were afoot for the Long Separation, had died, alone and in the snow of his birthing, a week after we had left in November. No one had plucked up the courage to tell us. "After that first snow had all melted," Wiget said, "one day I saw something up the hill among the trees above my house; and when I went up, there was your dog, dead among the leaves, with snow still on his fur.''

Dear Brown Wolf! It seemed hard indeed that he should have had his bleak heart wrenched so cruelly twice in his old age. Reminiscences were often upon Jack's lips: "Do you remember, Mate," he would say, "the day we started out for the afternoon on Belle and poor Ban, and Brown Wolf picked up a big juicy porterhouse some one had dropped, and nearly died because he couldn't decide between the beefsteak and the run with us? The red meat won out—he knew *we* would come back. But nothing could change his foreboding when we got ready for the *Snark*. . . . Funny about dogs: sometimes, as in his case, even before the traveling-gear is brought out they seem to sense what is coming to them.''

The dismantled Jack's House and Annex did not affect us cheerfully; and after a last ride to the Ranch, to see the completed stone and tile barn by moonlight, we bade final farewell to Wake Robin.

On the last night of the year, after wild funning with a chance party of acquaintances in the uproarious cafés and confetti-showered streets of Oakland, which had gained enormously in population after the great fire across the water, I closed my 1906 diary with these words:

"And so ends the happiest year of my life, with before us a great adventure."

CHAPTER XXXI

THE "SNARK" VOYAGE; TRAMP COLLIER "TYMERIC" VOYAGE;
ECUADOR; PANAMA; HOME

1907-8-9

"OUR friends cannot understand why we make this voyage," Jack elucidates his and my "I like," which, he always contended, is the ultimate, obvious reason for all human decision. "They shudder, and moan, and raise their hands," somewhat, he might have added, as did the Lily Maid's mother upon his departure for Alaska. "No amount of explanation can make them comprehend that we are moving along the line of least resistance; that it is easier for us to go down to the sea in a small ship than to remain on dry land, just as it is easier for them to remain on dry land than to go down to the sea in the small ship. . . . They cannot come out of themselves long enough to see that their line of least resistance is not necessarily everybody else's line of least resistance. . . . They think I am crazy. In return, I am sympathetic. . . . The things I like constitute my set of values. The thing I like most of all is personal achievement—not achievement for the world's applause, but achievement for my own delight. It is the old 'I did it! I did it! With my own hands I did it!' But personal achievement, with me, must be concrete. I'd rather win a water-fight in the swimming-pool, or remain astride a horse that is trying to get out from under me, than write the great American novel . . . Some other fellow would prefer writing the great American novel . . . That is why I am building the *Snark* . . . I am so made. I like it, that is all. The trip around the world means big moments of

162

living . . . Here is the sea, the wind, and the wave. Here are the seas, the winds, and the waves of all the world . . . Here is difficult adjustment, the achievement of which is delight to the small quivering vanity that is I . . . It is my own particular form of vanity, that it all.''

''The ultimate word,'' he says elsewhere, ''is I LIKE. It lies beneath philosophy and is twined about the heart of life. When philosophy has maundered ponderously for a month, telling the individual what he must do, the individual says in an instant I LIKE—and does something else and philosophy goes glimmering. Philosophy is very often a man's way of explaining his own I LIKE.''

To resume: ''There is also another side to the voyage of the *Snark*. Being alive, I want to see, and all the world is a bigger thing to see than one small town or valley.''

At the end of the voyage, he wrote:

''The voyage was our idea of a good time. I built the *Snark* and paid for it, and for all expenses. I contracted to write 35,000 words descriptive of the trip for a magazine which was to pay me the same rate I received for stories written at home. Promptly the magazine advertised that it was sending me especially around the world for itself. It was a wealthy magazine. And every man who had business dealings with the *Snark* charged three prices because forsooth the magazine could afford it. Down in the uttermost South Sea isle this myth obtained, and I paid accordingly. To this day everybody believes that the magazine paid for everything and that I made a fortune out of the voyage. It is hard, after such advertising, to hammer it into the human understanding that the whole voyage was done for the fun of it.''

The *Snark* exploit, so far as it lasted, was all and more to Jack London and to me than we had anticipated. Some feminine journalist, after reading my ''Log,'' described the cruise as ''a disappointment—nothing but a disappointment.'' It would have been—to her, who did not care to go down to the sea in ships, or having gone down to the sea in ships, dwelt only upon the little annoyances that enter sea-living as well as land-living. But I, with a firm philosophy that it is the Big Things which count, and with the memory of my Strong Traveler beside me, ask that no one shall entertain the opinion that it was not the most wonderful, victorious thing which ever happened to the right man and woman. What we set out to attain—the "purple passages," the glamor of Romance, the sheer emancipation from any possible boredom or commonplaceness of memory forever and forever, and, before everything, increased love and camaraderie between us two—became ours in unstinted measure.

One reporter, previously to our sailing, said: "When Jack London talks of his purposed voyage, he is all boy, all enthusiasm." So he appeared. But I, accustomed to look beneath the surface phenomena of him, realized throughout my life at his side that no matter how sincere his enthusiasms, the keen edge had been rubbed from adventure by pre-adventure, if I may coin a word—the super-adventure of, a too-early manhood. So, in his successful maturity, when he came to undertake, with all the zest in him, the conquest of dreams he had failed to capture in youth—like say exploring Typee Valley, or letting go anchor in uncharted bights of cannibal isles—it was with a *difference* which a less experienced, less thoughtful man would not have known.

Yet his ardors were many, once we were under way on the "Long Trail." Hawaii, that in later years he came to call his Love-Land, warmed his veins to the very deliciousness of our venture—the keenest zest of which was that we were seeing the world together. In the midst of his morning's thousand words, he would break off to remind me of the beauty and adventure we should find below the equator; and then, realizing that a half-hour had been lost from his busy time, he would pick up his charmed ink-pencil:

"There—don't talk to me any more, woman! How am I going to get my thousand words done, to pay for those pearls we're going to buy in the Paumotus and Torres Straits, and all that turtle shell from Melanesia, if you keep me from work now!''—Poor me, speechless, with clasped hands of transport in his own rapturous imaginings. But, since the youngling philosopher, who always dreamed with his two feet upon solid earth, seldom failed to bring his intentions to pass, safely enough I thought to count upon the gleaming sea-seeds and polished turtle-scales, the adventuring for which was to be seven-eighths of the prize. Again, looking up with visions in his deep eyes:

''Think, think where we are bound—the very names stir all the younger red corpuscles in one!—Bankok, Celebes, Madagascar, Java, Sumatra, Natal—oh, I'll take you to them all; and your lap shall be filled with pearls, my dear, and we shall have them set in fretted gold by the smiths of the Orient.''

As a sailor, I could not but feel that he was a consummate artist. As that matchless sea-writer, Joseph Conrad, reminds us, ''an artist is a man of action, whether he creates a personality, invents an expedient, or finds the issue of a complicated situation.'' And Jack London's was a facility of adjustment, a quickness of conception and execution, ''upon the basis,'' again to quote Conrad, ''of just appreciation of means and ends which is the highest quality of the man of action.''

All a piece of wonder it was, on and round about the narrow precipitous deck of the *Snark*, herself a mere scudding fleck of matter advancing upon the vast undulating plane of the Pacific. How could a true sailor be bored, the longest day under the arching blue sky—the excellent trades hunting his ship to its purple havens? For Jack found me sailor, too, albeit a lamentably untechnical mariner—ever he stood aghast at the hopelessness of getting me to present, ''so that the Man from Mars could understand,'' certain ordinary, primary principles of seamanship. But my love and true feel for the very shape of a boat, and for her performance, and for the whole world of water, easily he saw were not to be questioned; while always, in entering and leaving the most dangerous passages, he sent me to the wheel to coöperate with his piloting. "It's this way:" he had it. "There are many boats, but only one woman; boats will come and go, and captains will come and go, but Charmian will be with me always, at the helm."

Here I am tempted to digress, in order to word a still but not small worry that was mine during our married life. Jack's correlations between brain and body were exceptionally balanced. But there showed in him one inexactitude that led me to nurse a dread that my own hand, under his command, might some most inopportune time wreck a boat. I do not know when I first began to notice that at intervals he would say "right" for "left," but sometimes I would promptly call his attention to the mistake while his voice was still in the air. My principal fear was that, some irretrievable consequence having occurred, the responsibility might not be easy to place; and I prided myself upon unquestioning obedience aboard ship. Jack liked that, and only once did we personally come to grief. It was upon a midnight in the Solomon Islands, dark as a hat, and Jack, sick and apprehensive, was trying to make out a certain plantation anchorage on Guadalcanal. Suddenly, though the shore signal lights were identical, he discovered that we were almost on the rocks. It eventuated that another plantation than the one we sought had irresponsibly copied the other's lights. I started to put the wheel hard down at Jack's swift, tense command. "Hard down! Hard down! *quick!*" he repeated. Then I, like an idiot, "Oh, I am! I am!" It was too much for the disciplined sailorman. Not of babbling courtesies nor babies nor women was he thinking, but of saving the vessel that insured the safety of all the souls on board. And I let my own silly, mawkish, fever-warped nerves go up against this intellectually-cool, efficient manipulating of a real issue. Since

Jack never apologized for his sharp reproof, "Obey orders and don't talk back!" I truly believe that no realization of his harshness entered the mind so bent upon a life-and-death problem.

No, we did not know the meaning of boredom. And "Aren't you glad I'm your husband?" Jack would laugh over my enthusiasms. Or, tenderly, "You *would* marry a sailor!" when I floundered into the head-splitting fever attacks. But dearest of all was his assurance, reiterated in illness and discouragement: "You do not know what you mean to me. It is like being lost in the Dangerous Archipelago, and coming into safe harbor at last."

It is all a piece of wonder, the sea, to such as we: still magic of calms, where one's boat lies with motionless grace upon a shadow-flecked expanse of mirror; or when one laughs in the pelt of warm sea-rain from a ragged gray sky of clouds; or peers for blue-black squalls darkling upon the silver moonlit waves; or lifts prideful, fond eyes to the small ship's goodly spars standing fast in a white gale; or gazes in marvel at those same spars lighted to flame by the red-gilt morning sunrays from over some green and purple savage isle feared of God and man; or braces to the Pacific rollers bowling upon the surface of the eternal unagitated depths; or scans the configuration of coasts from inadequate charts; or steers, tense, breathless, through the gateways of but half-known reefs, into enchanted coral-rings below "the lap of the Line"; or looks with misleading candor into the eyes of man-eating human beings; or being received ashore on scented Polynesian "fragments of Paradise" aplume with waving palms, with brown embraces, into the "high seat of abundance." It is all wonder and deep delight, this "smoke of life"; and often and often we surprised ourselves thinking or voicing our pity for the "vain people of landsmen" who have no care for such joys as ours. Jack, embodiment of fearlessness, so vivid in thought, and action, and body, was a ringing challenge to any who were not half-dead.

On November 24, 1907, in 126° 20′ W.Lon., 60° 47′ N.Lat., Jack wrote George Sterling:

"Oh, You Greek:—

"I haven't received a letter for two months, and two months more will probably elapse before I pick up a mountain of mail in Papeete. You know what my mail is—think of four months of it coming in one swat!

"49 days next Monday since last saw Hilo and land, and we're in the Doldrums now, the Marquesas many hundreds of miles away.

"Did anybody ever tell you that it's a hard voyage from Hawaii to the Marquesas? . . . The South Sea Directory says that the whaleship captains doubted if it could be accomplished from Hawaii to Tahiti—which is much easier than the Marquesas. We've had to fight every inch of easting, in order to be able to make the islands when we fall in with the S. E. traders. . . . The first two weeks out of Hilo we met the N. E. trades well around to the east and even at times a bit north of east. Result was we sagged south (across a westerly current) and made practically no easting till we struck the Variables.

"But I'm working every day!

"Say, you've seen dolphin. Think of catching them on rod and reel! That's what I'm doing. Gee! You ought to see them take the line out (I have 600 yards on the reel, and need it all). The first one fought me about twenty minutes, when I hauled him to gaff—four feet six inches of blazing beauty.

"When they strike, they run away like mad, leaping into the air again and again, prodigiously, and in each mid-leap, shaking their heads like young stallions.

"I find it hard to go to sleep after catching one of them. The leaping, blazing beauty of it gets on my brain.

"I never saw dolphins really until this trip. Pale-blue, after being struck, they turn golden. On deck, of course, afterward, they run the gamut of color. But in the water, after the first wild run, they are pure gold.

"I am going to write up the voyage of the *Snark* and entitle it: 'Around the World with Three Gasoline Engines and a Wife.' "

And a postscript: "Talk about luck! I have played poker and I have now lost the ninth successive time, eight out of the nine times being the only loser. You can't beat that, you ever-blessed Greek!

"Wolf."

In Jack's ten-weeks' mail at Tahiti was a letter from his children's mother, announcing her approaching nuptials. His natural paternal interest in the prospective step-father of his two daughters, combined with news of the current panic in Wall Street, determined a break in the *Snark* voyage. We took a thirty-days' round-trip to San Francisco, on the old S.S. *Mariposa*, whose roomy portholes were model for the means of "Martin Eden's" suicide. Once more in Tahiti, Jack wrote Cloudesley Johns under date of February 17, 1908:

"Oh, you can't lose the *Snark*. By the time Charmian and I had arrived in Frisco, we were both saying: 'Me for the *Snark*' We were honestly homesick for her. We're a whole lot safer on the *Snark* than on the streets of San Francisco. Wish, often, that you could be with us on some of our jamborees and adventures. We sail from here in several days for Samoa, the Fijiis, New Caledonia, and the Solomons. Have just finished a 145,000 word novel that is an attack upon the bourgeoisie and all that the bourgeoisie stands for. It will not make me any friends. [This was "Martin Eden".]

" 'The Iron Heel' ought to be out by now. I wonder what you will think of it.

"Have just finished Austin Lewis' 'American Proletariat.' It's good stuff."

Somewhere along our gorgeous sea highway, the mail brought Jack word of the public's reception of "The Iron Heel," which cast him into temporary gloom.

"Just the same," he burst into his sunny chuckle, "I told the bourgeoisie a thing or two they didn't know about

the way their blessed laws are made!'' He referred especially to the Dick Militia Bill, passed by the Senate in 1903.
For some reason best known to the Solons, very few Ameri-
cans knew of this bill. Practically none but the Socialist
papers gave it notice. Chapter VIII of ''The Iron Heel''
started considerable publicity for both himself and Repre-
sentative Dick of Ohio. I have in my hand a clipping
as late as February 1917, headed: ''State Guards in a
Dilemma: Dick Bill and National Defense Act Conflict With
Some of the Units.''

Jack, pressed to relate our wildest experiences in can-
nibaldom, would sometimes tell the following:

''We had excitement enough, as Charmian will testify; but
there were no such hairbreadth escapes as that of a missionary we
heard of. This good fellow was preaching in one of the islands
where man-eating is practised, and was captured by a skeptical
chief. To his surprise, he was immediately released, but on the
condition that he carry a small sealed packet to a neighboring
mountain chief. The missionary was so grateful that, meeting a
detachment of English sailors from a battle cruiser, he declined to
accompany them to a safer territory. The sealed packet should be
delivered as he had promised. But an officer in the midst of the
discussion opened it. Therein, tucked among some small onions,
was a message to the chief:

'' 'The bearer will be delicious with these.' ''

During the space in time taken up by the *Snark* episode,
namely between April 1907 and July 1909, Jack London, in
addition to the administration of ship's affairs, recreation,
wide reading, sightseeing, and weeks idle from illnesses,
wrote the equivalent of more than eight full volumes, as
follows:

''The Cruise of the Snark,'' published serially in *The
Cosmopolitan* and *Harper's Weekly*.

''Martin Eden,'' begun in Honolulu in summer of 1907,
finished at Papeete, Tahiti, February 1908, and serial pub-

lication commenced in *The Pacific Monthly,* of Portland, Oregon, in September of same year.

"Adventure," a novel depicting the manner of life we lived ashore in the Solomons. Begun while cruising among that Group, and often interrupted for the writing of timely short work.

"South Sea Tales." These splendid stories, unlike the later ones in "A Son of the Sun," were written during the voyage.

"The House of Pride" collection of Hawaii romances.

"Burning Daylight." This novel was started in Quito, Ecuador.

And short stories, later dispersed throughout five different volumes:

"The Chinago" ("When God Laughs")

"A Piece of Steak" ("When God Laughs")

"Make Westing" ("When God Laughs")

"South of the Slot" ("The Night-Born")

"The Other Animals" (Article replying to Theodore Roosevelt's attack upon the "nature fakers," and collected in "Revolution.")

"Nothing that Ever Came to Anything" ("The Human Drift.")

In Australia, Jack, on condition that I should accompany him, reported the Burns-Johnson prizefight for *The Star,* Sydney, and the *New York Herald.* He also wrote a series of articles upon his general local impressions, as well as the labor situation in the Commonwealth from his socialist viewpoint. All of this work I shall collect at a future date for book publication.

Jack had much fun over the charge of "nature-faking," inasmuch as it arose over a misreading on the part of the President, of the incident, in "White Fang," of the wolf-dog killing the lynx; whereas Mr. Roosevelt erroneously attacked the author for having the lynx do away with the dog.

It must not be forgotten that throughout the traverse of the Pacific, Jack failed not in sounding his trumpet for the brotherhood of man. Wherever opportunity presented, he either debated, as in Honolulu, or lectured, as in Tahiti and Samoa, or used his pen when too ill to speak, as in Australia.

I might mention, if I have not previously done so, that Jack was accustomed, in the course of his literary career, to seek perspective upon his plots and motifs before developing them on paper; but during the *Snark* voyage he often went at the actual weaving of a story rather than merely filing notes upon it.

For the benefit of editors and readers who have scoffed at Jack London's novel "Adventure" as an inaccurate, over-drawn picture of savagery in the Twentieth Century, I select passages from his letter to George Sterling, from the Solomon Islands, October 31, 1908:

"For the last three or four months the *Snark* has been cruising about the Solomons. This is about the rawest edge of the world. Head-hunting, cannibalism and murder are rampant. Among the worst islands of the group, day and night we are never unarmed, and night watches are necessary. Charmian and I went on a cruise on another boat around the island of Malaita. We had a black crew. The natives we encountered, men and women, go stark naked, and are armed with bows, arrows, spears, tomahawks, war-clubs and rifles. (Have Fiji and Solomon war-clubs for you.) When ashore we always had armed sailors with us, while the men in the whale-boat laid by their oars with the bow of the boat pointed seaward. We went swimming once in the mouth of a fresh-water river, and all about us in the bush our sailors were on guard, while we, when we undressed, left our clothes conspicuously in one place, and our weapons hidden in another, so that in case of surprise we would not do the obvious thing.

"And to cap it all, we got wrecked on a reef. The minute before we struck not a canoe was in sight. But they began to arrive like vultures out of the blue. Half of our sailors held them off with rifles, while the other half worked to save the vessel. And down on the beach a thousand bushmen gathered for the loot. But they didn't get it, nor us.

"Am leaving here in two days to go to Sydney, where 1 go into hospital for an operation. And I have other afflictions, from a medical standpoint vastly more serious than the operation."

The one and only reason that our splendid adventure terminated in two years instead of seven, or ten, or unnumbered years, was that Jack London's supersensitive organism prevented. I remember him arguing, in Hawaii, with Dr. E. S. Goodhue, the point of his working-pace in the tropics. Neither Jack nor I was willing to forego any jot of our activity, mental or physical. In the end, the ultra-violet rays exacted their toll of his nervous system, as the Doctor had forewarned. In his own words:

"I went to Australia to go into hospital, where I spent five weeks. [The operation was for a double-fistula, caused we never knew how.] I spent five months miserably sick in hotels. The mysterious malady that affected my hands was too much for the Australian specialists. . . . It extended from my hands to my feet so that at times I was helpless as a child. On occasion my hands were twice their natural size, with seven dead and dying skins peeling off at the same time. There were times when my toe-nails, in twenty-four hours, grew as thick as they were long. After filing them off, inside another twenty-four hours they were as thick as before.

"The Australian specialists agreed that the malady was non-parasitic. and that, therefore, it must be nervous. It did not mend, and it was impossible for me to continue the voyage . . . I reasoned that in my own climate of California I had always maintained a stable nervous equilibrium.

"Since my return 1 have completely recovered. And I have found out what was the matter with me. 1 encountered a book by Lieutenant Colonel Charles E. Woodruff of the United States Army, entitled 'Effects of Tropical Light on White Men.' Then I knew . . . In brief, I had a strong predisposition toward the tissue-destructiveness of tropical light. 1 was being torn to pieces by the ultra-violet rays just as many experimenters with the X-Ray have been torn to pieces.

"In passing, I may mention that among other afflictions that jointly compelled the abandonment of the voyage, was one that is variously called *the healthy man's disease, European leprosy,* and *Biblical leprosy.* Unlike *True leprosy,* nothing is known of this mysterious malady . . . The only hope the doctors had held out to me was a spontaneous cure, and such a cure was mine." [This was simply *psoriasis,* as known in the United States, for which many cures are advertised, but none known that is efficacious.]

Finally, as a tribute to my own whole-hearted devotion to the voyage and all that it meant, Jack offers:

"A last word: the test of the voyage. It is easy enough for me or any man to say that it was enjoyable. But there is a better witness, the one woman who made it from beginning to end. In hospital when I broke the news to Charmian that I must go back to California, the tears welled into her eyes. For two days she was wrecked and broken by the knowledge that the happy, happy voyage was abandoned."

The venture definitely thrown over, Jack dispersed his crew, laid up the *Snark* in one of beautiful Sydney Harbor's green crannies, and shipped home our effects. The yacht eventually netted less than one-tenth of her original inflated price, and went to trade and recruit in the New Hebrides. Jack and I, loath to retrace our way across the ocean in conventional mode, watched for chance to ship on anything but a passenger liner. Our luck it was to catch, upon extremely short notice, a rusty leviathan of a Scotch collier, the *Tymeric,* Captain Robert McIlwaine, from Newcastle, N.S.W., to Guayaquil, Ecuador. With us sailed Yoshimatsu Nakata, the eighteen-year-old, fatherly Japanese soul who had joined the *Snark* as cabin boy when we left Hawaii. Nakata remained our loving and beloved shadow for nine responsible years; and I feel free to assert, for Jack London as well as myself, that when the faithful brown boy came to marry and resign from our service at the end of 1915, life never seemed quite the same again. Nakata is since a graduate of the San Francisco College of Physicians and Surgeons, and successfully wields his fashionable forceps in his own offices in Honolulu, with two assistants.

"No man is a hero to his valet" was not applicable in Jack London's household. Servants worshiped him, for he never tired helping them with his knowledge of all kinds.

For nearly three weeks after she stood out at sea, the *Tymeric*, resembling a log awash, fought a violent gale. I was time and again laid low with the terrible Solomon Island malaria. Jack and Nakata, suffering only occasional light attacks, nursed me like gentlest women. Jack was especially sympathetic in that I was missing the magnificent sight, from the bridge, of the plunging, submerging hull of the steamer, which he, "who lived with storms and spaces like a kinsman," as some one has aptly said, so reveled in. Here is his reference to the gale:

"We were a tramp collier, rusty and battered, with six thousand tons of coal in our hold. Life lines were stretched fore and aft; and on our weather side, attached to smokestack guys and rigging, were huge rope-nettings, hung there for the purpose of breaking the force of the seas and so saving our mess-room doors. But the doors were smashed and the mess-room washed out just the same."

Yet Jack compared all this as monotonous alongside sailing a small boat on San Francisco Bay.

We were forty-three days on this passage, seeing land but twice, and upon two successive days—first, fair Pitcairn Island of *Bounty* fame, on the southernmost edge of the farflung Paumotus whose northernmost edge we had skirted when westward-bound; and next, the low isle of Ducie, its tropic scents of blossom and cocoanut borne out across the water on the warm breeze.

Captain McIlwaine proved a mine of interest to Jack.

who wrote a brace of his most thoughtful stories, "Samuel" and "The Sea Farmer" (in "The Strength of the Strong") from notes made from the canny skipper's yarns. I worked up a County McGee, North of Ireland, vocabulary for Jack, often reporting the quaint speech under the table at meals. The Skipper caught me at it, I know; but he continued generously unabated in reminiscence.

Here is part of a letter Jack wrote off Pitcairn Island on May 2, to George Sterling:

"Never you mind N—— and all the other little bats, but go on hammering out beauty. If the urge comes from within to write propaganda, all right; otherwise you violate yourself. There are plenty who can do propaganda, but darned few that can create beauty. Some day you may see your way to fuse both, but meanwhile do what you heart listeth.

" 'Memory' is great! I've read it aloud a dozen times. (You should see us, George, when you send us a new poem! We sit and read it with tears in our eyes!)"

One could draw a sheaf of sketches upon that month in Ecuador. We climbed great Chimborazo, twelve thousand feet of its twenty-two thousand, on the wonderful American railway; thence descended two thousand feet to Quito, where, at the Hotel Royal, over a fortnight was spent; and before sailing upon the *Erica* for Panama, friends took us alligator-hunting up the River Guayas, where Jack, who never did anything by halves, laid in a large supply of salted skins.

As to this marvelous country, he ever afterward raved of its possibilities of agricultural development, and advised more than one ambitious young man that Ecuador would give him "the chance of his life."

There are many incidents that throw added light upon Jack London's individuality. Such as his indignation toward the unfair methods of the bull-ring, as against the "white-man's game" of prizefighting—his passion leading

1906. JACK LONDON AND HIS DAUGHTERS, JOAN (other) AND BESS

1905 'THE SEA WOLF'

1906   JACK LONDON AND ALEXANDER IRVINE AT YALE UNIVERSITY

FROM RIGHT TO LEFT—JACK LONDON LUTHER BURBANK (Plant Wizard) PROFESSOR EDGAR LUCIEN LARKIN (Astronomer)

him to write "The Madness of John Harned" (in "The Night-Born"); and his interest, for once, in American horse-racing as practised in Quito; and the Latin-American character as displayed about him, in public, and in the clubs where he took a look-in at the gambling of Ecuadorian gentlemen and their psychology as regarded payment of losses. He was in the best of humor for most of the sojourn, little troubled with fever, and spilled some of his whimsical disgust at the undependableness of Quito's inhabitants in a humorous skit, "Nothing that Ever Came to Anything" (in "The Human Drift"), which is the narration of an actual occurrence.

One sweet manifestation of himself shone out one day when I was strolling alone. A spic-and-span victoria was sent all over the shopping district to find me, because, forsooth, a peddler with her basket of laces had come to our rooms, and Jack did not want me to miss her. He hovered about the pair of us seated on the floor in a sea of needle-work, inciting me to satisfy my craving to the uttermost. A day he spent taking me to convents, in search for embroideries, and joined in a blanket-haggling revel in an old plaza —brilliant native dyes of hand-loom weaves from llama wool. He did balk, however, at adding a tiny, shivering green monkey to the menage.

In Panama, a rousing American military Fourth of July was followed by a ten days' stay at the Hotel Tivoli, whence we explored some of the surrounding country, saw the work of the great canal, and shopped in the Chinese stores. And I must take space for something that happened on the evening of the Fourth. The hotel was jammed, and we were obliged to share our small table with an American couple. The man appeared to be much the worse for the climate, and his wife evidently spent her life soothing him into a semblance of fitness for association with his kind. We extended the ordinary courtesies to them both, but it was no use.   After the man had sourly declined several things passed him, suddenly, to Jack, he burst:

"I don't want anything from *you!*"

Jack gulped.   I went chill, as when Manyoungi had invited destruction, but again misjudged my man.   Instead of blowing up as the terrified woman expected, Jack turned to her, and quietly, without interruption, at length and sans haste, told her exactly what he thought of her husband and how sorry he was for her.   The poor lady, already blanched and wilted, never raised her eyes nor opened her lips.   Nor did her companion.   They presently rose and left the table.

"I couldn't help it," Jack apologized to me.   "I was sorry for her, and I did her a service, I do believe—just in telling her, *before him*, what a skunk he is!"

I never saw Jack smite anybody except with a tongue-lashing; and, so far as I know, during our years together he never but once struck a man.

We sailed from Colon on the *Turrialba* for New Orleans.   My temperature on the day of arrival, if memory serves, was 104°, and I continued for a year to suffer intermittent attacks of malaria.   But Jack, again in his home-land, soon had cast all trace of fever, as well as of psoriaris, forever into the discard.

From New Orleans to Oakland his return was hailed by the newspapers, and reporters boarded the train at a number of towns.   We stopped over but once, at the Grand Cañon of the Colorado, where we found ourselves hospitably entertained by the Manager of the Hotel El Tovar and his wife, Mr. and Mrs. Brandt, as guests of the proprietor, Mr. Fred Harvey.   On July 24, 1909, we were once more at home in Wake Robin Lodge.

CHAPTER XXXII

RETURN FROM SNARK VOYAGE; A DAUGHTER IS BORN

End—1909-1910

HOMECOMING, after twenty-seven months of absence, was not the least of our enviable experiences. There was so much to see and do. The great stone barn was completed, roofed with red Spanish tile, and sheltered, besides horses and vehicles, all of our magnificent collection of South Sea curios. Concerning this small museum, much mirth had escaped from the Custom House into the press as to its value in dollars and cents. Jack's "declaration" had perforce been couched entirely in terms of stick-tobacco, which had been the sole medium of exchange with the savages of Melanesia.

Then Ranch improvements were to be inspected, together with the modest increase in stock—colts and calves, chickens, ducks, and pigeons. Most exciting of all, my Aunt, as Jack's agent, had added to our possessions the tiny "Fish Ranch" and the La Motte hundred and thirty acres adjoining Wake Robin, as well as a broad strip connecting the same with the Hill property—Jack's "Beauty Ranch." There was but one fly in the ointment as regarded the new acquisition. Certain men had so conducted negotiations as to leave Jack's agent in ignorance of a serious drawback to ownership of the land: upon it rested a thirteen-year lease of a valuable pit which furnished clay for the Glen Ellen brickyard. This was not so bad in itself, but the lease also covered standing timber, which might be cut at any time by the lessees for use in the brick-kiln furnaces.

Jack, in the face of unalterable circumstances, naturally made the most of the fact that he was entitled to "ten cents a yard" for all clay hauled down hill, and in course of time netted a tidy sum which, I must insert, did not compensate him for the annoyance of a dusty, rutted right-of-way over his land, to say nothing of the constant reminder, whenever plodding teams and creaking loads in clouds of dust crossed his vision, of the dishonest dealings of his fellow men. The nuisance was before long abated, and finally ceased altogether, for the brickyard went out of business previous to its requirement of any firewood from the La Motte land. It may interest travelers to know that the hollow brick used in the beautiful Hotel Oakland, in Jack's home town, was made at Glen Ellen from material mined on the Jack London Ranch.

Meanwhile, nothing daunted, Jack, with fabulous forests in his far-seeing eye, had hesitated not to set out 15,000 baby eucalyptus trees, bought from Stratton's in Petaluma, trying out their vitality on the most impoverished section of the La Motte holding.

My perspective of the latter months of 1909, from our return in mid-July on into the winter, is not one of unalloyed pleasure. For exuberance in our general happy estate was sorely tempered by anemia and sporadic attacks of the vicious malaria that so impaired my usefulness, as well as any fair qualities I may have possessed as hostess. And from the first week, Jack and I were not for a day without guests. Hospitality is a beautiful thing in itself; but I leave to the reader my frame of mind, when time and again I was obliged to lie up for days, my work going behind, and, not the least of my troubles, the pitiable effect this helplessness worked in Jack. Whenever anything interfered with "the Cheery One's" cheeriness, Jack, under no matter what merry dissembling, was lamentably at outs with existence.

Despair seemed to reach its height when during the duck season, I had to remain home from a long-contem-

plated yachting trip up-river which was to include a
house-guest, Louis Augustin, from Canada, and the Sterlings. Only at the last moment did I give in, and keep to
my bed. This cruise was made in a rented sloop, *Phyllis,*
and lasted for several weeks. Jack was not well, and returned quite ill, but was soon himself. In the interim, I
had patronized Burke's Sanitarium for a week—a lovely
Mecca in our own county, administered by a noble man, Mr.
J. P. Burke—and felt greatly improved. Burke's, by the way,
had formerly been Altruria, a coöperative colony of charming idealists, where I had spent more than one vacation,
going about the country on horseback for a month at a time.

But far be it from me to draw a veil of gloom over
that summer and autumn. There was ample *joie du vivre*
sprinkled throughout. Jack's work was as always the sus-
taining anchor for us both. "Burning Daylight," the novel
commenced in Quito, Ecuador, was duly "signed, sealed,
and delivered" unto the *New York Herald,* where it appeared serially, and was published by Macmillans in the
fall of 1910. And Jack wrote one short manuscript beside,
on a request to describe the most dramatic moment of his
life. This is entitled "That Dead Men Rise Up Never" (in
"The Human Drift"), a ghost-story founded upon his experience aboard the *Sophie Sutherland,* from which I have
made quotation in an early chapter.

A short-story collection, "Lost Face," and the novel
"Martin Eden," which has helped shape the purposes of so
many, were the two volumes brought out in 1909. There was
almost universal protest from readers of this novel as to
its author's wisdom in killing off the hero. Jack held that
Martin, robbed both of love and of pleasure in his too-hard-
won fame, and finding no faith in his fellow man to sustain him in his loneliness, had nothing left to do, logically
and artistically, but terminate a life that had become a
burden. "Which is where Martin Eden and I differed,"
Jack smiled contentedly. "To be sure, when my own battle

was won, I had little use for the spoils, so far as fame went; but I did not become self-centered. I solaced myself with warm interest in my kind, and I did find love—which is better than all.'' Whereupon, he presented his wife with the first copy in hand, in which he had generously written:

"You see, Martin Eden did not have you!"

Here is a letter, dated April 26, 1910, to one Lillian Collins who, neglecting to leave a forwarding address, never came into possession of Jack's argument in answer to her protest:

"In reply to your good letter of April 22. I don't know whether to take it as an unconscious compliment to me, or as a subtle compliment to me. I quote from your letter: 'He was not physically able to defend himself. He was heartsick; the nerves of action paralyzed by enormous strain, the power to weigh and analyze, compare and select, submerged under an overwhelming sense of loss.'

"From the foregoing, and much more that you have said in your letter, you point out to me that I did succeed in showing the inevitableness of his death. I was no more treacherous to Martin Eden than life is treacherous to many, many men and women. You continually point out to me where I took unfair advantages of Martin Eden, 'cramming his newly awakened mind with abstraction which his crude mental processes were not able to assimilate.' Granted; but do not forget that this was MY Martin Eden, and that I manufactured him in this very particular, precise and peculiar fashion. Having done so, his untimely end is accounted for. Remember that he was MY Martin Eden, and was made by me in this fashion. He certainly was not the Martin Eden that you would have made. I think the disagreement between you and me lies in that you confuse my Martin Eden with your Martin Eden.

"You say: 'I look upon Martin Eden's selfish individualism as a crudity adhering from the boy's early habits of life—a lack of perspective which time and a wider horizon would correct.' And you complain because he died. Your point is that if I had let him live, he would have got out of all this slough of despond. Again, to make a simile which I know will be distasteful to you, let me point out that the case is exactly parallel with that of a beautiful young man, with the body of an Adonis, who cannot swim, who is thrown into deep water, and who drowns. You cry out, Give the young man time to learn to swim while he is drowning, and he will not drown, but will win safely to shore. And the queer thing, reverting to the original proposition, is, that you yourself, in sharp, definite terms, point out the very reasons why Martin Eden couldn't swim, and had to drown.

"You tell me that I asserted that love had tricked and failed Martin Eden, and that you know better and that I know better. On the contrary, from what I know of love, I believe that Martin Eden had his first big genuine love when he fell in love with Ruth, and that not he alone, but that countless millions of men and women, have been tricked in one way or another in similar fashion. However, you are unfair in taking such an assertion and making the sweeping generalization that I deny all love and the greatness of all love.

"Then, it is an endless question. I don't think you and I have so much of a quarrel over Martin Eden as we have on account of our different interpretations of life. Your temperament and your training lead you one way—mine lead me another way. I think that right there is the explanation of our difference.

"Thanking you for your good letter,

"Sincerely yours,"

To one who had interpreted Martin Eden as a Socialist, Jack wrote:

"Contrary to your misinterpretation, Martin Eden was not a Socialist. On the contrary, I drew him a temperamental, and, later on, an intellectual Individualist. So much was he an Individualist, that he characterized your kind of Individualism as half-baked Socialism. Martin Eden was a proper Individualist of the extreme Nietzschean type."

As for public appearances in 1909, Jack read "The Amateur M. D.," (from "The Cruise of the Snark") in Oakland, before the Rice Institute in Old Reliance Hall; and he spoke a number of times, here and there, on other phases of the *Snark* voyage. Once he lectured in San Francisco for the Socialists in Dreamland Rink.

"Among those present" at Wake Robin Lodge that fall were the Sterlings; Jack's old friend Frank Atherton; Cloudesley Johns and his bride; "Lem" Parton, author and editor; Mrs. Lucy Parsons, a plucky widow of the Haymarket tragedy in Chicago; "A No. 1," the engaging gentleman-tramp who left his picturesque "monaker" carved on the Lodge veranda as well as along the railroad route to Glen Ellen, on which he "beat" his passage; and Emma Goldman and Dr. Ben Reitman, who, with friendly naïvete, tried to divert Jack from his socialism, which they derided, toward their unconstructive anarchism, at which he jeered, while not depreciating their martyr-sincerity and courageous, if (to him) misguided sacrifices. Of these and some others he later said: "The anarchists whom I know are dear, big souls whom I like and admire immensely. But they are dreamers, idealists. I believe in law . . . you can see it in my books—all down in black and white." I have more to say about this when presently drawing together the threads of Jack's life near its close.

And in his two or three days' entertainment of this woman and man, one of whom during the Great War fell into such evil fortune, he argued seriously as little as possible, devoting himself to laughing at and with them, and playing juvenile pranks. One of these was the placing at Dr. Reitman's plate of an attractive little red book, bearing the title "Four Weeks, a Loud Book." The guest, somewhat of a joker himself, met his Waterloo at Jack's hands. For when, the book opened, it exploded with loud report, "Never," Jack would laugh in retrospect, "did any one jump so high as that red anarchist! He must have thought it was a bomb, for he went positively green. He has the soul of a child—they're such soft people, anarchists, when it comes to actual violence—and when they do try it, they usually make a mess of it because they're dreamers and haven't learned practical brass-tack ways of doing the very things they so vehemently preach."

The ordinary camp recreations prevailed; and Jack, upon which tenderfoot, during the establishing of himself as a farmer, certain unreliable or unsound horseflesh was palmed off by traders for substantial returns, spent much time, that year and the next, subduing the creatures to his will. I was often worried when he failed to report for the evening meal and for hours afterward. After I had satisfied myself, from repeated successes, of his prudence and wisdom in forestalling the scant and often addled gray-matter of our equine friends, I said, perhaps carelessly:

"I don't worry about you any more when you are out with your incorrigible horses!"

For once our mental lines were crossed. Jack looked as puzzled and grieved as an abandoned child. I hastened to explain the reason for my lightened emotions—confidence in his methods; whereupon he was as proud as he had been taken aback and hurt. It was not wholly true—my flat statement that I had ceased to worry. There could not fail to be an undercurrent of apprehension, while an occasional minor accident, that left its scar upon my man, or further disqualified delicate ankle or wrist, prevented my nerves from becoming unresponsive.

How he gloried in it all—how he beamed and fairly quivered with achievement when, say, he had, with months of patient "staying with it," beguiled spidery little Fleet from her custom of bolting downhill with nose high in air to the detriment of all control; or his excusable bragging when, for fifteen hundred miles, he drove the notorious outlaw, Gert, as wheeler in our four-in-hand—she who had broken the spirit of every owner who had tried to hang harness upon her rebellious frame.

When, by Christmas of 1909, there was no doubt that, barring mishap, June should crown our enduring love with parenthood, our happiness was boundless. Jack was a new man—all himself and something ineffably more. It showed in his every look, the touch of his hands, the vibration of his voice. When the latest volume, "Revolution," came in the spring, this is what he wrote in the fly-leaf:

"My Mate-Woman:

"Not that I shall be able to tell you anything about revolution—you, who in a few short weeks from now, will be prime mover in turning our Wake Robin household upside down with the most delicious and lovable revolution that we can ever hope to experience.

"Mate Man.

"Wake Robin Lodge,
"April 24, 1910."

Always I shall cherish, I think above all others, the memories of those months. Never had I been so joyful, nor so strong. It seems as if all nature with lavish hands contributed to the making of the perfect child I desired and bore. "How the birds do sing and shout!" raves my diary. "—meadow-larks, blue-jays, orioles, linnets and wild canaries bickering at bath and play; gentle mourning-doves at twilight; chattering, whirring quail in the warm woods, and quaint little owls calling by night." And "Such flowered fields I never saw!" Not the least of our blisses was wandering in the eucalyptus "forest," not yet knee-high, dreaming of when they should some day be over our heads on horse-back. "They'll only be a few months older than our boy!" Jack would say.

We did not stay strictly at home, but harnessed young Maid and Ben in our light, yellow-wheeled run-about, packed writing materials and toilet articles, and drove for a week at a time about the country, stopping over wherever it looked good to us. "We three," Jack, at this sweetest height of living, would breathe leaning to my willing ear as the bays forged up mountainsides or dropped into the exquisite valleys. I have set down these words of his on an April morning: "Wife, little mother, sweetheart—I cannot express the love I feel for you these days!"

One night we spent in Petaluma, and attended a performance by an all but stranded company of itinerant players. "Tell you what, Mate Woman—if you're game for it," Jack whispered, "let me send word behind for them all to join us at supper."

It was done. The affair came off. The troupe looked hungry, but partook sparingly of a very good repast, as if hesitating to divulge their chronic emptiness. Jack was all keyed up to order cocktails, wine, champagne, anything to put them at their ease; but one spoke for light beer, and the rest, every soul of them, insisted upon milk.

Another journey was to Carmel-by-the-Sea, where we were guests of the George Sterlings.

There is a remark in the diary concerning lack of excitement in passing through the tail of Halley's Comet.

Ernest Untermann, socialist, author, painter, and perhaps best known as translator of Karl Marx, spent some time at Wake Robin, while other friends came and went. Eliza Shepard, with her boy Irving, had come to live in the little Fish Ranch house, under what, we always maintained, was the biggest madroño in California; and Eliza shortly began to assist Jack in the business of the ranch, attending to accounts and "overhead." For in May we had swelled our estate by the seven hundred acres of the Kohler property, and Jack needed such aid in carrying out his headful of ambitions. "He's burgeoning with all sorts of happiness," my journal recalls, "with love of the land, with his new mare, Gert the Outlaw—why, his eyes glisten when he speaks of her; and with life and its promises." In my copy of "Theft," a play he wrote for Olga Nethersole that spring, but which was never acted, he inscribed:

"Dear My-Woman:
    "How our days continue to grow fuller and sweeter!
                                    "Your Lover-Man."

Speaking of "Theft," this time Jack considered he had written a fairly good play; but it went the rounds of the dramatic agencies in New York without being placed—this after Miss Nethersole had decided against it. Besides "Theft," in the first half of 1910, Jack commenced a fantastic piece of long fiction, "The Assassination Bureau." This, interrupted by the death of the baby, he never finished. Only death itself, it would seem, could compel that man to stay his hand. It is noteworthy that his only uncompleted work is this "The Assassination Bureau," and the novel left less than half finished when he himself went "into the dark."

A short Klondike story, "The Night-Born," was also written that spring, and "The Human Drift," a synthesis of years of research into the great developing forces in human history.

How much one can live through—physically, mentally—and splendidly recover from! The baby was born upon high noon of Sunday, June 19, in an Oakland hospital. In my little old record I read: "Then came on the terrible hours, when Jack helped me, breathed with me, loved me and praised me——" "We named her Joy, Mate and I." She was a beautiful baby, they told me, all who saw her. I was so near to fading out that I feared my strength would fail through sheer emotion if I looked at the little soul until I had had time to gather my forces; so they carried her away. When Eliza had come from Glen Ellen at Jack's bidding, she found him so radiant with relief after his own sharp strain, so excited telling her of the small one's fair skin and gray eyes, "Just like Mate's and mine. Anglo-Saxon through and through!" that she had difficulty in learning whether he was father to a son or a daughter. The fact that he had prayed for a boy was forgotten in the larger matter of a living, breathing child of whichever sex.

What he said was: "Boy or girl, it does n't matter—so long as it's Charmian's!"

Poor little Joy! The severity of her birth, coupled with certain unwisdom, or ignorance, in the handling of the same, within thirty-eight hours had cost her life. "A perfect child," they said, after those perfect months that went into the creation of her. I go on from some notes headed "First Thoughts": "He came to me, and Eliza, and, one on either side my bed, Mate told me with a brave, bright face. And I did not make it harder for him than I could help. But oh! the pity of it! Our own baby, our little daughter, ours, our Joy-Baby, only thirty-eight hours old—gone in the twilight of the morning."

The New York *Herald* had long ahead engaged Jack to write up the Jeffries-Johnson prizefight, wherever it should be staged, together with ten days' observation, previous to the big event, of the contestants' camps. Jack was no more loath to break his pledge than I to have him; and it was with great satisfaction to me, for one, that I was pronounced out of danger from a slight operation, and that Jack could go away without apprehension. The prospective scene of the fight had been moved over California several times, and finally settled upon Reno, Nevada, so I could not see my husband for the best part of two weks. He departed June 22, and sent me daily "Lettergrams." On the morning of the fight, he wired: "I wish you were by my side to-day."

It was reported, I am reminded by news clippings of that month, that "Jack London lost heavily on the Reno fight." But this could not be, since he laid but a few dollars at most, and a hat, a dinner, and so forth.

And now, an episode, further to make clear Jack London's reactions to the corrupt injustices that may surround such a man:

Having fortified myself against shock by determining not to be shocked by anything, if I would live, on the third morning after the baby came I received in quiet the spectacle of my handsome husband with one large optic neatly closed and plastered with what appeared to be pink paint.

To my studiedly calm and interested inquiry, he frankly told me "all about it." I give the facts as he related them:

Leaving me the day before, after breaking the baby's death, he had gone into Oakland's business center to attend to final arrangements for his Reno journey. Winding up at the barber's, he then strolled, miserable and grieving, down Broadway.

"You know how I hate walking," he broke in. "And I usually seem to get into trouble when I do walk! I swear I'll never walk again. Listen to what happened:"

Noticing, in the windows of the Oakland *Tribune* office, a display of an "Autobiography of Jeffries," he bought several copies, thinking to pass them along to other correspondents at Reno. Continuing, absorbed in the morning's disaster to our hopes, he became aware that he had strayed into old haunts, down around Webster and Eighth and Ninth streets—in his boyhood a respectable residential neighborhood, but now infested with Chinese gambling houses.

As he went along, pondering the great change, he saw an American saloon, and near its main entrance a smaller door that suggested ingress to its lavatory. Entering, he found himself in a narrow passage-way, terminating in a large room behind the barroom proper, and evidently a night resort, judging from the tables and chairs. What appeared to be two lavatory doors were at the farther end, opening out of a short hall that led into still another apartment, where a lowering figure sat eating alone.

Jack, with a salutation to which the other growled something he did not hear, opened a door and passed through. Before he had time to shut it behind him, the man had thrust his foot inside, threateningly ordering him out.

"I believe he thought I was there to post on his walls some of the gaudy literature I had under my arm," Jack told me. "At any rate, I was not in the mood for trouble, especially in such cramped space, and spoke in a conciliatory way while I got into the big room and made for the passage out, intending to escape as quick as God would let me. I knew his kind, and wanted none of him. And I thought of you, and of my promise to the New York *Herald*."

What next took place—the man's unprovoked attack, Jack's scientific stalling, never striking a blow, the appearance from the barroom of an audience of pasty-faced night-birds who came to look on, and his difficulty, once he had worked his way to the street, of getting an officer to consent to arrest the dive-keeper—all this he has graphically described in a short story, "The Benefit of the Doubt" (in volume "The Night Born").

What he did not include in the story was that it turned out that the Hebrew police judge who dared to sit on the case, was in truth *owner of the resort*. Jack learned of this through a letter from a well-wishing stranger, who suggested he look up the records. When Eliza went to do this, every obstacle was put in her way; but she prevailed, and her homecoming with the notes she had made was an occasion for triumphant celebration in the London household.

The reporters, as always paid to "give Jack London the worst of it wherever possible," hinted at the vilest construction upon his presence in the low resort. The San Francisco *Bulletin* account was the most decent—because, according to Joseph Noel, in charge of the Oakland office, he offered to throw up his position rather than distort his friend's account of the one-sided scrimmage.

Jack was keen for the trial, but got it postponed until after the Reno prizefight. Never have I seen him so cut up as when the Judge dismissed the case, giving both complainants "the benefit of the doubt," as faithfully told in the story of that name. And the exasperating newspaper lie as to his shaking hands with the dive-proprietor and their "departing for the nearest saloon," is as accurately recorded.

Jack worked off, in the fiction, a fantastic revenge. The eastern weekly's editor, before accepting the yarn, made sure through the author that he would not be liable for libel. Quite different from his usual eventual tolerance, Jack never forgave the Hebrew Judge. "Some day, somewhere, I am going to 'get' him," he would say at long intervals. "I shall watch him all years, and some time, when he least looks for it, I shall get him. I don't know just how —perhaps it will be in thwarting his dearest ambition; but mark my words, I intend to get him." Jack's countenance, no matter how one sympathized with his viewpoint, was not good to look upon at such a time. But his cards were played squarely, as always, face up on the table. He sent the following open letter (I typed it for him during convalescence) to the newspapers of San Francisco and Oakland, the same post carrying a copy to the magistrate that he might be prepared for the writer's deadly interest in him:

"Some day, somewhere, somehow, I am going to get you legally, never fear. I shall not lay myself open to the law. I know nothing about your past. Only now do I begin to interest myself in your past, and to keep an eye on your future. But get you I will, some day, somehow, and I shall get you to the full hilt of the law and the legal procedure that obtains among allegedly civilized men."

One day, long afterward, out of a sudden whimsey, Jack had his sister telephone to arrange an interview for him in the office of that grafting judicator. "Oh, I intend no violence," he allayed my start; "I just want to tell him a 'few.'" But the other had hastily pleaded an imminent and important engagement elsewhere. Jack died unavenged, unless the Judge's conscience, or fear of his enemy, were punishment enough.

It was mainly grit that carried Jack through the Reno

1908. JACK AND CHARMIAN LONDON IN SOLOMON
ISLANDS

1914. "KOAIEK"

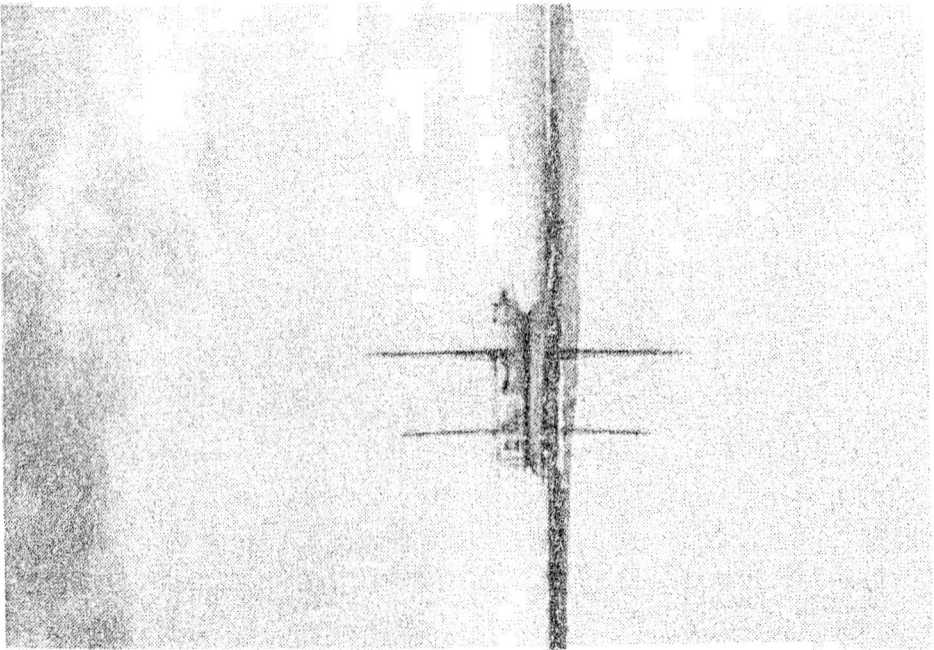

1907 "SNARK" AT PEARL HARBOR

1915   JACK LONDON AT FRICKEE WITH
"SCOTTY'S" DOGS

JACK LONDON'S IMPORTED ENGLISH SHIRE STALLION
"NEUADD HILLSIDE"

1913 JACK LONDON CONTEMPLATING HIS "BEAUTY RANCH"

period. He was miserably ill, probably from the effects of the Muldowney struggle, and coughed exhaustingly.

The fiasco of the fight did not improve his spirits— "It wasn't a fight," he wrote me, "It was awful."

Once back in Oakland, and the afternoons with me in hospital resumed, he told me he was having his sputum examined for traces of tuberculosis, for he was thoroughly alarmed at the obstinacy of the racking cough and soreness in his chest. With our customary rebound from carking care, the battered pair of us lost no time making tentative arrangements for a lengthy sojourn in high, dry Arizona, and presently were all alive with the details of equipment, saddles, clothing, books—and work! The analysis of the sputum brought to light no evidence of active "T.B.," although a scar that was located in Jack's bronchial tissue proved his own diagnosis not without foundation.

"Well, that settles our Arizona vacation," he smiled over a momentary regret.

Another hospital memory is the day Jack said to me:

"I went last night to the Macdonough to see the De Mille-Belasco production of 'The Woman.' And take it from me, my dear—that play never would have been written if I had not written 'Theft.'

I made him return to his Ranch and his writing, while I devoted every atom of energy to recuperating. In a letter of July 24, he begs me to "Come home right away; I'll cut out the Jinks this year if you will . . . I read your 'First Thoughts' and two of your later letters, to Eliza last night; and both she and I were in tears."

But it was more than six weeks from June 19, before I was fit to travel. It was a deep obligation I put upon myself, then as ever, to take the best care of my health, that I might be "on deck" as much as possible. Jack's content depended so vitally upon the brightness of his household.

The first day that I was able to mount a docile horse, Jack, bestriding his cheerful outlaw, led me from the idyllic site on the Beauty Ranch where we had decided to build, into the forested ravine of Asbury Creek. To my astonished exclamation at sight of a new bridle trail engineered upon its precipitous sides, he answered:

"It's the 'Charmian Trail,' Sweetheart, and I saved it for a surprise."

From that time on, similar trail-making was continually in progress, until there came to be miles of these green zig-zags within the boundaries of the Jack London Ranch, opening up breath-taking views of the surrounding valleys and mountains.

In addition to "The Benefit of the Doubt," the author, not yet in humor, from his aggregation of past troubles, to settle down to sustained effort, turned out some light stuff—an airplane story, "Winged Blackmail"; "Bunches of Knuckles," containing a conversation, with a skipper, just as I had heard it aboard the *Snark;* "When the World Was Young," with a double-personality motif. Then he penned what he called a picture, or, rather, two successive pictures, entitled "War," which he deemed one of his gems; and the story "To Kill a Man," which he also greatly liked. All the foregoing are bound in "The Night Born."

"Told in the Drooling Ward," a delightful study of the amiable egotism of a high-class idiot's psychology, but which Jack had difficulty in selling, was another 1910 production; also "The Hobo and the Fairy," a dainty and wholesome tale, both of which will be found in "The Turtles of Tasman."

While in Oakland, Jack had been called upon by "Bob" Fitzsimmons and his wife, Julia, and for their use in vaude-ville he wrote a rather inconsequential skit, "The Birth Mark," which appears in "The Human Drift." The Fitz-simmonses visited us the first week in September, and "Bob," to the joy of Glen Ellen, forged a mighty horseshoe in the village smithy, which adorns a door frame of our cottage.

Next was begun "The Abysmal Brute," hardly more than a long-short story, but subsequently published as a novelette—a cleanly conceived bit of propaganda for the purifying of the prize-ring. Before the year was out, Jack had made a start on a series of a dozen Alaskan yarns, which are built around the central figure of "Smoke Bellew."

Very little public speaking was heard from him that year—a Memorial Day address in Sonoma, a lecture in Oakland, and another, in December, in the Auditorium Annex at Page and Fillmore Streets, San Francisco, in protest at the current murders of educators and reformers in Russia, in Japan, and, in particular, Spain's inexcusable execution of Francisco Ferrer.

CHAPTER XXXIII

YACHT "ROAMER"

The End of 1910

AT last, at last, Jack's search for a suitable inland yacht ended in mid-October, when a friend discovered for sale the thirty-foot yawl, *Roamer*, once the fast sloop *Iris*. A personal try-out convinced us of her eminent qualifications, despite her ripe years which were rumored to be at least forty. We schemed a better galley for'ard, installed a little coal-stove for winter warmth and cooking, and had the hull and rigging overhauled.

For it was meant that I, from my salt heredity, and practice both before and after marriage, should be Jack's true shipmate. None so keenly as I, perhaps, can appreciate his own words, written on board the *Roamer* in Sonoma Creek, the next spring:

"Once a sailor, always a sailor. The savour of the salt never stales. The sailor never grows so old that he does not care to go back for one more wrestling bout with wind and wave. I live beyond sight of the sea. Yet I can stay away from it only so long. After several months have passed, I begin to grow restless. I find myself day-dreaming over incidents of the last cruise, or wondering if the striped bass are running on Wingo Slough, or eagerly reading the newspapers for reports of the first northern flight of ducks. And then, suddenly, there is a hurried packing of suit-cases and overhauling of gear, and we are off for Vallejo where the little *Roamer* lies, waiting, always waiting, for the skiff to come alongside, for the lighting of the fire in the galley-stove, for the pulling off of gaskets, the swinging up of the mainsail, and the rat-tat-tat of the reef-points, for the heaving short and the breaking out, and for the twirling of the wheel as she fills away and heads up Bay or down."

With Nakata and the cook, Yamamoto (an intellectual socialist later abstracted back to his native islands by the long arm of the Mikado), we set sail on October 17, from Oakland, across the Bay of San Francisco, "than which," to quote my captain, "no lustier, tougher sheet of water can be found for small boat sailing," for an up-river cruise.

Two days earlier I had found upon my desk a fresh, sky-blue volume entitled "Burning Daylight," into which Jack had woven so much of our daily blessedness. This is the inscription:

"A sweet land, Mate Woman, an almighty sweet land you and I have chosen—our Valley of the Moon,
"Your Own Man,
"Jack London."

My old, old dream come true—to see with Jack this stage of his youthful performances! He looked much like his piratical early self, I fancy, in blue dungaree and the time-honored "tam" pulled down, with a handful of curls, over his sailor-blue eyes that roved incessantly for changes and found comparatively few. I had the privilege, at Vallejo near the yacht club, of seeing the meeting between Jack and an old crony or two—as Charley Le Grant, so often mentioned in "Tales of the Fish Patrol"; and another time, threading Sonoma Creek's delta of sloughs to the tuneful sound of blackbirds' throats, into our own valley within eye-reach of our own mountain fastnesses, to Jack's unbounded delight we came upon a venerable, rickety little French Frank of *Idler* memory, keeper of a duck-hunting club shack. Debonair and gallant Frank still was, though all his jealous fires and furies had long since been drawn. And ludicrously tactful was he, before "Jack's lady," in references to the wild '90s he and the lady's husband had shared in common. Having convinced him I was no ogress his tongue loosened in spicy reminiscence, abetted by a bottle of red wine.

What a blissful passage it was, this first *Roamer* voyage, only to be surpassed by the second and the third, and so on. "*Snarking* once more," Jack named it; honeymooning upon the face of the winding waters; fanning into Benicia to the sunset melody of birds in the rushes; running across that "large, draughty, variegated piece of water," Suisun Bay, where the great scows we had both learned to respect came charging down, grain-laden; picking our way in the "Middle Ground" channels, and gliding close-hauled into Black Diamond "in the fires of sunset, where the Sacramento and the San Joaquin tumble their muddy floods together"—to port the hazy, Aztec unreality of the tawny-rose Montezuma Hills palpitating in the westering sunlight; to starboard the low brown banks with green upstanding fringes of rustling tules; all about red-sailed fishing boats homing for the night; and old Black Diamond's lazy water-front and lazier streets sloping upward toward the Contra Costa Hills; and, in the morning, Diablo crumpled against an azure dome.

Once, off a tree-plumed island in the pictureful delta, a gay "red-light" barge, with its painted ladies, anchored within hailing distance of the *Roamer*. "I'll take you aboard to-morrow evening early, if you'd like," Jack volunteered; and I was glad enough for a new experience with him. But the next day he was invited by the principal, Professor Vickers, to speak to the school children of the town across river, which he consented to do, in a brief talk on "The Call of the Wild"; and when we were once more aboard, he said soberly:

"I guess we won't go adventuring next-door to-night, Mate—it might offend the good people ashore if they found it out. They wouldn't understand how you and I go about together. Also, there might possibly be folks on the barge whom you've seen about and who wouldn't want you to see them there. So we'll just give it up and wait for a better chance."

I think it was about this time Jack illustrated his belief in the innate goodness of even very low unfortunates, by telling me how, when he was a mere stripling, his pockets had been rifled by one of the women companions of his associates up-river. "But do you know—she only took exactly *half* of what I had," he said. "I never forgot that. It was bad, of course, but it was only half-bad at worst, and showed she had some heart of softness left in her toward a mere boy like me."

It was while we lay off the town of Antioch, in this region, that Jack recounted to me the laughable story of how he and his mates netted a score of illicit fishermen; but that is for all to read—"Charley's Coup," in "The Fish Patrol" group.

Together we came to know the rivers and serpentine sloughs, with their foreign inhabitants, as Jack had known them aforetime; only, now, the dwellers upon and behind the willowed dykes had become increasingly foreign. This gave rise to many "human drift" speculations upon my skipper's part, later used in "The Valley of the Moon." I am reminded in passing, the young hero and his comrade wife run across a pseudo *Roamer* and its master and mate.

Among other features new to Jack, was the growth of the Japanese-Chinese village of Walnut Grove. Here we poked about among tortuous roofed streets lined with gambling dens, stores, geisha houses and tea-shops, entertained in these latter by the pretty toy-like women, with saki, and raw bonita soaked in soyu sauce, to the debatable harmony of samisens.

Jack, snugly at anchor, his work punctually disposed of, read intensively upon agriculture, devoured a plunder of countless old books he had been collecting upon western

Plains migration, and laid deep and deeper foundation for Ranch development and stock-raising. "I devoted two solid years," he has written, "to the study of the migrations toward the West of America, being moved to it perhaps by the fact that my people came from the Middle West."

Everywhere he used his eyes, bent upon seeing what the other fellow was doing in the vast fields of California, making me the willing repository of his plans as he worked them out. Often, while I shopped or walked or rowed in the skiff for exercise, he drifted about the towns, meeting men, going to their farms, inspecting cattle and horses. He bought a draft-mare, June, a striking creature, black and proud, who came to live on the Ranch and become the mother of several colts.

Jack was living so fully—a life balanced with essential interests and endeavor and simplest of amusements. The test, I am sure, he undertook deliberately. To him relaxation consisted not in cessation but in change of thought and occupation. The vessel all in order, laid against a river-bank for the night, he would sit, placidly smoking in the blue dungarees and old tam, humped comfortably on deck, his soft-shod feet hanging over the rail, line overboard for cat-fish or black bass. Meanwhile he would argue for long with Nakata or the cook, in all the ardent simplicity of a sailor in the fo'c's'le, some trifling point—say relative sizes of fish each had hooked the day before; or there would be a jokingly heated disagreement as to the payment of a penny wager a week old; or the three, stopping to catch laughing breath, feverishly laid new bets against the evening's basket. Jack was always ready to chuckle over it all, should I remind him of his reversion to fo'c's'le methods.

To a Sacramento reporter at this time, Jack said: "I am a Westerner, despite my English name. I realise that much of California's romance is passing away, and I intend to see to it that I, at least, shall preserve as much of that romance as is possible for me. I am making of 'The Valley of the Moon' a purely Californian novel—it starts with Oakland and ends in Sonoma."

He was an unfailing wonder to me, my Jack London—my mentor—his continuous cerebration to every impact, mental, physical, awake, and asleep; always young, always old, always wise, with "a bigness of heart that kept conscience with itself"; efficient dreamer, harnessed to his work for the sake of Heart's Desire, which included the discharge of so many responsibilities—penalties of patriarchy. How vivid he rises, standing on his handsome legs at the wheel, those robust, muscle-rounded shoulders leaning back upon a howling norther before which we fled, tense, caution on hair-trigger, uncapturable thoughts behind his deep, wide eyes, lips parted, and that great chest expanding to breeze and effort. One man has written me: "I remember Jack London above all by his beautiful chest. It was the most beautiful thing I have ever seen."

December saw us home at Wake Robin, trying to come abreast with work that had piled up during the cruise. "Poor little woman! She has to pay for her fun!" Jack turned from his desk to where I was filing letters and notes. "But it's worth it!" Again, suddenly wheeling around, "How good it is to have a *satisfying* love. Mate, I love you more than I ever did in my first days of madness. It's different—but I love you *more.*" And he had a way of blowing involuntary kisses in the air when I spoke to him. How good it all was! I am reminded of Browning's:

"There's your smile!
Your hand's touch! and the long day that brings
Half-uttered nothings of delight."

While we spent hours poring over the Wolf House drawings, twenty men were setting out twenty thousand additional eucalyptus. And Jack's funds, despite our boundless plans, were sinking low.

"Well, I've got five hundred dollars in bank, and an eight-hundred-dollar life-insurance premium due," he announced. "Doesn't balance up very well, does it? But never fear—'Smoke Bellew' will pull us even with the bills. Guess we'll accept that invitation from Felix Peano to move into his Los Angeles house for a month. It'll be a nice winter change, and I can forget my creditors easier at a distance, while I'm slaving to pay them!"

He always referred to "Smoke Bellew" as "hackwork," strictly excluding the last story, "Love of Woman," which he strove to make one of his best. The "hack" turned out to be a great favorite with the male readers of his average public. It would seem that Jack London's work, third-best, or worse, could never be bad. Light it might sometimes be, comparatively unimportant; but it was impossible—reservoir of learning, and imagination, and emotion that he was—that he should ever turn out trash.

The *Cosmopolitan* later asked for a continuation of "Smoke Bellew," and the while Jack considered its popularity in light of means to keep up the enormous expense of house-building, I suggested sailing Smoke and Shorty into the South Seas for a series of adventurings, for he had been longing again to dip his pen into tropic colors. This he considered; but all at once he threw up the whole thing:

"I'm tired writing pot-boilers! I won't do another one unless I have to!" And in March, the twelve off his hands, he went at the David Grief series, these romances, "crackerjacks," Jack referred to them, being issued as "A Son of the Sun."

So January, 1911, was spent in the Westlake District of Los Angeles, while "Smoke Bellew" went forward, and chance visitors were regaled with readings from the manuscript. We took along our two Japanese, and had my

Aunt, now Mrs. Edward B. Payne, and her husband, as
house-guests. It was a very jolly arrangement—we, accepting our sculptor-friend's roomy house, he, our hospitality of table and service. Jack's thirty-fifth birthday
was celebrated in this pleasant cottage. Besides entertaining, our amusements numbered much attendance at the
theaters, swimming in the city's salt tanks, a captive bal-
loon ascension, canoeing on Westlake hard by, feeding
the swans and reading aloud, and a run to Santa Catalina
Island. On this last excursion Jack said my Aunt and
her husband must go with us—she having visited the big
island with my own mother long before I was born.

One of my commissions while south was to look up a
suitable four-in-hand of light horses for a summer trip to
northern California and Oregon. I succeeded in obtaining
a trio, more or less ill-assorted, which was shipped home.
Upon our own return, Jack had up from Glen Ellen his
old friend "Bill" Ping—mentioned in more than one of his
books—to consult about reinforcing the Winship two-
seated "cut-under," for the heavy going, and the proper
harness. Mr. Ping, one of the splendid passing type of
old-time stage-drivers, who in his day had tooled his six on
the Overland Trail, was sent to San Francisco to order
harness; also a whip with an eleven-foot lash which Jack,
after a surprisingly short trial, learned to crack with a
brave report, but seldom used.

Mr. Ping being busy with his own affairs, another stage
driver, of a younger generation, was hired to put the
team in shape and instruct us in the gentle art of guiding
its four mouths and sixteen wayward feet. Jack, as always, mastered the thing perfectly, knowing, move by
move, precisely how he did it; while I, to his laughing,
almost mocking admiration, "got the hang of it" by way
of emulation and my "horse instinct," doing it well one
day and not so well the next.

The Lily Maid was one of our guests in March, and Jack never appeared to better advantage than in his kindness to her, still pleasuring in her mantle of yellow English hair. For her health was but poorly, and when she could not come to table, with Jack's own hands Nakata's nicely appointed trays were carried to one of the little woodsy guest-cabins we had built.

We had formulated a printed slip that frequently went into Jack's correspondence along with socialist and agricultural folders, reading as follows:

"We live in a beautiful part of the country, about two hours from San Francisco by two routes, the Southern Pacific and the Northwestern Pacific.

"Both trains (or boats connecting with trains) leave San Francisco about 8 a. m.

"The p. m. Southern Pacific train (boat) leaves San Francisco about 4 o'clock.

"The p. m. Southern Pacific train can be connected with at 16th Street Station, Oakland, also.

"If you come in the afternoon, it is more convenient for us if you take the Southern Pacific route, as it arrives here in time for our supper. We usually ask our guests to dine on the boat, if they come by the Northwestern Pacific.

"Write (or telephone) in advance of your coming, because we are frequently away from home. Also, if we are at home, word from you will make it so we can have a rig at the station to meet you.

"*Be sure* to state by *what route,* and by *what train,* you will arrive.

"Our life here is something as follows:

"We rise early, and work in the forenoon. Therefore, we do not see our guests until afternoons and evenings. You may breakfast from 7 till 9, and then we all get together for dinner at 12:30. You will find this a good place to work, if you have work to do. Or if you prefer to play, there are horses, saddles, and rigs. In the summer we have a swimming pool.

"We have not yet built a house of our own, and are living in a small house adoining our ranch. So our friends are put up in little cabins near by, to sleep."

I have come across a verse by Foss, which so expresses Jack's deep heart of hospitality that I steal space to quote:

"Let me live in a house by the side of the road,
    Where the race of men goes by——
The men who are good and the men who are bad,
    As good and as bad as I.
I would not sit in the scorner's seat,
    Or hurl the cynic's ban——
Let me live in a house by the side of the road
    And be a friend to man."

He was always buying blankets; never so happy as when all the beds were full. His heart was soft, and all were treated alike—friend, stranger, of whatsoever estate. I remember the pleased look that crossed his face when I related how, while I was buying a riding suit in a San Francisco shop, the fitter said to me:

"Mrs. Jack London?—Oh, I heard something so lovely about your place—that no one, even when you people are not home, is ever allowed to go away without being entertained!"

It was in October Jack placed in my hands the story of his wayward flight across the continent, "The Road." The inscription is one of his most generous:

"Dearest My Woman:—

"Whose efficient hands I love—the hands that have worked for me long hours and many, swiftly and deftly, and beautifully in the making of music, the hands that have steered the *Snark* through wild passages and rough seas, that do not tremble on a trigger, that are sure and strong on the reins of a Thoroughbred or of an untamed Marquesan stallion; the hands that are sweet with love as they pass through my hair, firm with comradeship as they grip mine, and that soothe as only they of all hands in the world can soothe. "Your Man and Lover,"

Of course many calls were made upon Jack's time and purse. And "purse" reminds me that he never carried other than the slender chamois gold-dust sack that he had learned to use in the Klondike. He was obliged to work out circular letters to cover such exigencies as he was unable to comply with. Here is an example in a copy of a letter written to a young writer:

"In reply to yours of recent date undated and returning herewith your Manuscript. First of all let me tell you that, as a psychologist and as one who has been through the mill, I enjoyed your story for its psychology and point of view. Honestly and frankly, I did not enjoy it for its literary charm or value. In the first place, it has little literary value and practically no literary charm. Merely because you have got something to say that may be of interest to others does not free you from making all due effort to express that something in the best possible medium and form. Medium and form you have utterly neglected.

"Anent the foregoing paragraph; what is to be expected of any lad of twenty, without practice, in knowledge of medium and form? Heavens on earth, boy, it would take you five years to serve your apprenticeship and become a skilled blacksmith. Will you dare to say that you have spent, not five years, but as much as five months of unimpeachable, unremitting toil in trying to learn the artisan's tools of a professional writer who can sell his stuff to the magazines and receive hard cash for same? Of course you cannot; you have not done it. And yet you should be able to reason on the face of it that the only explanation for the fact that successful writers receive such large fortunes is because very few who desire to write become successful writers. If it takes five years' work to become a skilled blacksmith how many years of work intensified into nineteen hours a day, so that one year counts for five,—how many years of such work, studying medium and form, art and artisanship, do you think a man, with native talent and something to. say, requires in order to reach a place in the world of letters where he receives a thousand dollars cash iron money per week?

"I think you get the drift of the point I am trying to make. If a fellow harnesses himself to a star of $1000 a week he has to work proportionately harder than if he harnesses himself to a little glowworm of $20 a week. The only reason there are more successful blacksmiths in the world than successful writers is that it is much easier, and requires far less hard work, to become a successful blacksmith than does it to become a successful writer.

"It cannot be possible that you, at twenty, should have done the work at writing that would merit you success in writing. You have not begun your apprenticeship yet. The proof of it is the fact that you dared to write this manuscript, "A Journal of One Who is to Die.' Had you made any sort of study of what is published in the magazines you would have found that your short story was of the sort that never was published in the magazines. If you are going to write for success and money you must deliver to the market marketable goods. Your short story is not marketable goods, and had you taken half a dozen evenings off and gone into a free reading room and read all the stories published in the current magazines you would have learned in advance that your short story was not marketable goods.

"There's only one way to make a beginning, and that is to begin; and begin with hard work, patience, prepared for all the disappointments that were Martin Eden's before he succeeded—which were mine before I succeeded—because I merely appended to my fictional character, Martin Eden, my own experiences in the writing game.

"Jack London."

The next letter here appended, he used to send out before he came to decide to read every manuscript that came his way, and encourage the sending to him. He found that in refusing to avail of such opportunities, he was depriving himself of just so many chances to study the wayward seed of man:

"Every time a writer tells the truth about a manuscript (or book), to a friend-author, he loses that friend, or sees that friendship dim and fade away to a ghost of what it was formerly.

"Every time a writer tells the truth about a manuscript (or book), to a stranger-author, he makes an enemy.

"If the writer loves his friend and fears to lose him, he lies to his friend.

"But what's the good of straining himself to lie to strangers?

"And, with like insistence, what's the good of making enemies anyway?

"Furthermore, a known writer is overwhelmed by requests from strangers to read work and pass judgment upon it. This is properly the work of a literary bureau. A writer is not a literary bureau. If he is foolish enough to become a literary bureau, he will cease to be a writer. He won't have any time to write.

"Also, as a charitable literary bureau, he will receive no pay. Wherefore he will soon be bankrupt, and himself live upon the charity of his friends (if he has not already made them all enemies by telling them the truth), while he will behold his wife and children wend their melancholy way to the poorhouse.

"Sympathy for the struggling unknown is all very well. It is beautiful—but there are so many struggling unknowns, something like several millions of them. And sympathy can be worked too hard. Sympathy begins at home. The writer would far rather allow the multitudinous unknowns to remain unknown, than allow his near and dear ones to occupy pauper pallets and potter's fields.

"Sincerely yours,

"Jack London."

In extreme cases, I have known him to send out copies of Richard Le Gallienne's "Letter to an Unsuccessful Literary Man," a document that leaves little to be said.

Requests for money usually found his responsive. He used some discernment, however, declining to be "touched" too often by certain men who took him more freely for granted than he liked; with some others, he blithely kissed hand to his dollars when telling me of his gifts and "loans." And——

"Oh, well, Mate—money's only good for what it can buy. It buys me happiness to buy happiness for others. Don't hoard money. You can't take it with you when you go into the dark"—that was a concept he had inculcated for all time into the rapidly simplifying philosophy that had followed his "opening of the books." The disadvantageous, soul-belittling influence of poverty had been practically banished for the span of his existence on this competitive planet. I smile as I handle the cancelled checks of many dates, to hear that husky, half-apologetic: "They've all dreamed their dream. Who am I not to help, now that I can. And these have realized their dream only a little less, after all, than the rest of mankind. . . . But it does give me joy," with a smile into my eyes, "when what my money does for others receives some little appreciation of the pleasure or comfort it buys!"

In mid-April the *Roamer* all "ship-shape and Bristol fashion" from Nakata's deft brown hands, sailed on a month's cruise, while Eliza superintended architect and house construction, and colts and calves increased, and orchard and house-vineyard took root in the gentle terraced amphitheater behind the rising red-stone pile that was to be our castle.

During this absence, Eliza saw her chance to buy, at a price her brother had been waiting for, a section of some twelve acres right in the heart of the big Kohler ranch already ours, on which stood the buildings large and small of the old Kohler and Frohling winery of other days, all in sad but picturesque disrepair from neglect topped with the Great Earthquake.

This out-door life was the best thing that could happen to Jack, who had been suffering from one severe cold after another, coupled with repeated sties on his eyelids, and much nerve-rack from his teeth—this last, of course, being nothing unusual. I marvel to think of his eternal patience with pain; probably he was never, for years at a time, free from pain or at least discomfort. And there was his ever present joy in my own good teeth —"Woman!" he would cry, "you don't know how lucky you are!"

Before launching out for the coast on our northern

trek, Jack asked me, what I had been anticipating for some time:

"Do you think we could fix up that old cottage on the Kohler, to live in until the Wolf House is done?"

It was a six-room, one-story frame house once occupied by the heads of the winery, and now in a shocking state. Subsequent Italian lessees of the vineyard had made a veritable dump of it and its old garden of foreign trees and shrubbery. I was dubious enough to reply:

"Honestly, I don't think we can."

But my partner had, for once, evidently made up his mind before consulting me, and presently I entered into the spirit of making the place as attractive as possible. Besides, it was, at worst, a consummation of our mutual desire to live in the very center of the Ranch activities now afoot.

The cottage came to be our sleeping and working quarters, including two guest-rooms, while in one side of the enormous winery were built others; workmen's family quarters being created on the other, and a new roof shingled over all.

Quite a ceremonial it was with the Japanese, getting ready Jack's bedside table for the night. Sharp pencils there must be plenty, scratch pads, big and little; many packages of "Imperiales," and fine Korean brass ashtray; his ubiquitous little red-velvet pin-cushion with pins driven in to their heads; files of papers and magazines neatly arranged on a lower section of the table, according to dates, the latest on top; a dish of fruit, or, lacking fruit, of some favorite dried fish or other "dainty." And finally, there were no less than three bottles of liquid of one sort or another. For Jack always maintained that it was a mercy, with his almost uninterrupted smoking, the alcohol he consumed, and certain sedentary spells when he took little exercise, that he "breathed through the skin" —by which he meant free perspiring. Therefore, he drank almost excessive quantities of this and that favorite beverage—grapejuice, buttermilk, and endless draughts of water. These, according to the whim, in cool thermos bottles, stood in an inviting row on the bedside table, and were always empty in the morning.

Papers and magazines, ravished of whatever in the way of information he wished to file as notes, were flung upon the floor; letters, envelopes, all small matter that was finished with, he carefully crumpled lest Nakata or the house-boy should put them back where he would have to handle them again. Sometimes, dropping off to sleep, cigarette between his lips, he singed his curls, exploded a celluloid eyeshade, or burned small round holes in sheet or pillow. As for pillows, he liked them large, three of them, with a very small one for that left elbow which supported him so many, many hours.

This dwelling was the only one of his very own in which Jack London ever lived—and in which he continued to live until he died within its old book-lined walls. It was into this house we moved upon our return from the four-horse adventure, which began in early June and ended in early September, 1911.

CHAPTER XXXIV

FOUR-HORSE DRIVING-TRIP; NEW YORK CITY

1911

FROM Glen Ellen to the Coast, and north to Bandon, Oregon, was our route; thence inland to Medford and Ashland, and southward through the interior—fifteen hundred miles altogether. Jack wrote forenoons before starting out, and our average drive was thirty miles. "Four Horses and a Sailor," written primarily for a Northern Counties promotion object, published in *Sunset Magazine* (collected in "The Human Drift"), is based upon this summer's journeying, as is also the wagon-travel episode in "The Valley of the Moon."

We did not camp. Before ever Jack London and I came to "hunt in pairs" he had had enough "roughing" to last out his life, and our migrations were invariably attended by one or more helpers. Nakata packed, put up lunches, on hottest afternoons hoisted the big brown sunshade that clamped to the back of the driver's seat, kept our "gear" in order and sometimes assisted in harnessing the antic four-footed quartet. I typed Jack's manuscript on a small machine, and he steadily ground out the wherewithal for our subsistence as well as the big things left doing at home. Watching him in this phase, exhilarated with the youth and beauty of the summer world of out-doors, I caught myself thinking of him as driving a team of stars; for he harnessed the very stars to do his work—his lines reaching to the stuff of which the stars are made.

But sometimes, as more often on days when I was not

so bright as usual (I drove little, finding my strength was not quite equal to the weight of those long leathers in my hands for hours on end) furtively I watched Jack's face; and there was that in it I had never seen before the death of our child. It made more difference to him than any one, even I, then realized. On the evenings of such days, our goal reached, horses properly housed, and hotel or farm accommodations made sure, he was most likely to drift off alone down-street, looking for "inhibitions"—a word he worked a great deal at the time—of man-talk, new association, and an extra glass or two. When he would return, there was a more than common glisten in his always lustrous eyes, a trifle of feverishness in the telling of what he had picked up in the way of local information or backwoods lore, a super-enthusiasm about the newest antlers of elk or deer for which he was bargaining, or the bearskin so-and-so had promised to bring for my inspection.

For a period of two or three years after the baby's loss, which included a second unlooked-for disappointment, my health was not of the best; but I was wary to avoid giving any possible impression to Jack that I linked my lack of freshness in any way with maternal misfortunes. I had early discovered that the slightest suggestion of such a thing irritated him instantly and beyond sympathy. He was as automatically touchy about this as he was concerning hysteria. Not much would he say, but his few words had showed me that he harbored a deep-rooted, resentful opinion that the majority of womenfolk held their men responsible for *all* the consequences of reproduction!

Beside a number of the David Grief episodes, Jack wrote among other stories "The Prodigal Father," and "By the Turtles of Tasman" (both in "The Turtles of Tasman"), "The End of the Story," and "The Mexican" (in "The Night Born").

Much he enjoyed the horses—their characters and caprices: Prince, his sugar-tongue hanging out on all occa-sions, Prince the "Love-Horse," Jack called him, with his laughing eye and friendly hoof-shake and the pocket-seek-ing of his mischievous muzzle; Sonoma Maid, the excellent and wise; Gert the irascible outlaw who yet did her work and came to bury all the other three when Jack himself had gone; and Milda, variously dubbed the Rabbit, the Rat, the Manger-Glutton—Milda, who asked nothing of anybody but to let her do her work and win to her supper by the least circuitous route.

For the sake of any who would care to follow in our track, I briefly outline the same. But first, there was a trial-trip of one week from Glen Ellen to Petaluma; thence to Olima on Tamales Bay; Point Reyes, and the Light House, Willow Camp on the coast; from there on the wonderful coast drive and across Mt. Tamalpais' feet to Mill Valley. The long uninterrupted trip was as follows:

Glen Ellen to Santa Rosa, and Sebastopol where one sees Luther Burbank's flowering and fruiting fields, to Bo-dega Corners; Duncan's Mills; Cazadero; Fort Ross, on the coast, of historic interest; Gualala—where one may fish and boat on the river; Greenwood; Fort Bragg; Hardy; Usal; Moody's; Garberville; thence along Eel River, where deer come down to drink, to Dyerville. From this section the tourist may cut inland to the Hoopah Indian Reservation. This we did, by automobile and saddle, coming out down the Trinity and Klamath Rivers in a dugout with Indian ca-noemen to Requa by the sea; next, to Fortuna, with fishing and hunting and old Indians along the way; Eureka; Trini-dad; Kirkpatrick's. Crescent City, in the northwest corner of California, where one gathers jewels, agates of marvelous colorings, in the ocean sands; on to Smith River Corners, and into Oregon, to Colgrove's Mountain Ranch; Laurence's on Pistol River; Gold Beach, on Rogue River; Port Orford; Langlois; then to Bandon, Coos County, whence we struck inland to Coquille; Rock Creek; Murray's, Roseburg; Canyonville; Wolf Creek; Grant's Pass; Medford, with a motor trip to that marvel, Crater Lake; Ashland; down into California again,—Montague; Weed; driving within sight of grand Mt. Shasta; Dunsmuir; Le Moyne; Kennett; Redding; Red Bluff; Orland; Willows; Maxwell; Leesville; Lower Lake; Middleton; Calistoga—and home to Glen Ellen by way of the Petrified Forest.

One sparkling afternoon on the Bay of Eureka, I had an opportunity to observe my husband in a crucial moment of judgment and fearlessness. What a ringing challenge that man was to the courage of all (except the spiritually deaf, dumb, and blind), who were privileged to know him! How seldom he ever reached into his own vocabulary for the word *fear!* Burned into my memory is something he said early in our comradeship:

"I think I am really afraid of but thing—being hit over the head from behind.—Oh, not from fear of death—never! But to live with my brain addled—it's unthinkable!"

It was our pastime, while visiting in a luxurious houseboat, to go fishing or to sail down the harbor and, if not too rough, cross the bar and cruise a little way toward the blue Pacific horizon that was forever a receding Paradise. On this day, tacking up-bay on the satin swell, a big rakish power-launch, full speed ahead, came bearing down upon us. There was plenty of room, and Jack, knowing the sailboat's traditional right of way, naturally kept on his course, expecting to pass the other to port. But her pilot kept right on for us, and to avoid being sliced squarely amidship, Jack in a flash spun his wheel to starboard, to bring her up into the wind, while the other, who must have been dreaming, suddenly with terrified face swerved to his left and took with him the starboard corner of our stern rail.

It all happened in the space of three seconds, but there remains, *snap, snap,* one of the sharpest moving-pictures in my experience. At the last least instant, with the high knife-edge bow right upon us, I, the first law of existence automatically superseding any sentimental desire to be cloven in twain even in company with the spouse of my bosom, had jumped just forward of where the crash would occur. Turning as instantly as I landed, ready to dive if necessary, I took in Jack's incredibly quick action with the wheel, his cool, calm, fighting face, and heard, saw, and felt the splintering of the rail.

"You did exactly the right thing," he reassured my tentative inquiry. "I had my hands full, and did not have to worry about you. I had to stay at the wheel and do the only thing that could be done to save the sloop. . . . Some day, though," and he more than once warned me of this, "my curiosity in seeing the thing through is going to be my finish!" But I always banked on his mental and steel-springed physical alertness to save himself just short of annihilation.

So I rested fairly comfortably upon his opinion that I had done "the right thing," until one day in his Bad Year, 1913, when he, in a dreadful depth, brought up the action. It followed upon something I had just done. We had been driving behind a wicked roan gelding, of irreproachable breeding, who bore an evil reputation for running away and smashing things—several on the Ranch, including Eliza, had at various times been thrown out and injured. The horse, this afternoon, had balked, and plunged sidewise, cramping the buggy until the wheels cracked. Unless I could have the reins in my own hands, I preferred being in Jack's care to any driver I knew—so expert had he become. But we were in a tight pinch, and without warning I sprang to the ground and to the animal's head to straighten him out. It was wrong, I admit, and mortifying to the driver. I should have stayed beside him and "seen it through," as I had before and many times afterward. It was the cap-stone to a series of vexations to Jack, ending in one of his superb "disgusts" with the universe of which I was an important part; and he brought up the Eureka incident.

"But I *know* I am not a coward," I remonstrated to an accusation he had not voiced but which smoldered in his purple eyes. "And *you* know it, too, *you!* I've nerves, but never cowardice!"

Jack's retractions and apologies, generous if rare, were among the sweetest of the silken ties that bound us forever. And, looking back over it all, the two utterances of his that now mean the most to me are his early "You are more kin to me than any one I have ever known," and this next, apropos of I know not what, in the last conversation we were ever to hold—suddenly, as if from a full heart: "Thank God, you are not afraid of anything!"

Once more, on September 6, we took up the round at home—replete with all that love, keen interest in life, work, and friends could bring. Jack began the day with a few moments in the garden:

"Gorgeous, tropic flowers!" he would murmur delightedly over the flaunting goldfish, their long tails waving like lazy veils in the sunny water of the pool, its fountain bowl an old Indian stone mortar. "And how I love the all-night drip and plash of your tiny fountain!"

He cared less for flowers in general than most men do, or are willing to own. His was joy in a single bloom. If he was caught momentarily by a mass of blossoms, it would be for a definite idea connected with it—perhaps that it was in my arms, and gave me pleasure; or that it enhanced me in some way. I can see him at his desk near a doorway, writing, interrupted by the flame of my basketful of poppies or rosies crossing his vision, coloring the sunlight. And the glance would rest, and dwell, and soften—his deep-gray, wide eyes full of the love that was my wonder and glory and guerdon.

Everything was in full swing on the Ranch, and guests' voices were in the air.

"This is what I like," Jack would pause in a dictation to me at the typewriter. "While we are together, carrying on our work, they can do whatever they want. Look—I love the rail out there under the oak, with our horses tied, saddled and waiting. And there go two lovers on horseback for the trails; and a married pair for a hike. Others are playing cards in the living room, where I shall join them as soon as this letter is finished. . . And if you don't mind, Mate," his eyes begging the favor, "you take the crowd that's coming for dinner, over the Wolf House trail, because I have just *got* to get even with George for the walloping he gave me at pedro last night!—Listen to those girls chattering up in the fig-tree—and who's practising on the piano? Mate, do you *really* know how I love it all!" To this day, as a friend said, the house "still breathes of the sweetness of you two toward each other."

Some notes for future work, made about this time, illustrate how simple was his initial preparation:

"*Series of Stories.*

"Why not write a superb short story from each of a number of diverse places, and collect in book-form under some suitable title that conveys the idea 'from all the world.'? 'The Purple Sea' might make a good title."

"*Novel.*

"Why not a series of past and future novels? For No. 1, I could use 'Before Adam;' No. 2, 'Christ Novel;' No. 3, 'The Middle Ages;' No. 4, some great proletarian-bourgeoise conflict story of the present; No. 5, I could use 'The Iron Heel;' No. 6, 'The Far Future,' the perfected and perishing human race."

"*Farthest Distant.*

"Radium engines, etc., for energy,—See Atoms and Evolution, in Saleeby's 'The Cycle of Life.'

"Collision of dark body from out of space (not large), one-tenth size of sun. And earth learns of coming by perturbations of outer planet. Then rush the earth away from the sun.

"When earth travels through space, all must be inclosed; and they must use stored heat of some sort. The oceans freeze, etc. A great preparation. See Direction of Motion chapter by Herbert Spencer. The initial momentum they have. The momentum in a straight line that is altered to a curve around the sun by the pole of the sun. Nullify the pole of the sun, select the right moment, and sail off into space to reach nearest neighbor sun. They make some mistakes the first time. Something goes wrong with the machinery, and they dash around the second sun like a comet and return to the old sun. They figure it out on the way, do not check at old sun, and like a comet return to new sun, where they succeed in checking."

The material for the Christ novel above referred to Jack had been compiling for years; but in the Christ episode of "The Star Rover" he concentrated his long-sought data. When he read me, aboard the *Roamer,* that chapter of "The Star Rover," I asked him what of the Christ novel. "This will suffice," he said. "I shall not do the longer work."

Jesus Christ and Abraham Lincoln were names of praise upon his lips. Tolstoy said of Lincoln that he was a Christ in miniature. Jack London: "The two men I reverence most are Christ and Lincoln," and spoke of them with shining, worshipful eyes. And Stephen French sends me the following from a letter Jack wrote him: "I don't know whether Jesus Christ was a myth or not; but taking him just as I find him, just as I read him, I have two heroes—one is Jesus Christ, the other Abraham Lincoln."

Our main meal was at 12:30. This hour better suited our work and Ranch plans generally. At twelve the mail-sack—a substantial leather one bought before we sailed on the *Snark*—arrived at the back porch, and Nakata brought it to me to sort the contents. In the half-hour before dinner, Jack had glanced over the daily paper, read his letters, indicated replies on some of them for my guidance, and laid the more important ones in their wire tray, one of many such nested on a small table beside the Oregon myrtle rolltop desk where he transacted business. I always endeavored to have his ten pages of hand-written manuscript transcribed—an average of two and a half typewritten letter-size sheets—before the second gong (an ancient concave disk of Korean brass) belled the fifteen-minute call to table. Jack implored me to be on time to the minute's tick, and attend to seating the guests, so that he might work to the last moment.

In many minds, I am sure, still lives the vision of the hale, big-hearted man of God's out-of-doors, the beardless patriarch, his curls rumpled, like as not the green visor unremoved, pattering with that quick, light step along the narrow vine-shaded porch, through the screened doorway and the length of the tapa-brown room to his seat in the solid red koa chair at the head of the table. "Here comes a real man!" was the prevailing sentiment.

How he doted upon that board with its long double-row of friendly faces turned in greeting, ever ready with another plate and portion! It was his ideal—carried from old days with the Strunskys'. "In Jack's house," one writes me, "I met the most interesting people of my life and of the world." And perhaps, while we fell to our portions, before his own was tasted he would read aloud newspaper items or newly received letters; or he might launch out in a fine rage of his eternal enthusiasm, upon some theme that claimed him, or strike into argument, whipped hot out of his seething brain and heart. Always there was in him the potent urge to gather all about him into knowledge of whatever claimed his attention. Years only added to his capacity to function in every potentiality. There were no numb or inactive surfaces in his make-up, mentally, physically. He reached in all directions, to play, to work, to thought, to sensation. His face, smiling, cracked with thought-wrinkles, weather-wrinkles, laughter-wrinkles.

At no time did he have more than a few gray hairs; and his hands, to his pride, were very firm, showing no dilated arteries. "One is as young as one's arteries," he was fond of saying. How he would pluck at the air with those young hands, in unconscious pantomime groping for illustration for the means that no man born of woman has ever been able to command by which to express a complete concept.

Many were more impressed by his eyes than any other feature or characteristic. "All steel and dew," one man wrote of them. "All sweetness and hidden ferocity . . . as though they masked profound and terrible secrets . . . eyes common enough, mayhap, when the world was young. . . . Alert, as though to him life were a constant battle-field."

They were eyes that look into one, and through and beyond—as if what they saw on the surface, in one's own, led his into the deeps behind, into the brain, conscious and unconscious and far behind again into the intelligence of the race down through all the drift of the human. Gray, or iris-blue, they were when mild, the large pupils giving them a splendid, brilliant darkness; but let him be angry, instantly they went cold, metallic, the enormous pupils narrowing to bitter points.

He had a way, sometimes, in common with his sister, of apparently not listening while his eyes looked through one, patently seeing beyond. "You haven't heard a word!" I would remonstrate. "Oh, yes, I have," he would return, and repeat a sentence or two. "That doesn't prove anything," I would challenge. "No, my dear, I will give you your whole argument," and he would disprove my assertion.

Another likeness of Jack's to Eliza was expressed by a woman who had heard her speak in public: "When others get up and talk, we *listen* to what they say; when *you* get up and talk, we *do* what you say!"

How his "living language" of colloquialisms and slang pierces time when we call up the arguments that flew about the table like missiles in a game! "Come on, now—let's tell sad stories of the deaths of kings!—Go to it; the day is young, and we're a long time dead!" "Oh, it's only my shorthand," he would mourn, cutting short to a conclusion, speaking to blank faces, perhaps. Or, when he had perhaps let himself go on some subject near his heart: "You miss me—you miss me totally," in distressed tone to a solemn egotist who had dared his logic; or, "There you go—trying to pass the buck; now stick to the point." Or, "Ah—ah— but you've missed the factors. Connotations, man, factors!" Then, "Still well, but not so well." Parsimonious was a word he enjoyed for a time: "I'm parsimonious!" he would cry in a discussion, "You'll have to show me—I don't believe anything till I'm shown. I'm parsimonious!" "But to get back: As I was saying when I was so rudely interrupted," with a twinkle; "I'm afraid I was always an extremist; so don't mind my violence." And suddenly, in the face of non-understanding: "I'm boring you?" "Piffle!" he would exclaim, full-tilt; and irascibly, "Silly! You mean to say, then . . . ?" Showing up the muddlement of a wrathful and impotent opponent. "No? Then what do you mean to say? We must agree upon a working vocabulary for a basis." "What do I think about so and so? Well, if anybody should drive up in a hack and ask me, I'd say . . ." When something was well said or done, he might praise, "Fine and dandy!" or "Booful, my dear!" But always he hewed to the core of the truth of things, and his meanings were clear to any who would clearly listen. Some poet has expressed my own sentiment:

> ". . . well I love to see
> That gracious smile light up your face, and hear
> Your wonderful words, that all mean verily
> The thing they seem to mean."

Once Jack wrote me: "Remember, dear, not only in being true to myself am I true to you, but before I knew you I was true to myself. I have always been true to myself. This is my highest concept of right conduct. It is my measure of right conduct.''

One prejudiced person, who rather against his will had been brought by a mutual acquaintance, had this to say:

"That friend of yours, Jack London, is all and more than you said. He made me love him even when I quarreled with him. Why, he is a marvel—I never saw his like.''

Another remembered Jack, the comrade-man, arm around the shoulder of a friend:

"At times he was funnily boyish, then in a flash splendidly exalted, pouring forth in his glad way his knowledge of life, his love of life, his sympathy with life, his creative force, his open-minded embrace of the most vital in life; he, life itself, impregnated by ripeness of thought and feeling most unusual for his years.'' And still again: "What a warmth there was about this dear fellow! Sunshine followed him everywhere. . . . Even in his harshest moments, his fine, open smile would burst forth. Never have I seen such faith, resultant of research and understanding, coupled with such doubt of the purely dreamy optimistic or the unproven.''

To the youngsters of his race, entranced with his genuineness and utter lack of swank, "He was a prince!'' And one associate honored him with this: "Jack London was a great man; but his friends loved him just the same.''

So much for his own countrymen; and how I wish the English, in greater numbers, could have known him personally. One, who had and appreciated that privilege, said: "I had to come to his own land to hear a word in his disfavor—though I will say it came not from any who knew him at first hand.''

One illuminating little flare of Jack's burns up in memory. Some one at table used the contraction "Frisco,'' and a very young miss rushed headlong into trouble with her host: "Oh, *don't say Frisco!* Say *San Francisco!*"

Jack landed full wroth into the breach:

"Let *Frisco* alone, you! We love the western tang of it, we oldsters who knew her by that name before you were dry behind the ears!—*Frisco, Frisco* . . ." he rolled it sweetly on his tongue. And mingled in the fiber of his tone were scorn and pity for the greenness of her who jeered at what seemed to her the common crudity of a sobriquet the very glorious roughness of which symbolized what the old town had stood for of romance in the days Jack London had known, so dear to all who knew it then. He would seldom go far out of his way to pronounce correctly a foreign word: "You know what I mean, don't you?—that's the main thing!"

Despite that Jack London was an excellent subject, and was widely photographed, many have written to know of his appearance and proportions. Among some forgotten souvenirs I have come upon a typewritten record, made up at Jack's suggestion, of our comparative measurements. His are appended:

JACK

Height	5 ft. 9 in.
Above knee	15½ in.
Below knee	12½ in.
Calf	14 in.
Ankle	8¾ in.
Wrist	6½ in.
Forearm	11 in.
Biceps (relaxed)	12 in.
Biceps (tensed)	13 in.
Neck	14⅞ in.
Chest	40 in.
Waist	36 in.
Size of Hat	7⅛ in.
Size of Shoe	Number 7

Near the end of the midday meal, Nakata would lay beside my plate a note-pad and pencil, upon which it was my daily task to figure the horses, saddles, bridles, and riding costumes of transient guests from two to a dozen—and, in season, as many swimming-suits beside. Or, the four-in-hand would be wanted, and in his wide stiff-rim Stetson, white soft shirt and khaki trousers, Jack, noisy, gay, swinging the jingling, fleeing leaders hither and thither in his blossoming valley, would be seen pointing out the beauties of it to a packed wagonful of rapt, if sometimes apprehensive, men and women and children, enlarging to them upon the character and idiosyncracies of each horse. A neighboring editor saw him—"Big, boyish, warm-hearted . . . Over our hills with the sunshine of his favorite vale shining upon his head he often rode or drove in carefree style the beautiful horses he loved. His manner cordial, his greeting cheery, it was little wonder he became the pal of all, and no matter how big his triumphs he was never the conceited genius but always the genial friend and natural neighbor."

As Jack himself put it: "I'm so afraid of slighting somebody I ought to recognize in the neighborhood, that I'm going to speak in good old country fashion to everybody I meet!" which became his habit; and many the prim provincial lady, loitering in her dusty old buggy under the hot midsummer sky, who sat up suddenly from daydreams to stare, first, at the abounding good cheer of the robust young driver avalanching by, and tipping a gray cowboy brim so respectfully; and, next, to melt into smiles under the warmth of the neighborly apparition.

That year the Sierra Club made its first pilgrimage to the Jack London Ranch. Also it marked the employment of Jack's first paroled man from the State Penitentiary at San Quentin. Jack's principles in general, and in particular his own Buffalo experience, had for years made him eager to give a chance to those unfortunate enough to have come inside the forbidding gray battlements so often seen from the deck of the *Roamer*. For years, on our place, these men came and, went. As for his opinion of ameliorating prison conditions, he wrote:

"I have little faith in prison reform. Prisons are merely a symptom. When you try to reform them, you try to reform symptoms. The disease remains."

One sojourner with us, as houseguest, was Ed. Morrell, whose astounding experience, growing out of his connection with the notorious outlaws, Sontag and Evans, was the motif for Jack's subsequent novel, "The Star Rover." I well recall Jack, fairly frothing over the straitjacket scars Morrell had been revealing, lurching in, spilling over with emotion, to tell me what he had seen.

While the foregoing busy season went forward, the Bay newspapers had Jack attending the birthday party, in Monterey County, of some one's lapdog—"Fluffy Ruffles!"

Sometimes guiding our friends on the steep trails, or riding hand in hand to look over progress at the Wolf House, we talked of the big schooner that some day we should rig out and start for another round-the-world voyage. There was never any hint of dullness in the present nor fear of future boredom.

Four books were issued in 1911: "When God Laughs," "Adventure," "The Cruise of the Snark," and "South Sea Tales." Of the inscriptions I choose two—this, in the spring, from "When God Laughs":

"My Own Dear Woman:

"The years come, and the years go, our friends come and go, some few of them stick—and you and I stick better than any or all."

From "South Sea Tales," in the fall:

"Dearest Mate-Woman:

"And can we say, after all these years, that we have ever been happier than we are happy right now?"

There was much to do—every waking moment. The thing was, to find time to sleep; yet we regarded that as rather a leisurely year—perhaps because we did not go very far from home. My diary records: "Mate works in the evenings. He is so very busy. It makes my own head tired when I think of all his head must keep track of."

It was in the late afternoon of October 10, 1911, that Jack returned on horseback from Glen Ellen, two miles from the house, and announced with solemnity that he had just cast his vote for Woman Suffrage. "Woman Suffrage," he expounded, "means Prohibition; and that is why I voted for it. The normal woman," he went on, "has no liking for alcohol; through all the ages John Barleycorn has hurt her heart. All that will be changed when she wins political power."

This scene stands forever in the Foreword of "John Barleycorn," the book in which Jack London focused his sensations and viewpoints in regard to alcohol.

Some time after its publication, he received the letter below:

"Oakland, California, May 27th, 1916.
"Mr. Jack London,
   "Glen Ellen, Calif.
"Dear Friend:
   "I take this opportunity in forwarding these few lines reminding you of the coincidences which happened in Our Half Day along the Oakland estuary.
   "I understand that my name Spider Healy, along with Soup Kennedy, Boche Pierrati, Joe Goose and M. J. Hynold has been heralded all over these United States and the rest of the world and that you have realized an abundance of wealth both in moving pictures and a book known as John Barleycorn. If you were to visit the old haunts of the oyster pirates of the present time you would find in a very decrepid condition. Financially and otherwise Soup Kennedy who you described in your book as a worthy opponent of Scratch Nelson has been following the sea as a means of livelyhood. But as time and tide wait for no man he has over-

looked an opportunity of acquiring a vast wad. Many times we have sat upon the deck listening to the strains of the chanties, hoping that a time would arrive when we would again get together either to talk of the old times or to make arrangements to go salmon fishing to Alaska or sealing to the Bonin Islands.

"I was surprised on more than one occasion to have individuals acost me on the street asking if my name was the Spider Healy of John Barleycorn fame. On answering in the affirmative I was reminded that my part of your John Barleycorn was one of most importance.

"There is not a day passes that tourists from the far east and all parts of the United States do not stand and gaze with astonishment at the old relics of the old St. Louis House and the first and last chance saloon where you have gained renown and fortune. A few nights ago at the foot of Franklin Street at which place you weighed anchor many a time I sat and listened to the strains of some of the Chanties of which you are quite familiar. Again it brought to mind the old day when you and I heard the same songs. (Lorenze was no sailor) (Blow the man down) (Whisky for my Johnies) (we'll pay Pattie Doyle for his boots) and (Bound for the Rio Grande and sailin Home to merry England town.)

"In conclusion the main object of calling your attention to these facts is to let you know the conditions that now exist with the pirates whose names have made you fames, in that book & plan known as John Barleycorn. Johnie Hynold and Joe Viergue are the only ones who accumulated a wad and I dare say buried it like a dog did his bone. To get a quarter from a turnip, is like extracting the same from these men.

"Johnie Hynold is estimated according to Bradstreet's to be worth about one hundred and sixty thousand dollars and Joe Viergue as you know as accumulating his fortune on our hard earned coin.

"I belief that Soup Kennedy has seen his last days as a seaman. Strength gone, health gone and eyesight failing what was once a big rough rovish stalwart fellow has dwindled to a mere nothing.

"I was talking to him a few days ago and in asking him what the matter was, he told me that a saw bones told him that his life was going to flicker out in a short time. He stated that it was not necessary for the old boy to put him on. On more than one occasion

I felt my heart slip a cog or two. Now you know Jack when your heart slips a cog or two there is no possible way to replace it by good smooth running gear. Soup is very much enthused when I told him that I was about to ask you for a small bit of assistance. I do not know what you are estimated to be by Bradstreet or Wall Street but I certainly would be ever grateful if you generously would be aroused to such an extent that it would be possible for you to loosen up and forward at once a check with a substantial amount to pull Soup and myself out of a hole.

"Now if you want to be a good fellow and have your name heralded as such along the water front where your childhood days were spent with the rest of the pirates you will please grant this request at once.

"Your old pals,
"Soup Kennedy,

"P. S.—We are living at present 416-2nd St. Oakland, Cal., and will await your earliest convenience, a reply, also that substantial check, Joe Goose is on his last legs.

"Spider."

As Jack did not invariably let his left hand know what his right hand did, I do not know what his reply, if any, was to the foregoing.

Jack's aversion to spending Christmas in the prescribed way caused many an outing to begin on the twenty-fourth of December. And so, that date in 1911 saw Mr. Kisich opening a bottle of champagne in his "Saddle Rock," to speed us on the way east. We slept aboard the Western Pacific Limited that night, headed for New York City. En route on the Denver and Rio Grande we stopped over at Salt Lake City to foregather with my friends the Harry Culmers; and among other trips, Jack and I went on a little pilgrimage to Fort Douglas, where in the '60's my father, Captain Willard Kittredge, had served under General Connor, his duties including those of Provost Marshal of the beautiful, romantic city.

The New Year was celebrated in New York. "And this time," Jack assured me, "we'll go home by way of Cape Horn."

Almost any passage in our companionship I contemplate with more pleasure than that 1912 winter in 'Gotham." The trip had been one of our happiest; but, once off the train, and his enthusiasm expressed over the new Pennsylvania Station, it was the old story. The city reached into him and plucked to light the least admirable of his qualities. Out of the wholesome blisses of his western life, he plunged into a condition that negated his accustomed personality. Nine-tenths of the two months' time we made our headquarters in Morningside Park East, he was not his usual self. During the other tenth, cropping up in unexpected moments, the manifestation of his dearest self and his love were never warmer nor more illuminating.

Coincident with our arrival, he warned that he was going to invite one last, thoroughgoing bout with alcohol, and that when he should sail on the Cape Horn voyage, it was to be "Good-by, forever, to John Barleycorn." To me, the promised end was worth the threatened means; and my comprehension and acceptance of his intention were appreciated. But I could not fail to regret that new friends should know and base their judgment of Jack London upon this unfortunate phenomenon of him.

In that Jack London, drunken, was not as other drunken men, the majority of those who contacted with him during a period of what he termed his "white logic" deemed they knew the true, sober Jack London in all his panoply of normal brilliance. Never, in all my years with him, did I see him tipsy. An old acquaintance of Jack's, asked concerning this phase of the author of "John Barleycorn," laughed: "I have known him more or less intimately for ten years, and I have never seen him intoxicated." And Jack himself: "I was never interested enough in cocktails to know how they were made." Except in rare cases when a single drink acutely poisoned his stomach, upon him the effect of alcoholic stimulus was to render preternaturally active an already superactive mind. Keen, hair-splitting in controversy, reckless of mind and body, sweeping all before him, passionately intolerant of man or woman who challenged his way—all this and more was he in his "white logic" extreme. This unnatural state, combined with the depression New York invariably put upon him, was dangerous. And there was wanting—and how were others to know?—the splendid, healthy charm of the big man he was, the finer potency of his moral integrities, the square truth of his fundamental faiths and their observance. Much, at the time, I sensed, watching the calendar day by day as the day of release from New York approached; more, beyond guesswork, afterward came to light. But I knew my man, and, content or not, waited, remembering that I had never yet waited in vain to welcome back the sane and lovable boy. More and more deeply am I convinced that it is not the irks of the wayside that should count in one's valuing of events or individuals. I knew my man. I could only wish that some others had had such vision for crises like these in Jack London's contact with his kind.

"New York is one wild maelstrom," he saw it that year. "Rome in its wildest days could not compare with this city. Here, making an impression is more important than making good." And I take an item from the N. Y. *Evening World*, which throws light upon another observation of Jack's:

"In this great city woman does not care for woman friends. She will boldly tell you so. She does not trust them. . . . The average so-called wise woman of New York City will not introduce her attractive men friends to her women friends."

There comes to me, across the years, something for many years forgotten. He had said to me, very early in our marriage:

"Don't forget what I have been and been through. There may, mark, I only say *may* come times when the temptation to 'drift'—for an hour, or a day, will stick up its head; and I may follow. I have drifted all my life—curiosity, that burning desire to *know*. Yet, I have knocked the edge off my curiosity about a lot of things. Still——" in his honesty he anticipated the possibility.

Once, after the baby had 'been lost to him, I asked innocently, "Where been?" To which, with a teasing look, he replied, "Oh, *pirooting*, my dear—I'll tell you, maybe, when we're in our seventies!" But long afterward, when some association of ideas called for it, there would leak out, among other hinted adventurings, the story of a hard-fought game of cards in a water-front public house in San Francisco, or a weird experience of one sort or another with some nameless waif he had elected to trot around with for an afternoon or evening.

Referring to John Barleycorn and his mental condition in New York, I once asked him if it would not have been better for me to withdraw from him at such times—even to letting him go alone: "No," he reassured. "You did exactly as you should have done. If you had left me, I don't know *what* I should have done."

Another chance affair he divulged when in reminiscent mood. One afternoon, in the Forum Cigar store in Oakland, he ran across a man who knew an old Klondike acquaintance, whose address he gave. Some mistake was made, and Jack found himself in a curious little pocket. A door, answering his ring, let him into a hall at the foot of a narrow stairway. From the upper end a handsome, flashy woman called down:

"Hello, you Jack London!"

"How do you know I am Jack London?" he countered in his surprise at her expectant tone, and mounted several steps to have a look at her.

The woman peered down at him, then drew back, fear

and puzzlement in every line and movement. To cut the tale short, it appeared that the lady had been keeping company for some time with a man who called himself Jack London, whom she had quite believed was the simon-pure article enjoying a double life. She assured Jack that he bore a strong resemblance to her friend.

Once, that winter of 1912 in New York, he had said with smoldering eyes: "If you've got the nerve, I'll take *you* drifting! It would be great fun. One lark would be to board a subway, any subway, and run to the very end of the line; get off, start in any direction, and ring the bell of the first house that took our fancy. Say 'Good evening,' cordially, to whoever came to the door, and *get inside,* talking a blue streak, acting as if we were old friends. Of course, they'd think we were crazy, and the more familiar we got, the more excited they. The police would be summoned——" he broke off in a giggle that was the only familiar thing in his manner, "—but what's the use?" he finished gloomily. "You wouldn't be game for a mess like that! but think of the fun!" and he regarded me quizzically, as if calculating the experiment he was making upon the stuff of my character. I flatly declined to be lured by this or kindred prospects. He knew I would go with him anywhere and back again, but not when he was in this extreme, unnormal state. So he resumed his "pirooting"— I really do not know how to spell the word, and the dictionary is no help.

A wonder it is that nothing happened to him. Settling in a barber's chair one day, he noticed the man was shaking as with violent ague:

"What's the idea?" he inquired kindly. "Made a night of it?"

"Several," the barber chattered under his breath, glancing warily around. "Don't know how I'm g-g-going to shave you or anybody."

And Jack, with the razor making oblique stabs against his windpipe, sensing the wielder was in danger of losing his job, told him to "go through the motions, anyway," and he would make no fuss.

"But, man," I expostulated, "you might have had your throat cut!"

"Oh, well," he said, "he was in an awful state, and I couldn't get up and go out and give him away to the whole shop. I didn't enjoy it a bit, I assure you!"

I have speculated if he ever thought to liken his act to that of Robert Louis Stevenson, who is reputed to have accepted and smoked a half-consumed cigarette from a leper, rather than cause affront. Jack had often brought up that story to illustrate his conception of gameness.

He would not take care of himself. Coughing badly, week in and week out, he declined to wear other than thin "low-cuts" with sheerest of silk socks. "Don't bother—I'll be all right," was all that I, or the small fatherly Nakata, could elicit.

The New York *World,* during the Equitable Life fire, sent him a badge that gave him the freedom of that precinct of ice and flame; but I, who should have liked to share this real adventure, was barred by my sex.

Dozens of plays we attended together; a dozen or so books Jack read aloud to me; and there was a trip to Schenectady, where Frank Hancock, whom we had met in New Orleans, introduced us to Professor Charles P. Steinmetz, genius of the General Electric, and took us through the leviathan plant; for Jack was always sharp-set to study the enormous achievements of the human in harnessing force. At Schenectady we were guests of Dr. and Mrs. Cyrus R. Baker. In their home Jack treated his soul to an orgy of music, for Mrs. Baker had been on the grand opera stage, and her husband was a masterly accompanist. Another out-of-town week-end was spent at Short Beach,

Connecticut, with Mr. and Mrs. Robert Wilcox—Ella Wheeler—of our Jamaica memories.

Attending a tea at the Liberal Club on January 27, 1912, given in his honor, Jack was asked by a socialist if he was a "Direct Actionist." Jack regarded his questioner cautiously for a moment, then asked him to define what he meant by the term. "One who favors strikes and the like," was the definition:

"Yes, I am a direct actionist, as you call it. Direct Action, as I understand it, is teaching us the true fighting spirit, which is going to be the greatest asset the people of the masses possess when the great struggle finally comes between them and their present masters. There is a hard time coming. We shall have a big fight, but the masses will conquer in the end, because they form the stronger and more stable body. The story of the struggle will be written in blood. The ruling classes will not let go until it is."

Some one asked him to give his ideas on the subject of universal peace. He replied that there would come a time when all human contention would be settled amicably with the aid of referees, but that we must use our fighting spirit to bring about this condition. We must fight to stop war.

"What will you do with the fighting spirit when this ideal state comes to pass?" some one asked.

"Dig potatoes with it!" Jack shouted vehemently. "Write books with it, govern with it. By turning this energy, now wasted in building up great armaments with which to kill, into civilized channels, civilization would mean twice what it does now."

Of writing on his novel, "The Valley of the Moon," he did almost none; but he transacted considerable business with publishers. He had left the Macmillans, and contracted with Doubleday, Page & Company for "A Son of the Sun." The Century Company brought out the next four volumes—"Smoke Bellew Tales," "The Night Born," "The Abysmal Brute," and "John Barleycorn." In the fall of 1913, with "The Valley of the Moon," Jack resumed relations with the Macmillans, and continued thenceforth with that house.

One writer whose company greatly illumined our sojourn in New York was Michael Monahan; and Jack and Richard Le Gallienne got together most pleasantly. Several afternoons were set aside for receiving callers. Alexander Berkman came to see Jack, for the purpose of enlisting his aid in the matter of a Preface to his "Prison Memoirs of an Anarchist." The two "scrapped" amiably, and Jack wrote the Preface, but, in the nature of their radical differences, it was repudiated by Berkman and his associate anarchists. I shall include the Preface in some future collection, together with Jack's comments upon Berkman's refusal, written several years thereafter. "Alexander Berkman," I quote from the latter document, "could not see his way to using my introduction, and got some one else to write a more sympathetic one for him. Also, socially, comradely, he has forgotten my existence ever since."

Late that year, asked by an Oakland *Tribune* man if, with his interest in the economic aspect of the world, he did not find New York the best place for his observations, Jack cried:

"Great Scott, no, no! I must have the open, the big open. No big city for me, and above all not New York. I think it is the cocksure feeling of superiority which the people of the metropolis feel over the rest of the country that makes me rage—when it does not remind me of something near home. Next to my Ranch is an institution for the feebleminded. When some of the inmates who are not as feeble minded as the rest, are through with their chores, one or another of them will shake his or her head and say with great thankfulness: "Well, heaven be praised, I'm not feebleminded."

"And yet," he concluded benevolently, "I feel that

way about New Yorkers only when I see or think of them collectively. When I meet them one by one it is another story.''

This reminds one of what R. L. S. said, as remembered by Robert S. Lysaght, to a similar question:

''It is all the better for a man's work, if he wants it to be good and not merely popular. Human nature is always the same, and you see and understand it better when you are standing outside the crowd.''

CHAPTER XXXV

CAPE HORN VOYAGE

1912

FOUR of us sailed around Cape Horn, from Baltimore to Seattle—Jack London, wife, Nakata, and an engaging fox terrier puppy, three months foolish, who was destined to play an important part in Jack's household till the end of life. "Possum" we named him, in memory of a rough-coated little Irish gentleman we had known in the South Seas—brother to dear Peggy of the *Snark*, immortal in our hearts. The fox Possum figures in "The Valley of the Moon," which was resumed and completed on the Cape Horn voyage, and also in "The Mutiny of the Elsinore," this book being an out-growth of that experience on a windjammer. Besides "The Valley of the Moon," Jack made copious notes for "John Barleycorn," and wrote a short sea story, "The Tar Pot," published serially as "The Captain of the Susan Drew," and not yet collected in book form.

It was a very subdued, much-himself Jack London who stopped over with me in Philadelphia en route to Baltimore to take ship. And Philadelphia unconsciously perpetrated a classic joke on itself: without knowing, it entertained for three days at the leading hotel "America's most advertised writer." It seemed so strange that I had no accustomed duties to perform in the way of answering telephone calls from reporters in the lobby! For not one ever discovered the sprawling signature in the hotel register. The silence of the brotherhood of scribes was certainly not due to any boycott on Jack London, for they had hitherto appeared unanimously kind to his work.

The morning of our sailing from Baltimore, on March 2, 1912, as I sat alone writing my farewell letters home, the door opened and I heard Jack in colloquy with Nakata. I caught the words, in a giggly whisper, "Wait till Mrs. London sees me!" Something told me what I should behold, and I refrained from raising my eyes until obliged to do so. He had long threatened to do it, but until then had withheld the act because of my pleading. His head was as naked as a billiard ball. I looked him over with assumed poise, and resumed my writing. Jack tittered. I said "Yes, I see; but it isn't funny." Jack tittered again. "But it isn't funny," I repeated, beginning to lose hold of myself. "Oh, now, don't feel badly, Mate Woman," he began, for my voice was becoming unsteady, I know. "It is such a good rest for my head—I often did it in the old days, at sea and around."

It was the last straw in a hard winter, to mix a metaphor. I wept uncontrolledly for nearly three hours. There is a photograph of the pair of us, taken that day beside Edgar Allen Poe's monument, in which a very heavily coated Jack London, hat pulled down most unbecomingly over a chill scalp, stands with a woman who tries to hide swollen eyes and forlorn mouth in a new set of very handsome red fox. Jack looked apprehensive when I remarked that my own head needed a rest, and started for the scissors. But I only sheared off eight inches. I did not again look directly at Jack until there was at least half an inch of hair on his head.

The *Dirigo*, 3000 tons net registered, seventeen years old, had been the first steel ship launched by the famous Sewalls of Bath, Maine. She was technically a four-masted barque. Jack chose the *Dirigo* over a much newer clipper for the reason that she carried skysails—fast becoming obsolete. "And how I'd like to take you around the Horn on a ship with *moonsails!*" he lamented the impossibility.

Captain Omar Chapman, of Newcastle, Maine, was one of the fast disappearing type of lean New England aristocrat, who always presented himself on deck immaculately attired, his especial hobbies fine hats and cravats. His quiet Yankee humor extended to these little foibles and a frank contempt for the common clay of modern deep-water sailors. The calm kingliness of his character was in cool contrast to that of the Mate, Fred Mortimer, hot-hearted, determined, all-around efficient driver of a crew that was composed, with a few exceptions well along in years, of landlubbers and weaklings.

Imagine our surprise to learn that Captain Warren, of the *Snark,* had applied for the berth of second officer, although in ignorance of our presence in the ship. As surprising was the fact that the man who was accepted bore the same name!

We paid $1000.00 for our passage, and, since such vessels carry no passenger license, had to sign on the articles, Jack as third mate, myself as stewardess, and Nakata as cabin-boy. It must have been attributable to Yankee thrift that, when it became known we traveled with a man, no cabin boy was taken along. Therefore many duties aft fell to our private servant, over and above his service to Jack and me, and Nakata put up with the gratuitous injustice with good grace rather than create unpleasantness.

The *Dirigo* stood out to sea in an abating icy gale that had held her bound for exasperating weeks. Rough and bitter cold it was, but nothing mattered to me except the fact that land was left behind, in prospect long months of blissful sea life with its cleansing simplicities.

In all the one hundred and forty-eight days, our eyes rested on land but once—or in one brief period of two or three days—literally land's-end, the end of the earth, the island of Cape Horn itself, with the continuous mainland

and islands. Even Diego Ramirez, sinister finger of stone to the south of the Continent, became visible in the war of water and cloud.

"Cape Horn on the starboard bow!" on May 10, was the most exciting tocsin, next to a savage war conch, I had ever awakened to.

"Gee—you folks are lucky!" Mr. Mortimer exclaimed, as, wrapped in heavy coats, we clung to the poop-rail and actually gazed upon the Cape. "I tell you, I've made this passage more times than I can remember, and I haven't laid eyes on that there island since 1882! The fog has never raised." And the day before, conditions being favorable for the risky feat, the Captain had been able to reduce time by passing through the Straits of Lemaire, instead of going around Staten Island. It was exciting business, made more breathless by sight of a great wreck, standing stark upright in her doom of shallow water off the mainland.

Our farthest south was Lat. 57° 32', Lon. 67° 28'. And though we had some little difficulty "making westing" and were driven back time and again, our traverse "from 50 to 50" was but fifteen days, which is almost better than a master mariner dare hope.

"How could you endure such a life!" women a-many have said to me. There was no single moment of wearisomeness to either Jack or me. Think of the industrious working hours—even I, suddenly inspired by one of the anecdotes from Captain or officers, wrote a sea yarn, "The Wheel," afterwards published at a round price by a newspaper syndicate. He had been much surprised and delighted when, without warning or comment, I laid my manuscript with his night-reading. And after I had benefited by suggestions from him: "It's quite good enough for you to go ahead and market!" he advised to my astonishment.

For at least three hours daily, on deck in fine weather,

otherwise sitting below on his high bunk with a bright "angle-lamp" at either end, Jack read aloud while I embroidered a new supply of fine lingerie. We read everything from Chinese lore to Robert W. Chambers. "And for once," my companion grinned, "I've time to read Sue's 'Wandering Jew.' I never could 'see' the time for it before."

Oh, the vivifying salt air, and the sea-food—good old "salt horse" and beef tongue, and the cook's inspired concoctions of tinned dainties! Captain Chapman had brought along a well-stocked hencoop solely because there was to be a woman aboard; but after he had been taken mysteriously ill the day before sighting the Horn, the fresh eggs had been a boon. Indeed, he lived many weeks because of the whites of eggs I was able to serve him; but he died two days after arriving at Seattle—and alas, before his wife could come to him from Maine. Cancer of the stomach, the doctors diagnosed. I spent a whole night, in the hotel, sadly enough, but glad of my detailed notes, writing Mrs. Chapman a log of the voyage from the day her husband was stricken.

So placidly and promptly his old self was Jack at sea, that I, slowly recuperating from acute nerve-strain, contemplated him with the amazement women must ever feel toward certain phases of their menfolk. My diary exclaims in wonder: "I do believe the man has utterly forgotten New York and its abominations!" But later, when I had hurt a finger, and developed a "run-around" that held me sleepless through nights of pain, his devotion seemed to carry a new note, and there were moments when I saw float up through the deeps of his eyes a knowledge of all that those weary eight weeks had meant to me.

The Master and Jack gathered fuel for everlasting fun at my expense. Two long connecting staterooms had been fitted up for us, that we might have separate bunks. It was to general systemic upset that I attributed an annoying attack of *hives* that followed sailing. With tin upon tin of cream of tartar from the ship's galley my offended stomach was dosed; I tried sleeping all over the vessel aft— in the main cabin, and even in the chart-room, where I seemed to rest the best. And the consumption of cream of tartar and sympathy in the cabin went on apace. Then a suspicion began to dawn in the Captain, which precipitated an investigation of my freshly painted wooden bunk. The secret was out. All the scrubbing and painting and fumigation had failed to dislodge the last of a nest of the ubiquitous bed-bug that a ship is never able quite to eradicate. A broad grin was evident from stem to stern of the *Dirigo* the day a young sailor had finally eradicated the pest, and I never heard the last of my "hives."

Would you pursue beauty indescribable, go to sea on a wind-jammer. I know no more exalted moments than when, a hundred miles off the coast of Brazil I have set my face to the four quarters of the heavens, upon which were painted as many astounding sunsets, with a heavy moon lifting to spill thick silver in a fading copper sea; or have clung in the eyes of her, the great steel body of the ship plunging enormously onward among the night-green rollers of her moonlit highway, her orderly forest of masts swaying, swerving, to the weight of full sails—gargantuan pearls, hard and bright, strung to the loftiest spars of the golden masts, white-gleaming in the very witchery of moonlight that transfigures all their majesty into the immateriality of a vision. Masefield knows it all:

"I have heard the song of the blossoms and the old chant of the sea,
And seen strange lands from under the arched white sails of ships."

How could I live such a life? Woe is me—how can I live without it!

Night after night, fair weather or foul—and it was all

of a magnificence, dead calm or great guns blowing—I took
a note-book and pencil to the poop hatch, and painted, as
well as I could in words, the sunsets and their mirrored
reflections on the vast dome. Bits of these "sketches"
are in "The Mutiny of the Elsinore." On a day I may
come upon the rest among Jack's own notes, and drop an
hour from a busy dozen to find my feet again treading the
deck or the fore-and-aft bridge of the *Dirigo*, stately and
beautiful moving house of ocean, now, along with our old
friend the *Tymeric*, at one with the slime. For the Huns
got them both. I would that mermen and mermaids could
people them for ay!

For exercise we boxed lustily, trained and played with
the puppy, and climbed into the "top" of the mainmast—
the first foot-hold of the same above deck, reached by precarious, lurching way of the shrouds from the rail. In Jack's
pocket was a book, in mine my embroidery. Here, remote,
ecstatic, above the "wrinkled sea" and the slender fabric
of steel, we lived some of our finest hours, enthralled by
the recurrent miracle of unbored days, love ever regenerate,
and contemplation of our unwasted years.

Once around the Horn, Jack took to hooking albatross,
catching quite a number. Some were liberated, but several
he kept. I still have the skins—twelve feet from tip to tip,
if I remember aright.

One of his activities was pulling teeth for the crew—
to say nothing of assisting Possum to shed her puppy-
molars which, in lack of normal food and bones, were
troublesome in letting go. For Jack had not forgotten to
bring along his *Snark* dentistry case.

The first news of an almost forgotten world in five
months was of the *Titanic* disaster, and, next, that our old
acquaintance, President Alfaro of Ecuador, and his son (a
West Point man) had been murdered in Quito and their
headless bodies dragged through the streets.

And would any one know what Jack London thought

of "enduring such a life," half a year away from the land spaces of the world:

"Mate," he said in all earnestness, as the dear, gray, battered hull towed up Puget Sound, looking pensively at the sailors aloft making all snug, "I wish it had been a year, or years!—You remember, don't you? how happy I was stocking up inexhaustible reading matter, in case we got driven back from the Horn and had to double the Cape of Good Hope, and on around the world that way!"

There had been one shadow upon me. One evening about three months out, at table, the Mate, Fred Mortimer, remarked:

"I never drink on duty. I drink very little anyway; just a glass now and again on shore with the fellows." Jack replied, to my dismay:

"That is what I am now working toward. I have, by putting myself, for the first time in my life, where I am absolutely free for months of alcohol, with alcohol entirely purged from my system—in a position, also for the first time in my life, to review the whole question of alcohol with reference to myself and that system, and my brain. I have learned, to my absolute satisfaction, that *I am not an alcoholic* in any sense of the word. Therefore, when I am on land again, I shall drink, as you drink, occasionally, deliberately, not because I have to have alcohol in the economy of my physical system, but because *I want to,* we'll say for social purposes. I never have been so happy in my life concerning alcohol with reference to myself, as I am right now this minute. It has never mastered me, I now know; it never shall. There is no danger of it mastering me."

Although I knew he was giving us the honest content of his best conclusions in the matter, I also felt that I knew he would fail of the perfection of such a plan. He did. But what counts in the end—is the end, and near that end he drank but little.

Four days in Seattle were spent, if the newspapers were to be trusted, in a lavender satin-lined suite, Jack attired exquisitely in pink silk pajamas and reveling in perfumed ablutions.

It was the old *Puebla* that carried us down the coast. There were two reasons for this voyage: one, we were not wearied of the sea; the other, it was feasible for us to have Possum with us more than would have been allowed by rail. The evening of August second we sat in the front row at the Oakland Orpheum, our seats ordered by wireless from "outside" the previous day. And it was one of our happiest homecomings, as will be seen.

For, the long voyage ended, we looked for another child in March—a child love-beckoned, to fill a heart's desire once bereft. But owing solely to the ignorance in which we had been left of certain conditions that should have been corrected before another birth was to be thought of, a second blighting disappointment was suffered within a month of our return.

Jack was sadly cast down, though he said little. But his somber state cropped out indirectly in a letter to me. He was entertaining a houseful of guests who had been with us when I was obliged to go into hospital for a few days. Some criticisms had been made of his supporting a trio or more of his pet hobo philosophers—so picturesquely and sympathetically delineated in "The Little Lady of the Big House" as "the seven sages of the Madroño Grove." The title was a reminiscence of his delving into Chinese Legend on the *Dirigo*. He wrote me in a strain that showed a cumulative discouragement with human things that had led him to take agriculture so seriously:

"As for ———, I get more sheer pleasure out of an hour's talk with him than all my inefficient Italian laborers have ever given me. He *pays* his way. My God, the laborers *never* have paid theirs. The Ranch has never lost much money on X———, and Y———, and Z———, and R———, and T———, and all the rest of the fellows who've had a few meals and beds out of me. The Ranch has lost a hell of a lot on the weak sticks of cash-per-day laborers who've battened off of me and on me. Don't forget that the Ranch is *my* problem. This one and that one never helped me. It was I, when I was ripe, and when I saw a flicker of intelligence in this one and that one, who proceeded to shake things down. What all these various ones have lost for me in cash is a thousand times more than the price of the few meals and beds I've given to my bums. And I give these paltry things of paltry value out of my heart. I've not much heart-throb left for my fellow beings. Shall I cut this wee bit thing out too?"

Yet right near this time, returning from a week's absence, he brought home with him a false friend of his early writing days, an old beneficiary who, for some fancied slight, had kept away from Jack for years and talked bitterly against him. I, at sight of Jack with this man in tow, was inwardly as mad as a much dampened mother-hen, although it was incumbent upon me to be courteous in my own house. Jack had taken me aside at first opportunity:

"The poor devil," he said, "—Mate Woman, be good to him; I know you will. It gave me pleasure to bring him. After all, he's only hypersensitive—I don't know what about, in my case; but at any rate, I decided to forget his silly treatment of me—it was only silly, after all."

Home from the Bohemian Club's High Jinks, Jack settled into his stride on the new book, "John Barleycorn," by some reviewers jocosely dubbed his "alcoholic memoirs" and "a bibulous epic." But the work, containing so much autobiographical material of serious portent, was far from humorous. Despite the author's sense of artistry that made it read like fiction and placed certain exaggerations to best advantage, during my typing, as it unfolded day by day, I was conscious of shock upon shock at the content of Jack's mind. Not only with regard to his past, far and near, was I impressed; but also by a realization of the restlessness and deep-reaching melancholy he suffered from the frustration of his dearest ambition—victorious fatherhood of my children. But our days together were happy, and here is what he wrote in my copy of "Smoke Bellew":

"I am still filled with the joy of your voice that was mine last night when you sang. Sometimes, more than any clearly wrought concept of you, there are fiber-sounds in your throat that tell me all the lovableness of you, and that I love as madly as I have always loved all the rest of you."
"Oct. 2, 1912."

Four hundred acres known as the Freund Ranch, had been annexed to the upper reaches of the Kohler, though Jack had to mortgage. The "Wolf House" was slowly mounting, story by story, Jack's big draft horses laboring four and four, from a quarry three miles across the valley and up our mountain, with the great volcanic boulders that were the same red-amethystine hue of the redwood logs also to be used in construction. "We gloat over the growing red arches," my diary reads; and to me, in Oakland, Jack wrote:

"The stone house grows. Two four-horse wagons hauling lumber to-day—20 loads of it. Bar accidents, we'll be in our *own* home next fall."

And he goes on in the same letter:

"Miss you! I've got to have you away from me for a couple of days truly to appreciate you. To myself, all the time, these days, I keep swearing: 'She's a wonder! She's a wonder!'
"For you are. You're the best thing that ever happened to me.
"When are you coming home? I miss you so dreadfully."

In early November, I went again into hospital for an overhauling that included a minor operation. We made it up that Jack should hold my hand during the taking of the ether, so that we might "keep up the lines" to the end of consciousness. I seemed to come to the Edge of Things, when another moment would yield me the Riddle of the Universe. Poised on the brink, I hung in an agony of desire to fix firmly what I should grasp, in order to pass the priceless gift to Jack—possessed by an overwhelming knowledge of what it would mean to his brain. Then something snapped, and I knew nothing until I heard:

"She's gone, Mr. London," and I felt him relax his clasp.

"Oh, no, I'm not, Mate!" protested I. But that was the last thought until I came out.

Jack's daily calls, with their tea-parties for two, were a source of joy to me; and one day, blowing into my room full of news of the day, laden with magazines and books, he burst forth:

"I simply cannot tell you what these afternoons mean to me—how I look forward to them from day to day!"

Then he went on to tell how he had signed a five-year serial contract with *The Cosmopolitan*, for all his fiction. This, so long as he delivered the pledged amount of fiction, was not to interfere with any non-fiction he might write and sell to other periodicals. Hence, when the semi-autobiographical "John Barleycorn" appeared serially, it was in the *Saturday Evening Post*. This work, while it created a sensation, had no phenomenal book-sale. Jack laid the fact to the *Post's* enormous circulation, and vowed that the next time he sold anything to that weekly it must pay him a larger rate to offset the diminished book-royalties. As to the *Post* itself, he said:

"I hate the sight of it—because, forsooth, when I open a number I can't lay it down, and it takes too much time from my other reading!"

Once, at a dance in a Honolulu hotel, Cyrus Curtis, standing alone, was pointed out to Jack. "I'm going to have some fun—watch me!" he whispered. Stepping over to the great publisher, he said:

"Mr. Curtis, I believe?—I've done some work for you now and again."

The older man, little dreaming that this was the author of two of his most successful serials, "The Call of the Wild" and "John Barleycorn," looked politely inquiring, probably thinking the modest-voiced, soft-collared man might be a typesetter.

"Jack London is my name."

"Jack London!—Man, do get me out of this!" And the two, arms linked, disappeared into a veranda and were seen no more until time to go home.

Recalling those afternoon teas in my hospital room, a very sweet thing happened one day. Somewhere I have referred to Jack's regret that he had never learned the soft, pretty ways of social intercourse. "I never bought flowers for a woman in my life," I had heard him say. One afternoon, lying and gazing into the sunny tree-tops, I caught myself wondering how Jack would look entering with a big bunch of double-violets. I turned to see whom the door was admitting, and there was he, red and flustering with an armful of flowers, and my double-violets—a bunch as large as his head! "There are yours, Mate Woman—and these others are for Joan." His elder girl was ill at her mother's home. Jack proceeded:

"Curious coincidence—I've just got your doctor-bill and Joan's nurse-bill. And they're identical—$125 each!"

"I'll tell you something queerer than that," I answered, handing him a New York check for the same amount. "This is in payment for my one and only story, 'The Wheel,' —and I mean for you to put it into the family pot to pay Joan's nurse!"

"I'll do it, I'll do it!" Jack looked at me steadily a moment, an odd expression in the eyes that were as blue at the moment as my violets.

But what could be sweeter than the tale of an incident

that came from his lips one day when he had slipped into the bedside chair and taken my hand—looking with affection upon where it lay, idle for once, in his palm:

"I'm a silly fool, I suppose—I don't know what ever made me do it; but down in the Forum Cigar Store this noon, matching for cigarettes, the men got to talking about adventure, and women, and what not. I don't know how it came about; but I found myself telling those fellows—I can't even remember their names—how I had once nearly signed on to go to the Marquesas; how I longed to see those and all the isles of the South Seas, with, in my eyes, more especially the romance of conquest among the brown maidens sung by poet and sailor. . . . All very well, my dear; but I didn't stop with that; I went on, the proudest, happiest man you ever saw, and bragged, positively bragged to those city men that when I had at last gone into those same South Seas, with the memory of an old longing, it was with my small white woman by my side. And that, co-adventurers, we lived our own faithful romance of the South Seas."

When I was able to leave hospital and sail on the *Roamer*, he brought her from Vallejo to Oakland, accompanied by a house-guest, Laurence Godfrey Smith, a concert pianist whom he had known in Australia. To him Jack declared:

"We chose a boat as small as this so that we could flee from even our best friends once in a while; but we're going to make an exception of you, Laurie. Though, I'm afraid," dubiously, "that we'll have to put you to bed on the floor beside the centerboard, with the aid of a shoe-horn!" And when, months afterward, we saw "Laurie" off to Australia, Jack, contemplating the silent grand piano, said: "It seems as if some one had died!"

CHAPTER XXXVI

THE BAD YEAR; AGRICULTURE

1913

1913, though it yielded a measure of good fortune, Jack was wont to name his "bad year." It did seem as if almost everything that could hurt befell him. First, there was the death of a woman friend, an invalid, whom for years he had seen seldom. Never had I observed him so stirred by the passing of any adult person. That this one, so bright, so brave, should have ceased, for once made his philosophy waver.

"I did something last night I never did before," he confessed. "I concentrated every thought and actually tried to call that girl back. If any one could, I think it would be myself. . . . Of course," he smiled half-foolishly, "there was no answer."

His sister's boy, Irving Shepard, was nearly electrocuted while playing in a tree during school recess, and lay precariously ill for months in our house.

Jack himself had to undergo a sudden operation for appendicitis.

One of the most valuable draft brood-mares, in foal, was found dead in pasture, from a bullet.

An old man ran amuck one night and "shot up the ranch." Jack landing upon the scene, in the space of three seconds had disarmed the lunatic, who, in retaliation, haled him into court for "choking an old man into insensibility." "Me, choking an old man into insensibility!" Jack fumed. "Can't you *see* me?"

Then, there was serious want of early rains, and a "false spring" brought out blossom and young fruit untimely, only to be frosted after belated showers. On top of that, the valleys of California were visited by a plague of grasshoppers. They fastened even upon Jack's baby eucalyptus trees, which were supposedly immune from pest and blight. Nature's beneficence, in his view, was more than counterbalanced by nature's cruelty. "Certainly," he would groan in unison with his harassed sister, "God doesn't love the farmer! Look at that beautiful half-grown cornfield scorched and withered by sun and north wind!"

One of the bitterest mischances was an attack upon him, in court, by a moving-picture promoter whose name enemies metamorphosed into "Porchclimber." The suit was brought to establish whether or not Jack London owned any copyright in his work. A noted eastern attorney was retained, one whom we heard had had a hand in the drafting of copyright law, to take charge of the infamous prosecution. The whole affair was so baldly pernicious that the Los Angeles judge threw it out of court.

Jack had gone into the fight with every atom of his energy, and, since his downfall would mean that of all American authors, he was backed, should he lose, by the Authors' League of America, in the determination to carry the fight into the highest courts of the Union. Very quietly the noted lawyer returned whence he came, and it has never come to my ears that he boasted of the part for which he had been cast.

Later on, as an outcome of the controversy, two film-versions of "The Sea Wolf" were being shown on opposite sides of the same street in Los Angeles. Of Hobart Bosworth's depiction of the hero Jack said:

"When I wrote 'The Sea Wolf,' the physical image of Larsen that took shape in my mind was more or less vague in outline and detail. Nevertheless, it was there, in my mind, and I carried it with me for years, until it was almost real to me. But it fled, like a ghost at daybreak, when I saw on the screen Mr. Hobart Bosworth, the real, three dimension, flesh-and-blood Sea Wolf. Until I die the image of the Sea Wolf will be Mr. Bosworth as I saw him on the screen."

There were moments, during the preparation for the copyright fight, when Jack became so enraged that I was alarmed about him. But one morning, after an untoward outbreak of "catastrophic red wrath" the preceding night, he came to me with a face of humility:

"I'm all right now, Mate. You needn't be afraid for me any more. I'll be good from now on.—Only, you know, it's awfully hard to sit by quietly and let these sons of toads try to take the earnings of your whole life's work away from you!"

"If they get me," he said one gloomy day when I had cheered him with the reminder that I shared his trouble equally, and that we must endure everything shoulder to shoulder, "If they get me, you might as well know that we'll lose everything we have—the Ranch, even; every-thing. But I've still my earning capacity, and we'll buy a big ship outright, one of those we were looking at last winter in the Alameda Basin. And we'll put in a fireplace, like Lord and Lady Brassey's on the *Sunbeam*, and take your grand piano, and be quit forever of a country where a man's life-work can be cheated out of him by a lot of thea-trical sharks and their crooked copyright lawyers—and we'll tell them all to go to hell!" he wound up out of breath. And later, "Why, we could even pick up odd freights here and there over the world," he became interested in spite of his righteous wrath, "and make the old tub pay for her-self! What do you say?"

Ranch guests can attest the incredulous delight my at-titude afforded him in this dark period. "Would you be-lieve it!" he was never tired of acclaiming, "I actually think she wanted me to ride to my fall! I rather thought the idea did not shock her much. By next morning she had got well under way with cabin-plans—and as the days went by and my troubles and my moods smoothed out, she seemed disappointed that I was not to be driven to embarking upon the endless voyage."

Perhaps I *was* disappointed—why not? Had he not always proved a calmer, happier soul in a sea-existence away from the warring frictions of the land?

It may be that hardest of misfortunes was the losing of Jack's "dream house" by fire. Everything else paled, however, when one day, overheated on a long walk while suffering from a bad attack of poison-oak, I fell ill. For some time Jack had been absorbed in work, ranch, and other problems; but now, faced with a human, vital consideration, all beside could go by the board. As he said:

"Mate Woman, I always suspected I had a heart, but now I know. I am the proudest man in the world—I have a heart. And when I was face to face with the possibility of losing you, that heart seemed to come right into my throat—I ate it, I tell you, and I forced it down. Truly, truly, I was near dying!"

It was about this time that he said to a man friend, who told me long afterward, "If anything should happen to Charmian, I'd kill myself. I wouldn't try to live without her."

There were strains and wounds unhealable dealt Jack in that unlucky twelve-month, trials of spirit that caused him to say in retrospect:

"My face changed forever in that year of 1913. It has never been the same since."

Still, midmost of all this, he protested having been called a pessimist by a Jewish cub reporter:

"I am not a pessimist at all. Why, I exploited to you that love is the biggest thing in the world, and held out my arms to you and to all the world in love while I was talking to you. No man who is a lover can be a pessimist.

When you have grown a few years older, you will realize that a man who disagrees with your political, economic and sociological beliefs, does not necessarily have to be a pessimist—especially if he be a self-proclaimed lover.''

I was not surprised when Jack announced that he had made a gamble. Two brothers-in-law of a famous writer, with alluring credentials, had approached him with a proposition to exchange his signature for certain Mexican land stocks. Jack looked very carefully into the business, and assured me he was safe in case the project fell through. ''I invest nothing, you see. They want my name in it, that is all; and I stand to win.'' But they got him in the end.

Then there was a so-called ''fidelity'' loan outfit that ''trimmed'' him for a similar amount. This matter was taken into court, and while the company was patently fraudulent, it won upon a technicality. Jack had chosen a youthful lawyer who had his career to make:

''Might as well give an unknown a chance! And he'll probably represent me as well as another.'' He was fond of saying: ''A 'practitioner' is one who practices upon his victims, anyway!''

These two ventures left Jack out of pocket about ten thousand dollars. Once I made reference to them, and he said:

''Please—I don't want to talk about them at all.'' Which was unlike his usual eagerness to elucidate his affairs. It must be recorded that when he went into speculations, he labeled them frankly:

''Remember what I tell you, in case these go wrong—that they are deliberate gambles. I think they are good gambles; but sheer gambles they are. There's nothing like playing a flyer on a long chance. Pure lottery. Sometimes a chance proves a big winner. I've never won anything yet. Maybe now's my chance!''

All I had to say was that a man who ''made good'' as he did, in all his obligations, had a right to ''take a flyer'' upon occasion. Jack smiled with pleasure; and his face bore the same expression when he told some one how, one day aboard the *Roamer*, lying off an inland city, I had said:

"Don't let yourself get stale aboard, if you feel like having a little recreation. Why don't you go ashore and look up a good card game of some sort. It will do you good."

He took the suggestion, but returned shortly.

"Oh, I pirooted around a while, and watched some playing; but I didn't see anything that looked half so good to me as this cabin and the little wife-woman who wanted me to do as I pleased! . . . Where's that pinochle deck? I can beat you a rubber of three out of five games before Sano has that fish-chowder ready."

January aboard the *Roamer* saw Jack drafting his first chapter of "The Mutiny of the Elsinore"—a whacking good sea-story, true, modern; beneath the romance and action a heartfelt protest against the decayed condition of the American merchant marine. It was finished in August, and serial publication, under title of "The Gangsters," begun in *Hearst Magazine* for November. For once, he was touched with his creation. This from my diary: "Mate has a great moment in creating the character of Captain West. Stopped me as I went by, to read me morning's work; and his eyes were shining with joy in our mutual appreciation of what he had done." In my gift-copy is written, dated September 21, 1914:

"We, too, have made this voyage together, and, in all happiness, known the winter North Atlantic, the pamperos off the Plate, and the Sou'west gales and Great West Wind Drift off the Horn. And we 'made westing,' as we have made westing in all the years since first we loved."

"Lying on the beach at Waikiki," wrote a Honolulu newspaperman, "I learned that 'The Mutiny of the Elsinore' was written to illustrate how the blond white man from the Northern countries of Europe is rapidly being crowded out of America, and that as he disappears, he will go down fighting to the last, but that he will go down beneath the weight of the Latin, the Slav, and other Southern European races that are pouring into America, whom he can rule as long as he lives, but with whom he cannot successfully compete in the continual struggle for existence.''

Home from our blissful river-drifting, Jack plunged deeper than ever into ranch development, the while we honeymooned amidst all the quickening farm activities. A ''frosty honeymoon,'' Jack laughed, for ice was in the ground, and there was an unwonted snowfall. In March he gave me ''The Night-Born,'' with this in its fly-leaf:

''Dear My-Woman:

''The seasons come and go. The years slide together in the long backward trail, and yet you and I remain, welded with our arms about each other moving onward together and unafraid of any future.''

In a new edition of ''The Call of the Wild,'' illustrated by Paul Bransom, he wrote:

''It was many dear years ago when I first gave you a copy of this book—in the days when I was hearing a love call; and never has that same love called more loudly than it calls now in this year 1913, when my arms are still full of you, and my heart still full of you.''

It was all a part of his yearning to escape from the world at large. Several times, without self-consciousness, even before others, he held out his arms to me when I came into the living room—as if he must clasp something, some one that came nearest to understanding his need.

To facilitate his heavy correspondence, a dictaphone was added to our office equipment—a spring machine, in anticipation of the installation of electricity. I was seriously concerned at this innovation, realizing its threat toward the old intimacy of working hours.

"But think, my dear," Jack explained, justly indeed, "I don't have to wait for you; I can dictate to the damned thing any moment, in bed, even, if I please, while you pursue your precious beauty sleep!"

After which he practised on the "damned thing" for an uninterrupted afternoon, reeling off half a hundred neglected letters. When I came to transcribe them, at the end of each cylinder I was greeted with a love message in a fair imitation of my husband's voice: "Her master's voice!" giggled he. How could any one try to obstruct the progress of such a being!

In April, he went to Los Angeles on moving-picture business, but was back in three days: "I never stay very long where you are not," he said upon returning.

In May "The Abysmal Brute," that "brief for the purification of the prize-fight game," came from the Century Company, catching its author in a darker phase than even I had guessed; for when he put the little book into my hands, I found this inside:

"The years pass, we live much, and yet, to me, I find but one vindication for living, but one bribe for living—and that vindication is you, the bribe is you.

"Your Lover,
"Jack London."

And here is something about love:

"Woman, beyond all doubt, remains the biggest thing in the world to-day. The love-motif is the highest thing that can exist between normal humans. To me, existence is impossible without love. Love does not lead nor direct. Love satisfies as no other thing in human knowledge satisfied. Love is the ultimate benediction of living. It ennobles; it makes the impossible possible; it makes life worth living.''

A portion of Jack's hypochondria might be laid to the bodily distemper that was leading up to an acute attack of appendicitis. I think he was subsequently in lighter humor. The history of his recovery from the knife, against illustrating that magnificent physical endownment, might be written down as ''uneventful'' in the annals of surgery, except for its astonishing rapidity.

On July 6, we rushed him to Oakland and into hospital. On the 8th, Dr. William S. Porter operated. Four days later, an important moving-picture conference was held in Jack's room. Other afternoons were filled with callers, and his room was banked in flowers. ''Only,'' the bed-ridden one grumbled sheepishly, ''I wish *men* wouldn't bring me flowers—somehow it makes me feel silly.'' Frolich, the sculptor, unwittingly mitigated the situation by contributing an absurd corbel, a cowled monk in the ultimate throes of seasickness, and Jack racked himself with mirth. Newspaper men and women came and went, and headlines featuring ''The Call of the Wild Appendix,'' and ''Jack London Takes the Count,'' beguiled his morning tray.

On the seventh day, the patient stood on his feet, then inspected the building from a wheeled chair. Next morning, Dr. Porter, in his own car, conveyed Jack London to the house on Twenty-seventh Street. The obstreperous convalescent insisted upon going out to dine the following night, as well as to the theater, enjoyed a Turkish bath and a café dinner on the tenth day after the operation; and on the twelfth he left for Los Angeles to jump into ''the hottest, hardest business fight'' of his life with the wily but ingratiating Hebrew, Mr. ''Porchclimber.'' The twentieth day beheld him at home and in the saddle—another tribute to his own vitality and to the cunning of his surgeon friend.

Jack could not abide ether as an anæsthetic. This time

he was first given chloroform, and when, once unconscious, ether was substituted, he resisted so violently that chloroform again had to be resorted to.

With that prescience of the Builder that brooks no delay, Jack mortgaged everything in sight, even our cottage and the new one he had erected for Eliza, to obtain funds needful for his big aims. On August 18, with but $300 in bank, and large obligations pressing, he negotiated another mortgage in order to complete the Wolf House before winter. But I always knew, beyond questioning, that no matter what hazards he seemed to be taking, he divined the way out.

The Bank placed an insurance on the Hill Ranch covering half the amount loaned. There was no other insurance on the huge purple-red pile, since every one agreed that rock and concrete, massive beams and redwood logs with the bark on, were practically fireproof unless ignited in a dozen places, owing to the quadrangular construction and cement partitions.

Nevertheless, three nights later, August 22, the entire inflammable part of the high stone shell was destroyed. I was awakened by voices from Jack's porch. Tiptoeing out, I saw Eliza, by his bedside, point in the direction of the Wolf House half a mile away, where flames and smoke rose straight into the windless, star-drifted sky.

Teams were harnessed, and leaving the Japanese to keep an eye on things at home, if incendiarism was in the air, we drove leisurely across the Ranch. "What's the use of hurry?" Jack demanded. "If that is the Big House burning, nothing can stop it now!"

All the countryside, that had come to feel a personal pride and ownership in "Jack's House," had gathered or was arriving. Public sentiment ran high: and I think, had the criminal or criminals who fired it been detected that night, there would have been a stringing-up to the nearest limbs, in lusty frontier fashion.

Already the beautiful red-tile roof had clattered down inside the glowing walls, and the only care that need be exercised was in regard to the adjacent forest. "Promise me," I said to Jack, so lately out of hospital, "that you won't forget yourself, and overdo." He made the pledge and kept it, very quietly walking about and directing the men.

"Why don't you cry, or get excited, or something, you two?" asked a neighbor. "You don't seem to realize what's happened to you!"

"What's the use?" Jack repeated his thought. "It won't rebuild the house.—Though it can be rebuilt!" he swore cheerfully, purpose in his eye.

But uneraseably beneath our contained exterior lay the vision of it six hours before, palpitating in the mid-summer sunset light, when we had emerged on horseback from the ravine Jack called his house-garden. He had burst out:

"How beautiful—Our House, Mate Woman! Did I tell you that Harrison Fisher, after I brought him home from the Jinks two weeks ago, told some one it was the most beautiful house in the West?"

Yes, Jack laughed and buoyed up the spirits of the Ranch while his dream castle ascended in lurid smoke that hot August night. But when at four in the dawn, the tension relaxed, and uppermost in his mind loomed the wicked, cruel, senseless destruction of the only home he had ever made for himself, he lay in my pitying arms and shook like a child. After a few moments he stilled, and said:

"It isn't the money loss—though that is grave enough just at this time. The main hurt comes from the wanton despoiling of so much beauty."

A long pause, and then, referring to the recent death of the bridegroom of a young friend:

"Do you know—thinking it all over, I'd be willing to go through this whole night again, and many times, if it could bring Tom back!"

We never did learn whose hand applied the torch. I had all but written "assassin." For the razing of his house killed something in Jack, and he never ceased to feel the tragic inner sense of loss. To this day the ruins of amethystine stone, arch beyond arch, tower above tower, stand mute yet appealing. Total strangers, not all of them women, have wept before them, have cried out, "Poor Jack!"

From his immediate actions, however, none but Eliza and I guessed the extent of his repining. Something had to be done, and quickly. Forni, the master-mason, must be taken in hand. He was like a father who had lost a child, and in danger of losing his reason. Two of his men, the big, blue-eyed Martinelli brothers, wandered around the unapproachably hot ruins like spirits suddenly bereft of Paradise, crossing their breasts and murmuring, "Mary!" "Christ!" Even Jack had to turn away when the man who had nailed the last Spanish tile before the conflagration, said with wet eyes: "Well, my roof never leaked, anyway!"

The fire was on Friday. On Monday, Jack had the entire crew putting up a splendid retaining-wall of mossy gray stone, that had long been in his eye, on the right of a driveway to the smoking walls which came to be known simply as The Ruins. Eliza was scarred to the soul by the sudden wiping out of her work—she had superintended the building from start to finish; but she met Jack wholeheartedly in showing the workmen and the country roundabout that the end of the world had not come. It was when we came to readjust that the loss became most evident.

My diary calls it up:

"We lay aside notes and samples, and plans drawn for this and that, and feel as if the bottom had fallen out of everything—light, queer, unreal."

I have been asked why Jack London, socialist, friend of the common man, built so large a house. And I have been glad that there were those who asked, for it has ever been my suspicion that some one who waited not to ask, set the brand to that house.

How shall I say? Jack could not traffic in small things, any more than he could deftly handle trifling objects with his fingers. All he did was in a large way. His boyish memories were of moving from one small, inadequate wooden domicile to another. Being what he could not help being, and remaining true to himself, lover of large and enduring things, he must invite spaciousness and solidity— room to breathe in, and for others to breathe in. The ancient frame cottage in which on the ranch he lived and worked and received all men at his table, was entirely disproportionate to his needs. Being so indefatigable and systematic a worker and thinker he required everything to his hand. A smoothly running domestic menage made for efficiency in other matters. Here, where he had to live during the three years while the Wolf House building went on intermittently, the rooms were crammed and jammed and spilling over with the very implements of his many branches of endeavor. Only the combined efforts of the two of us, and later a third, a secretary, made it anything less than distracting for Jack to function in the cramped apartments. Three-quarters of his library was packed away molding in the big stone barn half a mile away, and many the time he could not lay his hand upon some volume especially needed.

Wanderer, yet deeply fond of his own home, a place for the permanence of his treasures—curios, blankets, books, "gear"—he sighed with content knowing that in the big house there would be a story in one wing devoted to the library; above that, his roomy work-den; on the first floor, dining room and kitchen. The middle story of the opposing wing was to be mine—a place where I might retreat to rest and call my soul my own when the outside world was too much within our walls. Above, Jack's sleeping tower reared. Beneath mine were the guest chambers, and, still below, servants' quarters and the like. The connecting link of these two wings formed a two-story living-room, partially flanked by a gallery; and underneath this high hall lay what Jack termed the "stag room," where no female might venture except by especial ukase from the lords of creation who might lounge and play billiards and otherwise disport themselves therein. The house foundation measured roughly eighty feet from corner to corner.

It should be thought of, that house, in relation to Jack, not as a mansion, but as a big cabin, a lofty lodge, a hospitable tepee, where he, simple and generous despite all his baffling intricacy, could stretch himself and beam upon you and me and all the world that gathered by his log-fires. I know a friend who appreciated this largeness of the man, and who with man's tenderness calls him the Big Chief.

To one who suggests that this house would have been a recreation place for guests "acquired by the sole reason of Jack's fame and prosperity," I am able to protest that it would have been the contrary—in the Wolf House as in the rickety cottage, our transient household would have been made up mostly of the wanderers, the intellectual (and otherwise) hoboes, sometimes washed, sometimes not, while the master drove his pen for the multitude without. As always, these would have come to sit with us, and furnish grist for Jack's unsleeping brain-mill. That was the sort of "inspiration," to quote my inquirer, he would have continued to draw about him "within such walls of stone." Why, the very form of the rough rock hacienda was an invitation, with its embracing wings, its sunny pool between the wide, arched corridors and grape-gnarled pergola! The reason that seekers after the truth about Jack London find more reminder of him in the simple red boulder that lies upon his ashes than in the aching ruins of his great house, is because they do not know the all of Jack London. He was a man before all else—big and solid, and spacious, and unvaryingly true to himself.

And so with his ranching. There, too, he wrought largely: "No picayune methods for me," he would vow. "When I go into the silence, I want to know that I have left behind me a plot of land which, after the pitiful failures of others, I have made productive. . . . Can't you see? Oh, try to see!—In the solution of the great economic problems of the present age, I see a return to the soil. I go into farming because my philosophy and research have taught me to recognize the fact that a return to the soil is the basis of economics . . . I see my farm in terms of the world, and the world in terms of my farm . . . Do you realize that I devote two hours a day to writing and ten to farming?—my thought-work, my preparation, at night, and when I am out-of-doors."

Similar revelation of himself he gave on the witness stand only a few days before his death, when suit had been brought to restrain him from using his share of the waters of a creek boundary much needed in his scheme of agriculture. But in the whole sad affair, which contributed its weight toward his break-down, not one iota of understanding was accorded him by the prosecutors, among whom were some near and dear to him.

From time to time I would ask: "When, in the years to come, do you think you will ever pull even, financially, with your ranch project?" And it was always with a laugh that he would return: "Never, my dear—at least, I want and expect to have the place eventually sustain itself. That would be the natural object. But it will never make money for me, because there is so much developing I want to keep on doing, endless experiments I want to make."

A noted socialist lecturer, with misapprehension and prejudice in his eye, spent a day or two on the ranch. "At last I see," said he. "I was wrong. In your work here, as you unfold it to me, I see a social *creation!*"

Once more, let me impress: temperamentally Jack London was a Builder of books, of houses, of roads, of soil, of things that would outlast merely temporary uses. *My house will be standing, act of God permitting, for a thousand years. My boat, act of God permitting, will be intact and afloat a hundred years or five hundred years hence.* Little call to point out that he did not build for himself alone.

"Who will come after us, Mate Woman!" he looked into the distances. "Who will reap what I have sown here in this almighty sweet land? You and I will be forgotten. Others will come and go; these, too, shall pass, as you and I shall pass, and others take their places, each telling his love, as I tell you, that life is sweet!"

He was fond, at this time, of having me play Arthur Foote's Rubaiyat Suite, particularly the section illustrating

"How sultan after sultan, with his pomp,
Abode his destined hour, and went his way."

And Macdowell's "Sea Pieces" swept him out upon the tide of his dreams.

True to his determination not to be downcast over the houseburning, Jack redoubled ranch operations. "I am the sailor on horseback!" chanted he. "Watch my dust! . . . Oh, I shall make mistakes a-many; but watch my dream come true." And, as he loved the name of Sailor, Skipper, Captain, for the love he bore the sea, so he now loved as well to be greeted Farmer, what of his overmastering desire to make blossom the exhausted wilderness. Beauty, in his precincts, began to reveal itself more and more in the light of tillable soil, of food-getting efficiency. "Don't grieve about the clearing of that field, or that little clump of scrubby redwoods," he would say. "We get used to a certain view, and the idea of altering it is untenable. But when it is altered, we are surprised how soon we adjust, and even forget. Remember, there is endless wildwood farther back—it isn't as if I were depriving you of it. Try to dream with me my dreams of fruitful acres. Do not be a slave to an old conception. Try to realize what I am after.''

In step with the day-dream went the visions of his slumber, and he loved them: ''I am a keen dreamer, and I love to dream. It seems to me that my life is doubled by the amount of dreaming I do every night.'' Often he recounted to me a story of long hours spent in a verdant land where he seemed to be proprietor, rolling country where, just beyond each hill, great schemes of agricultural betterment were flourishing. Many times, he said, I was by his side: but for the most part he would be instructing intelligent foremen how to carry out his ideas. This trend in his unconscious mind increased until the day of his death.

The former quiet of the ranch gave place to a pervasive hum of important matters afoot. Rending blasts of dynamite far afield spoke of a new era in the somnolent order of the old land of the Spaniards. Jack founded his purebred English Shire stable by the purchase of nothing less than Neuadd Hillside, grand champion of California, and once prize-winner in England. He weighed a ton, and was wondrously shaped withal. Cockerington Princess, champion of her own sex, also came to gladden our eyes, while the converting into stables of theretofore unused stone winery buildings went on apace. Into each barn, for the men to scan and heed, was posted a long list of rules borrowed from a great western express corporation for the care and use of the horses.

''Although the tails of these imported horses are docked, we won't dock their colts,'' Jack remarked on the day the two grand beasts, pranked out show-fashion in colored worsted, were unloaded from the stock ''palace car'' amidst much comment in Glen Ellen. ''Do you know,'' he asked me, ''why horses like those aren't common sights on the country roads of the United States? I'll tell you: because

our farmers are so stupidly wasteful about saving feed!
I mean just that. Instead of crowding the development of
a colt, particularly the first year, by care and feeding, he
turns it out to grub for itself in pasture. That first year is
like the first year of any other baby. It's what so vitally
counts.''

Six days before his voice was silenced, Jack said something like the following to an interviewer:

''What is the difference between this good team and
that team of scrubs? Man alive! What is the difference
between that field, as it is now, and the same field as it was
two years ago? What is the difference between anything
that is strong and fine and well arranged—be it words or
stones or trees or ideas or what not—and the same elements
as they were in their unorganized weakness? Man—the
brain of man, the effort that man had put into man's supreme task—organizing! That is the work of man, work
that is worth a man's doing—to take something second-rate
and chaotic and to put himself into it until it becomes
orderly and first-rate and fine.''

He was, in short, really far more interested in intro-
ducing better farming into Sonoma County and the country
at large than he was in leaving behind masterpieces of
literature.

As usual, for him to think out a thing was to see it done;
and early he had learned, with his instinct for teaching and
for effort-saving, to instruct others now to act upon what
he thought out. Thus, he was pressing his sister hard and
ever harder, firing her with the depth and breadth of his
outlook. There were long, grilling hours of discussion—
he trying to inculcate his principles, she giving him the benefit of what her practical judgment, regardless of books,
prompted her to do.

Here are two loose notes among his many:

''Please, please, know that I carry only general principles in
my head, and do not carry details.''

"You must always allow me the latitude of a mind that is filled with a million other things that have nothing whatever to do with this ranch, so that when I query, I query honestly and sincerely and without ulterior purpose, so that all I want is what I ask for, and I don't want guessed replies to what you guess are ulterior questions on my part. I ain't got no ulterior questions or motives, but, just once in a while, I have a legitimate, overwhelming desire to know *what is*, which *what is* has occurred during my periods of being away from ranch, of being immersed in problems which have nothing whatever to do with ranch, save that they enable me to keep ranch going. I make *my living* out of the world. I must 90% of my time devote myself to the world. Please, please, give me that 90% latitude of ignorance and of non-remembrance of the per cent. of ranch happenings that hit you every moment of every day and that hit me possibly once in six months. Meet me in at least a 9 to 1 percentage sympathy."

Discussion but infrequently took place between Jack and the workmen, for he was fond of learning by argument. Little they could teach him. And so for the most part he kept from contact with them. "Eliza is the captain I have picked out to run this particular ship of mine," he would say to me, repository of his deductions upon each situation as it unfolded, "and you know how much I interfere between captain and man!" But there was often the irk of those who knew less than Jack, who tried to hold him back: "You can't make it work, Mr. London. We have never done it this way."

"Why not?" he would blaze. "Why can't I make it work? Do you think that I learn nothing from the greatest specialists in your profession, when I put in whole nights, month upon month, studying them? What do you know about government bulletins, government deductions based upon scientific principles that have been put to work?"

I take the following from a transcript of evidence in the water-suit before referred to:

"Aren't you a good enough agriculturist to estimate an acre of ground?" was the question put by opposing counsel.

"No," drawled Jack. "We all have our weaknesses. I never could master an acre, by looking at it. I always send somebody out to measure it for me." And to the question, "Have you ever acted as a farmer, practically tilling the soil yourself?" he explained as below:

"I have never had my hands on the handles of a plow in my life, but I know more about plowing than any plowman who ever worked for me. I have acquired practically every bit of my knowledge from the books. I never was a graduate of an university; I never finished the first half of my freshman year at a university; yet I have thought it nothing to face a group of thirty or forty professors hammer-and-tongs on philosophy, sociology, and all the other 'ologies—the group including David Starr Jordan and others of the same high intellectual caliber. I was able to do that and hold a table of debate—I, who had never been through a university—because I had gotten my knowledge from the same books they had got their knowledge from. The same with plowing and other branches of farm knowledge. I state that I am eminently fitted from my knowledge of the books."

He went on: "My knowledge of agriculture and farming is also derived from actual contact with the soil—looking at it, on occasion hiring experts to come and tell me their diagnoses of these thick soils or bad soils or wrong soils. I find very often that they disagree with one another; then I go back to my books and find the right clue, applying it, making my experiments year after year, whether in fertilizer or in methods of cultivation or drainage or the thousand factors that enter into successful tillage."

His aloof supervision was expressed in notes to be passed on. "But see that they are returned and preserved, so that I may refer to them at any time."

From a sheaf I choose almost at random:

"Watch out for the first unexpected rain catching lots of our equipment exposed. As for instance the wood-saw and engine. Months in the sun and fog and dew have not done them any good. A rain will do worse."

"Who left half a dozen sacks of cement in rain to spoil under roofless section of rock-crusher house?"

"Near rock-crusher is a shingled roof section, lying flat on the ground, going to hell."

"In any new building operations around the ranch, such as the bath-house, etc., are the men who do the work told to keep the nails cleaned up? Because if they are so told, and continue to let the nails lie around, fire them. To-day it was King who was lamed; some time ago it was one of the Shire mares. To-morrow it may be Neuadd. Is 'father' to sit back and pay for the Veterinary, for the stallion man's time, for the crippled horse's time?"

And first, last, and always, stood his creed:

"What we do must be adequate and permanent."

His plaint to me, aside, when confronted with the obstinate wall of farmer-brains smaller than his own, was like this:

"The reason a man works for me, is because he cannot work for himself. Stupid boobs, most of them, who do not wake up to avail themselves of the fund of knowledge ready for the asking. In the matter of government reports, over and above the price of a postcard of inquiry, knowledge is as free as air."

Out of his despair with the incapacity of employes, their unwillingness to be educated, he coined the phrase "Down the hill," which meant the discharge of those who could neither learn nor take orders. "The more I see of men," he would apostrophize, "the more I turn to the land; yet, in order to manipulate that land, I must deal with those very men who hurt me so with their blind ineffectiveness and lack of foresight. And they try to teach *me*, who spend my nights with the books. My work on this land, and my message to America, go hand in hand!" And he would ride away, waving his cowboy quirt, bent upon appraising a worn-out plot of ground with the intention of reclaiming it.

Of course, his experiment was being advertised far and wide by the press. He had, as one farm magazine declared, "ideas on the profession of farming that will do the world more good than all the stories he ever could write."

"When I bought one hundred and twenty-nine acres near Glen Ellen nine years ago I knew nothing of farming," Jack gave out. "I bought the place mostly for its beauty, as a place to live and write in.

"About forty acres was cleared and I tried to raise hay for my horses, but soon found I could scarcely get the seed back. The soil had been worn out; it had been farmed for years by old-fashioned methods of taking everything off and putting nothing back.

"The region was a back-water district. Most of the ranchers were poor and hopeless; no one could make any money ranching there, they told me. They had worked the land out and their only hope was to move on somewhere else and start to work new land out and destroy its value.

"I began to study the problem, wondering why the fertility of this land had been destroyed in forty or fifty years when land in China has been tilled for thousands of years, and is still fertile.

"My neighbors were typified by the man who said: "You can't teach me anything about farming; I've worked three farms out! Which is as wise as the remark of the woman who said she guessed she knew all there was to know about raising children—hadn't she buried five?

"I adopted the policy of taking nothing off the ranch. I raised stuff and fed it to the stock. I got the first manure spreader ever seen up there, and so put the fertilizer back on the land before its strength had leaked out. I began to get registered stock, and now I sell a blooded cow at nine months for $40 and an old-fashioned rancher comes along and wonders why he has to feed a scrub cow for two years and sell her for less than $40.

"An old-fashioned farmer has thirty milch cows and works eighteen hours a day taking care of them and milking them and can make no money. An up-to-date man comes along, buys the place, pays $10 for a Babcock tester and buys milk scales. Right away he gets rid of ten of the cows as non-productive, and he makes more with two-thirds of the work."

Jack's disappointment that so much of his main "punch" in "The Valley of the Moon" had been lost by wholesale deletion, in serial publication, was mended by the way the published book was received by the agricultural magazines. One of them declared that it "ought to be adopted for a text book by our 'back to the farm,' missionaries. Besides being a firstrate love-story, it is replete with knowledge of rural conditions. With that familiar universal touch of Jack London's, this book, while essentially Californian, applies and appeals to America at large. We wonder that it has not been made a part of the curriculum at the agricultural colleges. *It is worth dozens of lectures sometimes delivered to students.*"

"Why isn't 'The Valley of the Moon' the 'Great American Novel'?" a correspondent wanted to know. "It lets light in upon the question of why the old American stock is dying out. The ignorant, unlettered foreigners, Italians, Japanese, Scandinavian, and the rest, crowd out the good old American, because the American will not, for one thing, if he can help it, live the way the foreigner does. And because, also, the American will not use his head for the improvement of the land. Result, the carcass of the good old superior American fertilizes his own land for the crowding, thrifty, crafty foreigner."

That one man is more fit than another to become a law-giver, Jack London has laid down in "The Bones of Kahe-kili," written five months before he died, one of seven stories in "On the Makaloa Mat." The old Hawaiian commoner asks:

"Here is something stronger than life, stronger than woman, but what is it—and why?" And Jack, over and above his personal desire and sacrifices toward the masses, speaks his unwilling but inevitable conclusion through the mouth of Hardman Pool:

"It is because most men are fools, and therefore must be taken care of by the few men who are wise. Such is the secret of chiefship. In all the world are chiefs over men. In all the world that has been have there ever been chiefs, who must say to the mary fool men: 'Do this; do not do that. Work, and work as we tell you, or your bellies will remain empty and you will perish. . . . You must be peace-abiding and decent, and blow your noses. You must be early to bed of nights, and up early in the morning to work if you would have beds to sleep in and not roost in trees like the silly fowls. This is the reason for the yam-planting and you must plant now. We say now, to-day, and not picnicking and hulaing to-day and yam-planting to-morrow or some other day of the many careless days. . . . All this is life for you, because you think but one day at a time, while we, your chiefs, think for you all days and far days ahead."

And the old man: "Yes, it is sad that I should be born a common man and live all my days a common man."

To which Hardman Pool: "That is because you were of yourself common. When a man is born common, and is by nature uncommon, he rises up and overthrows the chiefs and makes himself chief over the chiefs. Why do you not run my ranch, with its many thousands of cattle, and shift the pastures by the rainfall, and pick the bulls, and arrange the bargaining and selling of the meat to the sailing ships and war vessels and the people who live in the Honolulu houses, and fight with lawyers, and help make laws, and even tell the King what is wise for him to do and what is dangerous? Why does not any man do this that I do? Any man of all the men who work for me, feed out of my hand, and let me do their thinking for them?—me, who works harder than any of them, who eats no more than any of them, and who can sleep on no more than one lauhala mat at a time like any of them?"

"I am out of the cloud . . ." the old man says. "We are the careless ones of the careless days who will not plant the yam in season if our *alii* does not compel us, who will not think one day for ourselves. . . ."

There were timely trips into the interior—Sacramento, Modesto, and to the University of California stock farm at Davis. Eliza Shepard went along further to imbibe and abet the game her brother wanted to play; and Jack came speedily to accept her judgment in the selection of livestock, for her choices came to be the prize-winners at State and County fairs.

A concrete-block silo, twelve feet in diameter, the first of two, and the first of their kind in California, was rising half a hundred feet into the air near the old cowbarns. Jack put his own and his neighbors' corn into the first silo that was finished, and neglected his writing to take a hand in the fascinating work of feeding the cutter. Houseguests and servants alike were unable to keep out of the busy scene, and remained to help. Their host boasted: "No material comes up the hill except cement. My own machinery has done the crushing of the rock that my own tools and dynamite have got out of my own land, and that my own draft animals have hauled. My own mixer has made the mortar. My ten-inch drain-tile for the alfalfa fields yonder, has been made right here on the ground. And all this paraphernalia will build a dam at the mouth of that natural sink up-mountain, to impound 7,000,000 gallons of water for irrigation. And think of the pressure for fire protection!"

The "piggery" which Jack invented, and which was built during our fall *Roamer* cruise, became famous the

world over, not only among farmers but with curious lay-
men as well. Entirely of rock and concrete, it is on a circular plan, surrounding, with graveled driveway between,
a handsome tower wherein feed is mixed and distributed
to the "suites" of apartments, with their individual run-
ways, that came to house, first, the white Ohio Improved
Chester hogs, and later, Jack's choice of what he deemed
a sturdier breed for our climate, the red Duroc Jerseys.
A system of flushing and antiseptizing both here and in
the barns, rendered premises and vicinity "sweet as a
nut," to quote an English visitor who lately registered in
the tower guest-book. Crowning a knoll for perfect drainage, surrounded by blossomy madroño trees with bark like
Korean red lacquer and glossy leaves so resembling the
magnolia, this farm yard "sermon in stone" is an object
of distinct beauty.

Jack had conceived the idea of demonstrating that he
could restore exhausted grainfields by a system of terracing
on a large scale—in his own words, "farming on the level."

"You increase the organic content by levelling, pre-
venting the destructive erosive effects that draw from it
the organic content—so that instead of one-tenth of one
meager crop a year you can grow three rich crops a year.

"The hillsides are first ploughed along contour lines,
and at intervals, depending on the slope of the land, balks,
or small ridges, are thrown up. The process is slow, but
its advantages from the start are great. Rains are held
back to sink into the soil instead of rushing down the hillsides, tearing out great gullies and carrying rich soil down
the streams to the ocean. . . . We have been letting our
rich hillsides go to waste, and by ignorant cultivation have
increased erosion rather than prevented it. The method I
have outlined will restore even impoverished hillsides and
turn them into productive fields."

A dozen acres of old French prune trees were brought
up to standard; vineyards, once famous, that had gone too

long neglected, were uprooted and given over to barley; and the barley was planted with inoculated vetch.

Beehives, likewise ducks, pigeons, geese, chickens, and a few pheasants, made their appearance on the Hill place as a side issue.

I heard Jack say that "the best blocks of vineyard did not have more than seventy-five per cent. of the vines standing when I took over the ranch. In some cases three out of every five vines were missing." But in time he had those "best blocks" yielding as formerly.

And here are his intentions with regard to fertilizing:

"The Chinese have farmed for forty centuries without using commercial fertilizer. I am rebuilding worn-out hillside lands that were worked out and destroyed by our wasteful California pioneer farmers. I am not using commercial fertilizer. I believe the soil is our one indestructible asset, and by green manures, nitrogen-gathering cover crops, animal manures, rotation of crops, proper tillage and draining, I am getting results which the Chinese have demonstrated for forty centuries.

"We are just beginning to farm in the United States. The Chinese knew the *how* but not the *why*. We know the *why*, but we're dreadfully slow getting around to the *how*."

Before long this modern husbandman had revolutionized the sleepy neighborhood, to say nothing of his employes upon whom he sprung timesheets, rigorously insisting that these be properly filled in each night. "Any man who isn't willing to give an account of his work and time, is welcome to go down hill," was Jack's ultimatum.

A blacksmith in the village went out of business. Jack relieved him of the entire establishment, which was installed in one of our cool winery buildings, pleasantly shaded by a "spreading chestnut tree," while a horseshoer and general blacksmith was added to the payroll. The village thought little about the transaction until a paper in a rival community came out with:

"Good boy, Jack! Why not make another trip with your wagon and take the rest of Glen Ellen up to the ranch?"

Then and always, when asked "What do you call your place?" the owner replied, "The Ranch of Good Intentions." Develop it as he might, it seemed to remain only in its merest beginning, in view of his ultimate hopes.

An old neighbor, whose boundaries carve sharply into our property, often suggested that Jack buy him out, lock, stock, and barrel. "But there are too many buildings on your place, for one thing," Jack would object. "It would cost too much to demolish them!" But once he said: "If I ever do buy the Wegener place, I'll turn it over, buildings and all, to my intellectual hobo friends. The community would wax, and oh, my!" As he had written to Anna:

"Some day I shall build an establishment, invite them all, and turn them loose upon one another. Such a mingling of castes and creeds and characters could not be duplicated. The destruction would be great!"

It has always been a sadness to me how, as before hinted, Jack's most intimate acquaintances, given every opportunity to view the magnitude of his interest in agriculture, without exception discounted the importance of it to him, and vice versa. In all the memorial gatherings met so generously after his passing, it never entered the mind of a single friend to whom Jack had expounded his dear ambition, to make mention of the great book he had begun to write upon the mountain fields. I, aghast at the vital omission, protested, and appealed to the lovers of his memory not to forget. The explanation dawned upon me before ever it was put in words by one, a sociologist, who had no inkling of the bearing of agronomy upon economics:

"You see, Jack's agriculture did not impress me as it should have done—probably because I have no interest in agriculture."

In September we made our first visit to the State Fair at Sacramento. Jack was averse to showing his own stock, holding that putting an animal in "show condition" was a harmful process. His presence at the Fair was for the purpose of getting in touch with "the other fellow" to see what he was doing in the matter of raising draft horses, beef cattle and hogs.

It was during this absence Jack told me that at intervals for months past he had had warning flutters in the region of the heart that gave him sudden moments of foreboding. "Haven't you noticed that I have got into the habit of laying my palm over my heart?" he asked. "I didn't realize I was, until I happened to catch myself at it." He also told me that there had been no report, after an examination by their physician, from a certain life insurance firm to whom he had applied some time back for an additional policy. I, to offset the tremor of my own heart at his intelligence, eliminated one reason after another for his condition, and finally asked if it might be laid to his excessive cigarette inhaling. But he did not take to the diagnosis. After a couple of years the symptoms disappeared.

In mid-October we "joy-sailed on the good, old, dear, and forever dear *Roamer*," to quote her skipper, spending one of our most care-free seasons, with the resilience that fortunate souls exhibit after an excess of work and emotional endurance. From my diary: "Let's look at the chart we've sailed off," says Jack at two p. m., after our exciting run in a howling norther. Things broke; we missed stays twice on one tack, and went aground in the glistening tules, that were laid flat by the wind. Spouting surf on lee shores. A big scow aground. Ducks flying low. Sierras white with snow, and Mt. Diablo and its range clear-cut sapphire. We did not have a ribbon of canvas on the *Roamer* except three-reefed spanker and our dandy jib. She eats right up into the wind with that big jib.

"In spite of all that has happened this year," Jack reviewed, surveying water and sky with calm, sure eyes, "somehow it seems now as if it has been one of my hap-

piest—at least, when I think what I have started on the
Beauty Ranch!—At any rate," he finished, pulling the old
Tam over his fore-top, "there has been no boredom in it
all—no danger of *rusting*."

One morning in the midst of his work he burst out:

"I'm going to live a hundred years!"

"Yes? Why?"

"Because I want to!"

"It's a good reason—couldn't be bettered. But let me
remind you that you're likely to become a widower!"

"That *is* a consideration," reaching for me. "I'll have
to think it over!"

CHAPTER XXXVII

NEW YORK; MEXICO; *ROAMER*

1914

FOR us, ending one year and beginning another aboard ship was the acme of good fortune. The holidays, spent partly ashore while the cook remained to guard the *Roamer* where she lay moored to one city wharf or another, were full of cheer. The "Porchclimber" episode settled, our future looked brighter, though Jack remarked more than once: "I'm riding to a fall, financially; but I'm not worrying—you've never yet seen me stay down long. I'll work harder than ever!"

Our New Year was ushered in at the Saddle Rock restaurant. Two nights before Christmas, with a big southeaster blowing, Jack and Nakata got me into an evening gown aboard the yacht where she rolled at Lombard Street wharf in San Francisco, then rowed me to a float, from which we mounted to water-front street and taxi, to attend the house-warming of friends uptown. In the early hours we were back, and casting off, on the way to Sausalito. A terrific ebb was running, and Jack breathed a sigh of relief when he had his vessel safely clear of the docks and speeding on the ebb, before the gale, under a little shred of a reefed jigger. When, not far from Sausalito, we ran into the great run-out that tears down through Raccoon Straits to the Golden Gate, it seemed as if the tiny yawl could not possibly make it across. Jack, in his most congenial element, was on the pinnacle of exhilaration. And in fifty-five minutes the thirty-foot craft, under that rag of canvas, had made a passage that regularly takes the huge screw-ferryboats thirty-five.

Threading his way among the tossing sloops and schooners and motor boats at anchor off the yacht clubs at Sausalito, Jack navigated over the mud flats, well on the way into Mill Valley, where in the falling tide he laid the *Roamer* in the mud and went to sleep for the afternoon, upon his lips the contented murmur, "This is the Life! We've got all others skinned to death, Mate!" The next day, Christmas, Nakata rowed us to a railroad station on the shore, and we dined with friends in Mill Valley. And on the 26th we were cruising once more.

While lying off Point Richmond, Jack developed an earache, and with bandaged head called upon a doctor. In no time the dailies came out with an exciting story of how, in a blow, Jack London had been knocked senseless by the mainboom, while his wife bravely and cleverly brought the vessel to safe anchorage! Jack was aggrieved out of all apparent proportion to the matter; but the reason was that he so especially prided himself upon never having unseamanlike accidents.

He became interested in Richmond real estate to the extent of buying a lot, thereby branding himself as a "booster" for the new harbor subdivision of the Ellis Landing and Dock Company.

Just as we began congratulating ourselves that certain hindrances had been overridden, and upon the general outlook for the New Year, fresh trouble broke that necessitated Jack's jumping out for New York within twenty-four hours, leaving the yacht at San Rafael, where the ill news had found us looking over ground familiar to our childhood. There was much I must attend to at home owing to the suddenness of his departure, and so our first long separation took place.

"While I'm straightening out this snarl, I can be looking into other details that need attention, such as advances from the publishers," Jack reminded me. "I'll be having good news for you soon, I hope." He often arranged for advances, either in bulk, or in monthly payments, upon contemplated work.

The "snarl," which took him over a month to smooth out, was with reference to dramatic rights in one of his novels. An old friend had held these rights for some years without having made a successful showing. Moving pictures had never been considered in the days Jack had signed contracts for speaking performances, and there were men who tried to befog the issue; hence it behooved Jack, now interested in cinema productions, to clear his way of misunderstanding.

But his friend had entered into a dramatic contract for a production of the novel in question, and borrowed money against future box office receipts, which later did not appear to be imminent. The agent was willing to release the playwright, but to the tune of forty thousand dollars. Jack, appalled by the ridiculous sum, bent all his powers to beat down the "robber." It took him four weeks, and in the end he resorted to what he called his "play acting" to bring about the signing of a "decent" release of the rights. Early in the combat, I would have this sort of message: "Outlook dark," or "Situation ticklish," or "Nothing good to write." But his old unnatural condition when in New York seemed to be absent.

"To hell with New York," he wrote in the midst of this and other difficulties that beset. "I am here to master this Babylon and its sad cave-dwellers, not to be mastered!"

Later: "Hereafter, either before or after *Roamer* winter trip, my impression is that you and I will spend a month in New York."

One night in a triple collision of taxicabs, he came near losing his life. A certain manager of burlesque had taken him to the playhouse, and afterward introduced him to the leading lights, three of whom the two men undertook to escort to their homes. When the cars crashed Jack found himself at the bottom of the heap of kindling-wood that had been his cab, his mouth full of glass, and with a sense of suffocation, since the other four passengers contributed to the weight. Aside from minor cuts and bruises, the party escaped uninjured, and in some way avoided revealing their identity, so that the newspaper clippings Jack sent lacked all names. The theatrical man longed to have the event featured with "scare-head" lines, for the advertisement of his star, but Jack would have none of it.

"I'd have looked well," he grumbled to me, "with the report flashed all over the country that I'd been 'joy-riding' with a bunch af actresses!—— I've never been joy-riding in my life," he teased; "but I'm going some time, for I'll never be satisfied until I come home to you with a pink-satin slipper in my pocket!"

Whatever else Jack London did or did not do in New York City, he always spent much time upon the theatres. About this time he enthusiastically applauded the idea of the Little Theatre, and hoped that San Francisco would take up the idea. Some time before the breaking of the Great War, friends were promulgating a widely ramified plan for a new opera house and conservatory in San Francisco, and Jack made regular contributions to the promoters. So far, nothing has come of it.

Having succeeded in obtaining a "decent" release of the dramatic rights in his book, and made some very satisfactory agreements for New York, he wired: "General future never looked brighter."

A word as to the "play-acting" which caused the "robber" to throw up his hands, or, rather put his hand to the signing of the "decent release." Jack, partly as a whim, partly in order to compose undisturbed, had hidden himself in a notorious hostelry of the "theatrical tenderloin." When he had telephoned to his publisher to send his money, that person cried out, "Great Scott, man! What

are you doing in a house like that? I'll have to bring it myself!"

Jack decided to inveigle the enemy into his room. He endeavored to turn the tables, but Jack, pleading indisposi-
tion, also that he was too rushed to come out, since he
must leave for California sooner than he had planned, con-
trived to gain the other's consent to call at an early forenoon hour. He then prepared the stage and made up for
the impish part he intended to play:

"You should have seen me," he giggled, "I was a
sight to throw the fear of God into any highwayman of his
feather. I had sized him up, you see.

"For two days I purposely let my beard grow, and you
know how black it comes out. I opened my pajama-coat so
that the mat of hair showed on my chest. And of course I
left out my upper teeth, mussed up my head and wore an
eyeshade. I was not pretty.

"So, when the clerk 'phoned up that he was below, I
said, 'Send him right up.' He answered, 'he's stepped
outside.' 'Outside,' says I, 'what for?' 'I don't know—he
said he'd wait for you there. 'Tell him,' I ordered, 'That
I'm in bed, and can't come down.'

"Well, when his tap came, I sat up in bed, and the high-
arm chair I had placed for him had its back to the door so
that if he tried to escape me he'd be in an awkward position getting out of his chair to do it.—— It sounds awful,
I can see from your face, Mate," Jack interpolated. "But
remember, I had wrestled for weeks with him. He had even
agreed to my figures and terms, and promised to send me
the release, and then I would wait for days without a word,
marking time, when I wanted to go home. It was my sheer
whimsey to bring him to his senses in this fantastic way. My
God! It was ten thousand times more legitimate than his
slimy methods and those of his kind!

"To get back. He came in, trying not to look queer
when he saw the object I was—haggard from the dark

growth on my chin and neck, hair showing on my chest, and a ghastly toothless smile of welcome! In his hand was the document, which I took from him and glanced over. And every little while I looked aside to one or the other of my fists, as if gloating over them. As I talked with him without appearing to study him I took in his sick, scared face and soul. He'd have given anything not to have got himself into that chair.

"And then, I went over the whole business again, all we had talked in our many interviews, and he finally consented to release for a tithe of his original claims. He said:

" 'I'll go right to my office to make the change, and send you the agreement immediately.'

"I had waited for just that, and didn't mean that he should elude me again. Said I:

" 'You'll sign that paper right here on that table, before you leave this room!'—and when he protested, I went on, closing and unclosing my fists, to tell him just exactly what I would do to him if he refused. He looked this way and that, at the telephone, and half around at the door, and knew his situation for precisely what I had made it. He signed the release and left it with me. . . . And as it is, it will take me months to pay him, month by month."

A little ill news greeted Jack's return—the best young shorthorn bull had broken his neck, and hog cholera had carried off nearly all his blooded hogs.

"I always seem to have to build twice—everything I undertake," Jack said thoughtfully.

In his workroom again, *The Little Lady of the Big House* was begun, in which were exploited his maturing concepts on farming and stockbreeding. Many readers take for granted that the "Big House" was copied from Jack's Wolf House. As a matter of fact, a picture of Mrs. Phoebe A. Hearst's home at Pleasanton, California, was roughly the model for that of his hero and heroine on an imaginary ranch in the interior foothills.

Margaret Smith Cobb, a poet of the northern California forest country, whose verse Jack had been the means of placing with eastern magazines, sent me the fragmentary thoughts given below. Jack, to whom I forwarded them, commented: "The poem is most sweet, most beautiful, most true. Tell Margaret Cobb the same, for me. I care not to utter another word on that sad topic."

"Love, let us wander, you and I,
Where but charred embers and pale ashes lie;
Here where my dreams and fancies took still shape,
In all their glory, laid in wood and stone.
* * * * * *
Here, blow thy kisses, many, for a stair,
That we may rise where was thy line of rooms——
Rooms for thyself alone—we had them thus,
Where none might enter but the moon and I.

Dear love, the smoke is yet about my heart,
The crackle of the fire yet sears my brain.
—You will be kind, and dream and care no more,
Nor sorrow for what was my house of dreams."

About this time it was rumored that the Prohibitionists wanted to nominate Jack London for President. He, when asked about it, gave his usual breezy consent: "Sure—I'll run for anything, if it will help, especially if there's no chance of my being elected!"

A grapejuice company was formed for the manufacture, on a large scale, of the incomparable unfermented drink that we were already pressing, from wine grapes, for our own table. Jack was elated over the prospect. It created a new market for his ranch product, and by the same effort furthered the cause of prohibition. He drank regularly of the clear, natural juice that bore so little resemblance to the commercial article that smacks of stewed fruit.

"Government recipe, my dear, government recipe!" he would gurgle, holding his little glass to the light. "Free advice to every one—and they wonder how I find out these things!"

There was crookedness in the grapejuice company, as there had been in the past year's ventures. Jack, who had no money in this, only his name, was ultimately sued for $41,000; but the case never came to trial.

With travel in his eye, Jack had been plotting to convince an eastern weekly of the value of a series of articles on all the world, and there was talk of having him begin with Japan. I was joyous at the prospect of realizing our old hope to visit those fascinating isles together. But the Mexican fracas in the spring of 1914 came in between and the other articles never were undertaken. Hearst had asked Jack the preceding autumn if he would go to Mexico in case trouble broke. When the time came, there was some disagreement upon the price, and Jack went for *Collier's* instead. This constituted no infringement of his fiction contract, so long as he delivered the appointed measure of the fiction.

"And now," he said, hopefully, "I may be able to redeem myself as a war correspondent, after what I was held back from doing by the Japanese Army!"

If he had been able to foretell how slim was the chance of attaining his wish, he would not have gone. As it was, *Collier's* wired to know how long it would take him to make ready to start for Galveston, Texas, should they telegraph him to go. "Twenty-four hours," was the response. Came the bombardment of the Naval Academy at Vera Cruz, and on April 16 the summons arrived. We left Glen Ellen the next morning, and Oakland the same afternoon.

"I'll see you on your way as far as Galveston," ventured

I, taking for granted that Galveston would be the end of my journey.

"You can't get ready in time!" Jack said, but with a bright expectancy that was balm to my apprehension, for I had not been enthusiastic about his going under fire.

"Oh, *can't* I!" and out came the trunks.

"Well," he paused from his own preparations to gladden my heart, "if you get that far, maybe we can get you to Vera Cruz at least—even if you have to stay there when we go on march to the City of Mexico."

Shortly before leaving, Jack handed me a copy of "The Valley of the Moon," inscribed:

"Dear My-Woman:

"This is our 'Book of Love,' here in our 'Valley of the Moon,' where we have lived and known our love ever since that day you rode with me to the divide of the Napa hills—Ay, and before that, before that."

It was at Galveston that Richard Harding Davis in the second instance rendered Jack London a service. Several days had passed, the date of departure with General Frederick Funston was nearing, and all the other correspondents who were to accompany him on the transport *Kilpatrick* had received their credentials from Washington and were gaily making ready. Jack's alone seemed to be withheld, for Edgar Sisson, editor of *Collier's,* kept wiring Jack to the effect that he was not to worry—everything would reach him in time.

On the morning of the transports' sailing-date, I was shocked from sleep and upon my feet by a burst of martial music that led a host of men in olive-drab who marched, with brave, ominous sound, along the sea-wall drive. Jack joined me at the window and silently we watched the stream of human life go down to the gulf in ships. Although thrilling to the spectacle, Jack could not forget, and quoted from Le Gallienne's *"The Illusion of War"*:

" 'War,
I abhor,
And yet how sweet
The sound along the marching street
Of drum and fife, and I forget
Wet eyes of widows, and forget
Broken old mothers, and the whole
Dark butchery without a soul.' "

As the morning wore, and still no word from Washington, we became genuinely concerned. Before others, Jack preserved a careless demeanor; but when he looked into my eyes I saw in his the baffled, pained expression that he must have worn in childhood.

"I can't understand it, I can't understand it," he puzzled. "Each time I've called on General Funston, his aide has courteously put me off. I know the General is not well, with that abscess in his ear, poor devil; but that isn't the reason. So there seems to be simply nothing I can do."

"I don't care for myself," he would reiterate. "I want to make good to Sisson, whose idea it was for me to go for *Collier's.* I don't want to throw him down." Presently, having dictated to me his final letters, and sent off his Article I to *Collier's,* he disappeared downstairs, murmuring:

" 'And even my peace-abiding feet
Go marching down the marching street,
For yonder, yonder goes the fife,
And what care 1 for human life!
. . .
And yet 'tis all unbannered lies,
A dream those little drummers make.' "

An hour passed, and I thought to reconnoitre in the lobby. Emerging from the elevator, my heart leaped to see Jack and the General's aide, Lieutenant Ball, each grasping the other by both hands, and laughing like schoolboys too pleased for words.

"Why, Mate," Jack explained as we hurried upstairs to put the last touches to his packing, "it's all up to Richard Harding Davis. He came to me and said he wondered if I knew what was going on. You remember that so-called 'Good Soldier' canard that was attributed to me? It has turned up again. As soon as Davis mentioned it, I could see the whole trouble in a flash. We looked up Lieutenant Ball, and—well, you saw us when you came down. Funny how pleased *he* was to get the thing cleared up!"

At luncheon, our table was near that of the General. He and his aide were consulting earnestly; and after a while the Lieutenant came toward us. Jack rose, and the two returned to the General.

"I gave him my word of honor that I did not write a line of that canard," Jack reported to me, "and upon that word he takes the responsibility of adding me to his already filled quota of correspondents. It seems that he had had word from Washington that my going was left up to him, but he, personally, was up in arms about the canard."

Next, a telegram came from Secretary Josephus Daniels that if Jack could not be accommodated on the transport, he should go on one of the convoying destroyers. "And that would be an experience new to me, too," Jack exulted. But a place was shaken down on the *Kilpatrick*, on which he sailed Friday afternoon. Any regrets that I may have felt at my inability to accompany him were tempered by the fact that I expected to depart twenty-four hours later, and to meet him on the very date of his arrival in Vera Cruz. This was made possible by our good friend Mr. Robert T. Burge, who had proffered me passage on a vessel of the Gulf Coast Steamship Company, of which he was President.

"I'm only too glad to present you with a ticket," he smiled, "but for goodness' sake, don't go. The steamers are not suitable for ladies' travel. . . . But go if you really must!"

Never shall I forget that evening the little old *Atlantis* (wrecked the next voyage) approached Vera Cruz. Across the mighty slopes of the storied land, Orizaba towered blue against a sunset sky; and to the south were raised the turrets of the "far-flung battle line" of our own Navy, its smoke mingling with the low tropic clouds. "War, I abhor, and yet——" that has nothing to do, per se, with just valuation of the magnificent machinery invented by brain of man. One of Jack's Mexican articles, in want of real war news, was devoted to what he saw at Tampico's oil-fields. Certain radical contemporaries raged against him, and one, a noted socialist writer, accused him publicly of having been subsidized by the oil interests—subsidized! Jack London! None but a stupid, or at best a warped creature, it would seem to those who knew him, could seriously conceive such a thing.

"Me! subsidized?" Jack stormed, "My worst capitalist enemies have done me the honor to know better than that. Why, no human being has ever dared even to *hint* subsidization to me, thank God!"

Here again, friend and enemy were like to convict him of paradox. Few could comprehend that universality which made him grasp the whole through all its parts. While decrying war, he could at the same time appreciate the romantic majesty of conquest, hail the bunting of great armadas, respect the courage and deeds of men who battled according to their lights. I have seen him almost weep over the exploits of British admirals and fearless midshipmen of old. "Look!" he would cry, following me with a dusty tome in his hands, "Listen to this, and this . . . this is the sort of stuff that went into the making of you, white woman, and me, and all of us who conquer ourselves and our environment!" In order to preserve a clear view of Jack, it must be held in mind that despite the warm human emotionalism of him he always came to rest upon his intellectual conceptions.

Achievement, to him, was achievement, though he saw all around and under it. "I take off my hat to it," he would say, whether inspecting the Culebra Cut, or the Harbor of Pago Pago, or the oil fields of Tampico, or the beneficial organization thrown into Vera Cruz by the army and navy. "If only the whole world could be made so clean and orderly," he said. "If such cleanliness and order could emanate, not from the idea of militarism, but as a social achievement. Let us not wantonly destroy these wonderful machines, these great world assets, that produce efficiently and cheaply. Let us control them. Let us profit by their efficiency and cheapness."

Upton Sinclair, commending upon Jack's detractors, made no mistake:

"He wrote a series of articles that caused certain radicals to turn from him in rage. But I felt certain that the exponent of capitalist efficiency who counted upon Jack London's backing was a child playing in a dynamite factory. . . . If a naval officer took him over a battleship, he would perceive that it was a marvelous and thrilling machine; but let the naval officer not forget that in the quiet hours of the night Jack London's mind would turn to the white-faced stokers, to whom as a guest of an officer he had not been introduced!"

While decrying war, in time of danger Jack said: "Although I am a man of peace, I carry an automatic pistol. I might meet somebody who would not listen to my protestations of friendship and amity. And so with nations —we're a long way from universal disarmament. The most peaceful nation to-day is likely to run up against some other nation that does not want peace. It would look as if we shall need armies for a weary while to come, to enforce the idea of peace."

He appeared to be surprised at the personnel of the

army and its officers. I must confess that my own general idea of the hard-bitten "regular" underwent a revelation. The rank and file were of a youthful and mostly blond Anglo-Saxon type. I noticed also that Jack was pleased to find many of the officers of both army and navy less "machinely crammed" than he had thought, quite able to stand on their own feet when it came to up-to-date, independent thinking. Jack held that the world would have no more big wars for a long time. "There will be wars, at one time or another," he believed. "You can't change man entirely from the primitive, fighting animal he is. But I do not think we of to-day shall see a big war. The nations are enlightened enough to stop short of that, and arbitrate their differences." I borrow this from *The Human Drift:*

"War is passing. It is safer to be a soldier than a workingman. The chance for life is greater in an active campaign than in a factory or a coal mine. In the matter of killing war is growing impotent, and this in the face of the fact that the machinery of war was never so expensive in the past nor so dreadful. . . . War has become a joke. Men have made for themselves monsters of battle which they cannot face in battle. Not only has war, by its own evolution, rendered itself futile, but man himself, with greater wisdom and higher ethics, is opposed to war."

But his uniformed acquaintances, sitting in the portales of the old Diligencias Hotel, sipping Bacardi rum cocktails, disagreed:

"Germany will start something before a great while—see if she doesn't. And she's dying to get her hands on the United States."

For once, Jack was a poor prophet.

Aside from his old associates of Jap-Russ memories—R. H. Davis, "Jimmy" Hare, "Bobbie" Dunn, Frederick Palmer—there were present in Vera Cruz the veteran war artist, Zogbaum, and Reuterdhal, who incidentally made a "*Collier*" cover from a sketch of Jack; J. B. Connolly, whom we had met in Boston; Burge McFall (Associated Press); John T. McCutcheon; Arthur Ruhl, Vincent Starrett, Stanton Leeds, Oliver Madox Hueffer from London, and Mrs. Dean, the "Widow" of the New York *Town Topics*. And from Mexico City, Mr. and Mrs. R. H. Murray, representing the New York *World*. There were others, whose names escape me.

Jack was not the only correspondent who chafed under the restraint imposed upon the army in Mexico; nor did the six weeks in that country strengthen his already weak regard for the Latin American. When the report came that Huerta had slipped out of Puerta Mexico to the south, the whole force was personally in mutinous humor with sitting inactive. Several of the newspapermen broke parole and made their precarious way to the capital, where some of them landed in prison. Jack had declined to go, saying he did not feel it was fair to General Funston. But later on he mitigated the control he had put upon himself, and sailed on the *Mexicana* for Tampico, the round-trip covering a week. He would not hear of my going to share any possible nip-and-tuck hazard. Realizing that I would be in his way, I did not urge, but remained, with Nakata, at the hotel. Jack charged me, in case orders should come for the army to march for Mexico City, to buy him a horse, and have all in readiness for him to go when he should jump back from Tampico. He also had me wait upon the good General, to discover if Nakata, being Japanese, might go along in such event. This the General did not think advisable; so I kept alert for some other man.

"If there is any advice you need, Mate," Jack adjured me, "any help at any time, apply to Richard Harding Davis." Which clinched what he thought of the "white man" who had so staunchly declined to see a brother correspondent labor under disadvantage. Davis died shortly before Jack; and six days before Jack's death, I heard him deliver an impassioned encomium on Davis as a man.

There being no military action about which to write, Jack employed himself turning out articles upon general observations and conditions as he saw them. For recreation, there were horseback rides and drives within the proscribed radius; swims at Los Baños; dinners and luncheons aboard the fleet or with the officers of army and navy ashore; shopping for laces, Mexican blankets, serapes and opals; visits to the little provost court where the natives gaped at a kindly dispensation of justice beyond all their conception; dancing in patios along the portales of the hotels; bull fights—General Funston watched these carefully, and allowed no horses in the ring. Aboard the *Solace*, the hospital ship, we found the wounded boys reading J. B. Connolly and Jack London, and forgetful of suffering in their pleasure at meeting the authors.

Those broken boys were forerunners of the thousands from all classes, one in pain and purpose, for whom in the hospitals of Europe Jack was to fill so many needs. "There, in hospital," wrote one, "I read *Burning Daylight* . . . then the doctor sent me to Blighty. There I left *Burning Daylight*—in the midst of volumes neat and clean and new, damp-stained and broken-backed, I left it . . ." And from our friend Major Harry Strange, at the Front: "I always knew somewhat, and Jack taught me more, and war has quite convinced me, that the only happiness and joy worth while is in service, good, big, noble, brave-hearted service." The Tommies called Jack's books "the Jacklondons"; and one of them, a hot-hearted young Celt, wrote me from Dublin: "I only know that the man who comprehends as he did is always right, and that every one else is wrong." Which voices my own conviction. Again I listen to Jack's appeal: "Be patient with me in the little things; I am really patient in the big ones—I have not winced nor cried aloud." And whereas he might be hasty in little things and little judgments, upon the big issues of mankind and of his own affairs in relation to mankind, he laid a divining finger that could not touch other than wisely and rightly.

There were visits to San Juan de Ulua, with its spew of filthy, dehumanized prisoners, whom, with their unthinkable dungeons, our navy cleansed and deodorized. Some of these unfortunates had no faintest notion as to what, if any, offense had condemned them to that living burial below sea level. Others recited haltingly the most trivial of incidents that had doomed them to exist for years without standing-room or light.

"Pretty awful, isn't it?—— But don't forget, Mate," Jack, who never forgot anything, would point out, "that we ourselves aren't half-civilized yet, in our treatment of convicts. Also, there's such a thing as 'railroad' still existing in the land of the free!"

All this time, busy working and playing in Vera Cruz, waiting while Washington held the army and navy bound in port, Jack, according to rumor in the capitalist press of the United States, was leading a band of insurrectos somewhere in the north of Mexico! Rumor, did I say? The large headlines read:

JACK LONDON LEADS ARMY OF MEXICO REBELS.

That some one was making use of his name, however, seems probable; for later on we heard of persons who had met "Jack London" in Mexico and in Lower California. And an American firm dealing in artist's materials, waited for years for this or another spurious Jack London in Mexico to settle his account.

Whether Jack gathered the bacilli in Tampico, or whether General Maas' blockade that prevented the ingress of fresh food to the occupied town of Vera Cruz, combined with the hotel's filthy kitchen, was responsible, we shall never know. But on May 30, the day set for him to go up in an army aeroplane, instead he went to bed in our lately bullet-riddled room, with acute bacillary dysentery. Nakata and I took charge of the nursing, under the resident American physician, Dr. A. R. Goodman, in consultation with Major Williams. The latter wanted him to go into army hospital, but Jack seemed to prefer a woman nurse, being myself. Thereafter, every spoonful of water that passed his lips or was used in nursing, was first thoroughly boiled in our room by means of electric appliances, "Thanks to American efficiency," he groaned from his bed; and his food we cooked by the same process.

It was a desperate, cautious campaign against death, but as usual the patient managed by his uncommon recuperative powers to make a spectacular recovery. After a few days he insisted that I take the air with our friends, and upon my accepting dinner invitations in the portales below. "And be sure you don't stint yourself at the lace shops!" he would call after, with indulgent eyes. Or he would turn to greet a decayed Spanish gentleman who tiptoed in, who must part with certain ornaments of coral and ancient gold filigree:

"Do you like it, Mate?" he would finger a bracelet or rosary. "If you do, say the word. A woman must have *some* loot of war, even if her husband has to buy it!"

Nine days after he was stricken, and with pleurisy to boot, he was able to go aboard the cattle transport *Ossabaw,* bound for Galveston. "If anything breaks in Vera Cruz, which I don't think likely, I can return," he said. "Meantime, me for the Ranch, where I can have white-man's climate and grub!"

"Do you know what are in the long boxes where those soldiers are sitting to play cards?" Jack pointed down to the main deck. And before I could gasp a reply, he finished:

"Those fellows were dead in four days of what I pulled through."

About this time occurred the riots in the hopfields at Wheatland, California, resulting from shocking conditions and treatment, and for once the high-handed methods of certain detectives had roused the ire of the public. Jack's opinion concerning this ''death hole'' was sought—indeed, looking over his clipping-books, I notice how frequently he was asked for his opinion upon widely variant subjects. I quote:

''The sheriff fired a shot in the air, and then, presto! it all happened at once. As a matter of fact, nobody knows what happened. I am willing to bet that if every one of these witnesses went before God Almighty and told, to the best of his recollection, no two would agree. It was the well-known crowd psychology on the job.

''These men were not organized. There was only one amongst the 2300 of them who held an I. W. W. card. They did not need organization. They had seen the cost of living soar and soar, their purchasing power grow less and less; they had all felt within themselves, 'Something must be done.' Above all, they have had force preached into them, pounded into them, from the beginning—by whom? The employers.

''The employers have always ruled the working class with force. One incident happened that is strangely typical. One of the Durst Brothers struck one of the leading workmen in the face. He said he did it 'facetiously.' Maybe he did; it isn't likely. But, facetious or not, that blow symbolized the whole relation between employer and employee. Where they do not actually strike blows, it is because they fear the blows will be struck back.

''Now, Sheriff Voss and District Attorney Manwell came on the scene not at all in the interest of equity, but in the interest of the employer. They were not there to see fair play; they were there to 'keep order.' The sheriff expected his shot in the air to cow them.

''Why didn't they cow? Simply because they are becoming more and more imbued with the belief that force is the only way. I look back over history and see that never has the ruling class relinquished a single one of its privileges except it was forced to.

''It is always the things we fight for, bleed for, that we care most for. This lesson of force is soaking into the workers—that's all.''

Another question upon which Jack's views were solicited was as follows: A grown man in the State of Illinois took advantage of a young girl, and was sentenced to thirty years in the penitentiary. A child being born, the young mother started a movement to free its father so that he might marry her for the sake of the child. Jack's answer to the Newspaper Enterprise Association is below:

"The world and civilization belong to the races that practice monogamy. Monogamy is set squarely against promiscuity. Wherefore monogamy, as the cornerstone of the state, demands a legal father for Vallie. Also the father and the mother of Vallie desire to make their parenthood legal. Therefore the only logical thing for the state of Illinois to do is to make possible this legalization of Vallie's birth and parentage. Otherwise the State of Illinois stultifies itself by kicking out the cornerstone of civilization on which it is found, namely, the family group that can exist only under monogamy."

No one could be more shaken than Jack, in July, by the beginning of war in Europe. And while he went on unremittingly with writing and ranch, the war was the undercurrent of every thought. More staunchly than ever before he reiterated his faith in England. "England is fighting her first popular war," he would say; and he could not forgive Germany, over and above her sworn Frightfulness, for having been stupid enough to think that England would not fight.

But to any proposition bearing upon his presence in France as correspondent, he practically turned a deaf ear, in 1914 and thenceforward until he died.

"Again I say, the Japanese settled the war correspondent forever, by proving him non-essential. Look at Davis and the rest, some of the best in the world," he would indicate as the conflict widened. "Eating out their hearts over there. Not for me. If I went, I would be unable to get what I went after. I have learned my lesson. If I ever do go to this war, it will be to fight with England and her Allies. . . . Meantime, I have a lot of mouths to feed, and irons in the fire, and I could not leave with my affairs in their present shape.''

Yet I knew that had there been the ghost of an opening for him to see what he wished, he would have managed to go.

He and *Collier's* corresponded upon the possibility, to find, in the end, that they agreed upon the matter. They wrote him:

''We learned . . . that of the twelve English correspondents chosen to join Sir John French's army not one has as yet been allowed the privilege, and the prospect seems that the thing has been indefinitely postponed. . . . The precariousness of the whole business of war correspondents at the present time seems to make it rather futile to put first-class men in the field, so to speak, and break their hearts by making it impossible for them to get anywhere of real importance. . . . We sent you a clipping some days ago which shows that finally all belligerents have decided to do away with correspondents. The result is that we can only get certain casual articles from roving writers of one sort or another with very little or real stuff from the front.''

Exasperated with the way he felt the Mexican crisis had been mishandled at Washington, Jack grew more so with the failure of his own country, as time went on, to take a hand in the European crisis. The effect of all this was to stimulate his brain to more thinking, while at the same time he increased his work and plans for work in every direction.

When in June he gave me ''*The Strength of the Strong*,'' the fly leaf reminded me of that in a book he had sent me the month before our marriage, in which was written: ''The red gods call to us. We fling ourselves across the world to meet again and not to part.'' And here, nine years later, I found:

"Back again from Vera Cruz, and all the world, you back with me from the war game, I am almost driven to assert that our little war game adventure was as sweet and fine as our first honeymoon."

In the Indian summer we rejoined the *Roamer* at San Rafael and spent months upon the big bay. The Exposition was rising from the water's edge and many the late afternoon we pulled up our fishing-lines where we lay off Angel Island, and sailed to where we could watch that dream city of domes and minarets in the flood of sunset rose and gold.

On December 8, Jack signed and dated the manuscript of *"The Little Lady of the Big House,"* and began working up notes for the Grove Play, which the Bohemian Club had asked him to prepare for the 1916 High Jinks.

CHAPTER XXXVIII

ROAMER; RETURN TO HAWAII; GLEN ELLEN FORTIETH YEAR

1915

WANT to hear some of your husband's verse?" he queried with mock gravity, inking a period to his first morning's work upon "The Acorn Planter." "Come below, and listen how it runs along!"

He had much sport writing this thin little volume. But let no one mistake that he was not in dead earnest with regard to its motif. Far from attempting formal versification, he but fixed more noticeably the runic tendency in earlier work which had dealt with the Younger World. When it was done and read aloud, he passed me the last slender sheaf to copy, sighing:

"I don't know what to think of it—and yet, I don't believe it is so bad! Good or bad, however, it is done; so send it along to the Secretary of the Bohemian Club. ——One thing about it, though: I'll bet the composers in the Club are going to have merry hell putting music to it. They've done Indian stuff before now; but this goes too far back into the raw beginnings of the race, I fear. . . . Ready to cast off, Nakata?" And Jack sprang to the *Roamer's* wheel, and in fine disdain of wind and wave forgot "The Acorn Planter," and all its works.

It was for the very reason feared by Jack that the Grove Play was finally written by some one else. "The Acorn Planter" has never been enacted, but appeared in book-form in 1916. "And somehow, I like the little thing," he would say, passing his hand over it.

"And now," he announced at nine the morning after it was finished," now for a dog-story. I just seem to have to write one every so often."

This was "Jerry," which was followed by a companion book, "Michael," as "The Call of the Wild" had preceded "White Fang." When, Jack gone beyond consulting, I was confronted with the dilemma of issuing "Jerry" simultaneously with a book of the same name from another house, I hit upon "Jerry of the Islands," with "Michael Brother of Jerry" to balance the sequel. Jack had planned, after bringing out both volumes, eventually to combine them under the title of "Jerry and Michael." I remember how he reveled in creating the Ancient Mariner.

"Michael," beneath its delightful romance and character portraiture, is frank propaganda for the stamping out of stage-training for animals. To this end, Jack had for years been quietly collecting data from every available source. No reader who would understand his motive should pass by the Preface of "Michael, Brother of Jerry," which states his views. Out of this book has grown a rapidly expanding, international organization known as The Jack London Club. There are no dues.

"Jerry" and "Michael" appeared duly in *The Cosmopolitan Magazine*, and the books were published in 1917 and 1918 respectively. "Jerry" was partly written in Hawaii.

Young friends in Stockton persuaded us to leave the yacht at anchor and join a week-end jaunt to Truckee, for the winter sports. There in the High Sierras we tobogganed and went on sleighing parties. A visit to the lake where the ill-starred Donner Party had made its last stand against odds, affected Jack—that frontier tragedy, with others of the brave old days, having always stirred his imagination. The skiing, while he watched it by the hour, and ice-skating, Jack would not attempt with his "smashed" ankles, which had been cramping at night. "Getting old, getting old," he would grit through his teeth while I manipulated the small feet. "Do you realize that your husband is in his fortieth year?"

Then he met "Scotty," otherwise Mr. J. H. Scott, champion dog-musher, with his prize teams of Malemutes and Siberian huskies, gee-pole sleds and all. Jack's pleasure knew no bounds—because, forsooth, beyond all personal joy in renewing acquaintance with the trappings of a wonderful phase in his youth, he could now show me the old way of the Northland. "Scotty" appreciated the situation, and we must drive with him. Two sleds swung up to the curb, one driven by Mr. Brady, and we took the novel airing for glistening miles to a neighboring mountain town—Jack behind the eight Malemutes, I drawn by the dozen lighter dogs, little chow-like things of fluff and steel, with plumy curled tails and the brightest, merriest eyes and manners in the world, ready to stampede the outfit any moment a rabbit hove above the white horizon.

"Gee! I wish it were possible to film 'The Call of the Wild,' Jack considered. "What good materials right here! But I don't see how it could be done—a dog hero would be necessary."

"How about your stage-training for animals?" I hinted. But he thought the "cruelty" would be negligible in preparing a dog, whose part at best could be but subsidiary.

"Remember," he worked it out, "a long time, in one place, with no harsh traveling conditions, would be taken to get the dog in shape. A few performances, at most, would do the trick, which is very different from the vaudeville circuit, my dear, where the animal is obliged, fair weather and foul, to go through the same act, often of most unnatural character, from two to four times a day, year in and year out."

Right here is a good place to make clear Jack London's position with regard to a much-mooted issue, that of vivisection. He subscribed to the use, not the abuse of vivisection, approaching this subject, as all others, through the scientific avenue.

"No, I'll admit, I'd run a thousand miles rather than see a pet dog of mine cut up. But if it were a choice between having my dog or any dog experimented upon, and my child or any child, I'd say the dog every time."

Thus, he had little time to waste in argument with men and women who made claim that no benefit had been derived from vivisection, no human life saved by the conclusions therefrom. He considered that he knew better, what of the time he spent with the books.

"There will always be fanatics, and there will always be abuse, in any field of research," he would declare. "But the legitimate practice of vivisection should not be interfered with. It should be subject to inspection and control—but not by ignorant and prejudiced sentimentalists, who won't listen to the good features of a proposition, and who exaggerate the regretable."

There was something inimical working in Jack's blood those days. No sooner were we back on the Ranch, than the sporadic cramps were succeeded by an attack of rheumatism in one foot.

"And gaze out of that window, at the weather," he grieved, pointing from his bed to the streaming landscape. "Last winter there wasn't enough rain. This year we're swamped! God doesn't love the farmer! But the drain-tile is carrying off a lot of the overflow—things are working, things are working!" he cheered up.

Severe pyorrhea of long standing contributed its quota of poison; and, in his acid condition, his yachting fare of twelve-minute-roasted canvasback and mallard, and red-meated raw fish, was hazardous menu. He experimented with emetine, and had the village doctor make tri-weekly calls at the Ranch to give him intramuscular hypodermic injections. Jack's mouth altered considerably in latter years, from loss of all upper teeth and wearing a plate.

The upper lip, once full and narrowing to the deep corners, grew thinner and more straight of line. It was no less beautiful—merely different from the more youthful feature. Jack's face, at whatever age, breaking into smile of lips and eyes, was one that, once seen, was never forgotten. It is undying. It will persist as long as the life of any one who beheld it.

Before sailing for Honolulu on February 24, we made several trips to that loveliest of evanescent cities, the Pan-Pacific Exposition. Jack cared little, as a rule, for that sort of spectacle and amusement. But the sunset metropolis enfolded him in its golden embrace, charmed him into hours of unwonted idleness, through afternoon and blue twilight, listening to the fountains and watching the Tower of Jewels blossom against the starlit skies. One day I particularly recall, when we had arrived early and stepped into the human, holiday atmosphere that pervaded the vast inclosure.

"I never drove a car in my life," Jack threatened. "It's time I began. Woman, climb in!" What I was so summarily invited to climb into was one of the handy electric-driven wheel-chairs that rest many tired limbs. How we laughed; and how the morning strollers laughed with the enthusiastic, noisy boy with the cap and curls, who coaxed the feeble mechanism into doing his will, and when it would not respond, talked to it eloquently before dismounting and lifting it around. It was Jack London, any of you who joined in gayety with the exuberant boy that crisp California morning. Once, stalled momentarily in a geranium nursery behind the giant arbor that was the Horticultural Building, he stopped to admire the floral flames. He did not live to learn that one of them, a large crimson single variety, had been named for himself.

Going to Hawaii had been farthest from our thoughts that winter of 1915, and our decision was a result of the merest turn of events. Jack, beneath almost more than he could stagger, even with his large earnings, intended to stay close at home and work out his financial salvation under double pressure of work. *The Cosmopolitan* had offered release from his fiction contract long enough for him to accompany the Atlantic Fleet, carrying the President, on its jaunt through the Panama Canal to the Exposition. Jack's personal desire, or lack of desire to leave home, is expressed in his telegraphic reply:

"Glen Ellen, December 18, 1914.

"Don't want to go anywhere. Don't want to do anything except stay in California and write two dandy novels, the first of which I am now framing up. However, since I like to be as good to my friends as I like my friends to be good to me, I am willing to fall for the Panama adventure if it does not compel me to lose too much financially.

"European war has hit me hard financially, wherefore in view of fact that Panama trip is short enough not to prevent my delivering next year's serials on time, the primary stipulation is that regular check comes to Ranch every month, including the month in which I do Panama. Wire me full business details, dates, and amount of stuff I am expected to write. Should like several days in New York before sailing."

It was not for me to sail on the battleship, and while I accepted my feminine fate, I declined again to remain in California during an absence of Jack. "I shall go to Honolulu and join Beth," referring to my cousin, Beth Wiley, who was wintering here. "I can be in San Francisco for your return."

Jack, though outwardly falling in with my plan, I think was rather taken aback at the idea of his small woman going her own way, alone. It was amusing to note his restlessness. Not once but many times he would boil over.

"I don't want to go on that damned Panama trip—I want to go to Hawaii with you, and work on 'Jerry' and 'Michael!'"

Or: "Somehow, I can't be content not to see the Islands again, with you."

The exigencies of the European conflict having made it necessary to call off the Fleet's Exposition voyage, Jack's voice rang with the good news:

"Look what I've got! And now, Mate Woman, I can go to Hawaii with you!"

But when, standing on the deck of the *Matsonia*, we waved farewell to our friends, he confessed:

"Do you know the true reason I am aboard this ship to-day? Because I could not bear to disappoint you—and incidentally myself. I ought not to go away, with all those important things needing my attention. But I just couldn't risk the sight of your face when I should tell you that you'd have to go alone after all!"

"But I wouldn't," said I, with a great relief that our feet were on the outward-bound planking. "I should have staid home, of course, where I belonged—and beside," I put in slyly, "if you had let business keep you home, it would be the first time! You've always been able to manage things from a distance, and the mails and cable facilities are still working."

"You're right," he acknowledged.

This and our next visit, as before written, are detailed in my book "Our Hawaii." In the 1921 edition, I have included three articles written by Jack in 1916, entitled "My Hawaiian Aloha," which one of the Territory's leading men pronounced "worth millions to the Islands."

We took our own servants and set up housekeeping, in the first instance on Beach Walk, whence we came and went on inter-island travels in the group. Our daily life in the pretty cottage included the same working habits as at home; and afternoons were spent on the beach. Each day, after luncheon, saw Jack, often robed in a blue kimono of bold design, carrying a long bag of similar fabric containing reading matter and cigarettes, with a bath-towel wound turban-wise around his head, soft-footing Kalia Road bound for the Outrigger Club. They were happy hours, lying on the shady sand among the barbaric black-and-yellow canoes, reading aloud, napping, and chatting with our friends. Later in the day we swam through and beyond the breakers and spent some of the most wonderful moments of our united lives floating in the deeper water where, in the swaying, caressing element, undisturbed betwixt sky and earth, all things lost their complicated aspect, and we talked simply and solemnly of the issues that count most in human relationship.

When "The Scarlet Plague," written just before the baby was born, had been received, in it he wrote:

"My Mate-Woman:

"And here, in blessed Hawaii, eight years after our voyage here in our own speck boat, we find ourselves, not merely again, but more bound to each other than then or than ever."

In March he wrote a Preface for "The Cry for Justice," by Upton Sinclair.

The following letter, written on June 3, is interesting:

"Dear Cloudesley:

"In reply to yours of May 15. First of all, whatever you do, read Conrad's latest—VICTORY. Read it, if you have to pawn your watch to buy it. Conrad has exceeded himself. He must have deliberately set himself the challenge, and it is victory for him, because he has skinned "Ebb Tide."

"He has made a woman out of nothing—out of sweepings of life, and he has made her woman glorious. He has painted love with all love's illusion—himself, Conrad, devoid of illusion.

"Lena goes without saying. She is Woman. But it is possible, absolutely possible, for the several such men as Mr. Jones, Ricardo, Pedro, Heyst, Schomberg, Morrison, Davidson, and Wang and his Alfuro woman, to exist. I know them all. I have met them all. I swear it.

"As regards the love of this book, the sex of this book—all the love and the sex of it is correct, cursedly correct, splendidly, magnificently correct, with every curse of it and every splendid magnificence of it duly placed, shaded and balanced. Yes, and the very love of Ricardo is tremendous and correct.

"In brief, I am glad that I am alive, if, for no other reason, because of the joy of reading this book.

"Jack London."

The next day, still filled with his emotion, he could not restrain himself from passing it on to the author of "Victory":

"Honolulu, T. H., June 4, 1915.

"Dear Joseph Conrad:

"The mynah birds are waking the hot dawn about me. The surf is thundering in my ears where it falls on the white sand of the beach, here at Waikiki, where the green grass at the roots of the cocoanut palms insists to the lip of the wave-wash. This night has been yours—and mine.

"I had just begun to write when I read your first early work. I have merely madly appreciated you and communicated my appreciation to my friends through all these years. I never wrote you. I never dreamed to write you. But 'Victory' has swept me off my feet, and I am inclosing herewith a carbon copy of a letter written to a friend at the end of this lost night's sleep. [The letter to Cloudesley.]

"Perhaps you will appreciate this lost night's sleep when I tell you that it was immediately preceded by a day's sail in a Japanese sampan of sixty miles from the Leper Settlement of Molokai (where Mrs. London and I had been revisiting old friends) to Honolulu.

"On your head be it.

"Aloha (which is a sweet word of greeting, the Hawaiian greeting, meaning 'My love be with you.")

"Jack London."

Never, before or since, have I taken such hazards with the water as during those months at Waikiki, under Jack's tutelage. Always relying upon that sixth sense of his in matters of life and death, I followed his lead wherever he thought by direction I could go, and accomplished what I would not have deemed possible for myself. But he never led me where he feared I could not safely swim. And when once or twice we had surmounted conditions that kept shorebound the canoes and even surfriders, and returned unexhausted, his joy and pride in his "one small woman" were unlimited.

"You're so little, so frail, white woman of my own kind," he would marvel, his great eyes looking into me as if to discern the fiber of which I was made. 'Look at that arm, with its delicate bones—I could snap it like a clay pipe-stem . . . and yet, those arms never faltered in that succession of smoking combers to-day . . ." He tapped his forehead: "That's where it resides—that's what makes the trivial flesh and bone able to do what it does!"

Deep thinker though he was, and worshipful of the brain-stuff of others, he ever found shining things of the spirit in courageous physical endeavor. I think, in a dozen close years with him, year in and year out, "in sickness and in health," till death did us part, that never have I seen him more elated, more uplifted with delight over feat of one dear to him, than upon one April day at Waikiki.

An out-and-out Kona gale had piled up a big, quick-following surf, threshing milk-white and ominous under a leaden, low-hanging sky. At the Outrigger beach no soul was visible; but a group of young sea-gods belonging to the Club sat with bare feet outstretched on the railing of the lanai above the canoes. Joining them, Jack inquired if they were "going out." "Nothing doing," one laughed. And another, "This is no day for surf-boards—and a canoe couldn't live in that mess!" "But we are going to swim out," Jack said. "You'd better not, Mr. London," the boys frowned respectfully. "You couldn't take a woman into that water." "You watch me," Jack returned. "I could, and shall."

We went. Now, understand: it was not to be spectacular that Jack led me into the sea that day. This was not bravado. With the several weeks' training he had given me in sizable breakers, he expected as a matter of course to see me put that training to account. And I felt as one with him. The thing was, first, to get beyond the diving-stage, for a freshet had brought down the little river a tangle of thorned algaroba and other prickly vegetation, which, with a wild wrack of seaweed, made the shallow almost impassable.

Very slowly we forged outward, and at length were in position where the marching seas were forming and over-toppling. Rather stupendous they loomed, I will confess; but, remembering other and smaller ones and obeying scrupulously Jack's quiet "Don't get straight up and down —straighten out—keep flat, *keep flat!*" I managed not badly to breast and pass through a dozen or more smoking combers that followed fast and faster.

When I finally ventured, "I think I have had enough," immediately Jack slanted our course channel-ward where the tide flows out toward the reef egress. But after half an hour we found we were, despite all effort, drifting willy nilly out to sea. By now, the young sea-gods had followed with their boards, fearing we might come to grief; and upon their advice we rejoined the breaking water, and "came in strong" with our best strokes to the Beach.

Which I tell, further to point his passion for physical courage and prowess that after all are but mental. "I'd like you to write books, if you wanted to," was his final word; "but I'd rather see woman of mine win through those great seas out there than write great books!"

Jack's health was fairly good that summer, though he seemed to be on tension, and prone to argue overlong and over-intensely. Indeed, as time went on, he battled with this and that opponent, or provoked skirmishes, with an increasing fervor and violence that ill-betokened a peaceful old age. "Oh, well, I'd rather wear out than rust out!" was his verdict on the matter.

And once Jack told me a thing that will abide like a dove of peace until I die, as one of my sweetest touches with this sweetest of men:

"I never said this to you," he began; "but many years ago, before I knew you existed, I lay one afternoon on a California beach—at Santa Cruz—in one of my great disgusts . . . you know—when I have dared look Truth in the face and become blackly pessimistic about the world and the men and women in it who cannot learn, who cannot use their puny minds. It was a warm, still day; and while I lay, with my face on my arms, over and above the steady breathing of the ocean and splashing of a small surf, there came to me, from very far off, almost like skylarks in the blue, the voices of a man and a woman.

"I couldn't for the life of me figure where the voices came from. I raised my head, but no one was in sight on the beach; and at last, the nearing conversation guided me seaward where I could just barely make out the heads of two persons very leisurely coming in, talking cozily out there in deep water, as unconcerned and comfortable as if sitting in the sand.

"Something inside me suddenly yearned toward them —they were so blest, those two together. And I wondered, lying there sadly enough, if there was a woman in the world for me who so loved the water—the little woman who would be the right woman who would speak my own language— with whom I could go out to sea, without boat or life-preserver; hours in the water holding long comradely talks on everything under the sun, with no more awareness of the means of locomotion than if walking.——I could have told you this eight years ago," he mused, "that wonderful morning we swam together across Urufaru Bay in Moorea, while the Tahitians worried about the sharks. . . . I thought of it at the time. But we were not alone. The stage was not set for you and me.''

I could see that the shame of civilization, the Great War, worked havoc in him. That any white nation, hunting for a place in the sun, should have made such a thing possible, was never out of his consciousness; and he raved in his choicest vocabulary concerning Germania. Still, he did not think the war would last long. We were on Hawaii, the "Big Island," with the 1915 Congressional junketing party from Washington, on which Jack had been made one of the entertainment committee, when the stunning intelligence came of the sinking of the *Lusitania*. Jack, for once, was shocked into something akin to silence. To his mind, the best characterization of that crime was the one made by I have forgotten whom: "When Germany, with paean of joy, committed suicide!"

To certain harsh comments upon a young English friend who, answering Great Britain's call, left his mother and his children in Honolulu, Jack pleaded with blazing eyes:

"You do not seem to understand: he *had* to go. There was no other way out, for him, than the one he chose; he could not have done other than he did . . . as well criticize the flame that burns, as criticize this royal thing of the spirit within him that drew him from success, and love of children, and fat security, half-way across the world to fling himself into the maelstrom of battle, pain and death—all for an Idea."

In the latter part of July, we bade good bye to Honolulu. Jack said: "We must go back soon. 1 feel as if our visit had been interrupted." For he had made many friends, conquered a few outstanding prejudices, and felt much at home in this neighboring "fleet of Islands" above the Line.

We landed into the annoyance of trouble with the grapejuice company, but it seemed as if difficulties of this sort were all in the day's work. "What am I to think? I go into the cleanest sort of business, to make the best non-alcoholic drink known, and I get it in the neck, *pronto*—just like that!"

"But the lake's full of water for my alfalfa," he checked himself, "and that means more life, more abundance of butter-fat from your little Jerseys, bigger Shire colts, heavier beef cattle, and the rest!"

To our mutual rejoicing, the water was warm enough for swimming, and Jack asked his sister to shift a gang from some other section of the ranch, "run up" a log bath-house of six rooms and lead the necessary piping for two showers. Inside of three days this convenience was a reality, as well as an appropriate accent in the scenery of the meadow. A rustic table and seats, set within a circle of redwoods, two canvas boats forgotten out of the *Snark's* dunnage, together with a diving float, perfected our equipment for al fresco entertaining.

Jack stocked the lakelet with catfish brought from the San Joaquin river, and these proved a great advantage, both for sport and table.

A trap-shooting outfit was purchased, but he never got around to having it installed. "1 can't find a place that seems exactly right," he complained; "nor a good spot for a tennis court. As for golf links—" he put it up to Joe Mather, "if you'll make suggestions where they can be laid out, I'll go ahead and have the work done."

There had been correspondence with Mr. Edgar Sisson, then editor of *The Cosmopolitan*, as to writing a "movie" novel based upon a scenario by Charles Goddard, author of "The Perils of Pauline" and other "thrillers" of the screen. Chapters of the novel were to appear in the string of Hearst newspapers, and simultaneously illustrated in the cinema theatres. Jack was not enthusiastic at first, but saw a possible way to recoup his pocketbook from his tremendous outlay on the ranch. His suggestion being agreed upon for a lump sum running into five large figures with temporary release from his regular measure of fiction, he launched into it with glee:

"Think—it'll be sheer recreation, though I double my usual daily portion, at double my usual rate! And I don't have to do a thing but reel off the stuff, upon Goddard's scenario notes. I don't have to worry about plot, or sequence of events, or contribute a single idea if I don't want to!"

He never ceased to maintain that he hated to write—had to drive himself to it. It made him flare when this was questioned. In reply to an unknown admirer, he wrote: ". . . Let me tell you that I envy you. You delight to write. You delight in your writing. You are enamored of writing, while I, with the publication of my first book, lost all joy in writing. I go each day to my daily task as a slave would go to his task. I detest writing. On the other hand it is the best way I have ever found to make a very good living. So I continue to write. But his best work was conceived in passion for its own sake, and I think one feels his urge of self-expression, while many were his enthusiasms over what he was doing. One short piece of work gave him a great deal of pleasure—a Preface for a new edition of Dana's "Two Years Before the Mast." Because of absence from California, his manuscript did not reach Macmillans in season, and it was a keen disappointment to Jack that the book was published without his appreciation. So the most he could do was to include it in a book-collection, and it appears, under the title of "A Classic of the Sea," in "The Human Drift."

Mr. Sisson and Mr. Goddard paid us a visit to discuss ways and means, because Jack avowed his determination of taking this work to Hawaii, where Mr. Goddard would have to send his installments of scenario for the novelist's guidance. When in the spring of 1916, at Waikiki, he completed this manuscript of what has been called "frenzied fiction" he wrote a Foreword explaining at length how he had come to lend himself to such a bizarre undertaking. "In truth," he says, "this yarn is a celebration. By its completion I celebrate my fortieth birthday, my fiftieth book, my sixteenth year in the writing game, and a new departure. I have certainly never done anything like it before; I am pretty certain never to do anything like it again." And he then goes deeper into his subject.

"Hearts of Three," they named it; and, as a sympathetic critic has suggested, it should be viewed as something of a joke—the most adventurous, high-spirited, rollicking, ridiculous, impossible stuff in the world, an outrageous thing of delightful absurdity. In this light Jack regarded it, and had the time of his life in its fabrication. He received his money, but died before the story was published in the newspapers; and for some reason it has not, up to 1921, been presented upon the screen.

Our loss of Nakata, to marriage and career, at the end of 1915, constituted more than a domestic flurry. He had nearly every prerequisite of the close and confidential servitor, and it is hard to decide which suffered more from his absence, Jack or myself. All in all, I think it was Jack. Next, our guests missed his cheery and charming service, for "Where is Nakata?" ordinarily followed greetings from our friends.

CHAPTER XXXIX

THE WAR; HAWAII

1916

AND now I come to the last and most difficult movement in my undertaking. The mere narrative is nothing —that in March, with our Japanese, we sailed on the *Great Northern* for Honolulu, rented a spreading old bungalow at 2201 Kalia Road, Waikiki, and lived the gay life of the sub-tropic city, breaking the round with wonderful inter-island explorations, and returning to California after seven months.

What is so difficult is the developing of this last earthly phase of Jack London, so that all who run may read and not wonder overmuch why, through sheer neglect, he cut himself off, or caused himself to be cut off from the larger fulfilment of himself. For I truly believe that his best work was yet to come. That he believed it, I am equally convinced. "Just wait, wait until I've got everything going ahead smoothly, and don't have to consider the wherewithal any more, and then I am going to write some *real* books!"

Jack's life is the story of a princely ego that struggled for full expression, and realized it only in a small degree. There were so few to heed his deeper self-manifestations. As a mere lad, he was conscious of that superiority and of its environmental discrepancy, and all the while fought for the congenial environment. As he grew in mental stature, he recognized himself as part of the whole ego-substance, and proceeded to fight for the proper environment for egos

1915. AT WAIKIKI, HONOLULU

1913 ABOARD THE 'ROAMER

1910. JACK AND CHARMIAN LONDON AT WAIKIKI, HONOLULU

1914. JACK AND CHARMIAN LONDON IN VERA CRUZ MEXICO

JACK LONDON TWO WEEKS BEFORE HIS DEATH

THE WORK-ROOM: LOW TABLE (left) WHERE HE WROTE, ROLL-TOP DESK (center) FOR BUSINESS. MARJEAN'S TYPEWRITER DESK (right)

other than his own. Hence, Jack the Individualist, and Jack the Socialist.

The result of his individual struggle for expression, when young, was Success, Recognition. Yet, as I have already written, such was the universal quality of his mind that he would have reached success, as the world regards it, by way of any medium of expression he had selected under ceaseless urge of that princely ego. Perhaps, as the years lapsed, if the world had demanded more, he might have been forced into an expression somewhere nearly adequate to his inner demand. But the world acclaimed what he did do, and the money that same world paid enabled him to search for happiness—a goal in itself. Yet happiness, as he saw it, was endeavor, always endeavor, the accumulation of knowledge, and to no small end. He created an environment which bade fair to balance in extent his royal requirement—the wide-reaching acres with their herds of the best, the lavish hospitality, the great house. Yet throughout he preserved the collective ideal, gave to others the unselfish help of his brain and time and money, impelled by an incorruptible ideal of making the world a better place for his having lived in it—of "causing two blades of grass to grow where one grew before."

But with all this in his grasp, the instinct to search still drove him on. He was doomed to remain unsatisfied, and unsatisfied he remained. The ultimate aim could not be fame, nor money, nor anything the world had in its gift. I had almost said that Love itself left him empty; but insofar as he loved Love, and could not live without Love and what understanding and ease of spirit Love could vouchsafe in his unguarded moments of despair, Love, I say, given and returned, kept him alive for many a year. This I know.

He had tried during his life all the ways known to man for getting away from an insatiable ego. And all he had really succeeded in was to obscure the demands that he had by his white logic interpreted, and had striven so hard to placate. It may be he sensed this long before he came face to face with and acknowledged it; and this probably led him more or less consciously to greater emphasis upon all the things with which he drugged his perception of futility—his work, his amusements, and the dream of scientific husbandry into which his unquenchable pioneering spirit had led him. And when, once in a while, he brought up and staggered before a flash of insight to the way he was bound, he called upon all the artifices of a superb intellect to prove he was right in defying the vision. It was a regal battle, and he lost—at least, so far as concerns the perceptions of most of us who are left. No man with his capacity could ever really bury the melancholy heritage that is coincident with the brain that seeks and scans too closely the fearful face of Truth. "My mistake in opening the books," he would repeat. "Sometimes I wish I had never opened the books." Still, except as he was warped by sickness, at any time he was glad to quote, " 'E liked it all." The game was worth the candle.

The conflict shows in the caliber of literature that first earned him renown, and the caliber of that which served his chosen end, preaching the things which filled his brain and hands with work that warded off the final capitulation he made to his fate. The first is distinguished by the impersonal note; the second marked equally by the personal. Had the human clay of him been equal to his mental capacity and urge, he might in time have stood out grand and free and his gift to the ages been of unequaled value. As note:

For months Jack had been reading, in his intensive method, in conjunction with the works of all the best alienists, upon the subject of Psychoanalysis—Freud, Prince, and, most of all, Jung. Much he read aloud, calling me to him, or following me about to instil certain passages. But it was one utterance, in that summer of 1916, that made me realize, distinct from the excitement that the conquest of

Knowledge always produced in him, that he had at last come upon something commensurate with his highest powers of penetration. His eyes like stars, his face still with a high solemnity I had never before seen upon it, in a voice so prophetic that my soul has been listening ever since, he said:

"Mate Woman, I tell you I am standing on the edge of a world so new, so terrible, so wonderful, that I am almost afraid to look over into it."

As I came to look with him over that brink into the possibilities of that new world which is as old as Time, I began to see what it was beginning to mean to him who had sensed its abysses as long ago as when he wrote "The Call of the Wild," ay, and before that. With his synthetic mind, he would have been a splendid exponent of what bids fair to be the limitless scope and application of the principles of Psychoanalysis. At times, when he expounded his hopes of what he would be able to accomplish in this research I was caught up into his vision. But so terrific was the marvel of what he dared dream he might do, that one's every-day senses reeled away from the contemplation. I have no words, no skill, with which to transfer to my reader this look into the gulf. But why, Jack thought, if he could learn to analyze the secret soul-stuff of the individual and bring it up to the light of foreconsciousness, could not he analyze the soul of the race, back and back, ever farther into the shadows, to its murky beginnings? His eyes, when he thus speculated, were those, not in the least of a fanatic, but of a seer, deep as the ages. He walked on air, yet the actual material practically of it appealed before all.

While he laid aside the heavy volumes read and annotated, until such time—say on a voyage to Japan in 1917—as he could review them with me, Jack applied their principle more than was entirely safe for the complacency of those with whom he came in contact. If he had ever before used the world and its inhabitants to keep him interested in the game of life, he now employed them in ways they never guessed in casual association with him. Applying his new system of approach, all in the way of social intercourse he was delving into the soul-stuff of men and women as they never would have dared analyze the significance of their own repressions. He went to startling lengths in this risky game of "playing with souls." Old curiosities, long since laid, were resurrected, to be dipped in the alembic of psychoanalysis, and he experimented with his own caprices in the most unexpected ways.

Perhaps the majority of the minds which he laid bare were not of a quality to make his investigation profitable. However that may be, it brought to him—and this was my greatest fear—yet more disillusion with the human element that had already suffered much in his regard. When the measure of a thinker's associates steadily shrinks in his estimate, that thinker, maddened by their immobility to ideas, is facing annihilation. The situation becomes insupportable. The "will to live" weakens and breaks down, no matter how fair the world nor Love how sweet. Jack's conclusions were saddening in the extreme. A paragraph from H. G. Wells's "The Discovery of the Future" so appositely expresses Jack's attitude from time to time, that I shall quote it instead of trying to reconstruct his own words:

"I do not think I could possibly join the worship of humanity with any gravity or sincerity. Think of it! Think of the positive facts. There are surely moods for all of us when one can feel Swift's amazement, that such a being should deal in pride. There are moods when one can join in the laughter of Democritus; and they would come oftener were not the spectacle of human littleness so abundantly shot with pain."

Wells goes on to say that the pain of the world is also shot with promise; but Jack at this stage was grudging of this expectation.

I was too close to it all to see the full drift of his fall; or, better, in my characteristic way, while doing my best in a given set of circumstances, I would not admit what I shrank from facing. The test of my endurance was severe, for Jack required so greatly of me in the capacities of wife, lover, friend, even confessor, for he withheld nothing— nothing, I repeat—of what he was passing through; and my responsibility, it may be guessed, was almost more than I could bear and preserve a cheerful poise. That he missed little of this, I am assured. More than thrice he suddenly remarked: "You are the only one in the world who could live with me!" Which was with direct reference to his intellectual vagaries, and not to any personal difficulties. It is all an inexpressibly dear heritage—the memory of that with which he entrusted me. I might think I had failed in many particulars, except for the continuance of his confidence and his almost childlike dependence upon me when his burden was too great. A generous friend, talking with him shortly before his death, has given me Jack's declaration, speaking of myself: "She has never failed me. I have had the comfort of her stedfastness, and have gained strength from it. She is always ready to act with and for me at any moment."

No matter how strange he seemed at times, nor how isolate, I learned I must stand by, night and day, for his instant need. There would be, say, a tirade against the infinitesimal natures of folk, or an argument, and he might work himself into a frenzy wherein I accused him of intellectual unfairness; or, we might disagree vitally upon some personal matter. Once, twice, I withdrew and left him to work out his humor by himself. But he could not, or would not. I found myself not daring to pursue this course; and thereafter, in the Islands and later at home, when the impulsion was upon him, I did my best to maintain my end in discussion, into the small hours if necessary, until he was exhausted, when, suddenly, in his fighting-face there would dawn the sweetness that disarmed anger and criticism alike in friend and foe. He would fall asleep in my arms, awakening penitent for the pallor of my cheeks that no smile could camouflage, and gratitude for the smile. A conversation something like this would ensue:

"Bear with me, Mate Woman—you're all I've got."

"I do. I do."

"Then, do more than that!"

"I will! I will!"

Any chiding that he was not taking sufficient nourishment, and neglecting his exercise, elicited the time-honored response:

"I'm all right—don't bother. And you're never up in time to see the huge breakfast I tuck away—three cups of coffee, with heavy cream, two soft-boiled eggs, half of a big *papaia!*"

But it was months before I learned that every morning the ample bedside repast, which he so enjoyed with his morning *Pacific Commercial Advertiser,* was completely lost. That abiding pride in his "cast-iron stomach" had suffered an eclipse; and with it his God-given ability to sleep whensoever he elected. This was indeed a desperate case, and I was frightened, because from birth on I myself had bedded with insomnia, and feared its consequences upon one of Jack's temperament. Only three times did he tamper with a narcotic, for he realized its peril. "Oh, have no fear, my dear," he reassured me more than once, "I'll never go that way. I want to live a hundred years!"

It being an unwritten rule that I was never to be disturbed from sleep, I awoke in swift terror one morning in Honolulu to find Jack, his face working with pain, at my door:

"I had to call you, Mate—I am sorry—but you must get a doctor. I don't know what it is, but it is awful!" And he crept back to his sleeping-porch. His friend Dr. Walters was out, and Dr. Herbert responded, as best he could help-ing Jack through the agony, diagnosing the cause as a calculus.

I suppose it is a wise wife who, rather than make mar-riage hideous by nagging, lets her husband destroy himself in his own uncaring way! Even with the excruciating omen of worse to come, Jack made little or no effort to put off his day of dissolution. The friendly physicians exhorted in vain: he clung to his diet of raw *aku* (bonita), and, aside from the breakfast fruit and occasional *poi,* which he termed a "beneficent food," quite neglected the vegetable nutri-ment his malady demanded, while the cramping of his ankles did not lessen.

As for exercise, save for the most desultory and infre-quent dips off-shore, he took none. My question, "Are you going to swim with me to-day?" was oftenest met with:

"Yes—believe I will . . . No, I'm right in the thick of this new box of reading-matter from home. Oh, I don't know—the water looks so good . . . But no; I'll go out in the hammock where I can read and watch you." And his bodily inertia won out.

But it would strike me, looking back across the seawall to where, in blue kimono, he swung under the ancient *hau* tree, that he read little; whenever I waved back to him there was an immediate response that bridged the jade and turquoise space. But the arm stretched out to me was all too white from seeking the shadows. If I did not ask him to go out, then, the same day or another, he would remind me of it, with a mild reproach.

Not a block would he walk to the electric tram, but called an automobile three miles from town whenever he wanted to go in for a shave. If he were not going out, and expected no company, he spent the day in bathing-trunks and kimono and sandals, not only for coolness at work, but because it was too much effort to dress. This calls up an incident that occurred one day in Honolulu, though I did not come upon the inwardness of it until long afterward. It goes to illustrate the sheep-mindedness of the mass of beings who wish to find famous men and women fashioned in the image of the quibbling, foppish, gnat-brained incarnation that is their own. Jack himself, small as was his respect for these, never failed to react to the clumsy stab of their inert yet harmful smugness—harmful because it influences and fixes the attitude of masses of humans who might, otherwise guided, attain a freer view of life.

A woman of Russian birth, passing through, wanted to meet this man Jack London, who so dominated the fancy of her countrymen. According to her story, certain tourist acquaintances warned her: "But he isn't decent—he's likely as not, we hear, to receive you dressed only in a kimono!" The lady was not to be balked; and one day, unannounced, she called during Jack's working hours. In spite of his irritation at being so unceremoniously interrupted, she found him courteous and interesting, and did not stop over-long.

"What did you think of him? What is he like?" her informants asked.

"I think he is a *very* decent fellow," the Russian began.

"But wasn't he in his kimono?"

"Why, yes—I believe he was," coolly she rejoined. "And I want to say that, in his kimono, he seemed to me more fully clothed than most of the men one meets in full conventional attire."

Except that he sat through long dinners without eating, Jack was normal enough to all intents. When anxious hostesses drew his attention to the untouched plate, he would repeat that story of the large breakfast, and declare that except at a Hawaiian *luau* (feast), where he made a practice of banqueting shamelessly, he would rather talk than eat; and thereupon he closed the topic by taking up the thread of his discourse where it had been cut.

He drank very moderately. "Sometimes I think I'm saturated with alcohol, so that my membranes have begun to rebel," he observed upon more than one occasion. "See —how little in the glass—and this is my first drink to-day!" A month before the end, in response to a telegram from Dr. W. H. Geystweit, Pastor of the First Baptist Church, San Diego, California, Jack wired:

"Never had much experience with wine-grape growing. The vineyards I bought were old, worked out, worthless, so I pulled out the vines and planted other crops. I still work a few acres of profitable wine grapes. My position on alcohol is absolute, nation-wide Prohibition. I mean absolute. I have no patience in half-way measures. Half-way measures are unfair, are tantamount to confiscation, and are provocative of underhand cheating, lying, and law-breaking. When the nation goes in for nation-wide Prohibition, that will be the end of alcohol, and there will be no cheating, lying nor law-breaking. Personally I shall continue to drink alcohol for as long as it is accessible. When absolute Prohibition makes alcohol inaccessible I shall drop drinking and it won't be any hardship on me and on men like me whose name is legion. And the generation of boys after us will not know anything about alcohol save that it was a stupid vice of their savage ancestors."

In Hawaii for the most part he ordered "soft" drinks or "small beer" during the nights we spent in the open-air cafés, I dancing, he visiting at the tables with his friends. But ever he kept an eye upon me, as if looking for some one stable in a crashing world. Seldom, swinging near, did I fail to catch his glance and a little indulgent smile he had for the "kid woman" who, loving the dance, had gone without it for so many traveling years after marrying him.

In a côterie of excellent players among Honolulu's men and women, both American and Hawaiian, much of Jack's recreation time was at cards—mostly bridge, with now and then a poker game.

To show the restlessness that was in him, I can instance

the entertaining we did. Day after day at our house it would be a luncheon, a bridge party, tea, swimming, a dinner, and theatre, or dancing either at home or on the Roof Garden or at "Heinie's," and, likely, a midnight swim before bed. Some of the luncheon guests might be included in the afternoon cards outside in the little jungle of that magnificent *hau* tree, but new players had also been bidden. A fresh bevy blew in for tea and bathing, and the diners would be still another party. Friends for noonday or dinner usually numbered an even dozen, since the round table accommodated just that number. We lived in a whirl; and many times, while I was at the telephone inviting for three different events for a certain day, Jack would come pattering in his straw sandals across the large palm-potted rooms, and whisper: "While you're about it, better plan the crowds for the day after."

A Honolulu neighbor, Charles Dana Wright, one day asked Jack:

"Why do you always have twelve at your table?"

"Because it won't hold any more!" was Jack's reply.

He seemed running away from himself, filling in every moment, as if uneasy with too many disengaged dates in prospect. Yet he would suddenly tire of it all, and there would be a lull. One night, after an undisturbed day when we had worked, and swam, read aloud, played pinochle, and eaten alone together, he breathed with satisfied demeanor: "Happiest day I ever spent in Hawaii!"

He had a way, at work in his cool green *lanai* (veranda) —a mile from where R.L.S. once wrote by Waikiki waters —of looking aside upon me as I walked about the long rooms; and when I caught him at it, his lips would frame kisses in the air. What was behind the inscrutable, star-blue eyes that were never so beautiful as that summer in his Happy Isles, when he made no attempt to retard an illness that could not be less than fatal if not checked? Was that mind that had "known the worst too young," and that

he had systematically overworked, now longing for surcease, "restless for rest," as William Herbert Carruth so
aptly put it? Does that account for the apparently deliberate want of resistance? He, the eternal fighter, patently
refused to fight for the reconstruction of a failing body,
or to exert his powerful will to conserve his physical
strength. On the contrary, it would seem as if the longing,
at least of his *unconscious* mind, for cessation of effort to
continue existence, swung him into a non-resistance which
made for destruction. When he looked at me as he would
look, was he hiding something he knew would fill me with
terror—did he have an intuition that I would be unthinkably
alone with the falling of the autumn leaves? One late afternoon, in the hammock, he read me "In Autumn," from
George Sterling's "The Caged Eagle," just received from
the poet. His voice broke at the last, and the eyes he raised
to mine in a long, long gaze, were deep pools in which I felt
us both drowning. But when at length he spoke, it was of
the wonder of the man who had written the poem.

I shall never know. All I do know is that he was upon
the nightward slope of living, and that all I had to cling to
was what sometimes fell from his lips when I had thought
him absorbed in book or writing—abruptly, as if wrung
from him:

"God!—Woman, if you knew how I love you!"

And again, his eyes burning:

"Child, child—you don't know what love is!"

Or he would murmur in a golden voice, across the length
of the house, so that I must harken closely to hear:

"I *love* you . . . I *love* you."

Once:

"Take my heart in both your hands, My Woman."

To me, who asked nothing from fate but to serve, he
said one day:

"I can refuse you nothing. Anything you ask for, in
seriousness, you may have. I am so entirely yours; you

can have anything you want of me. I'd do *anything* for you—actually, I believe I'd murder, if you asked me?" He added: "Some day, when we are seventy, you and I, in the autumn of our long years together, I'll tell you some things about myself—how I have come to know how *unthinkably* I love you."

All this intensity was part of the raw state in which he was, dying, the dear heart, and how were we to know? One morning, it seems he thought I had told him a deliberate falsehood in a vital connotation, and I was at a loss to account for his alarming recklessness throughout the day. That night, worried, for once I eavesdropped, and heard him with his own soul: "To think of it! To think of it!" he wrestled with despair. The next day, quite as unwittingly as I had dealt the erroneous impression, I undid the same. Then it all came out, with boyish jubilance in his relief, how he had agonized that "All I've got in the world" had thrown him down!

When he heard that the old bungalow, whispering of romance, was on the market, he came to me, his eyes dilating with the pleasure of giving:

"Do you want me to buy it for you, or do you prefer to wait till the war is done, and then get a sweet three-topmast schooner, fit her out, throw aboard your grand piano, a big launch, and a touring car, and start around the world for years!"

Naturally I chose the schooner, and told him that if for only selfish reasons, the war could not terminate any too soon to please me!—There he was, at it again—his "crowded hour of glorious life" all too short for the large plans for work, thought, play! I finger the sun-tanned note-pad upon which he scribbled expense calculations for that post-bellum voyage: Six men, so much; Captain, so much; Engineer, Mate, Cook, Servants, Doctor—with loose margins for his figures. "But, Mate," I objected, "that means no letup for you—harder work than ever." "What of it?"

cheerily he laughed it off. "I make my work easy—I've got 'em all skinned to death!"

Those little note-pads of Jack's—I find them at every turn. "Always carry a notebook," he advised. "Travel with it. Eat with it. Sleep with it. Slap into it every stray thought that flutters up into your brain. Cheap paper is less perishable than gray matter, and lead pencil markings endure longer than memory."

Certain photographs, one of himself and me in the garden, and one of myself on Neuadd Hillside, he kept near his work-table, and often looked at them. And at home afterward, "*Charmian, Charmian . . .*" he would murmur as he had murmured the day we first met, "I love your name. You've no idea how I stop all work and reading, and lie here just looking at your face in the frame."

There were six weeks on end in Hawaii that Jack seemed quite his healthy, hearty self. This was during what can best be termed a "royal progress" upon which, in company with Miss Mary Low, a part-Hawaiian friend, diamond-trove of information and imagination, who made it possible at that time, we encircled the "Big Island." The details of this journey I have related in "Our Hawaii." It was a passage of unalloyed pleasure, fraught with plans for the future when we should return to do the thousand things that this time must be left undone. In my hand at this moment is one of Jack's yellow note-pad leaves, scribbled with the most fragmentary penciled items:

"How not to know Hawaii . . . How the Tourist does it—the tourist route—never dreams.

"How to know Hawaii. Wait—under that surface excess of hospitality—the deeps of a remarkable people —really exclusive . . . Make no quick judgments. Come back, and come back, and then, some day, you will begin to find yourselves not only in their homes but in their hearts. And you will be well beloved . . ."

"I almost think," he said in retrospect, "that this has been the happiest month and a half I ever knew!"

On that trip, having finished "Michael Brother of Jerry," he wrote his last gift to the Islands, the three articles which were published in *The Cosmopolitan Magazine*, "My Hawaiian Aloha." A few short months thereafter one of the Territory's most distinguished mouthpieces said of him. "In the death of Jack London Hawaii suffered an irreparable loss. . . . Among our most lasting memories of him will be his earnest and enthusiastic assistance in the organization of the Pan-Pacific Union. There was nothing that he disliked more than making speeches; but at meeting after meeting his voice was heard advocating the principle of the brotherhood of mankind and the recognition of that principle as the guiding star of the peoples of the Pacific."

Next, Jack produced a short story, "The Hussy," dating the end of the manuscript at "Kohala, Hawaii, May 5, 1916." "The Hussy" is in book entitled "The Red One," issued posthumously. Followed the short story, "The Red One," in which is evidenced the author's profound meditation upon the reaching out of the most primordial toward the most cosmic—all in stride with his study in race consciousness. Sometimes I wonder if it can be possible, in the ponderings of the dying scientist, Bassett, that Jack London revealed more of himself than he would have been willing to admit—or else, who knows? more of himself than he himself realized. His ultimate discouragement with the endless strife of humanity even unto the modern horrors of the Great War, are in the mouth of his puppet, speculating upon the inhabitants of other planets, and playing square with the old cannibal, Ngurn, because, forsooth, the old man had, according to his lights, "played squarer than square," and "was in himself a forerunner of ethics and contract, of consideration, and gentleness in man."

"Had they won Brotherhood? Or had they learned that the law of love imposed the penalty of weakness and decay? Was strife, life? Was the rule of the universe the pitiless rule of natural selection?"

Some one has written of Jack London: "This Lord of Life was never far from the consciousness that he held a brief and uncertain sovereignty." He himself has said:

"Man, the latest of the ephemera, is pitifully a creature of temperature, strutting out his brief day on the thermometer." And: "All the human drift, from the first ape-man to the last savant, is but a phantom, a flash and a flutter of movement across the infinite sky of the starry night." He thrilled to George Sterling's line, "The fleeting Systems lapse like foam."

A couple of months before the "royal progress," Jack had sent in his resignation from the Socialist party, the reasons given surprising some of his radical acquaintances who had scoffed that he was becoming "soft."

"Radical!" he would snort, lurching about in his chair, "next time I go to New York, I'm going to live right down in the camp of these people who call themselves radicals. I'm going to tell them a few things, and make their radicalism look like thirty cents in a fog! I'll show them what radicalism *is!*"

Among his equipment of notes are the following addresses:

The Liberal Club, The Greenwich Village Inn (Polly's Restaurant) The Hotel Brevoort, James Donald Corley, Hippolyte Havel, Sadakichi Hartmann, Charles and Albert Boni, John Rampapas, Hutchins Hapgood, Il Proletario, J. J. Ettor and Iva Shuster, Carlo Tresca, Arturo Giovannitti, McSorley's Saloon.

Jack's action in resigning, though it had been gathering momentum for some time, was precipitated by the withdrawal of a friend whose reasons were based upon the prevalent "roughneck" methods of other than the "well-balanced radicals.'' I can still hear Jack's battle-tread, somewhat muffled by straw slippers, as he marched toward my door, and his peremptory voice: ''Take a letter— please!'' I can see him plant himself on the edge of my bed, curls towsled, wide eyes black with purpose under the brows that were like a sea-bird's wings, his full chest half-exposed by the blue kimono, and one perfect leg thrust forth to steady himself. And here is what he rapped out, as fast as I could click the keys:

''Honolulu, March 7, 1916.

''Glen Ellen,
　''Sonoma County, California.
''Dear Comrades:
　''I am resigning from the Socialist Party, because of its lack of fire and fight, and its loss of emphasis on the class struggle.
　''I was originally a member of the old revolutionary, up-on-its-hind-legs, fighting, Socialist Labor Party. Since then, and to the present time, I have been a fighting member of the Socialist Party. My fighting record in the Cause is not, even at this late date, already entirely forgotten. Trained in the class struggle, as taught and practiced by the Socialist Labor Party, my own highest judgment concurring, I believed that the working class, by fighting, by never fusing, by never making terms with the enemy, could emancipate itself. Since the whole trend of Socialism in the United States during recent years has been one of peaceableness and compromise, I find that my mind refuses further sanction of my remaining a party member. Hence my resignation.
　''Please include my comrade wife, Charmian K. London's, resignation with mine.
　''My final word is that Liberty, freedom, and independence, are royal things that cannot be presented to, nor thrust upon, races or classes. If races and classes cannot rise up and by their strength of brain and brawn, wrest from the world liberty, freedom, and independence, they never in time can come to these royal possessions . . . and if such royal things are kindly presented to them by superior individuals, on silver platters, they will know not what to do with them, will fail to make use of them, and will

1916   JACK LONDON
Taken 6 days before he died

JACK LONDON ON SONOMA MOUNTAIN OVERLOOKING THE VALLEY OF THE MOON

JACK LONDON'S GRAVE ON SONOMA MOUNTAIN

be what they have always been in the past . . . inferior races and inferior classes.

"Yours for the Revolution,
"Jack London."

The foregoing, published in the Socialist press, caused much comment. Jack's grim amusement can be pictured when it was reported that a distinguished member of the Party, upon reading it remarked: "I'd have done the same long ago, for the same reasons, if I had not been so prominent a figure in the movement."

"And now," I queried, when Jack had got the letter off his mind and cooled down, "what will you call yourself henceforth—Revolutionist, Socialist, what?"

"I am not anything, I fear," he said quietly. "I am all these things. Individuals disappoint me more and more, and more and more I turn to the land. . . . Well," he reconsidered, "I might call myself a Syndicalist. It does seem as if class solidarity, expressed in terms of the general strike, would be the one means of the workers tying up the world and getting what they want. It would raise Cain, of course, but nothing ever seems to be accomplished without raising Cain. A world-wide strike would produce inconceivable results.—But they won't stick together—there is too much selfishness and too much inertia."

Surely, surely, Jack's experience with the "inertia of the masses" was not unique in the annals of reform movements. In Doctor William J. Robinson's "The Medical Critic and Guide," I come across this sentence: "It is not the slave that rebels against his slavery; it is the free man who sees the injustice of slavery who starts the fight for its abolition." Other social seers had suffered unto death. I could not but pray that the healthier side of Jack's philosophy of life might preserve him from despair.

Concerning *sabotage,* he stood somewhat like this: Peaceful methods having failed, and with his views on the frightfulness of capitalist exploitation of labor, he would not hesitate, were he an underpaid wage-slave, insidiously to wreck the machinery of production by the means of which he had become the underpaid, underfed, overworked, exploited tool and fool of his economic masters. But when confronted with the futile, desultory methods of bombing innocent persons by mistake, his impatience knew no bounds. Following one such mishap that had shaken the country, I asked him what he thought of it; and he used a word I had never heard in seriousness from his lips:

"I think it is *wicked.*"

Many resignations followed Jack's—quite an avalanche, in fact, when the Socialist Party at the St. Louis Convention in 1917 pledged itself to oppose, by every means within its power, the prosecution of the war against Germany.

When James Howard Moore, because of heartbreak over the world, had put a bullet through his brain, Jack was deeply moved. In his handwriting, at the head of a printed address delivered by Clarence S. Darrow at the funeral services, I find this:

"Disappointment like what made Wayland (*Appeal to Reason*) kill himself—and many like me resign."

Reading over the mass of material for this Biography, I am struck anew by Jack's old faith in the workingman, and anew saddened by his ultimate disillusion. Let me quote a letter, written several years before he died, stating the nobilities upon which he had founded his hope:

"To the Central Labor Council,
"Alameda County:
"I cannot express to you how deeply I regret my inability to be with you this day. But, believe me, I am with you in the brotherhood of the spirit, as all you boys, in a similar brotherhood of the spirit, are with our laundry girls in Troy, New York.
"Is this not a spectacle for gods and men?—the workmen of Alameda County sending a share of their hard-earned wages three

thousand miles across the continent to help the need of a lot of striking laundry girls in Troy!

"And right here I wish to point out something that you all know, but something that is so great that it cannot be pointed out too often, and that grows only greater every time it is pointed out,—AND THAT IS, THAT THE STRENGTH OF ORGANIZED LABOR LIES IN ITS BROTHERHOOD. There is no brotherhood in unorganized labor, no standing together shoulder to shoulder, and as a result unorganized labor is weak as water.

"And not only does brotherhood give organized labor more fighting strength but it gives it, as well, the strength of righteousness. The holiest reason that men can find for drawing together into any kind of an organization is BROTHERHOOD. And in the end nothing can triumph against such an organization. Let the church tell you that servants should obey their masters. This is what the church told the striking laundry girls of Troy. Stronger than this mandate is brotherhood, as the girls of Troy found out when the boys of California shared their wages with them. (Ah, these girls of Troy! Twenty weeks on strike and not a single desertion from their ranks! And ah, these boys of California, stretching out to them, across a continent the helping hand of brotherhood!)

"And so I say, against such spirit of brotherhood, all machinations of the men-of-graft-and-grab-and-the-dollar are futile. Strength lies in comradeship and brotherhood, not in a throat-cutting struggle where every man's hand is against man. This comradeship and brotherhood is yours. I cannot wish you good luck and hope that your strength will grow in the future, because brotherhood and the comrade-world are bound to grow. The growth cannot be stopped. So I can only congratulate you boys upon the fact that this is so.

"Yours in the brotherhood of man,"

That Jack London expected no glory nor even lasting appreciation from his comrades for his life-long work in the interests of Socialism, was evident to me early in our association. It was with utter absence of bitterness that he said:

"In a few years the crowd I have worked for and with,

the Socialists, will have entirely forgotten that a fellow named Jack London ever did a stroke to help along. I shall be entirely forgotten, or counted out, or, at best, merely mentioned.''

And when, even in his own short time he had proved his own words, in spite of a cool intellectual attitude he showed the hurt to his affections. There is bitterness and to spare, though essentially toward the race of men who had disappointed his warm confidence, in the following, already referred to in part, written in his last months for a Socialist publication:

''Some years ago Alexander Berkman asked me to write an introduction to his 'Prison Memoirs of an Anarchist.' This is the introduction. I was naïve enough to think that when one intellectual disagreed with another intellectual the only difference would be intellectual. I have since learned better. Alexander Berkman could not see his way to using my introduction, and got some one else to write a more sympathetic one for him. Also, socially, comradely, he has forgotten my existence ever since.

''By the same token, because the socialists and I disagreed about opportunism, ghetto politics, class consciousness, political slates, and party machines, they, too, have dismissed all memory, not merely of my years of fight in the cause, but of me as a social man, as a comrade of men, as a fellow they ever embraced for having at various times written or said things they described as doughty blows for the Cause. On the contrary, by their only printed utterances I have seen, they deny I ever struck a blow or did anything for the Cause, at the same time affirming that all the time they knew me for what I was—a Dreamer.

''I'm afraid I did dream some dreams about their brains, which now I find knocked into a cocked hat by their possession of the pitiful humanness that is the birthright of all sons of men. My dream was that my comrades were intellectually honest. My awakening was that they were as unfair, when prejudice entered, as all the other human cattle entered to-day in the human race.''

There are some of Jack's compeers who do not forget, who give him his place, and a high place. And there are others who, perceiving him nurse his efficiency by decent living after his too-lean years, became fearful that he might lose his head through worldly success, but held judgment and were rewarded for their openmindedness. One socialist, not fussing as to whether Jack belonged to the Socialist Party, or any party, had this to say: "He was one of us. A genuine, strenuous American, he fought a good fight in the sacred cause of human progress. Against the predatory Big Interests' attempt to enslave the workers and the Booze Interests' attempt to degrade the workers, his pen was a mighty weapon. Like a true comrade he died fighting. Alas, my Comrade!" But sadly enough I note that only too often his name is missing from the roster that includes his intellectual friends such as Walling, Spargo, Hunter, Stokes, Heron.

Jack's especial *bête noir* was the type of socialist, of either sex, who heckled him because he declined to lecture before small groups. Wasted upon these hecklers was his argument that with a stroke of his pen, while following temperamental bents in manner of living, he could reach millions, whereas his voice could be heard by but a few. This being so, he did not see why he should misapply energy by speaking to a few, when he so disliked public appearances. Further, reports of his speeches were almost invariably garbled. His gospel as propounded in his books was not garbled. Ergo, and finally, he would write rather than talk. Incidentally, his voice had gone back on him, so that it became husky at any attempt to project it into large spaces. Far from regretting this break-down in his anatomy, he hailed it with frank delight as another excuse from lecturing. The failure of his throat was precipitated, happily enough, by an excess of laughter at the Bohemian Jinks. He had returned unable for a while to speak above a faint wheeze, the vocal cords ruptured forever.

He would add that he had done his share of platform

work, and why not step out and let the younger generation have a chance. Here is his somewhat impatient reply to a suppliant who had tried sarcasm upon him:

"Dear Comrade:

"In reply to yours of September 14. I don't see anything to laugh at. With courtesy and consideration, on an average of five letters a day, I turn down propositions of comrades that run all the way from gold mines to perpetual motion. I sent you what I thought was a fair, courteous, sweet-natured and comradely letter. If you choose to laugh at that letter and me—why, go to it! I, however, am very sorry that you should laugh.

"You say you had hoped that your letter would have inspired me to nobler things (those are your words). What nobler things?— to attend a meeting at your place which you say nobody attended? To put money in your project and raise for you a temporary fund, when I am worrying over my own overdue life-insurance? For heaven's sake, dear woman, be fair, play fair, and get away from your own self-centering long enough to remember that all the others in the world may not be persuaded nor clubbed into following your immediate lead and desire, and that because they are not to be so persuaded nor clubbed is no license for you to laugh at them.

"Yours for the Revolution,"

Much earlier than that, in answer to a call that he could not afford, he had written:

"It's this way: I feel that I have done and am doing a pretty fair share of work for the Revolution. I guess my lectures alone before Socialist organizations have netted the Cause a few hundred dollars, and my wounded feelings from the personal abuse of the Capitalist papers ought to be rated at several hundred more. There is not a day passes that I am not reading up socialism and filing socialistic clippings and notes. The amount of work that I in a year contribute to the cause of socialism would earn me a whole lot of money if spent in writing fiction for the market."

It is not remarkable, however, that Jack London was much misinterpreted by the general run of men lost in pettifogging. He would not even be circumscribed by his broadest conceptions, if I may be allowed a paradox. And there was where he invited trouble with economists, who wanted him to be what they called consistent. The many sparkling facets of his mind dazzled and befuddled merely average thought processes. I speak with feeling. Sometimes we would battle for hours, he and I, earnestly, hotly, because, although I was doing the best I knew how, he was thinking so far beyond the logic of ordinary mortals who think they think. "Don't you see? Can't you get it?" he would almost wail in ardor and onrush to convince. And we would metaphorically roll up our sleeves and go at it hammer and tongs. To me, who was more "kin" to him than the rest, he declined to mute his trumpets. His own woman must speak his language. And then, suddenly, out would slip some little key-word he had unwittingly left unsaid, the door would fly open, and I would seem to drop a thousand light-years in space, alighting softly, happily, yet excessively puzzled at last by the cosmic simplicity of his reasoning.

In logic he bowed to no one. His supple mind that never stiffened from disuse was of a clarity that allowed of no master. He but grasped and applied the conclusions of Master-minds, used them in the mosaic of his own. Yet here is a curious thing: In his dreams, at widely separated intervals, appeared the Man who would contest Jack's self-mastership, to whom he would eventually bend a vanquished intelligence. He never met such an one in the flesh, yet that entity stalked through more than the hallucinations of sleep. It was long ago he first told me of this ominous figure in his consciousness. The last manifestation was within a very few years of his death. The man, imperial, inexorable with destiny, yet strangely human, descended, alone, a vast cascade of stairways, and Jack, at the foot, looked up and waited as imperially for the meeting that was to be his unknown fate. But the Nemesis never, in that form at least, overtook him. Was it Death? Or may it have been a reflection of his own most exalted self that he came face to face with at these times? There showed a certain pathos in his accounts. I do not think he had yet brought his inklings of psychoanalysis to bear upon his interpretations.

What gifts Jack had for all who could see and hear! But the world is prone to look askance at gifts that are tendered freely, without price. And what he offered was so open-handed, so open-hearted. He never wore nor waved a flag—his flags, his colors, were in his eyes, streamed from his pen, and waved from his printed page. Every one who tried to understand him was better for it. When persons say, "I never met him," I can only return, "I am sorry." If it was a privilege to know his work, it was a greater privilege to know himself, if ever so slightly, for he was greater than his work. He had few enemies among those who came into personal contact with him. With all his self-knowledge, for the most part in social dealings he preserved that unconsciousness of self which is above modesty, yet which spells modesty to the casual observer. And no matter how firmly he believed himself right, fought for it, shouted it, he also respected a similar belief existing in his opponent. This charity, however, had been sorely taxed during earlier years, by dark and helpless souls incapable alike of clear reasoning or appreciating his superiority; hence his impatience with inconsequential minds. But with the majority of acquaintances, no frown of his, no stern word, ever outweighed the morning of his smile, that beautiful smile that lured the bitterest antagonist under his charm.

Much non-understanding arose from the misleading habit of others in quoting his isolated opinions without context, deleting them of the vital connotations that his catholicity brought to ripe consideration of any theme. Only a few of his fellows could anticipate or supply the thousand factors embodied in his thought. Myself, I learned to hesitate before leaping to conclusions, to wait for the full drift. Just about the time, say, that Jack would begin to sink into lowest disheartenment over the abysmal significance of the War, and our failure to bear a hand, all at once he would flame anew to the undying wonder of the human. A case in point arose when Hall Caine wrote him from London, asking a contribution for the "King Albert Book." Jack responded:

"Belgium is rare, Belgium is unique. Among men arises on rare occasions a great man, a man of cosmic import; among nations on rare occasions arises a great nation, a nation of cosmic import. Such a nation is Belgium. Such is the place Belgium attained in a day by one mad, magnificent, heroic leap into the azure. As long as the world rolls and men live, that long will Belgium be remembered. All the human world passes, and will owe Belgium a debt of gratitude, such as was never earned by any nation in the History of Nations. It is a magnificent debt, a proud debt that all the nations of men will sacredly acknowledge."

Yet the very sending of the foregoing from Oakland brought him face to face again with human smallness. He thought to see if the cable company would share in the tribute by standing half the expense of the message. They politely declined, and Jack shrugged his habitual "Cheap at the price to learn them," under such circumstances.
The murder of Edith Cavell,

"... a simple English nurse,
Slaughtered between a challenge and a curse,"

snapped something in Jack. Eyes and soul full of this and the rest of the mad slaughter, he became more and more furious with the brutal stupidity of the Hun. He lingered in almost speechless wonder over the monstrous bestiality of German cartoons, in nearly all of which lay a boomerang unguessed by that same bungling stupidity.
He did not believe this to be a capitalistic war, but that it was being waged for a principle at its best, and must be

fought to the death. He would have stamped his approval, I know, upon the "irreduceable minimum" of peace terms, and Mr. Balfour's deliverance: "Next to being enslaved by Germany, there is no worse thing than being liberated by her."

Jack would refer to Germany as the "Mad Dog of Europe."

"I am with the allies life and death. Germany to-day is a paranoiac. She has the mad person's idea of her own ego, and the delusion of persecution—she thinks all nations are against her. She possesses also the religious mania —she thinks God is on her side. These are the very commonest forms of insanity, but never before in history has a whole nation gone insane."

"God help them when the British turn savage!" he cried at the first rumor of hostilities. His opinion of the country has been very adequately expressed by one who fought in France: "Germany has no honor, no chivalry, no mercy. Germany is a bad sportsman. Germans fight like wolves in a pack, and without initiative or resource if compelled to fight singly."

A hundred times I have heard Jack say: "It will be a war of attrition." He saw no abrupt termination, no brilliant, decisive victory. But for the Armistice, he might have been proven right. He was also heard to say that he believed the nations would eventually repudiate their war debts.

The Pathé Exchange wrote on June 16, asking his views upon the meaning of the World War, and this was his reply:

"I believe the World War so far as concerns, not individuals but the entire race of man, is good.

"The World War has compelled man to return from the cheap and easy lies of illusion to the brass tacks and iron facts of reality. It is not good for man to get too high up in the air above reality.

"The World War has redeemed from the fat and gross materialism of generations of peace, and caught mankind up in a blaze of the spirit.

"The World War has been a pentecostal cleansing of the spirit of man."

Another of his public utterances:

"I believe intensely in the Pro-Ally side of the war. I believe that the foundation of civilization rests on the pledge, the agreement, and the contract. I believe that the present war is being fought out to determine whether or not men in the future may continue in a civilized way to depend upon the word, the pledge, the agreement, and the contract.

"As regards a few million terrible deaths, there is not so much of the terrible about such a quantity of deaths as there is about the quantity of deaths that occur in peace times in all countries in the world, and that has occurred in war times in the past.

"Civilization at the present time is going through a Pentecostal cleansing that can result only in good for mankind."

That none may misconstrue the central paragraph, but may know upon what the assertion was based, I append this item from the *Scientific American*:

"Industrial accidents cost this country 35,000 human lives and many millions of dollars annually, according to the Arizona State Safety News. In addition, dismemberments and other serious injuries total about 350,000 yearly, while the annual number of minor accidents, causing loss of time, exceeds 2,000,000."

It is interesting, while on the War, to quote his disagreement, when a youth, with David Starr Jordan:

"There is something wrong with Dr. Jordan's war theory, which is to the effect that, the best being sent out to war, only the second best, the men who are left, remain to breed a second-best race, and that, therefore, the human race deteriorates under war. If this be so, if we have sent forth the best we bred and gone on breeding from the men who were left, and since we have done this for ten thousand milleniums and are what we splendidly are to-day, then what unthinkably splendid and god-like beings must have been our forebears those ten thousand milleniums ago. Unfortunately for Dr. Jordan's theory, these forebears cannot live up to this fine reputation.''

His full emotions toward the United States in withholding help from

"... the embattled hosts that kept
Their pact with freedom while we slept!"

are expressed in a telegram sent in reply to a New York daily asking his choice at election time, and of which I have no record that the paper dared print it:

"I have no choice for President. Wilson has not enamored me with past performances. Hughes has not enamored me with the promise of future performances. There is nothing to hope from ether of them, except that they will brilliantly guide the United States down her fat, helpless, lonely, unhonorable, profit-seeking way to the shambles to which her shameless unpreparedness is leading her. The day is all too near when any first power or any two one-horse powers can stick her up and bleed her bankrupt. We stand for nothing except fat. We are become the fat man of the nations, whom no nation loves. My choice for President is Theodore Roosevelt, whom nobody in this fat land will vote for because he exalts honor and manhood over the cowardice and peace lovingness of the worshipers of fat.''

To Henry Meade Bland, a month before his death Jack wrote:

"I am inclosing you herewith a clipping about 'Martin Eden.' 'Martin Eden,' and 'The Sea Wolf' a long time before 'Martin Eden,' were protests against the philosophy of Nietzsche, insofar as the Nietzschean philosophy expounds strength and individualism, even to the extent of war and destruction, against coöperation, democracy, and socialism. Here is the world war, the logical outcome of the Nietzschean philosophy.

"Read both these books yourself to get my point of view. Also make note that no reviewer ever got my point of view in those two books, and that this is the first time I have ever shouted my point of view in those two books."

The theory of alternate eras of Evolution and Dissolution fought with his work for the human. Yet, casting back into the hopelessness of the ages, citing fourteen cities built one atop another, and all lapsed, gone, with their pomp and circumstance—yet, I say, Jack suffered unendurably over the Great War, and perished in the midst of his deepest of all Great Disgusts because of America's "Safety First" policy that held us from protesting even the Belgian atrocities. We blunder along. The times blunder along. History-making blunders along. And he saw the blundering way of the race.

His main comfort throughout that Armageddon was his Anglo-Saxonism, his pride in England in the conduct of her "popular" war. How he would have rejoiced in the invincible combination of American man-power and British sea-power! I am exasperated all the time, consciously and unconsciously, that he is not alive and quick, to function in the gigantic tangle of world events growing out of the war—to see his own prognostications taking shape, and to lend a hand in the reconstruction. Indeed, it is hard to write calmly of this creature who strove so manfully for the great and simple integrities of human intercourse, looking as he did far through and beyond the small, petty thing of the moment. Always, while responding to the little tragical affairs of men, he could but compare these with the big, cosmic facts and dreams that lured him on. This verse, by I know not whom, so well envisages the Jack London whom I knew:

"Your stark vision and cold fire,
Your singing truth, your vehement desire
To cut through lies to life.
These move behind the printed echoes here,
The paper strife,

The scurry of small pens about your name,
Measuring, praising, blaming by the same
Tight rule of thumb that makes their own
Inadequacy known.''

How often I start up to share with him the very things
he so missed and would love to know from the lips of fellow
authors. ''He was an honest writer,'' says an Englishman.
That would have pleased him above all things. And another: ''A strong and virile writer of clean prose—robust,
honest, straightforward, and an artist.'' Berton Braley's
''He never struck a ribald note,'' calls to mind a conversation in Honolulu. Alexander Hume Ford exclaimed:

''But, Jack, you have never written anything smutty
—you've done almost everything else!'' He had meant to
be facetious, but in a flash Jack was all gravity:

''No!—and I never shall. I have never yet written
a line for print that I would be ashamed for my two little
girls who are growing up to see and read, and I never
shall!''

To me he would say: ''When I swear my worst, I really
don't mean it—only words, letting off steam. But when *you*
say 'Damn!' you are positively evil in your ferocity!
Wicked woman!''

Never shall I forget his indignation, too vast for any
expletives at his command, when a minister of the Gospel
wrote him that his novel ''The Little Lady of the Big
House'' was unclean, unfit for the youth of America to
read. ''Show *me!*'' he raged, ''where there is a line in that
book 'unfit' for any young man or woman to read!''
Hard upon this accusation came a book-review in a con-
servative New England monthly, employing the most extraordinary nomenclature to interpret the alleged pruriency of
the book. Jack could not contain his ire, but started a battle
royal with the sons of Adam who had in his opinion so
degenerated as not to know clean frankness when they saw

it. There is no telling where the controversy might have fetched up, had he lived. "I've given over sitting back and listening to gross misinterpretation of my clean and healthy motives," he said with smoldering eyes. "It is like malicious slander, and whenever it appears I am going after it and knock off its ugly head in the open!"

How does the foregoing comport with this: "He was an uplift to the young. The world is better and purer for his having lived—an inspiration to thousands of men and women to work and keep on working, to create and keep on creating, to live the full life wherever they are or whatever may be their work."

My copy of "The Little Lady of the Big House," dated three months before Jack died, carries this inscription:

"The years pass. You and I pass. But yet our love abides— more firmly, more deeply, more surely, for we have built our love for each other, not upon the sand, but upon the rock.

"Your Lover-Husband."

In the last weeks of his life, that was often the burden of his talk with me—the firm foundation of the house of love we had builded in the decade of our close companionship. So, in my memories of that year of unusual vicissitudes in our fortunes, the warm and deathless love-message in his hand in "The Little Lady of the Big House" is a rock of ages, made yet more immovable by the declaration in Jack's next volume. "The Turtles of Tasman," the last he ever was to hold in his fingers:

"After it all, and it all, and it all, here we are, all in all, all in all.

"Sometimes I just want to get up on top of Sonoma Mountain and shout to the world about you and me. Arms ever around and around,

"Mate-Man."

"The Ranch,
    "Oct. 6, 1916."

CHAPTER XL

THE LAST SUMMER

1916

UPON returning from Hawaii in August, Jack went about making plans to get away to New York three months thence. His contract with Mr. Hearst was due to expire at the end of another year, and he wished to be timely in reconnoitering the market. His requirements, looking toward ranch expansion and rehabilitating the red ruins of the Wolf House, were not diminishing. From Honolulu he had urged his sister to gather the materials; but she has ever since contended that something more than want of funds held her back. The second cutting of logs had long been seasoning. There was what I can only call a telepathic impulse that had more than once warned her when all was not well with Jack—a sudden intuition that he was ill or in difficulties. She had not failed in this present instance, and I knew, when her eyes rested upon his telltale face at the dock, that some premonition had been verified. Jack's secretary, his sister Ida's widower, after Jack's death reported that Eliza had said that day:

"Our Jack has not come back to us."

When in Honolulu, he had first broached the New York trip, my unexpected decision to remain at home disquieted him as much as had my intention to go alone to the Islands on the occasion of his projected Fleet trip through the Canal.

"At least," he urged, "don't quite make up your mind that you are not going with me. Give it more thought."

I had been seized with determination that was not to be resisted, to revise old Hawaiian notes into the companion book of my "Log of the Snark," and knew beyond question that there could never be time nor strength to give to it unless Jack were absent. When he had gone to a farther port, never to return, a railroad ticket for New York, dated for just a week after his death, lay upon the roll-top desk beside his work-table. But he had not been happy about my consistent refusal to accompany him.

August 9 to 13 he spent at Bohemian Grove, bringing home George Sterling and James Hopper. On the 17th he finished a short story begun on the steamer, "The Kanaka Surf," and before leaving for the State Fair on September 3, had completed another, "When Alice Told Her Soul," both included in "On the Makaloa Mat."

In "When Alice Told Her Soul," underlying its rollicking humor, Jack evidences that his feet had crossed the threshold of psychoanalytical understanding, and it is fascinating to note, in Jung's "Psychology of the Unconscious," marked passages showing the concepts that quickened Jack's imagination to express itself in that tale. Knowing what I already knew of Jack's last days, it was wonderful to check up this knowledge by the aid of those markings. It was my privilege to have the guidance of a pupil of Jung's, our friend Mary Wilshire. Here is an underlined section:

"The possession of a subjectively important secret generally creates a disturbance."

"It may be said that the whole art of life shrinks to the one problem of how the libido may be freed in the most harmless way possible. Therefore, the neurotic derives special benefit in treatment when he can at last rid himself of its various secrets."

Upon this Jack based his picture of the woman struggling to free her soul from a life-long accumulation of secrets which led her to the confessional of a mongrel Billy Sunday type of evangelist.

In the last story ever written by this master of the short story, "The Water Baby," completed on October 2, the theme is more subtly presented through the medium of Hawaiian mythology. Throughout Dr. Jung's chapter on "Symbolism of Mother and Rebirth," there are penciled indications of Jack's grasp of the meaning of folk-lore and mythology of recorded time. Also the comprehension of how to raise lower desires to higher expressions. He has underscored Jesus's challenge to Nicodemus, cited by Jung:

"Think not carnally or thou art carnal, but think symbolically and then thou art spirit."

"The Water Baby" is clearly a symbolic representation of the Rebirth, the return to the Mother, exemplified by the arguments of the old Hawaiian Kohokumi. A similar chord is struck in the following paragraph from Jung's book, indicated by Jack:

"The blessed state of sleep before birth and after birth is, as Joel observed, something like old shadowy memories of that unsuspecting thoughtless state of early childhood, where as yet no opposition disturbed the peaceful flow of dawning life, to which the inner longing always draws us back again and again, and from which the active life must free itself anew with struggle and death, so that it may not be doomed to destruction. Long before Joel, an Indian Chief, had said the same thing in similar words to one of the restless wise men: 'Ah, my brother, you will never learn to know the happiness of thinking nothing and doing nothing; this is next to sleep; this is the most delightful thing there is. Thus we were before birth; thus we shall be after death.'"

Even in "Like Argus of the Ancient Times," written in the first half of September, is exhibited, in the "Freudian dream" of old Tarwater, as he faces extinction in the Arctic forest, the influence of Jack's probings into the stuff of the psyche. And to the lighter reader, I call attention to the fact that Jack himself walks across some of the pages as young Liverpool.

Jack's emphasis upon the primitive elements in life did not emanate from the fact that his readers especially wanted it, because upon this point he was in conflict from first to last, tooth and nail, with editors and reviewers. He was thorough, that is all. It can easily be seen how his early instinctive use of the methods of psychoanalysis abetted this thoroughness in seeking for the noumenon of things, the better to reveal the process by which man has become what he is to-day. Look in "Before Adam" and "The Star Rover," again to find evidence of his knowing how important a part is played in our lives by old, primal emotions, long thought extinct. To him the work of Freud and Jung and others of the school presented a psychological-philosophical key to the "understanding and practical advancement of human life" which leads to synthetic evaluation of human endeavor. It was inevitable that his brain, which was both analytic and synthetic, should first take hold of the analytic half of psychological understanding and quite as inevitably pass into the synthetic half which forms the whole of psychological understanding. With quick, incisive mind he apprehended the scope of the Freudian method in contemplation of the material thus acquired, and then with Jung moved on into the realm of cosmic urge of which man's psychic energy is a part.

A man of Jack London's fearless quality, who prized truth at its proper worth, could but accord a royal welcome to any form of philosophy which offered to render knowledge more complete. His was "the character and intelligence which makes it possible for him to submit himself to a facing of his naked soul, and to the pain and suffering which this often entails." This, from Dr. Beatrice Hinkle's Introduction to Jung's book, Jack had heavily underlined. To face his naked soul he dared to the uttermost, but that was not new with him. It was the old tragedy that began with his earliest gropings. Yet see, in another marked passage, how in his loneliness he realized himself as brother to all other human beings:

"To those who have been able to recognize their own weakness and have suffered in the privacy of their own souls, the knowledge that these things have not set them apart from others, but that they are the common property of all and that no one can point the finger of scorn at his fellow, is one of the greatest experiences of life and is productive of the greatest relief."

"My one great weakness," Jack once wrote to Cloudesley Johns, "is the study of human nature." And when human nature through its repressions baffled discernment, he suffered inexpressibly. He had us bared to the quick those last days. After a set-to with his sister, on ranch questions, or personal ones growing out of controversy, he cried, trying to pierce her brain:

"I'd give my right hand to know what you are *really* thinking of me!"

And to me, in privacy, after I had been almost overreaching myself in self-illumination—once or twice, alack, goaded even to resentment—he would grit out, intensely, with a gesture of despair:

"You tell me this and you tell me that, and you state your reasons. But your true inner impulsions are withheld in spite of yourself. Close as we are, you and I, hard as we strive to give ourselves to each other, the old reticences remain, repressing the utmost revelation. You do your best. It is not enough. Can't you see, oh, my dear, can't you let go completely, and let me see the real you that I want to fathom? . . . I'd give my soul to know what you are *actually* thinking!"

But when, in sudden unasked circumstances, our minds came together in almost superhuman enlightenment, the man was caught up into a supreme and wondrous exaltation. I can only think that to sustain such heights one must needs seek a new world in which to live!

Read this section of Dr. Hinkle's Introduction, which, noted by Jack, throws light upon the struggle extraordinary which he was making to come breast to breast with us in mental sympathy:

"There is frequently expressed among people the idea of how fortunate it is that we cannot see each other's thoughts, and how disturbing it would be if our real feelings could be read. But what is so shameful in these secrets of the soul? They are in reality our own egotistic desires, all striving, longing, wishing for satisfaction, for happiness; those desires which instinctively crave their own gratification, but which can only be really fulfilled by adapting them to the real world and to the social group."

"The value of self-consciousness lies in the fact that man is enabled to reflect upon himself and learn to understand the true origin and significance of his actions and opinions, that he may adequately value the real level of his development and avoid being self-deceived and therefore inhibited from finding his biological adaptation. He need no longer be unconscious of the motives underlying his actions or hide himself behind a changed exterior, in other words, be merely a series of reactions to stimuli, as the mechanists have it, *but he may to a certain extent become a self-creating and self-determining being.*"

I shall never cease to remember the day when, all a-tiptoe with discovery, Jack entered the dining room, slipped into his chair and repeated the foregoing italicized sentence. I, knowing his theretofore immovable position regarding free will, sat aghast at the implication upon his tongue. At length:

"Do you *realize* what you are saying? What you are implying?"

"I know how you feel—how surprised you are," he answered. "But it almost would seem that I can grasp, from

this, some sort of inkling of free will. I'll explain further
—we will read together."

Bear with me, in fairness to a comprehension of the
point Jack London, as an individual, a member of society,
and an 'artist, had reached when he descended "into the
dark," while I quote a few, so very few of the many, marked
sentences from Dr. Hinkle's introduction:

"He, Jung, saw in the term libido a concept of unknown nature,
comparable with Bergson's elan vital, a hypothetical energy of life,
which occupies itself not only in sexuality but in various physio-
logical and psychological manifestations such as growth, development, hunger and all the human activities and interests. This
cosmic energy or urge manifested in the human being he calls
libido and compares it with the energy of physics. Although recognizing, in common with Freud as well as with many others, the
primal instinct of reproduction as the basis of many functions and
present-day activities of mankind no longer sexual in character,
he repudiates the idea of still calling them sexual, even though
their development was a growth originally out of the sexual.
Sexuality and its various manifestations Jung sees as most important channels occupied by libido, but not the exclusive ones
through which libido flows.

"In this achievement lies the hopeful and valuable side of this
method—the development of the synthesis."

"—an absolute truth and an absolute honesty."

"—the often quite unbearable conflict of his weaknesses with
his feelings of idealism."

"The importance of this instinct (sexual) upon human life is
clearly revealed by the great place given to it under the name of
love in art, literature, poetry, romance and all beauty from the
beginning of recorded time."

I was convinced that no mortal frame could out-last
the terrific strain Jack was putting upon his own. Something had to break. And one can only give thanks forever
that it was the body. That was the lesser sacrifice.

At this late date there rises out of my mind, quite
humbly, the question as to whether certain independent

manifestations of myself to which he had been unaccustomed, were upsetting Jack more than he cared to voice—as notably my insistence, in face of his dissatisfaction, upon remaining at home alone to do work of my own. I have come to see it as an inevitable self-liberation after an association that had held me like one enchanted, my faculties paralyzed in every function except as toward him and what of assistance I could be to him. If, as may have been the truth, my ego was unconsciously making effort to win to itself, it was probably due to the impetus of the tuition Jack's superior ego had contributed. I am only trying to clear up phenomena that it now seems might have been more or less portentous to him, and the inner meaning of which he was bending every nerve to discover.

"For the first time in my life," he remarked one day, "I see the real value to the human soul of the confessional."

The effect of this budding impetus in me did not terminate with the termination of his dominating personality. It went marching on, evident in the most amazing ways. Instead of still requiring, in order to go on, that superb domination under which I had so loved to dwell, suddenly I stood free, an ambitious, sure soul for the first time, almost unrecognizable to friends and self, bent upon making the best of that self and its remaining span upon earth; this, if only to prove its appreciation of the gifts that had been bestowed upon it, in the discharge of its tender obligation to the one who had gone. Life-long, inherited insomnia fell from me, and nights were none too long to compass the rejuvenation that was mine, and that prepared me for each looking-forward day of the many days of hard work which had descended upon my willing shoulders. No task, in contemplation, discouraged—even the most exacting, this Biography.

It hardly matters that I am ahead of my story, inasmuch as the events immediately preceding and succeeding Jack's death are all of a piece.

Closely following his passing "into the Silence," on every hand speaking evidence of his thought and achievement, even lacking the maturer masterpieces we shall never know, it came to me this way:

"It seems clear that there was no limit to his mind. Could he have lived, that cerebration would have gone on and on, stretching incredibly, interminably, no bounds to its elasticity in every direction. It was enormous."

This to George Sterling, sad beyond despair above his friend's "holy ashes." And he repeated after me:

"There was no limit to his mind. It was enormous."

Jack was so tired that hot evening we arrived at Sacramento, September 3, that he went to bed after dinner instead of joining Mrs. Shepard at the Fair. We were hardly ready to "turn in" when a general fire-alarm called us to the hotel window, and in the direction of the Fair Grounds we could see the flames rising.

"It's the Exhibition going up, all right," Jack said, peering through the glare for the towers of the buildings.

"But aren't you going to dress and drive out to see if the stock is safe—Neuadd and the rest?" I asked, surprised at his lack of excitement.

"Oh, no—Eliza's there, or will get there, and she'll do everything that can be done."

And surely enough, his indomitable superintendent, already bound back to the hotel, had turned about and somehow bluffed her way through the cordon of police thrown about the place, and marshaled our stockmen to convey her precious charges to an unthreatened open space.

As before written, she and Jack had disagreed upon the question of showing animals, at least thus early in the establishment of his reputation as a stockbreeder. But having seen, upon his return from the Islands, the prime state of his beasts which she had ready for the journey, he had relented, admitted her standpoint, and was loyally on hand to see them win. That they did; and no one, even Eliza, so proud as he with his handful of gold medals and blue and gold ribbons to prove that the Jack London Ranch was "on the right track."

But not with his own eyes did he behold our proud grand champions carry off their honors. Only the one day after arrival was he able to leave the hotel, for he was obliged to keep to bed for eight days with a session of rheumatism in his left ankle. Fortunately the torture was intermittent, or it would have been unbearable without a hypodermic. As it was, the doctor had to prescribe powders for the worst nights, or there would have been no rest for either of us. I went out of the house but three times, and then to buy books for the invalid, who seemed not to want me out of his sight.

In the longer pauses between recurrences of grinding misery that drenched the poor boy with sweat, we made genuinely merry over games of pinochle and cribbage, and read aloud, turn about; or he entertained callers, while I gently rubbed the ankle by the hour. Often I could put the sufferer to sleep by this means. Evenings, from the window, Jack enjoyed following the starry trail of Boquel's aeroplane flights.

For once, stung alert by pain, he was seriously anxious about the future as regarded bodily comfort. "Although, if I became permanently crippled, I'll have endless time in bed to do all the reading I can never get around to, and be the happiest fellow that ever came down the pike," he grinned with native paradox. But I noticed that he did not hasten that glad day by disobeying the physician, who told him he was in a precarious state and must mend his diet and work off some of his excess fat. He weighed in the neighborhood of one hundred and ninety-four pounds.

So all toothsome fleshpots were missing from the tray, while I was pressed to invent salad dressings and suggest the most tempting vegetable dishes.

Upon one especially precious day, when we two were reviewing our long run of years together, calling up memories sacred to our companionship, I asked Jack if he could remember a sweet thing, the idea of which, coming from him, had astonished me one day in Honolulu. I challenged:

"I'll wager anything you say, that you cannot repeat it just as you said it."

"Which sweet thing?" he came back; "There were many, if I remember aright. I'll subscribe to it, whatever it was, even if I can't remember it! Be kind, though, and give me a tip!"

When I had done so, he said very soberly:

"Yes, I not only remember and subscribe to it, but I can repeat it word for word. I told you: If I should go into the dark, and wake again—which I do not for a moment expect to do—but if I *should* open my eyes again, yours would be the first face I should want them to rest upon!—— And I mean it, Mate Woman. I surrender to you, you are the only one.—— Ask me for something that I can do for you!"

I have no personal evidence that Jack did not die a firm unbeliever in any hereafter—materialist monist to the end. In a story, "The Eternity of Forms," included in "The Turtles of Tasman" collection, he has given his lifelong confession of faith, "simple, brief, unanswerable":

"I assert, with Hobbes, that it is impossible to separate thought from matter that thinks. I assert, with Bacon, that all human understanding arises from the world of sensations. I assert, with Locke, that all human ideas are due to the functions of the senses. I assert, with Kant, the mechanical origin of the universe, and that creation is a natural and historical process. I assert, with Laplace, that there is no need of the hypothesis of a creator. And, finally, I assert, because of all the foregoing, that form is ephemeral. Form passes. Therefore we pass."

Two years before his death, he had more briefly stated his old position in a letter to a young socialist in Chicago:

"June 25, 1914.

"Dear Ralph Kasper:

". . . I have always inclined toward Haekel's position. In fact, 'incline' is too weak a word. I am a hopeless materialist. I see a soul as nothing else than the sum of the activities of the organism plus personal habits, memories, experiences, of the organism. *I believe that when I am dead, I am dead. I believe that with my death I am just as much obliterated as the last mosquito you or I smashed.*

"I have no patience with fly-by-night philosophers such as Bergson. I have no patience with the metaphysical philosophers. With them, always, the wish is parent to the thought, and their wish is parent to their profoundest philosophical conclusions. I join with Haeckel in being what, in lieu of any other phrase, I am compelled to call 'a positive scientific thinker.' "

Yet it was the same Jack London, caressing the thought of Death at the close of "The Human Drift," who wrote:

"There is nothing terrible about it. With Richard Hovey, when he faced his death, we can say: 'Behold! I have lived!' And with another and greater one, we can lay ourselves down with a will. The one drop of living, the one taste of being, has been good; and perhaps our greatest achievement will be that we dreamed immortality, even though we failed to realize it."

Jack's sister thinks he was on the way, those last weeks, to modify his uncompromising attitude. At least, she considers, judging from things said and unsaid in their closer moments, that he was shaken in his certitudes about a number of subjects. He had always smiled or good-naturedly scoffed at her telepathic "hunches," as he termed them; but himself underwent a puzzling experience. Midmost of his forenoon work, all at once he obeyed a call that his mortal ears had not heard, and discovered himself standing by the window straining his eyes toward Eliza's cottage, on a slight eminence several hundred yards away. Everything looked as usual in the serene prospect, and he came to himself with a laugh, turned to watch the big Shire mares hauling his prided manure-spreader, and returned to the interrupted manuscript. But he continued uneasy. Odd it seems to me that Jack did not tell me of the incident; for later in the day Eliza reported that the husband of her new cook had arrived unheralded and with a gun threatened herself, who had been totally ignorant of her cook's marriage status, for keeping his wife away from him.

I repeat that I have no evidence at first hand that there was any radical change in Jack's method of thinking. He only showed an intensification of his old instinct for the "inexorable logic of the shadowland of the unconscious." What he did say to me, and more than once, was the old: "If you should ever go 'soft,' I'd never forgive you!"

It was not until after the Fair had closed and his sister gone home, that Jack was fit to make the journey by automobile. About sunset we had a breakdown, and I remember him hobbling about a little village while the repairing went forward, and halting to watch some small boys spinning tops.

"But don't you do this, and this?" he said, all interest in the new generation, taking the toy from an urchin, and trying to resurrect his own cunning. No, they couldn't spin it his way—had never seen it done, in fact; nor could they, as did he, make it spin on the vertical trunk of a tree. Suddenly one of the lads sprang away to the side of the road and glibly named the make of an approaching car while the headlights were still distant.

"Well, I'll be——" Jack left it becomingly unsaid. "How did *you* know what was the name of that machine?"

"Know its engines, of course—I can tell most of 'em a long way off," the boy bragged, nicely even with his interlocutor for superior skill in the top-game.

"See, Mate," Jack lit a cigarette and contemplated the group, "I'm getting old. I'm out of touch with the younger generation. All they know is gasolene—but I will say they know it pretty thoroughly!"

He was very quiet the rest of the ride, and I recall a curious misapprehension displayed by him as we made ready to leave the town of Napa in a moonlight haze. Though we had often visited here, this time we differed as to an avenue that led into the twenty-mile road to Glen Ellen. Jack's sense of locality was usually faultless, mine far from being so. But on that night I was so positive that finally he relapsed into silence, sending forward the parting shot:

"Very well—have your way; but you'll soon find you are entirely off the route."

It happened otherwise; but I made no comment as the dim moonlit leagues were left behind. And then I became conscious of a pressure as Jack's hand clasped my shoulder, and over it came the love-husky, golden whisper I knew of his most humble and generous moments:

"I love you to death, my dear."

A return hand-caress, and "I know you do," closed the incident, and no reference to it was ever necessary.

To the tune of a merry household, after finishing "Like Argus of the Ancient Times" Jack went at a fantastic, whimsical tramp study entitled "The Princess," last of the "On the Makaloa Mat" cluster. The denouement is founded upon an after-dinner story once told at our table by a Bohemian clubman, an inimitable raconteur. Jack seemed to enjoy making this tale, and could hardly wait each day to catch me with his "Come on and see how it goes!" The accomplished ease of his method seemed only to increase; too much, some friends and critics thought. Yet, reading over his last stories, with their sure technique and character-drawing, profound thinking in the processes of the human soul, I cannot consider that he had fallen off.

How gay were host and guest, outside of what might be called natural sports such as swimming, and swimming the horses, "hiking," boating, riding, and the like, may be judged by a reckless prank that broke up one noonday meal. I do not remember how it started, nor whose was the suggestion, but some one was dared to swallow, alive and whole, the tiny goldfish that swam among plants in a low cut-glass bowl on the long table. In the babble among the horrified girls, Jack shouted:

"We'll play a hand at poker for it, and the fellow who loses must not only swallow the fish, but keep it down for ten minutes, no matter what is said to him."

Remonstrance was in vain—the trio, Jack, Finn Frolich, and Joe Mather, were "on their way." Joe, slender, fastidious, was "stuck," and exhibited, in paying the forfeit, the keenest courage I ever have witnessed.

"Gee," gasped the chesty Frolich, "I *couldn't* have got it down!"

"I'd have died if I'd had to do it!" Jack said in awe-struck admiration when confronted by the tragic face of the man who had "put away" the scaly morsel. And "I never can feel *quite* the same toward you again," Joe's young wife murmured betwixt laugh and sob.

"That was an awful thing to allow," afterward I chided Jack.

"It was a wild thing," he giggled concurrence, "but think of the fun!"

"How about the fish?"

"Now you're saying something," he admitted. "Just the same, it was quicker 'curtains' for the fish than your fish in the garden pool get, *slowly* smothering in the gullets of the water-snakes! And how about live oysters, now, my dear . . . *think, think!*—— Anyway, I'd rather have been the fish than Joe!" he grimaced in conclusion.

When, on October 2, "The Water Baby" was sent off to *The Cosmopolitan*, Jack went at his notes for a new novel, "Cherry," which was left less than half completed. This romance is laid in Hawaii. The heroine, Cherry, is a Japanese girl, mysteriously wrecked in the Islands when a baby, and evidently, by the trappings and the dead servitors on the abandoned sampan, infant of high degree. She is adopted and given every cultural advantage by a wealthy white couple who were childless. The motif of the work is a racial one, the climax depending upon Cherry's choice of a husband among the many, of various nationalities, who sue for the hand of this tantalizing oriental maid whose brain has divined her situation in every connotation. There are enough notes to guide a reader to the conclusion; but up to the end of the year 1921, I have not matured my plans for this book and that other incomplete manuscript, "The Assassination Bureau."

Evenings were spent in cards, or games like "packing peanuts," in which Jack nearly died of mirth. Or he would be inclined to read aloud, poetry, or perhaps his own stories. And I know there were listeners, captured and enchained by his charm, in whose ears still rings his rich and solemn voice in the stately numbers of Ecclesiastes. He had read from this favorite several times to certain friends in Honolulu, and now recurred to it with increasing appreciation. At these times Jack was extremely handsome, with something hard to describe—a fine nobility in expression and pose, but something also of the unconscious hauteur of isolation, of the aristocrat, of the imperator.

One little party that was with us for a day or two consisted of my uncle, Harley R. Wiley, of the University of California faculty, who had brought up his long poem "Dust and Flame" to read to us; and Blanche Partington, whose contribution, in this instance, beside her own ever-welcome personaliy, was the young Irish revolutionist's, Kathleen O'Brennan, whom she wanted to see lock horns with Jack London. She was not disappointed. The pair went into the arena in fine form, while the rest of us sat panting with emotions that ranged from serious to comic. "Never in my life,'' Blanche revives the occasion, ''did I hear such a racial dressing-down as Jack gave Ireland!''

More often than he went himself, Jack sent me over the trails with parties, and never did we twain go on any of the long rides once so reveled in. When guests were absent, the ranch claimed all his daylight recreation hours, and he forewent the Outlaw, and Sonoma Maid, and Hilo, preferring Prince, the ''Love-Horse'' of our fore-in-hand, on whom leisurely he explored the uplands, testing with eye and hand for soils he ached to ''put to work.'' This was not sufficient exercise for me, and I rode my colts longer distances, usually hunting for Jack in the woods, when we would descend together. Many was the day he said, though uncomplainingly:

''I got in a lot of reading last night, but not much sleep. I'll nap this afternoon.''

But it was seldom, homing alone from a canter, that I failed to see his tumbled handful of curls bobbing out of the door to meet me.

''You'll never know,'' he said again and again, ''how I love to hear your horse galloping toward me. I wouldn't miss being here to see you come in for anything!''

I was far from easy about him. There was a twilight stealing over our lives—was it to be ever this way, that I rode solitary while he must sleep? Whither were we trending?

''Near the end,'' an author has told me, ''he wrote me about my book, and in that letter he complained of being ill. Said he had been down with rheumatism . . . complained of having had a severe time of it. Complaint of any kind from him seemed unusual. My impression was that he was not himself when he wrote this way. It came stealing over me that his work was nearly done.''

Jack had expected to go east in the early part of October, but the water-suit intervened. He was supposed to be away, however, and I am always grateful to fate that we had those last few weeks uninterrupted save by a few loved ones. To one, my cousin Beth, he gave a book in which the inscription verified my fear in that he was going too fast, his mind increasing upon itself with an insupportable rapidity, wave upon wave, factors climbing upon the backs of factors, the thousand-thousand connotations that might have suggested the loom of madness to any who could not know his natural scope. But to me it represented an enormous sanity, a huge, normal functioning, only a madness if to be super-sane is to be mad; and the only question was, how long could a man live in so unchecked a mind-functioning, while neglecting his body?

"It is a long time," he complained in the inscription to Beth above referred to, "since I've seen you to renew acquaintance with you. When you were here, the world was here, and the world was very much and too much with me. Darn the wheel of the world! Why must it continually turn over? Where is the reverse gear?"

Evening after evening he read aloud from Percy's "Reliques of Ancient English Poetry," and reread certain of these to Beth and to his two "saints," my sister Emma Growall, and my uncle's wife, Villa Wiley. Two large volumes we went through, and the third and last to Page 288. The next selection is "St. George for England," and Jack's book-mark, the ubiquitous safety-match, still rests between the leaves. Dryden's "Jealousie Tyrant of the Mind" was an especial treasure to us. I shall hear until I die Jack's voice of the lover in "The Nut-Browne Mayd," which he never tired of repeating, and which I called for over and over, if only for the spell of the "viols" in his throat, and to see, under the long curl of lashes, the eyes he raised to mine at the verse-ends:

"I love but you alone."

He fastened upon the sweet old-English spelling of Darling—"Dearling"—and thenceforward used it exclusively when addressing me, his voice like a prayer.

Interspersed with these poems we also read the Beaumont and Fletcher Elizabethan plays, the power and beauty of some of these affecting Jack profoundly.

He frequently asked me to play or sing for him, and was strangely touched by a song-relic of my girlhood, "Recompense," in which occur the lines:

"And at the last, I found that she
    Was more than all the world to me."

Handel's "Largo," Wagner's "Pilgrim's Chorus," and the trio of funeral marches, favorites of all his adult life, were resurrected and rendered him as much pleasure as ever. Whenever he went to Oakland, he put in an hour or so in some music store, after which there was sure to arrive in Glen Ellen a box of phonograph records, most of them operatic. Many he retained, and while we had supper at a card-table on my glass porch, it was the duty of Sekinè or the house-boy to run off a succession of disks laid out by Jack. In line with tracing back into race-consciousness, he showed increasing preference for folk-songs, and the American negro melodies. After supper he would throw himself on the couch by my side, and have these reeled off, while he dreamed beyond all following of the significance of these human cries for rest.

"It's always been that way," he would reflect. "Mankind has always bowed under some galling yoke, physical or mental, that has made it supplicate for rest, to escape 'the dreary agitation of the dust.' Can't you hear it, beating down the ages—listen to that—play it over, Sera, so Mrs. London can hear it again."

Sometimes he was very calm, and evenings were of our sweetest, he reading aloud or talking, I embroidering the beloved "L" upon absurd little "guest-towels" for the Wolf House that was soon to be rebuilt. His dislike to see me sew had been modified these many years. My philosophy upon needlework had so pleased him that he incorporated it in "The Little Lady of the Big House."

Again, over-intense, on hair-trigger to snap up any word as a pretext to start an argument, if he caught me trying to placate or turn him into smoother channels he flew into a mental fury, at times hot, at others deadly cool. Sometimes, as before noted, I let him wear himself out. And when, as might happen, he was soon over the mood, resting in my embrace he would tell me what it meant to unburden to me in any way at any time.

On October 22, precisely a month before Jack went out, Neuadd Hillside, the "Great Gentleman," our incomparable Shire Horse, died overnight while we slept. Rupture, they pronounced it, and veterinaries were summoned from all quarters.

It was a heavy blow to Jack. Aside from the monetary loss this was an incalculable set-back in his far-seeing plans, already under way, for breeding and in-breeding. I learned of the event when at nine of the morning I found Jack still in bed, lying quite idle. I had not time to ask the reason for his stricken face when he said, reaching out to me:

"Come here and sit beside me. I have bad news for you —your Great Gentleman is gone."

"What? Who?—what do you mean?"

"Good old Neuadd died last night."

. . . And a little later: "I'm not ashamed, Mate-Woman," looking at me like a lost child through his man's tears. He followed me around much that day, telling more than I had ever dreamed of what the glorious animal had meant to him.

"l tell you, Mrs. London," said Hazen Cowan, our cowboy, who had had the care of the stallion, "I hadn't cried since the last time my mother spanked me, until Neuadd fell down. He wouldn't lie down till he was dead, but stood there shaking all over." Hazen pulled a freckled hand across his hazel, black-lashed eyes: "I'd really slept with him, lived with him, for months, you know."

"Cherry" was laid aside, and Jack went to making notes for a novel upon the horse. "You, too, make me some memory-pictures of him," he begged. He now believed that he had been right in the first place about "show-condition" for live stock, and that had Neuadd been maintained in proper working-flesh, he would have been saved to the farm.

He did not begin that book. After making a sufficient sketch to fix his motif, he returned to what was already begun—how vain the endeavor we were not then to know. But the death of the "chief of the herd" weighed more than we shall ever realize. At times he gave way to a listlessness I had never before seen in him.

Next, the gentle Prince developed what eventually proved an incurable rheumatism, and could not be used. One day his master charged: "If anything should happen to me, and Prince's case become hopeless, don't ever let him go off the ranch." So the "Love-Horse" came to sleep with Neuadd, Sonoma Maid and Milda, in a wooded ravine on the "Beauty Ranch." The only one remaining of our joyous coaching team is the indefatigable Outlaw, Gert, who lives and moves and delivers the finest of colts each and every renascent springtime.

When, in mid-October, the duck-hunting season opened, Jack flung caution to the four winds and with gusto consumed two large birds, canvasback or mallard, each day. An Oakland market kept him supplied. Poisoned as he already was with uremia, this richest of diets was nothing less than suicidal, and put him out of the world of human affairs in less than six weeks. "Oh, I love them so," was his incorrigible waive of my remonstrance. "I've been good as gold ever since Sacramento, you've seen; and now it won't hurt me to fall off my diet. Don't forget I'm naturally a meat-eater!"

The last guest Jack ever entertained, and who left

three days before he died, was a frail little stranger who came to ask if he would accept a joint guardianship of her children. "Sure!" said that obliging friend of the needy. "Put my name down with the rest!" She had studied medicine, and writing to me later inquired if Jack was accustomed to the amazing menu she had seen him consume twice daily while she was with us. None but a plowman could have survived it.

On the 28th, shaking off the dejection of the court proceedings in the water-suit begun two days previously, Jack with apparent joy read a letter from the Newspaper Enterprise Association, of New York City, and appended is his reply to their self-evident query:

"Gentlemen:

". . . When I lie on the placid beach of Waikiki, in the Hawaiian Islands, as I did last year, and a stranger introduces himself as the person who settled the estate of Captain Keller; and when that stranger explains that Captain Keller came to his death by having his head chopped off and smoke-cured by the cannibal head-hunters of the Solomon Islands in the West South Pacific; and when I remember back through the several brief years, to when Captain Keller, a youth of twenty-two and master of the schooner *Eugenie,* wassailed deep with me on many a night, and played poker to the dawn, and took hasheesh with me for the entertainment of the wild crew of Pennduffryn; and who, when I was wrecked on the outer reef of Malu, on the island of Malaita, with fifteen hundred naked bushmen head-hunters on the beach armed with horse-pistols, Snider rifles, tomahawks, spears, war-clubs, and bows and arrows, and with scores of war-canoes, filled with salt-water head-hunters and man-eaters holding their place on the fringe of the breaking surf alongside of us, only four whites of us including my wife on board—when Captain Keller burst through the rain-squalls to windward, in a whale-boat, with a crew of niggers, himself rushing to our rescue, bare-footed and bare-legged, clad in loin-cloth and sixpenny undershirt, a brace of guns strapped about his middle—I say, when I remember all this, that adventure and romance are not dead as I lie on the placid beach of Waikiki."

Here is a letter to his London agent, Mr. Hughes Massie, dated November 5:

"I have not replied by cable because of two things.

"First, I expect to be in New York sometime after the middle of November. I should then be able to talk the matter of such an autobiography of 50,000 words, about my writing, with my magazine publisher. In any such event, I would personally handle the sale of the American first serial rights.

"Second, I am not sure about what the contemplated 50,000 words would be concerned. From reading your letter it would seem that what is asked is how I obtained at first hand the experiences that are at the back of my writing. I do not see how I could write on such a subject—at least no more than several thousand words. My idea would be to give my writing experiences from my first attempt at writing right on down the line to the present date, I mean my experiences with newspaper editors, magazine editors, book publishers, etc., etc., entering intimately into my various books and short stories themselves, I mean in relation to the sale of them to the purchasers.

"If you could write me a letter conveying more adequately the subject that would be acceptable, as well as some sort of suggestions about the rate that the *Wide World Magazine* would pay for the first serial rights in Great Britain, I would be better equipped to discuss the matter with my people when I get to New York."

"The money I get for this," he exulted, "will buy more farm machinery, more seed to plant, and the rest!"

On the afternoon of the second court-hearing in the riparian rights contest, Jack was threatened with a repetition of the severe attack he had suffered in Honolulu, and drilled me again in the use of the hypodermic, should the pain get beyond him. He was very wretched, but the calculus passed without resort to the needle.

His fourth appearance in court was on November 10. He came home looking ill, and complained of distressing symptoms which toward evening so strongly resembled ptomaine poisoning that finally, as the pain increased, I got him to take an antidote, which produced the desired effect. Very gravely I talked with him, and he owned that he was shockingly out of condition, with an increasing tendency to dysentery. "I've never been quite right in that respect since my sickness and operation in Australia—and Mexico didn't help matters any. —But don't worry, don't bother; I'll be all right, my dear!"

And still he made no alteration in his diet of underdone wild fowl.

Philosophically, and helped by psychoanalysis, Jack better and better understood and sympathized with human frailty; but temperamentally, due largely to physical and nervous breakdown, he became more and more intolerant under the torment of his uncovered sensibilities. Those last days were not the first wherein he had gone stark against the apparent truism that any one who accepts benefits never forgives the benefactor.

As I sit at my typewriter, I can see him, back to me, elbows on desk, head in both hands, and hear him say, not for the initial time:

"It's a pretty picayune world, Mate—what *am* I to think? Are they all alike? Every person I've done anything for—and I've not been a pincher, have I?—has thrown me down: near ones, dear ones—and the rest."

"Some of us are still standing by," I reminded him soothingly.

"Oh, I don't mean you, of course, nor Eliza. But the exceptions are so rare—friend and stranger alike. Run over the list. Take that socialist woman east—I've forgotten her name—who wrote begging me to stake her to a small sum for a certain number of months, so she could devote herself to writing a book. It's ages since she acknowledged the last check Eliza sent, and she has never written me one line of thanks, nor even reported progress.

And she's but a sample of the whole hopeless, helpless mess! And take cases nearer home. The hand I feed smites. It's only the ones I have helped. What *am* I to conclude?" he finished, swallowed in gloom, suffering damnably.

"But even so," I argued, trying to offset the somber discord induced by those raw sensibilities that made him pierce too easily through even the unconscious petty shams of civilization—"even so, it is nothing new to you; do not forget that it has always been that way. Do not think you are the only one who suffers from this lamentable tendency of the human. Your kind has plenty of company in the world. No man who ever made money and played Santa Claus to many, has escaped your fate. So don't isolate yourself as a martyr. Be a *real* philosopher, and 'forget it.'" Then in a vain attempt to sting him out of his lethargy to a normal sense of values, I dared: "Be careful, or you'll find yourself nursing a persecution mania!"

But the only reaction to this last bolt was a rather spiritless challenge to show him where he was wrong in his facts.

Although Judge Edgar Zook urged the plaintiffs to allow him to apportion the water, which he was empowered to do, their lawyer declined to consider this. "We stand or fall," was his ultimatum. On November 14, the injunction was dissolved. Jack, desiring in neighborly manner to convince the plaintiffs of the veracity of claims upon which his testimony had been based, drove around inviting one and all to break bread with us at noon on Friday the 17th, and accompany him on a little tour of inspection. Nearly all accepted, and with one or two exceptions it was their last meeting with the big neighbor whose visions for agricultural welfare were for the most part incomprehensible to them. Jack appeared very bright during the meal, and no business was talked until its conclusion. But when we started out of doors, he became all earnest enthusiasm to persuade his opponents to the worth of his moral as well as legal rights in the matter at issue. One of them was heard to sigh:

"We should never have gone into this fight with you!"

And another: "What a pity we didn't get together with you in the first place and thrash out this matter instead of rushing into court with it!"

Saturday I myself went to bed. I cannot, to this day, name my illness; but looking back it seems that I was on the verge of a nerve-collapse. I must have been laboring under too great anxiety. The Thursday before, when Ernest Hopkins and two camera men had been photographing Jack both for "movies" and "stills," I had suddenly, in one or two of the poses, noticed something in Jack's face, or an accession of something more than dimly felt of late, that struck fear into me. It might be described as a *deadness*—or an absence of life; something that no face, upon an upright figure, should be. Others were full of vivacity, with all that Jack could command of charm and aliveness—sitting with his rifle, laughing from the high seat of the water cart, or driving two monster Shire mares in the manure-spreader. How eloquent, like a message of the year's increase, that oval ring of fertilizer lay for weeks upon his field until erased by the winter rains! How eloquent was the whole fruitful prospect, when he lay, in his own White Silence, in the midst of the fair land of his devising! To me, then, wandering among his kindly herds, in the effort to orient myself with a new universe, came the thought that he, our Jack, was the most eloquent dead man in all the world. That small, potent hand had written a deathless scroll upon the hills, and he seemed to live and speak and move at one with the growth he had encouraged in the pregnant dust of his Sweet Land. One could not quit and lie down in the face of such vital challenge to make short shrift of tears and rise to carry his banner as long as fate should be generous enough to let one work.

When on a day I gallop along the blossoming ways to Jack's mountain meadows, missing my Strong Traveler, it takes little effort still to hear his blithe, companionable "*Toot! Toot!*" I would feel no startlement did he emerge, reining the Outlaw from the shadows of the trees, laughing from under the cowboy hat.

He had been radiant in his hope that had no horizon. "I want to live a hundred years!" was his lusty slogan, repeated within a fortnight of his death. "See the dozens of boxes of notes filed away? Why, writers I know are looking about for plots, and I've enough here to keep me busy with twice a hundred novels!"

It was the expression of just such exuberance that Jack felt in this stanza of John G. Neihardt's:

> Let me live out my years in heat of blood!
> Let me lie drunken with the dreamer's wine!
> Let me not see this soul-house built of mud
> Go toppling to the dust—a vacant shrine!

When he was gone, I smiled with appreciation of an enthusiastic, but uninformed, reviewer who, despite Jack's fifty-odd books written within seventeen years, credited him with more than double that number, "to say nothing of other forms of literature."

And there was also a letter that pleased me, written on November 20, and never read by Jack:

"I have just seen your picture, driving two huge draft-horses to a manure-spreader. This is the picture of a man with a wagonload of fertilizer. He is going to spread it over an acre of ground and make it fertile. In reality the man has an inexhaustible supply of mental pabulum which he spreads over the whole world, the dark spots are made lighter, the sloughs of despond are drained and made to blossom . . . the weary and heavy laden are lifted up. . . . In reality you are subsoil-plowing the world, preparing it for the seeds of Universal Brotherhood, the while you dream dreams."

It would not be hard to imagine him a happy ghost revisiting his beloved lands or the running tides of San Francisco Bay, irresistibly drawn back to

"... The horses in the wagons with their kind long faces,
And little boats that climb upon the waves."

I could but think, viewing the excellence he left behind, the purity of his purpose, the way he went straight to his goal, that he made a shining exception to the rule that

"The evil that men do lives after them;
The good is oft interred with their bones."

I was sad when, on Saturday the nineteenth, our tenth wedding anniversary, I was unable to join Jack and a quaint woman guest at dinner. Jack brought her in to meet me, and later, having settled her somewhere with a book, returned to stroke my throbbing head. I remember reminding him of the fact that I was born and married in the same month, and that eight days hence, the twenty-seventh, would be my birthday. How little I imagined that there would intervene the date of my widowhood! Yet doom was in the air. Subtly I felt its clutch, and this was all my malady.

Jack wrote with unabated industry on Monday morning, and in the afternoon he came and coaxed me in a cheery and loving way to pull myself together and accompany him up-mountain. He wanted to see again a piece of land that adjoined the ranch, which he recalled as being well watered by springs.

"I may buy it," he said. "I could develop the springs, and that would mean bigger crops, bigger and better cattle and horses, life, more life, Mate-Woman! Oh, it's big, and I have so many plans and so much to do! Come on up with me."

It hurt to refuse, but I felt too weak and tired to face the long ride; so he went out alone, looking unusually disappointed. Yet what strength was mine but half a hundred hours later to meet the worst and not fail—so strangely are we constituted.

Upon his return he came breaking through the house with his merriest step to tell me every detail of his exploration.

"I found the trail without any trouble," he told me, "and when I came to the field I had in mind, there was a young farmer plowing. We talked quite a while, and I got off old Fritz to handle the soil myself. I found it of very good quality. It ran through my fingers, so *friable*, you know. I've discovered who owns it, and I'm going to take up the matter as soon as I can land the prospect of some money in New York. Maybe that autobiographical stuff will pay for it." Then further: "I'm planning to go on the twenty-ninth. And you're *still* not coming with me?" he finished wistfully. Then he resumed the tale of his projects for increasing the abundance upon his acres.

There followed a wakeful night for Jack, and he rose very late, frankly blue, and complaining of fatigue. The dysentery was so much worse that I protested at his taking no measures to check an alarming condition. He worked but a short time, and the few pages of manuscript were the last he ever set hand to. The several letters he dictated to the machine were transcribed afterward by his secretary. The very last letter he ever talked into the horn was the following:

"Editor *Every Week,*
  "My dear sir:
  "Curses on you, 'Every Week'! You keep a busy man busy over-time trying to get rid of you while unable to tear himself away. I wish the man who writes the captions for your photographs had never been born. I just can't refrain from reading every word he writes.
  "And the rest of your staff bothers me the same way.
  "Hereby registering my complaint,
                    "Sincerely yours,
                    "Jack London."

The last literary notes he ever penciled, I take from his bed-side tablet:

"Socialist autobiography.

"Martin Eden and Sea Wolf, attacks on Nietzeschean philosophy, which even the socialists missed the point of."

Another page:

"In late autumn of 1916, when Adamson Bill (8 hrs. for Railroad Brotherhoods) rushed at the last tick of the sixtieth second of the twelfth hour, through Congress and Senate and signed by President Wilson, agreed with my forecast of favored unions in Iron Heel."

"Novel. ·

"Historical novel of 80,000 words—love—hate—primitiveness. Discovery of America by the Northmen—see my book on same, also see Maurice Hewlett's 'Frey and his Wife.' Get in interpretation of the genesis of their myths, etc., from their own unconsciousness."

He did not go out all day, and slept in the afternoon, rousing himself with an effort. Eliza came over to talk ranch business, and they were still at it when the first and then the second gong sounded for our supper. Having shaken off the half-stupor in which he had awakened, he had become very excited outlining his immediate intention to erect on the ranch a general store, a school, and a post-office. I heard him wind up:

"There are enough children on the ranch to open a school. The ranch people can have their homes here, trade here at better prices, be born here, grown up here, get their schooling here, and if they die they can be buried on the Little Hill, where the two Greenlaw children's graves are. . . . No, I haven't in mind a community in the usual sense of a reform colony. I only look forward to making the place self-sustaining for every soul upon it."

Five days after that utterance, Jack London's own ashes were laid there on the whispering ridge.

Eliza told me later that in those days she worried about the over-working of Jack's brain. As far as possible she met him, yet wondered how he expected her to put into prompt execution the enormous tasks he prepared. A lesser man, in the throes of the toxemia that was destroying him, would have evinced a lesser "mania." Jack's mental vigor was spent logically along the lines of his ambition.

Even with modern familiarity with body chemistry, scientists are not able to determine with exactitude the nature of the toxins that produce uremia. "A gastro-intestinal type of uremia," the doctors pronounced Jack's disorder. The symptoms had been present for a long time —stomachic disturbances, insomnia, sporadic melancholia, dysentery, rheumatic edema in ankles, and dull headaches alternating with the speeding up of his mental enginery. Convulsions were absent, and the only coma was that in which he breathed his last.

When Jack at length parted from Eliza that night of the twenty-first, he brought with him into the warm and cozy veranda the sweeping current of his fervor, and continued talking in the same vein. But I saw that he was strung to a breaking pitch of excitement.

"Your duck was perfection half an hour ago," I said, "but I'm afraid it is far from that by now."

But he was not interested in ducks, and spoke much more than he ate, roving into a future heydey of the ranch. I distinctly recall one part of his conversation, and am again made glad for his clean soul:

"There's a big slump coming in real estate, country, not city. Recollect that man who came the other day to interest me in some of the land among the little hills north of us?

I didn't like the looks of his speculation. But if I cared to play the dirty business game, I could buy in largely when the slump comes, cut up the property and later on sell, as that man expects to do, to poor people at big profit. But I don't care to make money that way, Mate-Woman," he broke off earnestly. "My hands are pretty clean, aren't they?"

I could thankfully respond to that. His business was clean: his vocation, the making of books; his avocation, agriculture.

He did not ask for music, nor did he frolic with the fox terrier, Possum, as he had done so much of late, testing that keen little brain and great heart in a hundred ways. In half an hour, Jack's exuberance had worn out; and with an apprehension to which I had been no stranger of late, I saw that he was getting argumentative, as if looking for trouble lest he fall into melancholy. He picked up two wooden box-trays of reading matter that he had brought with him, and lifted them to the table on which stood his almost untasted supper.

"Look," he said, his voice low and lifeless, "see what I've got to read to-night."

"But you don't *have* to do it, mate," I said, trying to stir his spirit. "Always remember that you *make* all this work and overwork for yourself, and it must be because you choose to do it rather than to rest. My ancient argument, you know!"

There followed a colloquy upon relative values, and then he stood up abruptly, came around the small table, and flung himself on the couch into my arms.

"Mate-Woman, Mate-Woman, you're all I've got, the last straw for me to cling to, my last bribe for living. You know. I have told you before. You *must* understand. If you don't understand, I'm lost. You're all I've got."

"I *do* understand," I cried. "I understand that there's too much for you to do, and that you're straining too hard to get it done. Are you so bound on the wheel that you cannot ease up a little, both working and thinking? You are going too fast. You are too *aware*. And you are ill. Something will snap if you don't pull up. You are *tired*, perilously tired, tired almost to death. What shall we do? We can't go on this way!"

The green shade was well down over his face, and I could not see his eyes. But the corners of his mouth drooped pathetically. Poor lad, my poor boy—he was, indeed, tired to death.

We lay there for perhaps an hour, he resting, sometimes sighing, saying little except by an exchange of sympathetic pressures which were our wont. How thankfully I remember an old vow that never, under any provocation, would I ignore caress of his! A few sentences of that Hour are too sacred and too personal to be repeated, and yet they were the frequent expressions of our daily round—in the last analysis they were an expression of the ever-narrowing values of life, working the changes upon his "bribe for living."

All at once, turning slightly, he put his arms around my neck.

"I'm so worn for lack of sleep. I'm going to turn in." Rising, he gave voice to that which so startled me.

"Thank God, you're not afraid of anything!"

Never shall I know why it came from him unless it was he knew the unthinkable was upon him, that I would very shortly lose his dear comradeship, and felt that I would be gallant to cope with that disaster.

When in the days to follow Jack's holographic will was read, first in the family circle, next by Judge T. C. Denny, in court, and tacit responsibilities were made known, I could not help reverting to that fervent exclamation. Or was it an entreaty, a supplication? If a prayer, at least he had answered it by his own passive action in neglecting, during the half-decade the Will had lain in deposit, to alter a line of it. In effect it is a love letter, written by a wise man who knew our metal, and he named Eliza Shepard and my cousin Willard L. Growall, as executors. But Jack gave loophole for discontent and criticism in that, beyond trifling provision for various beneficiaries, he stipulated:

"Whatever additional may be given them shall be a benefaction and a kindness from Charmian K. London and shall arise out of Charmian K. London's goodness and desire."

Having not forfeited his trust, I am proud to append his closing paragraph:

"The reason that I give all my estate to Charmian K. London, with exceptions noted, is as follows: Charmian K. London, by her personal fortune, and, far more, by her personal aid to me in my literary work, and still vastly far more, by the love, and comfort, and joy, and happiness she has given me, is the only person in this world who has any claim or merit earned upon my estate. This merit and claim she has absolutely earned, and I hereby earnestly, sincerely, and gratefully accord it."

After he had gone to his room, I thought to cool my distressed head by a stroll in the blue starlight. The burden of my thought was that matters could not go on in this way, that I must make an effort to shake Jack into recognizing that he would have to change his physical habits.

When I reëntered the house at about nine, it was on tiptoe. Jack's light was burning. Peeping across from my own quarters, I saw that his head had fallen upon his chest, the eyeshade down. As I looked, he made a slight movement, as if settling to sleep; and knowing his sore need of repose, I did not venture a chance of disturbing his first slumber. The last work in which he read that night, was a small, rusty, calf volume, "Around Cape Horn, Maine to California in 1852, Ship *James W. Paige.* Myself half-exhausted from emotion and lack of rest, I went to bed, read a few moments in "The Wayside Lute," by Lizette Woodworth Reese, and fell asleep for the first unbroken eight hours I had known in weeks—thereby shattering any latent faith I may ever have entertained in the sweet code of telepathy between those close in sympathy.

As if to me a prophesy, one of the poems on which I went to sleep was this:

"House, how still you are;
Hearth, how cold!
He was vital as a star,
As the April mold.
Friend and singer, lad and knight,
Very dear;——
Hearts, how bare the dark, the light,
Since he is not here!"

But the last lines I scanned, and which keep impinging now upon memory, were these:

"Loose me from tears, and make me see aright
How each hath back what once he stayed to weep;
Homer his sight, David his little lad!"

When, at ten minutes past eight the next morning, my eyes opened upon Eliza standing by my bed, with Sekinè, our Japanese boy, in the background, I said, "Yes, what is it?" knowing well that only the gravest urgency brought them there. And just as quietly Eliza replied:

"Sekinè could not wake Jack, so came right to me. I think you'd better come in and see what you can do."

The stertorous respiration could be heard before we entered the sleeping-porch. Jack, unconscious, was doubled down sidewise, showing plain symptoms of poisoning. By means of strong coffee we had succeeded in producing some reaction before the doctors arrived and the real battle for Jack's life began, but not at any time did we succeed in coaxing the limp form to any effort. The physicians first summoned were A. M. Thompson and W. B. Hayes of Sonoma; followed by J. Wilson Shiels from San Francisco, and Jack's own surgeon, W. S. Porter. It was only by holding him up, one on a side, that Jack could be kept in a sitting posture on the edge of the bed: and when ranchmen, waiting all day at call, had him on his feet, equilibrium of the heavy and nerveless figure was maintained only by sheer strength of his supporters. Body and will could not coöperate, and but several times, in the middle of the day, was there a flicker of intelligence. Every legitimate kind of shock was resorted to. Physically he was for the most part beyond effort, but half-conscious response was obtained when we shouted alarming tidings across the abysm of coma:

"Man, man, wake up! The dam has burst! Wake, man, wake!" This caused a shudder in the congested, discolored countenance, the head jerked, the fixed and awful eyes made a superhuman effort to focus. There was a glimmer of consciousness, evanescent as the dying light along the wires in an electric bulb that has been snapped off. The awareness faded, faded. But oh, the pang of happiness even this brief acknowledgment lent us who stood by, together or by turn, in the struggle of those midday hours!

When the news of harm to his dam had been reiterated to the point of intolerable agony of rousing from so deadly lethargy, we were rewarded by observing that he protested, with the leaden vigor of one half-thralled in nightmare, by slowly beating the mattress with a loosely-clenched right fist. The left was never raised. Whereupon shaking and shouting were resumed, with a like outcome. Although on verge of tears of pure joy at this encouragement, I could but note, with a sickening sense of futility, that body and will were at sharp variance—the closer we forced cognition of our intent to resuscitate, the more rational became the opposition. He was, I see it, setting the last fleeting effort of his life, of his reasoned will, against rehabilitation of that life and will.

Then, realizing this in spirit, I desisted, inwardly at least, to fight, to hope. One thing, however, I must do: establish one last mental contact, to serve me all the deprived years that should befall.

"Let me try something," I said, and they set him upright upon the edge of the bed, his helpless feet upon the fur rug.

Face to face, seizing him firmly by the shoulders, I shook him, not roughly, but decisively, and repeated:

"Mate! mate! You must come back! Mate! You've got to come back! To me! Mate! Mate!"

He came back. Of course he came back. Slowly, as something rising from the unfathomable well of eternity, full knowledge brimmed into those eyes that drew to mine in a conscious regard, and the mouth smiled, a fleeting, writhen smile. It seemed as if my unbodied soul went out to meet his in that instant. Instant it was, ineffable, brief. But it contained as great, as glorious, a meeting of two as ever took place upon this planet. Yet it was not enough. Again I sent out the call to him upon the brink—and again the smile. Was it of hail and farewell to life as he had known it? Or of love, and the bliss of one perfect moment of understanding? Or was it of victory, that he, by lack of resistance, had beaten us all out, and thus invited "the ultimate nothingness," his passing behind the curtains into "The darkness that rounds the end of life"? Perhaps there was, too, upon the lips that smiled awry and vainly strove to speak, the twist of contempt for the dissolution that was upon him. What would we not give to know those words he could not frame!

What I love to believe, when all else is said, is that he, who gave life and death an equal supremacy in his affection, was redeeming a promise made so long ago that it is woven into the fabric of all memories of him.

"Death is sweet. Death is rest. Think of it!—to rest forever! I promise you that whensoever and wheresoever Death comes to meet me, I shall greet Death with a smile."

How the great ones have walked arm-in-arm with Death! Thus Robert Louis Stevenson to the beloved Assassin:

"I have been waiting for you these many years. Give me your hand, and welcome."

Where was he, our Jack, all that day we warred with his fate? What was it he so hated to forswear in order to answer our importunity? Judging reasonably enough by the dreams of his latter years, I hazarded that he was wandering purposefully in that same land of green fields, intent, watchful, happy. It had been the same with his father during a longer period of alternate unconscious periods—the long life-desire fulfilled. This, oh, surely, is what we tortured the son from!—But with the last breath which left his body—what of the bright dream? When the splendid head, no longer instinct with resolution, ceased from its cerebration, hard it was to agree with that same cerebration that the Thing that Thinks is one with the Thing that Dies! How I should love to believe that he, liberated, opened eyes upon the range of illimitable possibilities that had hitherto been bounded by failing mortality. Yet who am I to invoke for him, who declared for perfect *rest* otherwise than Ambrose Bierce's wish to a friend:

"Light lie the earth upon his dear, dead heart,
　　And dreams disturb him never.
Be deeper peace than Paradise his part
　　For ever and for ever."

Or, "the supreme beatitude of rest," as Jack's friend John Myers O'Hara has it.

Months after Jack's death I had the first and only "vision" of my experience. When a great asking comes upon me, in ungifted hours when my lamp burns low, think of it. Rising one morning with a renewed cheerfulness that bubbled over into song, suddenly, as clearly as ever I had looked upon the man, I saw Jack stepping blithely in a green domain, the very picture of an Elysian pastoral, whistling comradely to an unmistakable friend shadowing his heel—Peggy the Beloved, our small canine

Irish saint of the Southern Seas. What was it—a miscalculation of my Unconscious that let the dear dream spill over into Foreconsciousness to rejoice the day?

The sun went down upon our endeavor. They had brought him across into my glass porch, scene of so much quiet happiness, and there he died upon the couch where, a scant twenty-four hours earlier, he had cried to me: "You *must* understand my need! You're all I've got left!"

We watched. The good breathing that had upborne expectation of recovery began to lag, and more labored became intake and suspiration. I became aware that one of the Sonoma physicians was leading me from where I stood at Jack's head. Mechanically we sat down in my room. Minutes passed, a few, an eternity of them, it seemed. Longer were the intervals between those breaths so plainly heard, a very great interval, another, and then silence absolute, the sheerest vacuum of sound I had ever known. No one moved until Sekinè, his face an oriental mask of ivory, stepped in and bent his head to me.

I, who had never before lost any one essentially close; I, who had been protected from all outward semblances of death, half an hour later went out with my own dead and sat by the sheeted form until, with every atom of understanding I possessed, I had reckoned for all time with the hitherto unthinkable: that ultimate silence lay upon the lips of my man. Let me review that day a thousand-thousand times, there is nothing new to face. The worst had befallen; the future was plain, a horizonless expanse of ready work in which one must in good time build out of the wreck a renewed, if different, joy of living and serving. It was good. It has worked. It has continued to work, test incontrovertible. I proclaim to these who mourn overmuch, the worth and solace of my remedy.

When, later in the evening, we crept, his true sister and I, into Jack's old sleeping-place, all was restored to order by Sekinè. The broad bed was laid and turned, the pillows piled ready for the reader, the little table set to rights, even to cigarettes, freshly-sharpened pencils, and thermos bottles of water and milk. It was incredible that the one-time tenant should be lying, cold and insensible, across the house. We looked at each other dumbly, and I sought the Japanese lad.

"We always do it in our country for those who have died," he said unsteadily. "And I thought——" His explanation trailed into silence as he turned away. As long as he remained with the household, the bed was always in order, and we kept a single flower there and on the worktable.

Once, twice, in his later years, Jack, in chance reference to the possibility of his dying first, departed from his familiar careless injunction of "Oh, if I should go, scatter my ashes to the winds, or, if you prefer, upon the bay or ocean!" Eliza and I both recalled the time, when, speaking of his love and hopes for the ranch, he remarked:

"If I *should* beat you to it, I wouldn't mind if you laid my ashes on the knoll where the Greenlaw children are buried. And roll over me a red boulder from the ruins of the Big House. I wouldn't want many to come. You might ask George."

But before his chosen ceremonial there were thrust in occasions which, left to his own choice, he would not have stipulated. Clothed in his favorite gray, as in gray I had first seen him sixteen years before, for a day in his workroom he lay, in a gray casket that was like nothing so much as a cradle. Passing by I was touched by the smallness of it. I had thought Jack a larger man.

The neighbors came and went, in tearful awe of the unexpected demise of the lovable friend they yet had never understood. Little as he would have approved of exhibiting the discarded shell of him, it would have been needless affront to the tribute these people were accustomed to pay to the dead. And they had loved him more than they thought. As one of them said:

"I tell you, the death of Jack means a sorry day to many. He gave away a meal ticket and added to it a bit, too. His heart went out to the fellow who carried a roll of blankets— or no blankets."

On Friday, at dawn, I was awakened from fitful sleep by the rumble of the death-wagon coming up the hill. When, delaying, I slipped in to the abandoned workroom, the open window through which he had so often passed alive told of the manner in which Jack London had gone from his house.

Sekinè came to where I sat, thinking, adjusting, and held out a handful of keys, the dingy Klondike coin-sack of chamois, and a few stray notes, all taken from the ranch suit Jack had last worn. Sekinè murmured something about having put some notes in the breast-pocket of the burial clothes, together with a pencil and pad—"Just as he always had them, Missis," he whispered.

"But, Sekinè, the notes, what notes?" I asked, biting back the trembling of my lips at thought of the pitiful last service the boy had rendered, but fearful lest some latest words of Jack's had gone beyond recall.

"Something *I* wrote, and sent with him—no one will know," Sekinè explained. "I wrote," raising his head, 'Your Speech was silver, your Silence now is golden.' That was all. It was my Good-by."

My next step was to Jack's work-table, upon which lay the unfinished manuscript of "Cherry," just as he had laid down his pen. There, in that moment, looking at what was but an example of the myriad things he had left, in a flash it came to me:

"My life cannot be long enough to mend the broken things—to carry on the tasks that are left for me."

Eliza did me a supreme service that morning, when she accompanied Jack's casket from Glen Ellen to the Crematory in Oakland. One who met the little cortège in Oakland was Yoshimatsu Nakata, whom Sekinè had succeeded. No, I was not ill, as the report went out. I preferred to remain away from a funeral which represented Jack's idea so little, but which I felt should be accorded to his daughters and their mother. Several friends, including Frederick Bamford and others of the old Ruskin Club, were also there, and two or three persons who had corresponded with Jack now saw him for the first time. A short address was delivered by the Rev. Edward B. Payne, who was familiar with Jack's unorthodox views; and a poem, which had been asked of George Sterling, was read above his friend.

As regards the manner of his disposal, Jack himself, only a few weeks before, had had this to say, in reply to a query from Dr. Hugo Erichson, writing for the Cremation Association of America, the same having been submitted to a number of persons of national prominence:

"Glen Ellen, California, October 16, 1916.
"Dear Doctor Erichson:—

"In reply to yours of recent date, undated——

"Cremation is the only decent, right, sensible way of ridding the world of us when the world has ridden itself of us. Also, it is the only fair way, toward our children, and grandchildren, and all the generations to come after us. Why should we clutter the landscape and sweet-growing ground with our moldy memories? Besides, we have the testimony of all history that all such sad egotistic efforts have been failures. The best the Pharaohs could do with their pyramids was to preserve a few shriveled relics of themselves for our museums."

I have little connected memory of Friday and Saturday. I know there was work to do, and that I slept long night hours under the ministering hands of dear women. And I walked about the farm precincts, looking rather curiously at the young life, animal and vegetable, which Jack had fostered into being. Yet he, the biggest "mote of life between the darks" had vanished in a day! Wherever I appeared, I was conscious of some workman slipping away, or a face turned aside in a handkerchief. The half hundred men, many of whom had never conversed with their employer, seemed unnerved by the sudden gap in their little universe.

Jack, himself, would not have believed the warmth there was toward him in the skeptical old earth. As one expressed it:

"To me it seems like having a light turned off, with too few already burning, leaving the road darker and more dismal and difficult."

It was almost as if his actual death purged the mankind who knew him and his work, of jealousy, hate, and carping criticism; put a seal upon the lips of the meanest. Even his bitterest detractors tried to be fair and charitable. If I needed corroboration of my own belief in this man of mine, I could recall the mourning of his world. It must have arisen from his usefulness, his big contribution of heart's blood to humanity. Praise of him from all quarters and in many tongues from every class of society, literally from rich man, poor man, beggar man, chief, doctor, lawyer, and the rest—aye, thief, and worse! Out of prisons has come to me a wail at his passing; for the immaterial sweetness of Jack and his code, squareness, his long-suffering charity, that patriarchal kindness, had passed in and still live behind the bars.

To him, so articulate in the Great Common Things: "Three common pitmen in Durham will keep his memory green while hearts are able to respond to the bounteous thought of his love," reads a letter from England. "The sweetness of his life and work can never die."

And another, no less than his trail-mate, Hargrave, wrote:

"Always I have been assaulted by doubts; and then, coincident with the message that Jack had passed the portal that bars the Unknown from the Known, those doubts (independent of mental processes) were dispelled. I gave no reason for it—the reasons of men are such vain things in the presence of the Infinite."

This from one more "sour-dough": "I loved the man because—because he was a man; By the Turtles of Tasman, He was a man!"

And this for the premanency of his message:

"He touched the lowly side of life with a pen born of love and bitter experience. . . . He had lived with down and outs, and with animals. . . . And he wrote their tragic lives as no human ever wrote them before. . . . So long as there are human hearts that feel the tender touch of love, so long as there are honest souls that revolt at cruelty and oppression, so long will Jack London's books and stories live and be read."

"If Jack London had had faith, what a great preacher he would have made!" Dr. H. J. Loken, of Berkeley, exclaimed to his congregation, and went on to declare that his subject was of a deeply religious nature, pointing out that his criticisms had been of religion as found in the churches and not against Christianity itself.

One thing I do clearly recollect of those two days before Jack's ashes were placed upon the Little Hill: Eliza and I walked there alone in a wintry sunset. Hazen, who had preceded us with a spade to mark the spot, received his instructions about the red boulder. Six horses were needed to move it upon the steep knoll.

On Sunday morning, November 26, Ernest Matthews, accompanied by George Sterling, brought the urn from Oakland. We wreathed it with ferns and with yellow primroses from the sweet old garden. With the primroses, as a tribute to Jack's adopted home, Hawaii, I wound the withered rust-colored *leis* of *ilima* once given Jack in Honolulu by Frank Unger and Colonel Sam Parker, now, too, both under the ground. One terrible moment was mine when, in the rain, I carried the small, light vessel to the wagon, the same in which Jack had so blithely driven his four. The urn seemed to gather weight until I thought I should be pressed to the earth, but I reached the hands that placed it upon the hight seat before it had become insupportable.

Eliza and I, together, and my people, followed the horses at a distance. When we had all gathered upon the dripping slope, Mr. G. L. Parslow, our oldest ranchman, received the urn from Ernest Matthews, and set it, with its flowers, in the tile already cemented into the ground. At that moment a great flood of sun-gold spilled upon us from a break in the leaden sky.

As the trowel relentlessly filled the space within the tile, with that curious transparency of mind in crises in which details stand out, I observed with satisfaction that was a reflection of Jack's effective sense of proportion, that exactly the right proportion of mortar had been mixed, not a trowelful too much or too little.

No word stirred the hush. No prayer, for Jack London prayed to no God but humanity. The men, uncovered, reverent, stood about among the trees, and when their senior had risen, the stone was rolled into place.

Before we turned to retrace our forlorn steps to the house, it had come to me, once and forever, that this unpretentious sepulture beneath the tall pine was but a self-chosen memorial. Death, with Jack, had not seemed like death. Nature had slipped the moorings, and he, "bold sailor of the grey-green sea," had gone out with the tide, gallant, victorious, cruising beyond the outer reef, into the West, to a paradise of green lands with an ocean of sails just over the hill. This rugged monument, by his own wish, could never be a place for mourning, a spot to sadden his sweet and happy mountainside. And, by that wish and whatever gods may be, it never has been. Beautiful, singing with birds, vocal with winds among the tree-tops, Jack's Little Hill appeals only to contemplation and tender melancholy. There is nothing better than that the pilgrim, standing above the mellow purple boulder, should say:

"By the Turtles of Tasman, he was a man!"

APPENDIX

JACK LONDON BIBLIOGRAPHY

SERIAL PUBLICATION

1893

Typhoon off the Coast of Japan—SAN FRANCISCO CALL, November 12, 1893.

1894

An Old Soldier's Story—EVENINGS AT HOME (Oakland, California), May.

Old Baldy—EVENINGS AT HOME, September.

1895

'Frisco Kid's Stories—series in Oakland High School AEGIS.

1896

A Problem—AMATEUR BOHEMIAN (Oakland), March.

1899

To the Man on Trail—OVERLAND MONTHLY (San Francisco), January.

The White Silence—OVERLAND MONTHLY (San Francisco), February.

The Son of the Wolf—OVERLAND MONTHLY (San Francisco). April.

He Chortled with Glee (triolet)—TOWN TOPICS (San Francisco), April 20.

If I Were God One Hour (poem)—TOWN TOPICS (San Francisco), May 11.

The Men of Forty Mile—OVERLAND MONTHLY (San Francisco), May

On Furlough—ORANGE JUDD FARMER, May 20.

A Thousand Deaths—BLACK CAT MAGAZINE, May.

From Dawson to the Sea—BUFFALO EXPRESS, June 4.

Through the Rapids on the Way to Klondike—HOME MAGAZINE, June.

In a Far Country—OVERLAND MONTHLY, June.

Unmasking of the Cad (tableau)—TILLOTSON SYNDICATE, July.
What Are We to Say?—AMERICAN JOURNAL OF EDUCATION, July.
Strange Verbs—AMERICAN JOURNAL OF EDUCATION, July.
The Priestly Prerogative—OVERLAND MONTHLY, July.
The Handsome Cabin Boy—THE OWL, July.
The Wife of a King—OVERLAND MONTHLY, August.
Eggs Without Salt (Joke)—TOWN TOPICS, August 31.
In the Time of Prince Charley—CONKEY'S MAGAZINE, September.
On the Writer's Philosophy of Life—THE EDITOR, October.
The King of the Mazy May—YOUTH'S COMPANION, November.
The Rejuvenation of Major Rathbone—CONKEY'S MAGAZINE, November.
The Wisdom of the Trail—OVERLAND MONTHLY, December.
A Daughter of the Aurora—CHRISTMAS WAVE (San Francisco), December.

1900

Economics in the Klondike—REVIEW OF REVIEWS, January.
An Odyssey of the North—ATLANTIC MONTHLY, January.
Pluck and Pertinacity—YOUTH'S COMPANION, January 4.
The Impossibility of War—OVERLAND MONTHLY, March.
A Lesson in Heraldry—NATIONAL MAGAZINE, March.
When He Came In (triolet)—TOWN TOPICS, April 26.
A Reminiscence of Boston—BOSTON TRANSCRIPT, May 26.
The End of the Chapter—S. F. NEWS LETTER, June.
The Husky—HARPER'S WEEKLY, June 30.
Which Make Men Remember (Uri Bram's God)—S. F. SUNDAY EXAMINER, June 24.
Even Unto Death—S. F. EVENING POST, July 28.
The Dignity of Dollars—OVERLAND MONTHLY, July.
Grit of Women—MCCLURE'S MAGAZINE, August.
Jan, the Unrepentant—OUTING MAGAZINE, August.
On Expansion (editorial)—THE WAVE (S. F.), August 11.
The Shrinkage of the Planet—CHAUTAUQUAN MAGAZINE, September.
Their Alcove—WOMAN'S HOME COMPANION, September.
The Man with the Gash—MCCLURE'S MAGAZINE, September.
Housekeeping in the Klondike—HARPER'S BAZAAR, September 15.
The Phenomena of Literary Evolution—THE BOOKMAN, October.
"Girlie"—THE SMART SET, October.
Thanksgiving on Slav Creek—HARPER'S BAZAAR, November 24.
What a Community Loses by the Competitive System—COSMOPOLITAN MAGAZINE, November.
Dutch Courage—YOUTH'S COMPANION, November 29.
The Question of a Name—THE WRITER, December.
The Material Side (First Aid to Rising Authors)—JUNIOR MUNSEY MAGAZINE, December.
The Great Interrogation—AINSLIE'S MAGAZINE, December.

Semper Idem—BLACK CAT MAGAZINE, December.
Where the Trail Forks—OUTING MAGAZINE, December.
Bald Face—THE NEWS, December.

1901

A Relic of the Pliocene—COLLIER'S WEEKLY, January 12.
Sonnet—THE DILETTANTE (Oakland), February.
Lover's Liturgy—THE RAVEN (Oakland), February.
The Law of Life—MCCLURE'S MAGAZINE, March.
The Lost Poacher—YOUTH'S COMPANION, March 14.
At the Rainbow's End—MCCLURE'S SYNDICATE (PITTSBURG LEADER),
    March 24.
Siwash—AINSLIE'S MAGAZINE, March.
Editorial Crimes—THE DILETTANTE (Oakland), March.
The Scorn of Women—OVERLAND MONTHLY, May.
Minions of Midas—PEARSON'S MAGAZINE, May.
The God of His Fathers—MCCLURE'S MAGAZINE, May.
Chris Farrington: Able Seaman—YOUTH'S COMPANION, May 23.
Oregon Article—S. F. EXAMINER, June 13.
Washoe Article—S. F. EXAMINER, Sunday, June 16.
Review of The Octopus (Norris)—IMPRESSIONS (San Francisco),
    June.
A Hyperborean Brew—METROPOLITAN MAGAZINE, July.
Girl Fighting Duel (article)—S. F. EXAMINER, July 21.
The Schuetzenfest Articles—S. F. EXAMINER, July 15 to 24.
Daybreak—NATIONAL MAGAZINE, August.
Peter de Ville (article)—S. F. EXAMINER, October 14.
Villanelle: The Worker and the Tramp—THE COMRADE, October.
Review of Lincoln and Other Poems (Markham)—S. F. EXAMINER,
    November 10.
Ruhling-Jeffries Fight—S. F. EXAMINER, November 16.
Review of Foma Gordyiéff (Gorky)—IMPRESSIONNS (S. F.), November.

1902

Interview of Governor Taft—S. F. EXAMINER, January 22.
Keesh, Son of Keesh—AINSLEE'S MAGAZINE, January.
Interview with a Millionaire Socialist—S. F. EXAMINER, April 18.
The Stampede to Thunder Mountain—COLLIER'S WEEKLY, May 3.
To Build a Fire—YOUTH'S COMPANION, May 29.
An Adventure in the Upper Sea—N. Y. INDEPENDENT, May 29.
To Repel Boarders—ST. NICHOLAS MAGAZINE, June.
Batard (Diable, a Dog)—COSMOPOLITAN MAGAZINE, June.
Moon Face—THE ARGONAUT (S. F.), July 21.
The Cruise of the Dazzler—ST. NICHOLAS MAGAZINE, July.
The Fuzziness of Hookla Heen—YOUTH'S COMPANION, July 3.
Nambok the Unveracious—AINSLIE'S MAGAZINE, August.

Li Wan the Fair—ATLANTIC MONTHLY, August.
Wanted: A New Law of Development—INTERNATIONAL SOCIALIST
REVIEW, August.
Rods and Gunnels—THE BOOKMAN, August.
The Salt of the Earth—ANGLO-AMERICAN MAGAZINE, August.
In the Forests of the North—PEARSON'S MAGAZINE, September.
Again the Literary Aspirant—THE CRITIC, September.
The Master of Mystery—OUT WEST (Los Angeles), September.
The Story of Jees Uck—THE SMART SET, September.
The Sickness of Lone Chief—OUT WEST, October.
The League of the Old Men—BRANDUR MAGAZINE, October.
The Hearst Memorial Building—S. F. EXAMINER, November 19.

1903

In Yeddo Bay—ST. NICHOLAS MAGAZINE, February.
Getting into Print—THE EDITOR, March.
How I Became a Socialist—THE COMRADE, March.
The One Thousand Dozen—NATIONAL MAGAZINE, March.
Contradictory Teachers: Our Benevolent Feudalism, Social Unrest
(A Review)—INTERNATIONAL SOCIALIST REVIEW, May.
The Terrible and Tragic in Fiction—THE CRITIC, June.
Faith of Men—SUNSET MAGAZINE, June.
The Shadow and the Flash—THE BOOKMAN, June.
The Call of the Wild—SATURDAY EVENING POST, June 20-July 18.
People of the Abyss—WILSHIRE'S MAGAZINE, March-January, 1904.
Article on Boy Criminal—S. F. EXAMINER, June 21.
These Bones Shall Rise Again—THE READER, June.
Gold Hunters of the North—ATLANTIC MONTHLY, July.
The Leopard Man's Story—LESLIE'S MAGAZINE, August.
Stranger Than Fiction—THE CRITIC, August.
The Marriage of Lit-Lit—LESLIE'S MAGAZINE, September.
Local Color—AINSLIE'S MAGAZINE, October.
The Class Struggle—N. Y. INDEPENDENT, November 5.
Amateur Night—THE PILGRIM, December.
Too Much Gold—AINSLIE'S MAGAZINE, December.

1904

The Golden Poppy—THE DELINEATOR, January.
The Story of Keesh—HOLIDAY MAGAZINE, January.
The Scab—ATLANTIC MONTHLY, January.
The Sea Wolf—CENTURY MAGAZINE, January-November.
The Tramp—WILSHIRE MAGAZINE, February-March.
Russian-Japanese War Correspondence—HEARST PAPERS, February-
June.
On the Banks of the Sacramento—YOUTH'S COMPANION, March 17.
The Yellow Peril—S. F. EXAMINER, September 25.
Explanation of the Great Socialist Vote of the United States—S. F.
EXAMINER, November 10.

1905

White and Yellow—YOUTH'S COMPANION, February 16.
The King of the Crooks—YOUTH'S COMPANION, March 2.
A Raid on the Oyster Pirates—YOUTH'S COMPANION, March 16.
The Siege of the "Lancashire Queen"—YOUTH'S COMPANION, March 30.
Charley's Coup—YOUTH'S COMPANION, April 13.
Demetrios Contos—YOUTH'S COMPANION, April 27.
The Game—METTROPOLITAN MAGAZINE, April-May.
Yellow Handkerchief—YOUTH'S COMPANION, May 11.
The Walking Delegate (Review)—S. F. EXAMINER, May 28.
The White Man's Way—SUNDAY MAGAZINE SYNDICATE, July.
Britt-Nelson Fight—S. F. EXAMINER, September 10.
The Long Day (Review)—S. F. EXAMINER, October.
Love of Life—MCCLURE'S MAGAZINE, December.
All Gold Canyon—CENTURY MAGAZINE, November.
The Sun Dog Trail—HARPER'S MAGAZINE, December.
Holy Jumpers Article—BOSTON AMERICAN, December 19.

1906

What Life Means to Me—COSMOPOLITAN MAGAZINE, March.
A Nose for the King—BLACK CAT, March.
White Fang—OUTING MAGAZINE, May-October.
Earthquake Article—COLLIER'S WEEKLY, May 5.
Planchette—COSMOPOLITAN MAGAZINE, June-August.
Brown Wolf—EVERYBODY'S MAGAZINE, August.
The Unexpected—MCCLURE'S MAGAZINE, August.
Review of THE JUNGLE (Sinclair)—N. Y. JOURNAL, August 8.
Review of THE JUNGLE (complete)—WILSHIRE'S MAGAZINE, August.
My Best Short Story—THE GRAND MAGAZINE (London), August.
The Apostate—WOMAN'S HOME COMPANION, September.
Before Adam—EVERYBODY'S MAGAZINE, October, '06 to Feb., '07.
Up the Slide—YOUTH'S COMPANION, October 25.
A Wicked Woman—THE SMART SET, November.
Letter to H. M. Bland—STORY CLUB MAGAZINE, November.
Moyer-Haywood Article—Chicago DAILY SOCIALIST, November 4.
First Boat Letter (Snark Voyage)—WOMAN'S HOME COMPANION, November.
The Somnambulists—N. Y. INDEPENDENT, December 20.
The Wit of Porportuk—TIMES MAGAZINE, December.
The Cruise of the Snark—COSMOPOLITAN MAGAZINE, December.

1907

When God Laughs—THE SMART SET, January.
My Castle in Spain—THE HOUSE BEAUTIFUL, January.
Is Jack London a Plagiarist?—N. Y. INDEPENDENT, February 14.
Just Meat—COSMOPOLITAN MAGAZINE, March.

Created He Them—THE PACIFIC MONTHLY, April.
Finis ("Morganson's Finish")—SUCCESS MAGAZINE, May.
Confession—COSMOPOLITAN MAGAZINE, May.
A Day's Lodging—COLLIER'S WEEKLY, May 25.
Holding Her Down—COSMOPOLITAN, June.
Pinched—COSMOPOLITAN MAGAZINE, July.
The Pen—COSMOPOLITAN MAGAZINE, August.
Pictures—COSMOPOLITAN MAGAZINE, September.
Chased by the Trail—YOUTH'S COMPANION, Sept. 26.
Two Thousand Stiffs—COSMOPOLITAN MAGAZINE, October.
A Royal Sport (Riding the South Sea Surf)—WOMAN'S HOME COM-
    PANION, October.
The Intercollegiate Socialist Society—POTENTIA SYNDICATE, October.
Gay Cats and Road Kids—COSMOPOLITAN MAGAZINE, November.
Hoboes that Pass in the Night—COSMOPOLITAN MAGAZINE, De-
    cember.

1908

Revolution—CONTEMPORARY REVIEW (New York), January.
The Passing of Marcus O'Brien—THE READER, January.
Trust—CENTURY MAGAZINE, January.
The Lepers of Molokai—WOMAN'S HOME COMPANION, January.
That Spot—SUNSET MAGAZINE, February.
Bulls—COSMOPOLITAN MAGAZINE, March.
The Inconceivable and Monstrous—HARPER'S WEEKLY, July 18.
Adventure—HARPER'S WEEKLY, July 25.
To Build a Fire—CENTURY MAGAZINE, August.
Finding One's Way About—HARPER'S WEEKLY, August 1.
The First Landfall—HARPER'S WEEKLY, August 8.
The Other Animals—COLLIER'S WEEKLY, September 5.
The Nature Man—WOMAN'S HOME COMPANION, September.
Flush of Gold—HAMPTON'S BROADWAY MAGAZINE, October.
The Enemy of All the World—THE RED BOOK, October.
The High Seat of Abundance—WOMAN'S HOME COMPANION, No-
    vember.
Martin Eden—PACIFIC MONTHLY, Sept., 1908, to Sept., 1909.
Lost Face—N. Y. HERALD, December 13.
A Curious Fragment—TOWN TOPICS, December 10.
Burns-Johnson Fight—N. Y. HERALD and Syndicate, and Sydney,
    Australia, STAR, December 27.

1909

The House of Mapuhi—MCCLURE'S MAGAZINE, January.
The Dream of Debs—INTERNATIONAL SOCIALIST REVIEW, January-
    February.
First Impressions of Australia—THE STAR, Sydney, Australia.
    (This series of articles published January.)
On Strikes.

The Japanese Question.
Fortune in a Newspaper.
Sobraun Article.
The Yankee Myth.
The Seed of McCoy—CENTURY MAGAZINE, April.
Bêche de Mer English ("Too Much English")—WOMAN'S HOME COMPANION, April.
Make Westing—SUNSET MAGAZINE, April.
Aloha Oe—THE SMART SET, May.
South of the Slot—SATURDAY EVENING POST, May 22.
Good-by, Jack!—THE RED BOOK, June.
The Chinago—HARPER'S MONTHLY, July.
The Sheriff of Kona—AMERICAN MAGAZINE, August.
A Piece of Steak—SATURDAY EVENING POST, November 29.
Letter to Arthur Stringer (Nature-Faking)—CANADA WEST MONTHLY, November.
Koolau the Leper—THE PACIFIC MONTHLY, December.
Mauki—HAMPTON'S MAGAZINE, December.
The Japanese Question—SUNSET MAGAZINE, December.

1910

The House of the Sun—PACIFIC MONTHLY, January.
The Whale Tooth—SUNSET MAGAZINE, January.
A Pacific Traverse, PACIFIC MONTHLY, February.
Goliah, THE BOOKMAN, February.
Typee—PACIFIC MONTHLY, March.
Chun Ah Chun—WOMAN'S MAGAZINE, March.
The Terrible Solomons—HAMPTON'S MAGAZINE, March.
The Stone-Fishing at Bora Bora—PACIFIC MONTHLY, April.
An Amateur Navigator—PACIFIC MONTHLY, May.
Cruising in the Solomons—PACIFIC MONTHLY, June-July.
Burning Daylight—NEW YORK HERALD, June 19-August 28.
Jeffries-Johnson Fight articles—NEW YORK HERALD and Syndicate (Eleven articles) June 24 25, 26, 27, 28, 29, 30, July 2, 3, 4 (training camp); 5 (fight).
The Unparalleled Invasion—MCCLURE'S MAGAZINE, July.
Letter on Young Authors' Endowment—N. Y. INDEPENDENT, July 28.
The Amateur M.D.—PACIFIC MONTHLY, August.
The Heathen—EVERYBODY'S MAGAZINE, August.
When the World Was Young—SATURDAY EVENING POST, September 10.
Winged Blackmail—THE LEVER (Chicago), September.
Adventure (Novel)—POPULAR MAGAZINE, Nov. 1-Jan. 15, 1911.
The Benefit of the Doubt—SATURDAY EVENING POST, November 12.
Under the Deck Awnings—SATURDAY EVENING POST, November 19.
The Madness of John Harned—EVERYBODY'S MAGAZINE, November.

The Inevitable White Man—BLACK CAT MAGAZINE, November.
The House of Pride—PACIFIC MONTHLY, December.
To Kill a Man—SATURDAY EVENING POST, December 10.
Yah! Yah! Yah!—COLUMBIAN MAGAZINE, December.
Bunches of Knuckles—NEW YORK HERALD, December 18.

1911

The Human Drift—THE FORUM, January.
The Hobo and the Fairy—SATURDAY EVENING POST, February 11.
The Eternity of Forms—THE RED BOOK, March.
The Strength of the Strong—HAMPTON'S MAGAZINE, March.
A Son of the Sun—SATURDAY EVENING POST, May 27.
War—London NATION, May.
An Alaskan Vacation—PANAMA MAGAZINE, May.
SMOKE BELLEW: The Taste of the Meat—COSMOPOLITAN MAGAZINE, June.
The First Poet (play)—CENTURY MAGAZINE, June.
The Proud Goat of Aloysius Pankburn—SATURDAY EVENING POST, June 24.
The Goat Man of Fautino—SATURDAY EVENING POST, July 29.
The Night Born—EVERYBODY'S MAGAZINE, July.
SMOKE BELLEW: The Meat—COSMOPOLITAN MAGAZINE, July.
The Mexican—SATURDAY EVENING POST, August 19.
SMOKE BELLEW: The Stampede to Squaw Creek—COSMOPOLITAN MAGAZINE, August.
Navigating Four Horses North of the Bay—SUNSET MAGAZINE, September.
The Abysmal Brute—POPULAR MAGAZINE, September 1.
SMOKE BELLEW: Shorty Dreams—COSMOPOLITAN MAGAZINE, September.
A Little Account with Swithin Hall—SATURDAY EVENING POST, September 2.
A Gobotu Night—SATURDAY EVENING POST, September 30.
SMOKE BELLEW: The Man on the Other Bank—COSMOPOLITAN MAGAZINE, October.
The Pearls of Parlay—SATURDAY EVENING POST, October 14.
SMOKE BELLEW: The Race for Number Three—COSMOPOLITAN MAGAZINE, November.
Nothing that Ever Came to Anything—SUNSET MAGAZINE, November.
The Jokers of New Gibbon—SATURDAY EVENING POST, November 11.
The End of the Story—WOMAN'S WORLD, November.
By the Turtles of Tasman—MONTHLY MAGAZINE SECTION (Hearst), November.
SMOKE BELLEW: The Little Man—COSMOPOLITAN MAGAZINE, December.
A Classic of the Sea—N. Y. INDEPENDENT, December 14.

1912

SMOKE BELLEW: The Hanging of Cultus George—COSMOPOLITAN MAGAZINE, January.

SMOKE BELLEW: The Mistake of Creation—COSMOPOLITAN MAGAZINE, February.

SMOKE BELLEW: A Flutter in Eggs—COSMOPOLITAN MAGAZINE, March.

The Sea Farmer—THE BOOKMAN, March.

The Grilling of Lorrin Ellery—NORTHERN WEEKLY GAZETTE (TILLOTSON SYNDICATE), March.

Feathers of the Sun—SATURDAY EVENING POST, March 9.

Smoke Bellew: The Townsite of Tra-Lee—COSMOPOLITAN MAGAZINE, April.

The Prodigal Father—WOMAN'S WORLD, May.

SMOKE BELLEW: The Wonder of Woman—COSMOPOLITAN MAGAZINE, May, June.

Small Boat Sailing—COUNTRY LIFE IN AMERICA, August.

The Captain of the Susan Drew (The Tar Pot)—MONTHLY MAGAZINE SECTION, November 24.

1913

John Barleycorn—SATURDAY EVENING POST, March 15-May 3.

The Valley of the Moon—COSMOPOLITAN MAGAZINE, April-December.

Samuel—THE BOOKMAN, May.

The Scarlet Plague—AMERICAN SUNDAY MONTHLY MAGAZINE, June 8-Sept. 14.

The Mutiny of the Elsinore (The Sea Gangsters)—HEARST'S MAGAZINE, Nov., 1913, to Aug., 1914.

1914

Mexican War Correspondence from Vera Cruz—COLLIER'S WEEKLY:
  The Red Game of War, May 16.
  With Funston's Men, May 23.
  Mexico's Army and Ours, May 30.
  Stalking the Pestilence, June 6.
  The Trouble-Makers of Mexico, June 13.
  The Law-Givers, June 20.
  Our Adventures in Tampico, June 27.

Told in the Drooling Ward—THE BOOKMAN, June.

The Star Rover—AMERICAN SUNDAY MONTHLY MAGAZINE, September 6, 1914-October 3, 1915.

1915

The Little Lady of the Big House—COSMOPOLITAN MAGAZINE, April, 1915, to January, 1916.

1916

Our Guiltless Scapegoats, the Stricken of Molokai (article)—PUB-
LIC LEDGER, Philadelphia, June 21.
Politics and Leprosy—PUBLIC LEDGER, Philadelphia, August 6.
My Hawaiian Aloha (three articles)—COSMOPOLITAN MAGAZINE,
September-November.
The Hussy—COSMOPOLITAN MAGAZINE, December.

1917

Jerry—COSMOPOLITAN, January-April.
The Kanaka Surf (Man of Mine)—HEARST'S MAGAZINE, February.
Like Argus of the Ancient Times—HEARST'S MAGAZINE, March.
Michael—COSMOPOLITAN, May-October.
The Bones of Kahekili—COSMOPOLITAN, July.

1918

When Alice Told Her Soul—COSMOPOLITAN MAGAZINE, March.
The Princess—COSMOPOLITAN MAGAZINE, June.
The Tears of Ah Kim—COSMOPOLITAN MAGAZINE, July.
The Water Baby—COSMOPOLITAN MAGAZINE, September.
The Red One—COSMOPOLITAN MAGAZINE, October.
In the Cave of the Dead (Shin Bones)—COSMOPOLITAN MAGAZINE,
November.

1919

On the Makaloa Mat—COSMOPOLITAN MAGAZINE, March.
Hearts of Three—N. Y. JOURNAL, May 11, June 21.

BOOKS

1—THE SON OF THE WOLF, Houghton, Mifflin Company, April 7, 1900.
(Collected stories)
 The White Silence
 The Son of the Wolf
 The Men of Forty Mile
 In a Far Country
 To the Man on Trail
 The Priestly Prerogative
 The Wisdom of the Trail
 The Wife of a King
 An Odyssey of the North

2—THE GOD OF HIS FATHERS, McClure, Phillips & Company, May, 1901.
(Collected stories)
 The God of His Fathers
 The Great Interrogation
 Which Makes Men Remember
 Siwash
 The Man with the Gash.
 Jan, the Unrepentant
 Grit of Women
 Where the Trail Forks
 A Daughter of the Aurora
 At the Rainbow's End
 The Scorn of Women

3—A DAUGHTER OF THE SNOWS, J. B. Lippincott Co., October, 1902.
(Novel)

4—CHILDREN OF THE FROST, The Macmillan Company, September, 1902.
(Collected stories)
 In the Forests of the North
 The Law of Life
 Nam-Bok the Unveracious
 The Master of Mystery
 The Sunlanders
 The Sickness of Lone Chief
 Keesh, the Son of Keesh
 The Death of Ligoun

407

Li Wan, the Fair
The League of the Old Men

5—THE CRUISE OF THE DAZZLER, The Century Co., October, 1902.
(Juvenile)

6—THE CALL OF THE WILD, The Macmillan Company, July, 1903.
(Novel)

7—THE KEMPTON-WACE LETTERS, The Macmillan Company, May,
1903.
(A series of Philosophical Letters on Love. Written in Collab-
oration with Anna Strunsky.)

8—THE PEOPLE OF THE ABYSS, The Macmillan Company, November,
1903.
(First-hand observation of the East End of London.)

9—THE FAITH OF MEN, The Macmillan Company, April, 1904.
(Collected stories)
A Relic of the Pliocene
A Hyperborean Brew
The Faith of Men.
Too Much Gold
The One Thousand Dozen
The Marriage of Lit-Lit
Batard
The Story of Jees-Uck

10—THE SEA WOLF, The Macmillan Company, October, 1904.
(Novel)

11—WAR OF THE CLASSES, The Macmillan Company, April, 1905.
(Sociological essays)
The Class Struggle
The Tramp
The Scab
The Question of the Maximum
A Review (Contradictory Teachers).
Wanted: A New Law of Development
How I Became a Socialist

12—THE GAME, The Macmillan Company, June, 1905.
(Novel)

13—TALES OF THE FISH PATROL, The Macmillan Company, Septem-
ber, 1905.
(Juvenile)
White and Yellow
The King of the Crooks
A Raid on Oyster Pirates
The Siege of the "Lancashire Queen"

Charley's Coup
Demetrios Contos
Yellow Handkerchief

14—MOON-FACE ANE OTHER STORIES, The Macmillan Company, September, 1906.
(Collected stories)
Moon-Face: A Story of a Mortal Antipathy
The Leopard Man's Story
Local Color
Amateur Night
The Minions of Midas
The Shadow and the Flash
All Gold Canyon
Planchette

15—SCORN OF WOMEN, The Macmillan Company, November, 1906.
(Play)

16—WHITE FANG, The Macmillan Company, September, 1906.
(Novel)

17—LOVE OF LIFE, AND OTHER STORIES, The Macmillan Company, September, 1907.
(Collected stories)
Love of Life
A Day's Lodging
The White Man's Way
The Story of Keesh
The Unexpected
Brown Wolf
The Sun Dog Trail
Negore, the Coward

18—BEFORE ADAM, The Macmillan Company, February, 1907.
(Novel)

19—THE ROAD, The Macmillan Company, November, 1907.
(Tramping Experiences)
Confession
Holding Her Down
Pictures
"Pinched"
The Pen
Hoboes that Pass in the Night
Road-Kids and Gay-Cats
Two Thousand Stiffs
Bulls

20—TKE IRON HEEL, The Macmillan Company, February, 1908.
(Novel)

21—MARTIN EDEN, The Macmillan Company, September, 1909
(Semi-autobiographic Novel)

22—LOST FACE, The Macmillan Company, March, 1910.
(Collected stories)
> Lost Face
> Trust
> To Build a Fire
> That Spot
> Flush of Gold
> The Passing of Marcus O'Brien
> The Wit of Porportuk

23—REVOLUTION, The Macmillan Company, March, 1910.
(Sociological Essays and Others)
> Revolution
> The Somnambulists
> The Dignity of Dollars
> Goliah
> The Golden Poppy
> The Shrinkage of the Planet
> The House Beautiful
> The Gold Hunters of the North
> Foma Gordyéeff
> These Bones Shall Rise Again
> The Other Animals
> The Yellow Peril
> What Life Means to Me

24—BURNING DAYLIGHT, The Macmillan Company, October, 1910.
(Novel)

25—THEFT, The Macmillan Company, November, 1910.
(Play)

26—WHEN GOD LAUGHS, The Macmillan Company, January, 1911.
(Collected stories)
> When God Laughs
> The Apostate
> A Wicked Woman
> Just Meat
> Created He Them
> The Chinago
> Make Westing
> Semper Idem
> A Nose for the King
> The *Francis Spaight*
> A Curious Fragment
> A Piece of Steak

27—ADVENTURE, The Macmillan Company, March, 1911.
(Novel)

28—THE CRUISE OF THE SNARK, The Macmillan Company, June, 1911.
(Articles)
Foreword.
The Inconceivable and Monstrous
Adventure
Finding One's Way About
The First Landfall
A Royal Sport
The Lepers of Molokai
The House of the Sun
A Pacific Traverse
Typee
The Nature Man
The High Seat of Abundance
Stone-Fishing of Bora Bora
The Amateur Navigator
Cruising in the Solomons
Beche de Mer English
The Amateur M.D.
Backword

29—SOUTH SEA TALES, The Macmillan Company, October, 1911.
(Collected stories)
The House of Mapuhi
The Whale Tooth
Mauki
"Yah! Yah! Yah!"
The Heathen
The Terrible Solomons
The Inevitable White Man
The Seed of McCoy

30—A SON OF THE SUN, Doubleday, Page & Company, May, 1912.
(Collected stories)
A Son of the Sun
The Proud Goat of Aloysius Pankburn
The Devils of Fuatino
The Jokers of New Gibbon
A Little Account with Swithin Hall
A Gobotu Night
The Feathers of the Sun
The Pearls of Parlay

31—THE HOUSE OF PRIDE, The Macmillan Company, March, 1912.
(Collected stories)
The House of Pride

Koolau the Leper
Good-by, Jack!
Aloha Oe
Chum Ah Chun
The Sheriff of Kona

32—SMOKE BELLEW TALES, The Century Co., October, 1912.
The Taste of the Meat
The Meat
The Stampede to Squaw Creek
Shorty Dreams
The Man on the Other Bank
The Race for Number Three
The Little Man
The Hanging of Cultus George
The Mistake of Creation
A Flutter in Eggs
The Town-Site of Tra-Lee
Wonder of Woman

33—THE NIGHT BORN, The Century Co., February, 1913.
(Collected stories)
The Night Born
The Madness of John Harned
When the World Was Young
The Benefit of the Doubt
Winged Blackmail
Bunches of Knuckles
War
Under the Deck Awnings
To Kill a Man
The Mexican

34—THE ABYSMAL BRUTE, The Century Co., May, 1913.
(Novel)

35—JOHN BARLEYCORN, The Century Co., August, 1913.
(Autobiographical novel)

36—THE VALLEY OF THE MOON, The Macmillan Company, October, 1913.
(Novel)

37—THE STRENGTH OF THE STRONG, The Macmillan Company, May, 1914.
(Collected stories)
The Strength of the Strong
South of the Slot
The Unparalleled Invasion
The Enemy of All the World
The Dream of Debs

The Sea Farmer
Samuel

38—THE MUTINY OF THE ELSINORE, The Macmillan Company, September, 1914.
(Novel)

39—THE SCARLET PLAGUE, The Macmillan Company, May, 1915.
(Novel)

40—THE STAR ROVER, The Macmillan Company, October, 1915.
(Novel)

41—THE ACORN PLANTER, The Macmillan Company, February, 1916.
(Play)

42—THE LITTLE LADY OF THE BIG HOUSE, The Macmillan Company, April, 1916.
(Novel)

43—THE TURTLES OF TASMAN, The Macmillan Company, September, 1916.
(Collected stories)
By the Turtles of Tasman
The Eternity of Forms
Told in the Drooling Ward
The Hobo and the Fairy
The Prodigal Father
The First Poet
Finis
The End of the Story

(This was the last book published before Jack London's death on November 22, 1916.)

44—THE HUMAN DRIFT, The Macmillan Company, February, 1917.
(Articles arranged by Jack London for publication shortly before his death, and published posthumously.)
The Human Drift
Nothing that Ever Came to Anything
That Dead Men Rise Up Never
Small-boat Sailing
Four Horses and a Sailor
A Classic of the Sea
A Wicked Woman (Curtain Raiser)
The Birth Mark (Sketch)

45—JERRY OF THE ISLANDS, The Macmillan Company, April, 1917.
(Novel)

46—MICHAEL BROTHER OF JERRY, The Macmillan Company, November, 1917.

47—THE RED ONE, The Macmillan Company, October, 1918.
    (Collected stories)
        The Red One
        The Hussy
        Like Argus of the Ancient Times
        The Princess

48—ON THE MAKALOA MAT, The Macmillan Company, September,
    1919.
    (Collected stories)
        On the Makaloa Mat
        The Bones of Kahekili
        When Alice Told Her Soul
        Shin-Bones
        The Water Baby
        The Tears of Ah Kim
        The Kanaka Surf

49—HEARTS OF THREE, The Macmillan Company, September, 1920.
    (Novel for moving-picture, with explanatory Preface.)

Other collections, such as War Notes (Japanese-Russian, and Vera
    Cruz, 1914), and Prize-Fight articles, will be issued in course
    of time.

Printed in the United States
26278LVS00001B/11